KIDS KATAMARUS

SAINT **SHENOUDA**PRESS

KIDS KATAMARUS

By: FR: ANTONIOS KALDAS

ST SHENOUDA PRESS

SYDNEY, AUSTRALIA

2023

Kid's Katamarus

By: Fr: Antonios Kaldas

ST SHENOUDA PRESS
8419 Putty Rd,
Putty, NSW, 2330
Sydney, Australia

www.stshenoudapress.com

ISBN 13: 978-0-6455543-8-0

Cover Design:

Lidia Abdallah

CONTENTS

ANNUAL

LORDLY FEASTS

GREAT LENT

HOLY PENTECOST

Holy Gospel

Stand up in the fear of God and listen to the Holy Gospel, A chapter from the Holy Gospel according to Saint Matthew, May his blessings be with us all, Amen

From the psalms of our teacher David the prophet and king, May his blessings be with us all, Amen

"In You, O Lord, I put my trust; Let me never be ashamed; Deliver me in Your righteousness. Oh, how great is Your goodness, Which You have laid up for those who fear You, Which You have prepared for those who trust in You In the presence of the sons of men! Alleluia. - Psalm 31:1,19

Blessed is He who comes in the Name of the Lord Our Lord, God and Saviour and the King of us all, Jesus Christ, the Son of the living God. Glory be to You forever more, Amen

Now when He came into the temple, the chief priests and the elders of the people confronted Him as He was teaching, and said, "By what authority are You doing these things? And who gave You this authority?" But Jesus answered and said to them, "I also will ask you one thing, which if you tell Me, I likewise will tell you by what authority I do these things: The baptism of John—where was it from? From heaven or from men?" And they reasoned among themselves, saying, "If we say, 'From heaven,' He will say to us, 'Why then did you not believe him?' But if we say, 'From men,' we fear the multitude, for all count John as a prophet." So they answered Jesus and said, "We do not know." And He said to them, "Neither will I tell you by what authority I do these things. Matthew 21: 23-27

Glory be to God Forever, Amen

Pauline

Paul, the servant of our Lord Jesus Christ, called to be an apostle, appointed to the Gospel of God. A reading from the First Epistle of our teacher Paul to Timothy. May his holy blessings be with us. Amen.

Dear Timothy,

Sometimes, I want to say a very big 'thank You!' to God, because He was so, so kind to me! Before, I used to be really mean and cruel to the Christians. But Jesus knew that my meanness was because I didn't really understand.

Jesus was so kind to me. By His grace, He filled my heart with His grace and love, and He allowed me to change and to even become His servant! These words are just so true: "Christ Jesus came into the world to save sinners, of whom I am chief." I think Jesus used someone as cruel as I used to be to show that anyone at all can change, and believe in Him, and live with Him forever. Glory and honour be to our God and King, Who has no beginning or end, Who is invisible, And who is the only really wise One. I trust you, my son Timothy, to care for God's people just as God chose you to. Remember that, and be brave in your fight for what is good, having a strong faith, and a good conscience. (1 Timothy 1:12-19)

Bye for now!

Signed, Paul

The grace of God the Father be with you all, Amen.

Catholicon

The Catholic Epistle from the Epistle of our teacher St James. May his holy blessings be with us. Amen.

Hello Everyone!

Do you think it matters whether we do what Jesus taught us or not? If we don't do what Jesus taught us, this is what we'll be like, Imagine someone who looks at himself in a mirror and then walks away and quickly forgets what he looks like. He doesn't even know who he is! How silly! But we should look at the beautiful and perfect things Jesus teaches us And REMEMBER them And DO them!

Then Jesus will help us to know who we really are! Do you think you are a good person? Well, what you doreally matters. If are not careful about the things you do and say, and you end up hurting other people, then you are really just tricking yourself—you are not really a good person after all. This is what God the Father says will make you a good person: Help the needy, like widows and orphans. And don't be like those who do bad things. (James 1:22-27)

Signed, James the apostle

Do not love the world, nor the things which are in the world. The world shall pass away and all its desires; but he who does the will of God shall abide forever. Amen.

The Acts

A reading from the Acts of our fathers the pure apostles, who were invested with the grace of the Holy Spirit. May their blessing be with us all. Amen.

St Paul the Apostle was travelling, and stopped at a place where there was a Jewish synagogue which is a place where the Jews gathered to pray and read the Bible. And after they had read the Scriptures, they asked if anyone wanted to say something. St Paul certainly had something to say! So he got up and started to tell everyone about how the Old Testament Scriptures tell us all about Jesus! He started with the prophets, and then he came to St John the Baptist.

"John told us himself," said Paul, "that he was only preparing the way for Another, whose sandals he was not worthy of loosening; "And you, my brothers, being Jews and children of Abraham, you need to understand the words of your own prophets,which you read every Sabbath (which is Saturday). "But instead, you asked Pontius Pilate to kill Jesus on the Cross, even though Jesus never did anything wrong "And Jesus died, just as the prophets in the Scripture said, and He was buried in a tomb, but then something really amazing happened.

"God raised Jesus from the dead!Jesus was alive again!"We know this, because lots and lots of people saw Him; "So that's why I'm telling you all this Good News."Jesus died and rose for you and me.

That's what the Scriptures of the Old Testament were telling you, all this time; "That's why the second Psalm says,'You are My Son,Today I have begotten You' "We are the children of Abraham and the prophets "Jesus rose for you and for meand for everyone!" (Acts 13:25-33)

The word of the Lord shall grow, multiply, be mighty and be confirmed in the holy Church of God. Amen.

Holy Gospel

Stand up in the fear of God and listen to the Holy Gospel, A chapter from the Holy Gospel according to Saint Luke, May his blessings be with us all, Amen

From the psalms of our teacher David the prophet and king, May his blessings be with us all, Amen

> Love the Lord, all you His saints, For the Lord seeks out truth. How great, O Lord, is the abundance of Your goodness You hide for those who fear You. Alleluia. - Psalm 31:23,19

Blessed is He who comes in the Name of the Lord Our Lord, God and Saviour and the King of us all, Jesus Christ, the Son of the living God. Glory be to You forever more, Amen

For I say to you, among those born of women there is not a greater prophet than John the Baptist; but he who is least in the kingdom of God is greater than he. And when all the people heard Him, even the tax collectors justified God, having been baptized with the baptism of John. But the Pharisees and lawyers rejected the will of God for themselves, not having been baptized by him. And the Lord said, To what then shall I liken the men of this generation, and what are they like? They are like children sitting in the marketplace and calling to one another, saying: `We played the flute for you, And you did not dance; We mourned to you, And you did not weep.' For John the Baptist came neither eating bread nor drinking wine, and you say, `He has a demon.' The Son of Man has come eating and drinking, and you say, `Look, a glutton and a winebibber, a friend of tax collectors and sinners!' But wisdom is justified by all her children. Luke 7:28-35

Glory be to God Forever, Amen

SECOND SUNDAY OF THOUT

Holy Gospel

MATINS

Stand up in the fear of God and listen to the Holy Gospel, A chapter from the Holy Gospel according to Saint Mark, May his blessings be with us all, Amen

From the psalms of our teacher David the prophet and king, May his blessings be with us all, Amen

O Lord, our Lord, How excellent is Your name in all the earth, Who have set Your glory above the heavens! What is man that You are mindful of him, And the son of man that You visit him? Alleluia. - Psalm 8: 1&4

Blessed is He who comes in the Name of the Lord Our Lord, God and Saviour and the King of us all, Jesus Christ, the Son of the living God. Glory be to You forever more, Amen

Now in the morning, having risen a long while before daylight, He went out and departed to a solitary place; and there He prayed. And Simon and those who were with Him searched for Him. When they found Him, they said to Him, "Everyone is looking for You." But He said to them, "Let us go into the next towns, that I may preach there also, because for this purpose I have come forth." And He was preaching in their synagogues throughout all Galilee, and casting out demons. Mark 1: 35-39

Glory be to God Forever, Amen

Pauline

Paul, the servant of our Lord Jesus Christ, called to be an apostle, appointed to the Gospel of God. A reading from the Second Epistle of our teacher Paul to Timothy. May his holy blessings be with us. Amen.

Dear Timothy,

You know I've been through quite a lot! But I really don't mind that at all. Because I know that I have done it all for Jesus. And I know He will treasure me till the Last Day. And you too—may the Holy Spirit who lives in us both help you to treasure the faith and love of Jesus that I taught you. Some of my friends have done that, but sadly, some have not.

Remember Phygellus [Fie-gell-us] and Hermogenes [Her-modj-en-eez]? They turned away from me. But good old Onesiphorus [Oh-ness-ee-for-us]—the one who looked after me in Rome when I was in gaol, and in Ephesus— has always been faithful. May God bless him and all his family! So, dear Timothy, my son, be strong in Jesus, and try to find more faithful people like Onesiphorus. I told you about Jesus. You can tell good people what I told you about Jesus. They can tell more people what you told them about Jesus. But be ready! We are like soldiers, fighting against evil! Sometimes it's really hard, so we have to be really prepared and concentrating. If you run in a race, you can't win if you don't know and follow the rules. We are Jesus's soldiers. We are His athletes, training and running for Him. We are His farmers, growing many hearts to love Him. Jesus, the seed of David, rose from the dead! I want to tell the whole world about Him, even if it means they put me in gaol for it! But they can never put the Word of God in gaol! They can never stop the beautiful Truth of Jesus! So, I really don't care what they do to me. Because I love Jesus so much, and I love all His children. (2 Timothy 1:12-2:10)

Bye for now!

Signed, Paul

The grace of God the Father be with you all, Amen.

Catholicon

The Catholic Epistle from the Epistle of our teacher St James. May his holy blessings be with us. Amen.

From James,

My beloved brothers and sisters, You all know that Jesus loves everyone just the same don't you? But, Do you love everybody the same, just like Jesus? Or do you treat people differently? What about if a rich or important person comes to Church? Do you treat him really, really nicely? Good! But, what if a poor person comes to your Church? Do you treat him as nicely as you treated the rich person? Or do you treat him really badly, ignore him, or even insult him or make fun of him? Listen carefully now: God chose to love the poor people to be rich in faith, and to go to Heaven. If God treats them so nicely, how can you treat them so badly? And, it is usually the rich and important people who are greedy for money, and take people to court, and don't care about anyone else. So why do you treat the rich and important people so much better than you treat other people? If you really want to follow God's laws, listen to what He says:

"You shall love your neighbour as you love yourself". If you do that, you are doing the right thing. But if you love some people more than others just because they are rich or important, then you are certainly doing the wrong thing. You are actually breaking God's law. That's right! If you break one law of God, then you are a law-breaker. You have saddened God, just as much as if you had broken any other law, like killing someone! So don't do the wrong thing. Love everyone just the same, just as Jesus love all of us. If you show kindness and mercy to others, then God will show kindness and mercy to you. And we know how important it is for God to show us His mercy. If He didn't, we would all be in BIG trouble!!! (James 2:5-13)

Signed, James the apostle

Do not love the world, nor the things which are in the world. The world shall pass away and all its desires; but he who does the will of God shall abide forever. Amen.

The Acts

A reading from the Acts of our fathers the pure apostles, who were invested with the grace of the Holy Spirit. May their blessing be with us all. Amen.

After the Stephen the Archdeacon was killed, many Christians left Jerusalem and travelled to Syria and Lebanon and Cyprus Mostly they preached about Jesus to other Jews, but some of them were very brave and preached to the Gentiles too (Gentiles are all those people who are not Jews - like us).

And the Lord was with them. Heaps and heaps of people believed their words and became Christians! When the Church in Jerusalem heard about what was happening, they sent out a very good and holy man called Barnabas to help them and encourage them.

He was so happy with all that he saw God doing there. Barnabas went to Tarsus and brought back St Paul with him, and together, they stayed with this new Church for a whole year. And in Antioch in Syria, they were the first ones to come up with the name "Christians". Now all of us are called Christians! - Acts 11:19-26

The word of the Lord shall grow, multiply, be mighty and be confirmed in the holy Church of God. Amen.

Holy Gospel

Stand up in the fear of God and listen to the Holy Gospel, A chapter from the Holy Gospel according to Saint Luke, May his blessings be with us all, Amen

From the psalms of our teacher David the prophet and king, May his blessings be with us all, Amen

> O Lord, the king shall be glad in Your power, And in Your salvation he will greatly rejoice. You gave him his soul's desire, And You did not deprive him of his lips' request. Alleluia. - Psalms 21:1-2

Blessed is He who comes in the Name of the Lord Our Lord, God and Saviour and the King of us all, Jesus Christ, the Son of the living God. Glory be to You forever more, Amen

In that hour Jesus rejoiced in the Spirit and said, I thank You, Father, Lord of heaven and earth, that You have hidden these things from the wise and prudent and revealed them to babes. Even so, Father, for so it seemed good in Your sight. All things have been delivered to Me by My Father and no one knows who the Son is except the Father, and who the Father is except the Son, and the one to whom the Son wills to reveal Him.

Then He turned to His disciples and said privately, Blessed are the eyes which see the things you see; for I tell you that many prophets and kings have desired to see what you see, and have not seen it, and to hear what you hear, and have not heard it. And behold, a certain lawyer stood up and tested Him, saying, Teacher, what shall I do to inherit eternal life? He said to him, What is written in the law? What is your reading of it? So he answered and said, `You shall love the Lord your God with all your heart, with all your soul, with all your strength, and with all your mind' and `your neighbour as yourself.' And He said to him, You have answered rightly; do this and you will live.- Luke 10:21-28

Glory be to God Forever, Amen

THIRD SUNDAY OF THOUT

Holy Gospel

Stand up in the fear of God and listen to the Holy Gospel, A chapter from the Holy Gospel according to Saint Matthew , May his blessings be with us all, Amen

From the psalms of our teacher David the prophet and king, May his blessings be with us all, Amen

> And those who know Your name will put their trust in You; For You, Lord, have not forsaken those who seek You. Sing praises to the Lord, who dwells in Zion! Declare His deeds among the people. . Alleluia. - Psalms 9:10-11

Blessed is He who comes in the Name of the Lord Our Lord, God and Saviour and the King of us all, Jesus Christ, the Son of the living God. Glory be to You forever more, Amen

Now when Jesus had entered Capernaum, a centurion came to Him, pleading with Him, saying, "Lord, my servant is lying at home paralyzed, dreadfully tormented." And Jesus said to him, "I will come and heal him." The centurion answered and said, "Lord, I am not worthy that You should come under my roof. But only speak a word, and my servant will be healed. For I also am a man under authority, having soldiers under me. And I say to this one, 'Go,' and he goes; and to another, 'Come,' and he comes; and to my servant, 'Do this,' and he does it." When Jesus heard it, He marveled, and said to those who followed, "Assuredly, I say to you, I have not found such great faith, not even in Israel! And I say to you that many will come from east and west, and sit down with Abraham, Isaac, and Jacob in the kingdom of heaven. But the sons of the kingdom will be cast out into outer darkness. There will be weeping and gnashing of teeth." Then Jesus said to the centurion, "Go your way; and as you have believed, so let it be done for you." And his servant was healed that same hour. Matthew 8: 5-13

Glory be to God Forever, Amen

Pauline

Paul, the servant of our Lord Jesus Christ, called to be an apostle, appointed to the Gospel of God. A reading from the First Epistle of our teacher Paul to the Corinthians. May his holy blessings be with us. Amen.

Dear Corinthians,

When I first met you, I did not try to trick you with my words. No! I just told you the truth about Jesus and His crucifixion. We went through a lot together. Sometimes we felt weak and afraid. But it was the strength we got from the Holy Spirit that got us through! I want you to be wise. That means being able to understand things really well. But I want you to know that God's wisdom is much, much wiser than the wisdom of any human being, even a king! If they were really wise, do you think they would have crucified Jesus on the cross? Of course not! But God's wisdom and understanding is so deep, sometimes it is hard for human beings to really understand it. We call this "mystery".

What is heaven like? It is a mystery. That's why the Bible says "Eye has not seen, nor ear heard, nor have entered into the heart of man the things which God has prepared for those who love Him." "Eye has not seen, nor ear heard, nor have entered into the heart of man the things which God has prepared for those who love Him." But God gave us a way to understand these mysteries just as the spirit of a human understands humans, so the Holy Spirit of God understands the mysteries of God. And we have the Holy Spirit in us! And the Holy Spirit in us is happy to teach us about these wise mysteries! This teaching of the Holy Spirit is not like the teaching of the world. Other people hear it but they don't want to listen to the Holy Spirit. They think it makes no sense! But we know just how beautiful and true the spiritual wisdom of God is. We learn, little by little, to think and understand just like Jesus did. We have the mind of Christ. (1 Corinthians 2:1-16)

Signed, Paul

The grace of God the Father be with you all, Amen.

Catholicon

The Catholic Epistle from the First Epistle of our teacher St Peter. May his holy blessings be with us. Amen.

Hello Everyone!

How should we live our lives on earth? What kind of people should we be? We should learn how to think well, always hoping in the grace—the generous good gifts—Jesus gives us. We should be obedient to God, who is Good and Holy. We should not be obedient to bad people, or to our own bad thoughts. God says: "Be holy, as I am holy."

That means we should try hard to be good people, with good hearts, doing good things. Our Good and Loving Father is always watching over us!

Let's make Him happy with our lives! Our Father gave us a very special gift indeed, to help us to be good people who live good lives. Do you know what that is? He gave us His own beloved Son, Jesus Christ! Jesus loved us before world was even created. Jesus came to the world to save us from sin and death. Jesus bought us back and set us freely paying a very expensive price; Jesus did not pay with silver or gold or money. Jesus paid with. His own precious Blood, with His own life, on the Cross. Just like a gentle, innocent lamb—the 'Lamb of God'—He died, so we can live. And His Father raised Him gloriously from the dead! And because we believe in Him, because we try to be good and holy like Him. Then we will also share in His glorious victory! Our hope and faith is always in God. (1 Peter 1:13-21)

Signed, Peter the apostle

Do not love the world, nor the things which are in the world. The world shall pass away and all its desires; but he who does the will of God shall abide forever. Amen.

The Acts

Do you remember St Paul, who used to be called Saul before he saw Jesus and became a Christian? And do you remember how St Paul travelled around the world, bravely telling people how much Jesus loves them? Paul was always getting into trouble, because some people were bad, and they didn't like what Paul was saying. Some of these bad people came up with a very nasty plan. They wanted to kill Paul! Oh no! Whatever are you going to do, Paul? So Paul came up with a clever plan. When it was dark, some of his friends got a big basket, and they put him inside. But he wasn't hiding.

They tied a rope to the basket, and they carefully let it down the outside of the walls of the city. Paul had escaped! Next he went to Jerusalem. But the Disciples there were really scared of him! They remembered that when he was called Saul, he used to help people to kill the Christians. But Paul's friend Barnabas took him to the Disciples and told them the story of how Jesus had appeared to Saul, and changed him, so that now he loved Jesus.

The Disciples were really happy to hear that! So Saul began to tell people in Jerusalem about Jesus. He told lots and lots of people! But some of the people in Jerusalem didn't like what he was saying, so guess what they wanted to do? They wanted to kill him! When his friends found out, they snuck him out of Jerusalem, and he went to other cities. And everywhere he went, he told everyone about Jesus.

So the Christian Churches in all these places were growing and growing and growing. And walking in the fear of the Lord and in the comfort of the Holy Spirit, they were multiplied. - Acts 9:22-31

Holy Gospel

Stand up in the fear of God and listen to the Holy Gospel,A chapter from the Holy Gospel according to Saint Luke,May his blessings be with us all, Amen

From the psalms of our teacher David the prophet and king,May his blessings be with us all, Amen

> The Lord lives, and blessed is my God. Let the salvation of my God be exalted. Therefore I will give thanks to You among the Gentiles, O Lord, And sing to Your name. Alleluia. - Psalms 18:46,49

Blessed is He who comes in the Name of the Lord Our Lord, God and Saviour and the King of us all, Jesus Christ, the Son of the living God. Glory be to You forever more, Amen

Then Jesus entered and passed through Jericho. Now behold, there was a man named Zacchaeus who was a chief tax collector, and he was rich. And he sought to see who Jesus was, but could not because of the crowd, for he was of short stature. So he ran ahead and climbed up into a sycamore tree to see Him, for He was going to pass that way.

And when Jesus came to the place, He looked up and saw him, and said to him "Zacchaeus, make haste and come down, for today I must stay at your house.", So he made haste and came down, and received Him joyfully. But when they saw it, they all complained, saying, He has gone to be a guest with a man who is a sinner.

Then Zacchaeus stood and said to the Lord, Look, Lord, I give half of my goods to the poor; and if I have taken anything from anyone by false accusation, I restore fourfold. And Jesus said to him, Today salvation has come to this house, because he also is a son of Abraham; for the Son of Man has come to seek and to save that which was lost. - Luke 19:1-10

Glory be to God Forever, Amen

FOURTH SUNDAY OF THOUT

Holy Gospel

Stand up in the fear of God and listen to the Holy Gospel,A chapter from the Holy Gospel according to Saint Matthew,May his blessings be with us all, Amen

From the psalms of our teacher David the prophet and king,May his blessings be with us all, Amen

> Our soul waits for the Lord; He is our help and our shield. For our heart shall rejoice in Him, Because we have trusted in His holy name Alleluia. - Psalms 33:20-21

Blessed is He who comes in the Name of the Lord Our Lord, God and Saviour and the King of us all, Jesus Christ, the Son of the living God. Glory be to You forever more, Amen

Then Jesus went out from there and departed to the region of Tyre and Sidon. And behold, a woman of Canaan came from that region and cried out to Him, saying, "Have mercy on me, O Lord, Son of David! My daughter is severely demon-possessed." But He answered her not a word. And His disciples came and urged Him, saying, "Send her away, for she cries out after us. But He answered and said, "I was not sent except to the lost sheep of the house of Israel." Then she came and worshiped Him, saying, "Lord, help me!" But He answered and said, "It is not good to take the children's bread and throw it to the little dogs." And she said, "Yes, Lord, yet even the little dogs eat the crumbs which fall from their masters' table." Then Jesus answered and said to her, "O woman, great is your faith! Let it be to you as you desire." And her daughter was healed from that very hour. Matthew 15:21-28

Glory be to God Forever, Amen

Pauline

LITURGY

Paul, the servant of our Lord Jesus Christ, called to be an apostle, appointed to the Gospel of God. A reading from the Second Epistle of our teacher Paul to the Corinthians. May his holy blessings be with us. Amen.

Dear Corinthians,

God is so kind to us all. Whenever we are sad, He makes us feel better. And then, we can make other

sad people feel better! Because we love Jesus, we are happy to suffer with Him. But then, that means we also get to be happy with Him! In the same way, if you are suffering with us, you will also be happy with us! Can I tell you why I and my friends were suffering when we were in Asia?

Things were so tough, we thought we were going to die! But then we remembered how Jesus suffered and died on the Cross. And we KNEW we were going to be OK, because that same Jesus rose from the dead! And we also knew that you were praying for us! Saying "thank You" to God because He always helps us. That made us feel better! Something else that made us feel better is that we always behaved honestly and simply with everyone including you! With us, what you see is what you get!

I hope you know just how proud of you we are and I hope that you will be proud of us too in the Last Day, the Day of our Lord Jesus. (2 Corinthians 1:1-14)

Bye for now!

Signed, Paul

The grace of God the Father be with you all, Amen.

Catholicon

The Catholic Epistle from the First Epistle of our teacher St John. May his holy blessings be with us. Amen.

My dear brothers and sisters,

Do you know why Jesus, the Son of God, became a human being? Jesus became a man so that He could stop the devil and all the bad things the devil does. That is how you can tell which side a person is on: If a person does bad things, then that person is on the devil's side, not God's side. And if a person does good things, then that person is on the God's side, not the devil's side.

So if you don't do the right thing, and if you don't love others, you are not really on God's side, are you? This is what God has been telling us from the beginning: That we should love one another. We should not be like Cain. Do you remember the story of Cain and Abel? Remember how Cain was so jealous of his brother Abel that he killed him? Oh, how horrible! Cain did that horrible thing because he chose to be on the side of the devil. So he ended up doing what the devil does: Something really horrible. But we are on God's side. We would never be on the bad, bad devil's side! (1 John 3:8-12)

God loves you!

Signed, John the beloved

Do not love the world, nor the things which are in the world. The world shall pass away and all its desires; but he who does the will of God shall abide forever. Amen.

The Acts

Today we have a story about St Peter, one of the 12 Disciples,

There was once a lovely lady named Tabitha (or Dorcas) who lived in a town called Joppa Tabitha was ever so kind and gentle. She helped so many people. But one day, she fell sick and she died! Everyone was so, so sad. They washed her body and put it in her room.

Then someone remembered that Peter was in the next town, a town called Lydda. "Hey", he said, "let's send a couple of men to call Peter to come and pray with us. Lydda is not very far from Joppa!" When they brought Peter, he saw just how sad everyone was. They really loved Tabitha because she was such a kind and helpful person. Tabitha's friends were crying and remembering how kind she was, and looking at the lovely clothes Tabitha had made when she was still alive.

But Peter had a plan. He asked everyone to leave the room where Tabitha was. Guess what he did next? Peter knelt down on the ground next to Tabitha's body. And he prayed for her. Then he lifted his eyes, he looked at Tabitha and he spoke to her "Tabitha!" he said, "Arise!" And Tabitha opened her eyes! She was alive!

When she saw Peter, she sat up! So Peter took her by the hand and called everyone back so they could see her. When the people of Joppa heard about this great miracle, lots of them came and became Christians! (Acts 9:36-42)

Holy Gospel

Stand up in the fear of God and listen to the Holy Gospel, A chapter from the Holy Gospel according to Saint Luke, May his blessings be with us all, Amen

From the psalms of our teacher David the prophet and king, May his blessings be with us all, Amen

> The Lord is the strength of His people. Save Your people, bless Your inheritance and raise them up forever. Alleluia. - Psalm 28:8-9

Blessed is He who comes in the Name of the Lord Our Lord, God and Saviour and the King of us all, Jesus Christ, the Son of the living God. Glory be to You forever more, Amen

Then one of the Pharisees asked Him to eat with him. And behold, a woman in the city who was a sinner, brought an alabaster flask of fragrant oil, and stood at His feet behind Him weeping; and she began to wash His feet with her tears, and wiped them with the hair of her head; and she kissed His feet and anointed them with the fragrant oil. Now when the Pharisee who had invited Him saw this, he spoke to himself, saying, "This man, if He were a prophet, would know who and what manner of woman this is who is touching Him, for she is a sinner." And Jesus answered and said to him,

"There was a certain creditor who had two debtors. One owed five hundred denarii, and the other fifty. And when they had nothing with which to repay, he freely forgave them both. Tell Me, therefore, which of them will love him more?" Simon answered and said, "I suppose the one whom he forgave more." And He said to him, "You have rightly judged." Then He turned to the woman and said to Simon, "Do you see this woman? I entered your house; you gave Me no water for My feet, but she has washed My feet with her tears and wiped them with the hair of her head. You gave Me no kiss, but this woman has not ceased to kiss My feet since the time I came in. You did not anoint My head with oil, but this woman has anointed My feet with fragrant oil. Therefore I say to you, her sins, which are many, are forgiven, for she loved much. But to whom little is forgiven, the same loves little." Then He said to her, "Your sins are forgiven. Your faith has saved you. Go in peace." - Luke 7:36-50

Glory be to God Forever, Amen

FIRST SUNDAY OF BABAH

Holy Gospel

Stand up in the fear of God and listen to the Holy Gospel, A chapter from the Holy Gospel according to Saint Matthew, May his blessings be with us all, Amen

From the psalms of our teacher David the prophet and king, May his blessings be with us all, Amen

> O God, You are my God; Early will I seek You; My soul thirsts for You; My flesh longs for You In a dry and thirsty land Where there is no water. So I have looked for You in the sanctuary, To see Your power and Your glory. Alleluia. - Psalm 63:1-2

Blessed is He who comes in the Name of the Lord Our Lord, God and Saviour and the King of us all, Jesus Christ, the Son of the living God. Glory be to You forever more, Amen

Now after the Sabbath, as the first day of the week began to dawn, Mary Magdalene and the other Mary came to see the tomb. And behold, there was a great earthquake; for an angel of the Lord descended from heaven, and came and rolled back the stone from the door, and sat on it. His countenance was like lightning, and his clothing as white as snow. And the guards shook for fear of him, and became like dead men. But the angel answered and said to the women, "Do not be afraid, for I know that you seek Jesus who was crucified. He is not here; for He is risen, as He said. Come, see the place where the Lord lay. And go quickly and tell His disciples that He is risen from the dead, and indeed He is going before you into Galilee; there you will see Him. Behold, I have told you." So they went out quickly from the tomb with fear and great joy, and ran to bring His disciples word. And as they went to tell His disciples, behold, Jesus met them, saying, "Rejoice!" So they came and held Him by the feet and worshiped Him.

Then Jesus said to them, "Do not be afraid. Go and tell My brethren to go to Galilee, and there they will see Me." Now while they were going, behold, some of the guard came into the city and reported to the chief priests all the things that had happened. When they had assembled with the elders and consulted together, they gave a large sum of money to the soldiers, saying, "Tell them, 'His disciples came at night and stole Him away while we slept.' And if this comes to the governor's ears, we will appease him and make you secure." So they took the money and did as they were instructed; and this saying is commonly reported among the Jews until this day. Then the eleven disciples went away into Galilee, to the mountain which Jesus had appointed for them. When they saw Him, they worshiped Him; but some doubted. And Jesus came and spoke to them, saying, "All authority has been given to Me in heaven and on earth. Go therefore and make disciples of all the nations, baptizing them in the name of the Father and of the Son and of the Holy Spirit, teaching them to observe all things that I have commanded you; and lo, I am with you always, even to the end of the age." Amen. Matthew 28:1-20

Glory be to God Forever, Amen

Pauline

Paul, the servant of our Lord Jesus Christ, called to be an apostle, appointed to the Gospel of God. A reading from the Second Epistle of our teacher Paul to the Corinthians. May his holy blessings be with us. Amen.

Dear Corinthians,

I have recently been to the city called Troas. There God helped us to tell lots and lots of people about Him. But I was a little worried, because I expected to find my friend Titus there, but he wasn't there; so I went on to another place, called Macedonia. I am so thankful to God! He always helps us! He makes us like a sweet smelling perfume that everyone loves to smell! I know that some people who don't like Jesus think we are more like a bad smell. But to God, we are like a beautiful fragrance, a sweet-smelling perfume that gives life to others. God is so kind to us! So much more than we really deserve. Helping people to know God and to love Him is not just a job like other jobs, you know? It is something we do from our hearts—don't you know this already?

We spoke to you from our hearts about Jesus, and you loved Him from your hearts. And so you became like a letter written by us, not with pen and ink. No, you became a letter written in our hearts and everybody reads that 'letter' and knows God. We trust God, through our Lord Jesus Christ, and we know that it is HE who teaches people through us, we don't do it ourselves. He uses us to tell others about His New Promise to everyone, not the Old Promise where people had to be so strict about every little tiny thing. but the New Promise, the Promise of the Spirit, the Promise of LOVE. You see; being picky about every little thing doesn't make God happy, or anyone else! But LOVING God? That makes God very, very happy, And everyone else too! (2 Corinthians 2:12-3:6)

Signed, Paul

> *The grace of God the Father be with you all, Amen.*

Catholicon

The Catholic Epistle from the First Epistle of our teacher St Peter. May his holy blessings be with us. Amen.

My little children,

Now that you have believed in the Truth of Jesus Christ, through the help of the Holy Spirit. Do you know what is really, really important for you to do?

To love one another from all your heart! Have you seen the flowers that spring up on the grass at Spring time? They're beautiful, aren't they? But they don't last! After a little while, they wilt and droop and turn brown. And then they die. That's sad. We were like those flowers before Jesus came to us. We all had to die. But then Jesus came and He taught us how we can live forever!

You were born again in Jesus when you were baptised. Only this time, you were born so you could live forever. Not like a little flower that fades and dies. So if you have indeed got to know Jesus, and follow His word that lasts forever, and if you really, really love Him. Then you will NOT do any of these things:

You won't HATE anyone. You won't LIE to anyone. You won't be TWO-FACED. You won't be JEALOUS of anyone. And, you won't SAY BAD THINGS about anyone. For you see: if you don't do any of these horrible things, you will be like a precious stone to God. Jesus Himself was like a very special stone. Jesus is like the biggest stone in the corner, and we are like the bricks that make up the wall. The wall of the holy House of God, where God's Spirit lives. And Jesus is the Cornerstone of our lives—our lives and everything we say or do is built around Jesus. (1 Peter 1:22-3:5)

Signed, Peter the Apostle

Do not love the world, nor the things which are in the world. The world shall pass away and all its desires; but he who does the will of God shall abide forever. Amen.

The Acts

A reading from the Acts of our fathers the pure apostles, who were invested with the grace of the Holy Spirit. May their blessing be with us all. Amen.

Today we have a story about St Peter, one of the 12 Disciples. One day, St Paul was preaching about Jesus in the synagogue, the meeting place where all the Jewish people came to pray. After telling them about the story of how God has helped human beings from the very beginning, Paul was up to the bit about King David: You all know, said St Paul, That after King David had served his people well, he grew old and died. But Jesus served His people, died, and rose again from the dead! This is why Jesus can do something that no one else could ever do. Moses couldn't do it and King David couldn't do it, Do you know what it is?

Yes! Jesus can forgive sins! Even Moses and King David made prophecies about Him. They believed in Him, even though they hadn't seen Him yet. So, if YOU don't believe in Jesus, be careful! be very, very careful, because your own prophets warned you about the punishments of those who don't believe in God.

And now, God has done an amazing miracle when He sent His Son to earth. And you have heard all about Him. So, what are you going to do?

After the service was finished, they all went out, and lots of the Jews came out and asked St Paul to tell them more about this wonderful Jesus. And even their friends who were not even Jewish, they said to St Paul: Can you PLEASE speak to us next week? We want to hear about this Jesus too!" (Acts 13:36-43)

The word of the Lord shall grow, multiply, be mighty and be confirmed in the holy Church of God. Amen.

Holy Gospel

Stand up in the fear of God and listen to the Holy Gospel, A chapter from the Holy Gospel according to Saint Mark, May his blessings be with us all, Amen

From the psalms of our teacher David the prophet and king, May his blessings be with us all, Amen

> I will bless the Lord at all times; His praise shall continually be in my mouth. My soul shall be praised in the Lord; Let the gentle hear, and be glad. Alleluia. - Psalm 34:1-2

Blessed is He who comes in the Name of the Lord Our Lord, God and Saviour and the King of us all, Jesus Christ, the Son of the living God. Glory be to You forever more, Amen

And again He entered Capernaum after some days, and it was heard that He was in the house. Immediately many gathered together, so that there was no longer room to receive them, not even near the door. And He preached the word to them. Then they came to Him, bringing a paralytic who was carried by four men. And when they could not come near Him because of the crowd, they uncovered the roof where He was. So when they had broken through, they let down the bed on which the paralytic was lying. When Jesus saw their faith, He said to the paralytic, "Son, your sins are forgiven you." And some of the scribes were sitting there and reasoning in their hearts, "Why does this Man speak blasphemies like this? Who can forgive sins but God alone?" But immediately, when Jesus perceived in His spirit that they reasoned thus within themselves, He said to them, "Why do you reason about these things in your hearts? Which is easier, to say to the paralytic, 'Your sins are forgiven you,' or to say, 'Arise, take up your bed and walk'? But that you may know that the Son of Man has power on earth to forgive sins"--He said to the paralytic, I say to you, arise, take up your bed, and go to your house." Immediately he arose, took up the bed, and went out in the presence of them all, so that all were amazed and glorified God, saying, "We never saw anything like this!" - Mark 2:1-12

Glory be to God Forever, Amen

SECOND SUNDAY OF BABAH

Holy Gospel

MATINS

Stand up in the fear of God and listen to the Holy Gospel, A chapter from the Holy Gospel according to Saint Mark, May his blessings be with us all, Amen

From the psalms of our teacher David the prophet and king, May his blessings be with us all, Amen

> When I remember You on my bed, I meditate on You in the night watches. Because Your lovingkindness is better than life, My lips shall praise You. Thus I will bless You while I live; I will lift up my hands in Your name. Alleluia. - Psalm 63: 6,3-4

Blessed is He who comes in the Name of the Lord Our Lord, God and Saviour and the King of us all, Jesus Christ, the Son of the living God. Glory be to You forever more, Amen

Very early in the morning, on the first day of the week, they came to the tomb when the sun had risen. And they said among themselves, "Who will roll away the stone from the door of the tomb for us?" But when they looked up, they saw that the stone had been rolled away—for it was very large. And entering the tomb, they saw a young man clothed in a long white robe sitting on the right side; and they were alarmed. But he said to them, "Do not be alarmed. You seek Jesus of Nazareth, who was crucified. He is risen! He is not here. See the place where they laid Him. But go, tell His disciples—and Peter—that He is going before you into Galilee; there you will see Him, as He said to you." So they went out quickly and fled from the tomb, for they trembled and were amazed. And they said nothing to anyone, for they were afraid. - Mark 16:2-8

Glory be to God Forever, Amen

Pauline

LITURGY

Paul, the servant of our Lord Jesus Christ, called to be an apostle, appointed to the Gospel of God. A reading from the Second Epistle of our teacher Paul to the Corinthians. May his holy blessings be with us. Amen.

Dear Corinthians,

We didn't come to tell you about ourselves! We came to tell you all about Jesus! We are here to serve you! It's not about us. It's all about God. Do you know what God has done for us all? God made His Light shine to save us from the darkness. That Light is Jesus Christ! But we are like jars made of clay. The Light shines on us and makes us glow too. Jesus is our Light, and it is Jesus who is our power. Through the power of Jesus, even if we are squished we are never crushed!

Even if we are confused, we never lose hope! Even if we are treated badly, we are never left alone! Even if we are struck down, we are never destroyed! Our bodies might look like we are suffering—just like Jesus, but we are alive! Just like Jesus. That is what our suffering means—sharing with Jesus. Our bodies suffer with Jesus, And our bodies live with Jesus. And the same Life, which is living with Jesus, is happening in your life too because we believe and speak the same things about Jesus. And we know that He who raised up the Lord Jesus will also raise us up with Jesus, and will present us with you. God does all these things for us! When His kindness and His grace spreads to lots of people; Lots of people will thank and glorify God! (2 Corinthians 4:5-15)

Bye for now!

Signed, Paul

The grace of God the Father be with you all, Amen.

Catholicon

The Catholic Epistle from the Epistle of our teacher St James. May his holy blessings be with us.

Hello Everyone!

Do you know how to tell if you are wise and clever at understanding things? You are clever if your behaviour and actions are good and humble and thoughtful. On the other hand, If you are selfish and always fighting with others, then don't fool yourself! You are not clever or wise at all! You are not following God, you are following the devil! Wherever you find people being selfish, and arguing, and fighting, that's where you find confusion and evil. How sad! But the true cleverness and wisdom that comes from God is different. It is pure. It is peaceful. It is gentle. It is willing to give in happily. It does not cheat. It doesn't say one thing but do the opposite.

Good and wise people spread peace everywhere and make peace to grow in everyone's hearts and lives. So, why do you fight with each other? Isn't it because you are selfish? You say, "I want this I want that! Waaah!!!" But you never get what you want. You don't get what you ask for because you are selfish. That is not wise! That is just being silly! Don't you know that if you want to be a friend of the world and all its selfishness, you cannot be a friend of God? Have you forgotten just how much God loves you, and wants you to be loving, just like Him? But God is patient with us and gives us more grace. So remember what God says: God resists the proud, but gives grace to the humble. Don't be a proud, selfish person. Be a humble, loving person. Just like Jesus. (James 3:13-4:6)

Signed, James the Apostle

Do not love the world, nor the things which are in the world. The world shall pass away and all its desires; but he who does the will of God shall abide forever. Amen.

The Acts

St Paul and St Barnabas were travelling all over the world to tell people about Jesus. They came to a city called Antioch and they got all the Christians there together in the Church, and told them about their great adventures. They told them how God was bringing many people who were not Jewish (they're called Gentiles) to become Christians. And they rested in Antioch for many days. While they were in Antioch, some Jewish Christians came from Judea. But these men were trouble-makers! The trouble-makers started to tell everyone that you couldn't really be a Christian unless you became Jewish first!!! Do you think that's right? Well, Paul and Barnabas said, "NO!" Jesus accepts people from any country and any race. Sadly, Paul and Barnabas couldn't convince the trouble-makers, so they all agreed on a plan: Paul, Barnabas and some other men would go to Jerusalem and ask the apostles and the elders to settle this question, once and for all! So off they went to Jerusalem. And all along the way they met many Christians. And Paul and Barnabas told everyone they met stories about how so many Gentiles were becoming Christians, which made them so happy! (Chapter 14:24-15:3)

Holy Gospel

Stand up in the fear of God and listen to the Holy Gospel, A chapter from the Holy Gospel according to Saint Luke, May his blessings be with us all, Amen

From the psalms of our teacher David the prophet and king, May his blessings be with us all, Amen

> Shout to God, all the earth; Sing now to His name; Give glory to His praise. Let all the earth worship You and sing to You. Alleluia. - Psalm 66:1-2, 4

Blessed is He who comes in the Name of the Lord Our Lord, God and Saviour and the King of us all, Jesus Christ, the Son of the living God. Glory be to You forever more, Amen

So it was, as the multitude pressed about Him to hear the word of God that He stood by the Lake of Gennesaret, and saw two boats standing by the lake; but the fishermen had gone from them and were washing their nets. Then He got into one of the boats, which was Simon's, and asked him to put out a little from the land. And He sat down and taught the multitudes from the boat. When He had stopped speaking, He said to Simon, Launch out into the deep and let down your nets for a catch. But Simon answered and said to Him, Master, we have toiled all night and caught nothing; nevertheless at Your word I will let down the net. And when they had done this, they caught a great number of fish, and their net was breaking. So they signalled to their partners in the other boat

to come and help them. And they came and filled both the boats, so that they began to sink. When Simon Peter saw it, he fell down at Jesus' knees, saying, Depart from me, for I am a sinful man, O Lord! For he and all who were with him were astonished at the catch of fish which they had taken; and so also were James and John, the sons of Zebedee, who were partners with Simon. And Jesus said to Simon, Do not be afraid. From now on you will catch men. So when they had brought their boats to land, they forsook all and followed Him. Luke 5:1-11

Glory be to God Forever, Amen

THIRD SUNDAY OF BABAH

Holy Gospel

Stand up in the fear of God and listen to the Holy Gospel, A chapter from the Holy Gospel according to Saint Luke, May his blessings be with us all, Amen

From the psalms of our teacher David the prophet and king, May his blessings be with us all, Amen

> Awake, my glory! Awake, lute and harp! I will awaken the dawn. I will praise You, O Lord, among the peoples; I will sing to You among the nations. Alleluia. - Psalm 57:8-9

Blessed is He who comes in the Name of the Lord Our Lord, God and Saviour and the King of us all, Jesus Christ, the Son of the living God. Glory be to You forever more, Amen

Now on the first day of the week, very early in the morning, they, and certain other women with them, came to the tomb bringing the spices which they had prepared. But they found the stone rolled away from the tomb. Then they went in and did not find the body of the Lord Jesus. And it happened, as they were greatly perplexed about this, that behold, two men stood by them in shining garments. Then, as they were afraid and bowed their faces to the earth, they said to them, "Why do you seek the living among the dead? He is not here, but is risen! Remember how He spoke to you when He was still in Galilee, saying, 'The Son of Man must be delivered into the hands of sinful men, and be crucified, and the third day rise again.' " And they remembered His words. Then they returned from the tomb and told all these things to the eleven and to all the rest. It was Mary Magdalene, Joanna, Mary the mother of James, and the other women with them, who told these things to the apostles. And their words seemed to them like idle tales, and they did not believe them. But Peter arose and ran to the tomb; and stooping down, he saw the linen cloths lying by themselves; and he departed, marveling to himself at what had happened. Luke 24: 1-12

Glory be to God Forever, Amen

Pauline

Paul, the servant of our Lord Jesus Christ, called to be an apostle, appointed to the Gospel of God. A reading from the First Epistle of our teacher Paul to the Corinthians. May his holy blessings be with us. Amen.

Dear Corinthians,

St Paul the Apostle was writing a letter to the Christians who lived in the rich city of Corinth.

Dear Corinthians, I want you to know that I encouraged our friend Apollos to come to visit you, but he couldn't just now. I want you to be awake! Hold on tight to your faith! Be brave! Be strong!

Whatever you do, do it with love. Be sure to listen and obey those who serve with us, like Stephanas and his family who have given their whole lives to serving God. I was so glad when Stephanas and Fortunatus and Achaicus came to visit me! They brought us all your love and kindness!

Oh, and some other people also wanted me to say a big hello to you from them: All the churches in Asia, and Aquila and Priscilla who have a church in their own house. Actually, all our brothers and sisters say a big, hearty, "hello"! Greet one another with a holy kiss. And here is my signature written by my own hand.

PS. If anyone does not love the Lord Jesus Christ, I feel sorry them. O Lord, come! The grace of our Lord Jesus Christ be with you. My love be with you all in Christ Jesus. Amen. (1 Corinthians 16:12-24)

Bye for now!

Signed, Paul

The grace of God the Father be with you all, Amen.

Catholicon

The Catholic Epistle from the Epistle of our teacher St James. May his holy blessings be with us.

From James,

Give in to God! Stand up to the devil, and he will run away from you! Come closer to God and He will come closer to you. If you have done the wrong thing, tell God that you are sorry. Don't be all mixed up! Don't try to get away with doing the wrong thing! That's crazy!

It is so much better to own up and confess before God. Be sad for your sins, so God can forgive you and make you happy again. He will lift you up high!

Don't say bad things about each other - who made you the Judge??? There is only one true Judge— so leave the judging to Him. And don't be so proud as to say "I will do this", or "I am certainly going to do that". Our life is only short, and we are weak, like smoke that soon blows away in the wind. So it's better to say, "If God wills, I will do this or that". If you know how to do the right thing, and you still don't do it, that's bad: that's a sin. (James 4:7-17)

Bye for now!

Signed, James the Apostle

Do not love the world, nor the things which are in the world. The world shall pass away and all its desires; but he who does the will of God shall abide forever. Amen.

The Acts

Do you remember last week, how Paul and Barnabas had an argument with some troublemakers, who said the only way to be Christian was to be Jewish first? And finally they agreed that they should go back to Jerusalem, to ask the rest of the Apostles to tell them if this was right or wrong?

Well, they finally made it to Jerusalem! And they told all the apostles and elders there about all the wonderful things God had done with them. And some Christians who were also Pharisees stood up and insisted: "Every Christian simply has to become Jewish! And they have to keep all the Jewish laws of Moses!" Oh dear! However were they going to solve this problem? So they all got together for a big meeting.

Then Peter the Apostle got up and started to speak, "My friends," said Peter, "you all remember that God chose me a while ago to tell some people who are not Jewish about Jesus, don't you?" "And when those people believed in Jesus, God filled them with the Holy Spirit, just like He filled us with the Holy Spirit." "God knew what was in their hearts, but He didn't treat them any different to the way He treated us. His Holy Spirit made their hearts just as pure as ours." "So why do you want to be tougher than God?! Why do you want to force them to obey a million rules that we couldn't obey, and even our grandfathers couldn't obey?" "But we believe that through God's love and grace, all of us will be saved, whether we are Jews or not." When Peter finished, everyone listened with amazement as Barnabas and Paul told them all the wonderful miracles God had done among those who were not Jewish. (Chapter 15:4-12)

Holy Gospel

Stand up in the fear of God and listen to the Holy Gospel, A chapter from the Holy Gospel according to Saint Matthew, May his blessings be with us all, Amen

From the psalms of our teacher David the prophet and king, May his blessings be with us all, Amen

And You are my strong helper. Let my mouth be filled with Your praise, That I may sing of Your glory And of Your magnificence all the day long. Alleluia. - Psalm 71:7-8

Blessed is He who comes in the Name of the Lord Our Lord, God and Saviour and the King of us all, Jesus Christ, the Son of the living God. Glory be to You forever more, Amen

Then one was brought to Him who was demon-possessed, blind and mute; and He healed him, so that the blind and mute man both spoke and saw. And all the multitudes were amazed and said, Could this be the Son of David? Now when the Pharisees heard it they said, This fellow does not cast out demons except by Beelzebub, the ruler of the demons. But Jesus knew their thoughts, and said to them: Every kingdom divided against itself is brought to desolation, and every city or house divided against itself will not stand. If Satan casts out Satan, he is divided against himself. How then will his kingdom stand? And if I cast out demons by Beelzebub, by whom do your sons cast them out? Therefore they shall be your judges. But if I cast out demons by the Spirit of God, surely the kingdom of God has come upon you. Matthew 12:22-28

Glory be to God Forever, Amen

FOURTH SUNDAY OF BABAH

Holy Gospel

MATINS

Stand up in the fear of God and listen to the Holy Gospel, A chapter from the Holy Gospel according to Saint John, May his blessings be with us all, Amen

From the psalms of our teacher David the prophet and king, May his blessings be with us all, Amen

> I will give You thanks in the great assembly; I will praise You among many people. And my tongue shall speak of Your righteousness And of Your praise all the day long. Alleluia. - Psalm 35: 18,28

Blessed is He who comes in the Name of the Lord Our Lord, God and Saviour and the King of us all, Jesus Christ, the Son of the living God. Glory be to You forever more, Amen

Now the first day of the week Mary Magdalene went to the tomb early, while it was still dark, and saw that the stone had been taken away from the tomb. Then she ran and came to Simon Peter, and to the other disciple, whom Jesus loved, and said to them, "They have taken away the Lord out of the tomb, and we do not know where they have laid Him." Peter therefore went out, and the other disciple, and were going to the tomb. So they both ran together, and the other disciple outran Peter and came to the tomb first. And he, stooping down and looking in, saw the linen cloths lying there; yet he did not go in. Then Simon Peter came, following him, and went into the tomb; and he saw the linen cloths lying there, and the handkerchief that had been around His head, not lying with the linen cloths, but folded together in a place by itself. Then the other disciple, who came to the tomb first, went in also; and he saw and believed. For as yet they did not know the Scripture, that He must rise again from the dead. Then the disciples went away again to their own homes. But Mary stood outside by the tomb weeping, and as she wept she stooped down and looked into the tomb. And she saw two angels in white sitting, one at the head and the other at the feet, where the body of Jesus had lain. Then they said to her, "Woman, why are you weeping?" She said to them, "Because they have taken away my Lord, and I do not know where they have laid

Him." Now when she had said this, she turned around and saw Jesus standing there, and did not know that it was Jesus. Jesus said to her, "Woman, why are you weeping? Whom are you seeking?" She, supposing Him to be the gardener, said to Him, "Sir, if You have carried Him away, tell me where You have laid Him, and I will take Him away." Jesus said to her, "Mary!" She turned and said to Him, "Rabboni!" (which is to say, Teacher). Jesus said to her, "Do not cling to Me, for I have not yet ascended to My Father; but go to My brethren and say to them, 'I am ascending to My Father and your Father, and to My God and your God.'" Mary Magdalene came and told the disciples that she had seen the Lord, and that He had spoken these things to her. John 20:1-18

Glory be to God Forever, Amen

Pauline LITURGY

Paul, the servant of our Lord Jesus Christ, called to be an apostle, appointed to the Gospel of God. A reading from the First Epistle of our teacher Paul to Timothy. May his holy blessings be with us. Amen.

St Paul the Apostle was writing a letter to his good friend Timothy.

Dear Timothy, I am very concerned that there are some people in church who don't follow what Jesus taught us. These people think that THEY know everything, and love nothing better than arguing and arguing and arguing for hours over nothing. They blame everybody else and make friends become enemies. They think that church is a place for them to become rich and popular! They just want to boss everyone around. You really should just stay right away from people like this. The best thing in life is to do good things and to be happy with what you have. We were born owning nothing, weren't we! And when we die, can we take our riches with us? Of course not! But some people love money more than they love God, and this has made them greedy and sad and really nasty to other people. So if you really love God, don't be like that. Try to be kind, and generous, and patient and gentle instead. Fight the good fight of faith which you believe in, and have shared with others. Remember always that Jesus is with us and He can see everything we do. So do your best to follow Jesus Follow Jesus until He comes back in His own time, for He is the King of Kings and Lord of Lords. Jesus never dies. He is Light that no one can come near, and no one can describe, to Him be honour and everlasting power. Amen. And Timothy, tell those who are rich not to be proud, and not to depend on their money, but to depend instead on the Living God who gave us all we have. Tell the rich people to be rich in doing good things, ready to give, willing to share, because then they will be rich in heaven! O Timothy, my friend! Take good care of everything that has been given to you. Don't pay attention to wrong and silly teachings. Because some people did listen to wrong teachings and they lost their way. (1 Timothy 6:3-21)

Bye for now!

Signed, Paul

The grace of God the Father be with you all, Amen.

Catholicon

The Catholic Epistle from the Epistle of our teacher St James. May his holy blessings be with us.

From James,

Hello Everyone! I have some more very important advice for you; If you know how to do the right thing, and you still don't do it, that's bad: that's a sin. You who are rich— I feel so sorry for you! You should cry and weep for yourselves too! Do you know why? Because you thought your gold and your silver were going to protect you. But when Jesus comes, your money isn't going to do you any good at all! In fact, because you got your money by cheating and stealing and lying. Because you were selfish and didn't share your riches with anyone else - boy, are you going to be in BIG trouble, on that Last Day, when Jesus comes back!

So, my brothers and sisters, all of us should get ready for the coming of the Lord. You know how farmers sow their seeds, then they wait for the early rain. And then they wait the late rain. They are very patient, waiting and waiting, but always ready to gather the precious fruit as soon as it is ready. So we also should be patient and always ready, until Jesus comes. Be strong, for the Lord is near. Don't grumble about each other, so that you don't get in trouble. The Judge is at the door! (I mean Jesus, of course). And remember the prophets? How patient they were? Let's try to be like them. Indeed we count them blessed who endure. Remember how patient Job the Righteous was? See what a beautiful ending his story had? Yes, God is just so kind and so, so gentle! (James 4:17-5:11)

Signed, James the Apostle

Do not love the world, nor the things which are in the world. The world shall pass away and all its desires; but he who does the will of God shall abide forever. Amen.

The Acts

A reading from the Acts of our fathers the pure apostles, who were invested with the grace of the Holy Spirit. May their blessing be with us all. Amen.

Do you remember last week, we read about how Barnabas and Paul came to Jerusalem, and they agreed with all the apostles and the Christians that you don't have to be Jewish to be Christian? Well, after that big meeting was finished, Paul said to Barnabas, "Hey, why don't we go back and visit all those places where we set up Churches? Let's see how they're going." "Great!" said Barnabas. "And look, Mark is back! He can come and help us. It will be just like old times." Except, there was problem; You see, some time ago, Mark had left Barnabas and Paul half-way through one of their trips. Paul wasn't happy about that. Not at all. So Paul didn't want Mark to come with them. What if he just leaves them in the middle of the trip again? When Barnabas and Paul couldn't agree, they just decided to split up into two teams, instead of one. So Barnabas took Mark, and they sailed for Cyprus

While Paul took Silas, and they travelled to Syria and Cilicia [Si-li-see-yuh]. And both teams brought lots of love and strength to all the places they visited. Paul and his team came to Derbe and Lystra, and there they found a Christian called Timothy (remember him from Paul's letter?) whose father was Greek, but his mother was a Jewish Christian. Everybody told Paul that Timothy was an excellent Christian. So Paul added him to his team, after he circumcised him, so no one would complain about Timothy not being Jewish. So they all travelled around, telling the Christian Churches about the decisions that they took in Jerusalem with the apostles. And all the Churches were getting stronger and stronger in their faith and more and more people were becoming Christian and joining the Church. (Chapter 15:36-16:5)

The word of the Lord shall grow, multiply, be mighty and be confirmed in the holy Church of God. Amen.

Holy Gospel

Stand up in the fear of God and listen to the Holy Gospel, A chapter from the Holy Gospel according to Saint Luke, May his blessings be with us all, Amen

From the psalms of our teacher David the prophet and king, May his blessings be with us all, Amen

> For we are Your people and the sheep of Your pasture; We shall give thanks to You freely and openly forever; From generation to generation we will proclaim Your praise. Alleluia. - Psalm 79:13

Blessed is He who comes in the Name of the Lord Our Lord, God and Saviour and the King of us all, Jesus Christ, the Son of the living God. Glory be to You forever more, Amen

Now it happened, the day after, that He went into a city called Nain; and many of His disciples went with Him, and a large crowd. And when He came near the gate of the city, behold, a dead man was being carried out, the only son of his mother; and she was a widow. And a large crowd from the city was with her. When the Lord saw her, He had compassion on her and said to her, "Do not weep". Then He came and touched the open coffin, and those who carried him stood still. And He said, Young man, I say to you, arise. So he who was dead sat up and began to speak. And He presented him to his mother. Then fear came upon all, and they glorified God, saying, "A great prophet has risen up among us; and, God has visited His people". And this report about Him went throughout all Judea and all the surrounding region. Luke 7:11-17

Glory be to God Forever, Amen

FIRST SUNDAY OF HATHOR

Holy Gospel

MATINS

Stand up in the fear of God and listen to the Holy Gospel, A chapter from the Holy Gospel according to Saint Matthew, May his blessings be with us all, Amen

From the psalms of our teacher David the prophet and king, May his blessings be with us all, Amen

> You visit the earth and water it, You greatly enrich it; The river of God is full of water; You provide their grain, For so You have prepared it. You water its ridges abundantly, You settle its furrows; You make it soft with showers, You bless its growth.   Alleluia. - Psalm 65:9-10

Blessed is He who comes in the Name of the Lord Our Lord, God and Saviour and the King of us all, Jesus Christ, the Son of the living God. Glory be to You forever more, Amen

Now after the Sabbath, as the first day of the week began to dawn, Mary Magdalene and the other Mary came to see the tomb. And behold, there was a great earthquake; for an angel of the Lord descended from heaven, and came and rolled back the stone from the door, and sat on it. His countenance was like lightning, and his clothing as white as snow. And the guards shook for fear of him, and became like dead men. But the angel answered and said to the women, "Do not be afraid, for I know that you seek Jesus who was crucified. He is not here; for He is risen, as He said. Come, see the place where the Lord lay. And go quickly and tell His disciples that He is risen from the dead, and indeed He is going before you into Galilee; there you will see Him. Behold, I have told you." So they went out quickly from the tomb with fear and great joy, and ran to bring His disciples word. And as they went to tell His disciples, behold, Jesus met them, saying, "Rejoice!" So they came and held Him by the feet and worshiped Him. Then Jesus said to them, "Do not be afraid. Go and tell My brethren to go to Galilee, and there they will see Me." Now while they were going, behold, some of the guard came into the city and reported to the chief priests all the things that had happened. When they had assembled with the elders and consulted together, they gave a large sum of money to the soldiers, saying, "Tell them, 'His disciples came at night and stole Him away while we slept.' And if this comes to the governor's ears, we will appease him and make you secure." So they took the money and did as they were instructed; and this saying is commonly reported among the Jews until this day. Then the eleven disciples went away into Galilee, to the mountain which Jesus had appointed for them. When they saw Him, they worshiped Him; but some doubted. And Jesus came and spoke to them, saying, "All authority has been given to Me in heaven and on earth. Go therefore and make disciples of all the nations, baptizing them in the name of the Father and of the Son and of the Holy Spirit, teaching them to observe all things that I have commanded you; and lo, I am with you always, even to the end of the age." Amen. Matthew 28: 1-20

Glory be to God Forever, Amen

Pauline

Paul, the servant of our Lord Jesus Christ, called to be an apostle, appointed to the Gospel of God. A reading from the Second Epistle of our teacher Paul to the Corinthians. May his holy blessings be with us. Amen.

St Paul the Apostle was writing a letter to the Christians who lived in the rich city of Corinth. Dear Corinthians, I know how wonderfully generous you are, when it comes to giving donations to help the poor. Your generous giving has encouraged lots of other people to give generously too! So I wanted to let you know that I and my friends will be coming to your city very soon. Do make sure that you have your donations all ready for when we come. I know that you always give your donations with joy and happiness, and you are never grumpy about it. But this I say: If you give a little you will also get a little, and if you give a lot you will also get a lot. So I hope you will all give your donations with joy, not because you "have to". For God loves a cheerful giver. And God is most generous of all, and He will give you all you need, so that you, always having all sufficiency in all things, may have an abundance for every good work. Just like the Bible says: God has spread His love everywhere, He has given to the poor, God's goodness is forever! (2 Corinthians 9:1-9)

Bye for now!

Signed, Paul

The grace of God the Father be with you all, Amen.

Catholicon

The Catholic Epistle from the Epistle of our teacher St James. May his holy blessings be with us.

My little children, this is the Apostle James writing to tell you about something that is little, but very, very dangerous! I wonder if you can guess what it is? When you ride a horse, you put a little tiny 'bit' in the horse's mouth so you can make him go wherever you wish. And big huge ships can be steered by the tiny little rudder that pokes out from the back. A little tiny match can set a whole forest on fire! Well, this dangerous little thing can change the whole life of a big strong human being. Have you guessed what it is yet? It's the tongue! You see, we use our tongues to speak, and our little words can do so much damage! We use our tongues to pray to God, Yet we use the same tongue to tease people who are made in the image of God! We use our tongue to say kind things, Yet we use the same tongue to say mean, hurtful things! My little children, this should not be so. Does a spring pour out sweet water and bitter water from the same place? Does a fig tree bear olives? Can a grapevine bear figs? That's just crazy! But people find it so hard to control their tongues! We have tamed every kind of animal, or bird, or reptile, or even sea creatures! But we still seem to have so much trouble taming our tongue! Please, please, please be careful about what you say! (James 3:1-12)

By for now!

Signed, James the Apostle

Do not love the world, nor the things which are in the world. The world shall pass away and all its desires; but he who does the will of God shall abide forever. Amen.

The Acts

A reading from the Acts of our fathers the pure apostles, who were invested with the grace of the Holy Spirit. May their blessing be with us all. Amen.

One day, St Peter the Apostle got a strange message. It was from a man he'd never met before, whose name was Cornelius. And the odd thing was Cornelius wasn't Jewish, like Peter, And he wasn't a Christian, either. Whatever could he want? So Peter went to the house of Cornelius, where he got a big surprise! God had sent a dream to Cornelius, and told him to call for Peter, so that Peter could tell him all about Jesus. Peter was very happy indeed! He told Cornelius and his family all about Jesus! How Jesus is the Word of God and how the Holy Spirit came upon Jesus in the River Jordan, when St John the Baptist baptised Him. How Jesus healed so, so many people from sickness, and cast our demons and how Jesus died on the Cross, but He rose again on the third day, and the how the disciples saw Him, and ate and drank with Him. So, continued Peter, Jesus commanded us to go out and tell everyone all about Him, and about how He will come at the end of the world, to judge the living and the dead. Jesus is the one that all the prophets in the Old Testament spoke about. Whoever believes in Him will have all his sins forgiven! And while Peter was speaking, a miracle happened! All Peter's friends were shocked and amazed. Do you know what it was? The Holy Spirit came down on Cornelius and his family! They began to speak other languages! It was a miracle! So Peter said, Hey, why don't we baptise you right now? So guess what they did? Peter baptised Cornelius and all his family, right away, in the name of the Lord. Then Cornelius asked Peter to stay with them for a few days, so they could learn even more about Jesus from him. So he did. And the news about all that happened spread everywhere, even all the way back to Judea, where the rest of the apostles and the Church heard about it. (Chapter 10:37-11:1)

The word of the Lord shall grow, multiply, be mighty and be confirmed in the holy Church of God. Amen.

Holy Gospel

Stand up in the fear of God and listen to the Holy Gospel,A chapter from the Holy Gospel according to Saint Luke,May his blessings be with us all, Amen

From the psalms of our teacher David the prophet and king,May his blessings be with us all, Amen

> Water its furrows; multiply its fruits; With its raindrops the earth will be gladdened when it produces fruits. You will bless the crown of the year with Your goodness, And Your fields will be filled with fatness. Alleluia. - Psalm 65:10-11

Blessed is He who comes in the Name of the Lord Our Lord, God and Saviour and the King of us all, Jesus Christ, the Son of the living God. Glory be to You forever more, Amen

And when a great multitude had gathered, and they had come to Him from every city, He spoke by a parable: A sower went out to sow his seed. And as he sowed, some fell by the wayside; and it was trampled down, and the birds of the air devoured it. Some fell on rock; and as soon as it sprang up, it withered away because it lacked moisture. And some fell among thorns, and the thorns sprang up with it and choked it. But others fell on good ground, sprang up, and yielded a crop a hundredfold. When He had said these things He cried, He who has ears to hear, let him hear! Then His disciples asked Him, saying, What does this parable mean? And He said, To you it has been given to know the mysteries of the kingdom of God, but to the rest it is given in parables, that `Seeing they may not see, And hearing they may not understand.' Now the parable is this: The seed is the word of God. Those by the wayside are the ones who hear; then the devil comes and takes away the word out of their hearts, lest they should believe and be saved. But the ones on the rock are those who, when they hear, receive the word with joy; and these have no root, who believe for a while and in time of temptation fall away. Now the ones that fell among thorns are those who, when they have heard, go out and are choked with cares, riches, and pleasures of life, and bring no fruit to maturity. But the ones that fell on the good ground are those who, having heard the word with a noble and good heart, keep it and bear fruit with patience. Luke 8: 4-15

Glory be to God Forever, Amen

SECOND SUNDAY OF HATHOR

Holy Gospel

Stand up in the fear of God and listen to the Holy Gospel, A chapter from the Holy Gospel according to Saint Mark, May his blessings be with us all, Amen

From the psalms of our teacher David the prophet and king, May his blessings be with us all, Amen

> Then the earth shall yield her increase; God, our own God, shall bless us. God shall bless us, And all the ends of the earth shall fear Him. Alleluia. - Psalm 67: 6-7

Blessed is He who comes in the Name of the Lord Our Lord, God and Saviour and the King of us all, Jesus Christ, the Son of the living God. Glory be to You forever more, Amen

Very early in the morning, on the first day of the week, they came to the tomb when the sun had risen. And they said among themselves, "Who will roll away the stone from the door of the tomb for us?" But when they looked up, they saw that the stone had been rolled away—for it was very large. And entering the tomb, they saw a young man clothed in a long white robe sitting on the right side; and they were alarmed. But he said to them, "Do not be alarmed. You seek Jesus of Nazareth, who was crucified. He is risen! He is not here. See the place where they laid Him. But go, tell His disciples—and Peter—that He is going before you into Galilee; there you will see Him, as He said to you." So they went out quickly and fled from the tomb, for they trembled and were amazed. And they said nothing to anyone, for they were afraid. Mark 16: 2-8

Glory be to God Forever, Amen

Pauline

Paul, the servant of our Lord Jesus Christ, called to be an apostle, appointed to the Gospel of God. A reading from the Epistle of our teacher Paul to the Hebrews. May his holy blessings be with us. Amen.

St Paul the Apostle was writing a letter to all the Christians everywhere who were Hebrews—that means Jewish people. Dear Hebrews, Have you ever seen a lovely garden that thirstily drinks up the rain water? Then, when you plant some seeds in that garden, it helps the seeds to grow and to make lots of beautiful herbs and fruits! But if the garden just makes weeds and thorns instead of herbs and fruits, the gardener just burns them. I am sure that you are like the nice garden, not the one with the weeds and the thorns. God will never forget how hard you have worked— your labour of love— to serve His name and to serve His children. I hope you never become lazy but always keep serving God and His children, so that one day you will inherit what God has promised to those who love Him. Just like the time when God promised Abraham so long ago: "Surely, in blessing I will bless you and multiplying, I will multiply you." And when Abraham as very patient, God fulfilled His promise! (Hebrews 6:7-15)

Bye for now!

Signed, Paul

The grace of God the Father be with you all, Amen.

Catholicon

The Catholic Epistle from the Epistle of our teacher St Jude. May his holy blessings be with us.

My little children, This is the Apostle Jude writing to warn you about false teachers!

You have to be very careful about these people, the ones who try to confuse you about Jesus. The prophets long ago warned us that false teachers would come and teach the wrong things about Jesus, and about how we should follow Him. They warned us that the false teachers will be judged by God, when He comes back with His angels! These false teachers are not nice at all! They like to grumble and complain about everything, They like to boast and show off, They like to make people turn against each other, They like to crawl and suck up to people so that they can get what they want for themselves. But I don't want you to be tricked by them, my beloved. Remember how Jesus warned us that evil people like these would come. So make sure that you stick to the true faith, remembering the love and kindness of God, and always praying for the Holy Spirit to guard you. Be gentle with those who go wrong, but with some people you have to be really tough to save them from the fire! God is able to keep you from stumbling, until you stand happily in front of His Throne at the end. To God our Saviour, Who alone is wise, be glory and majesty, dominion and power, Both now and forever. Amen (Jude 14-25)

Bye for now!

Signed, Jude the Apostle

Do not love the world, nor the things which are in the world. The world shall pass away and all its desires; but he who does the will of God shall abide forever. Amen.

The Acts

A reading from the Acts of our fathers the pure apostles, who were invested with the grace of the Holy Spirit. May their blessing be with us all. Amen.

The High Priest of the Temple had arrested some of the Apostles of Jesus and thrown them in jail. But then God had the answer to their problems. That night, God sent an angel to the jail, and he opened the doors for them! And the angel said: "Don't be scared – God wants you to keep on telling people about Him. Go to the Temple and tell everyone about Jesus and the new life He brings to those who believe in Him." So the Apostles went early the next morning and began to tell people about Jesus again. Guess who was going to get the surprise of his life? Meanwhile, the High Priest called a meeting of the elders and the leaders to judge the Apostles, thinking they were still locked up in jail. And they sent some soldiers to the jail, to bring the Apostles to be judged. But when they got there the jail was empty! There was no one there! What? How? The surprised soldiers ran back to the High Priest as quick as they could. He would never believe them "You won't believe this!" they said. "We got to the jail, and the guards were standing guard as usual outside the door of the jail" "and the door of the jail was locked, nice and safe, as usual" "And the guards said everything was fine" "But when we opened the door to get the prisoners" It was empty! "There was no one inside! "It's impossible! How could they possibly have got out without anyone seeing anything?" The High Priest and the Captain of the Temple were shocked! Then someone came up to them and said, Hey, I just saw those men you put in jail. They were in the Temple! They were talking to everyone! The Captain sighed. Let's try again, he said. And he took his soldiers, and arrested the Apostles again. He brought the Apostles in front of the High Priest again. And the High priest said, Didn't we tell you to quit teaching people about Jesus? Look, you've filled the whole city of Jerusalem with your nonsense! Stop causing trouble, will you!?! Do you think Peter and the other Apostles stopped teaching people about Jesus? They did not. They said to the High Priest

Which one do you think we ought to obey? A man? Or God? We will obey God, of course! (Chapter 5:19-29)

The word of the Lord shall grow, multiply, be mighty and be confirmed in the holy Church of God. Amen.

Holy Gospel

Stand up in the fear of God and listen to the Holy Gospel, A chapter from the Holy Gospel according to Saint Matthew, May his blessings be with us all, Amen

From the psalms of our teacher David the prophet and king, May his blessings be with us all, Amen

> The trees of the plain shall be full of fruit, The cedars of Lebanon, which You planted; You are He who sends springs into the valley; The waters shall pass between the mountains. Alleluia. - Psalm 104:16,10

Blessed is He who comes in the Name of the Lord Our Lord, God and Saviour and the King of us all, Jesus Christ, the Son of the living God. Glory be to You forever more, Amen

On the same day Jesus went out of the house and sat by the sea. And great multitudes were gathered together to Him, so that He got into a boat and sat; and the whole multitude stood on the shore. Then He spoke many things to them in parables, saying: Behold, a sower went out to sow. And as he sowed, some seed fell by the wayside; and the birds came and devoured them. Some fell on stony places, where they did not have much earth; and they immediately sprang up because they had no depth of earth. But when the sun was up they were scorched, and because they had no root they withered away. And some fell among thorns, and the thorns sprang up and choked them. But others fell on good ground and yielded a crop: some a hundredfold, some sixty, some thirty. He who has ears to hear, let him hear! Matthew 13:1-9

Glory be to God Forever, Amen

THIRD SUNDAY OF HATHOR

Holy Gospel

MATINS

Stand up in the fear of God and listen to the Holy Gospel, A chapter from the Holy Gospel according to Saint Luke, May his blessings be with us all, Amen

From the psalms of our teacher David the prophet and king, May his blessings be with us all, Amen

> From the rising of the sun to its going down The Lord's name is to be praised. The Lord is high above all nations, His glory above the heavens Alleluia. - Psalm 113: 3-4

Blessed is He who comes in the Name of the Lord Our Lord, God and Saviour and the King of us all, Jesus Christ, the Son of the living God. Glory be to You forever more, Amen

Now on the first day of the week, very early in the morning, they, and certain other women with them, came to the tomb bringing the spices which they had prepared. But they found the stone rolled away from the tomb. Then they went in and did not find the body of the Lord Jesus. And it happened, as they were greatly perplexed about this, that behold, two men stood by them in shining garments. Then, as they were afraid and bowed their faces to the earth, they said to them, "Why do you seek the living among the dead? He is not here, but is risen! Remember how He spoke to you when He was still in Galilee, saying, 'The Son of Man must be delivered into the hands of sinful men, and be crucified, and the third day rise again.' " And they remembered His words. Then they returned from the tomb and told all these things to the eleven and to all the rest. It was Mary Magdalene, Joanna, Mary the mother of James, and the other women with them, who told these things to the apostles. And their words seemed to them like idle tales, and they did not believe them. But Peter arose and ran to the tomb; and stooping down, he saw the linen cloths lying by themselves; and he departed, marveling to himself at what had happened. Luke 24:1-12

Glory be to God Forever, Amen

Pauline

Paul, the servant of our Lord Jesus Christ, called to be an apostle, appointed to the Gospel of God. A reading from Second Epistle of our teacher Paul to the Thessalonians. May his holy blessings be with us. Amen.

St Paul the Apostle and his friends, Silvanus and Timothy, were writing a letter to the Christians who lived in the big city of Thessalonica. Dear Thessalonians, Grace and peace from God our Father and the Lord Jesus Christ. Our dear brothers and sisters, we say a huge "Thank You" to God every day for you, because you have a strong faith and you love each other so much. And we tell everyone how proud we are of your patience and trust in God, even when things are not going so good for you. We think you are ready for Heaven! God is very fair. When the end comes— when Jesus comes back with the angels— you who suffered will find rest with Jesus, and with us. But those who were mean to you and who weren't kind and loving, like Jesus—they will get exactly what they deserve— it will be horrible for them! On that last day, everybody will see and praise and glorify the goodness of God in Jesus Christ and in His saints. We pray that you will glorify God right now, by following Jesus every single day of your life, and by being strong in being good. May the grace of our God and the Lord Jesus Christ help you to do this always. (2 Thessalonians 1:1-12)

Bye for now!

Signed, Paul

The grace of God the Father be with you all, Amen.

Catholicon

The Catholic Epistle from the First Epistle of our teacher St Peter. May his holy blessings be with us.

Hello Everyone! Don't you think we have spent enough time doing the wrong thing? Sometimes other people want you to be bad with them and they are surprised when you tell them "no". Then they make fun of you! But do you know what? One day, they will have to stand in front of the Great Judge (that's Jesus) and they will have to explain all that bad stuff they did. I wouldn't want to be them! Would you? That's why Jesus went down to Hades and preached to the people down there who had died. He wanted to give them a chance to live! We never know when our end will come, so, please, always be ready, always be praying. And most important of all: Love one another, truly, from your heart, for "love will cover a multitude of sins"— if you love others, God will forgive their sins, and your sins too! So look after each other well, with great kindness, and do it happily, without grumbling and complaining about it. God has given each one of you their own special gifts, their own talents or abilities. Use them to serve each other, so that we all get the most out of the gifts God gave us. If your gift from God is being a good speaker, then speak the words of God! If your gift from God is to help others, then help as much as you can! That way, the goodness and love of God will spread far and wide, and everyone will glorify and praise God through Jesus Christ to whom belong the glory and the dominion forever and ever. Amen. (1 Peter 4:3-11)

Bye for now!

Signed, Peter the Apostle

Do not love the world, nor the things which are in the world. The world shall pass away and all its desires; but he who does the will of God shall abide forever. Amen.

The Acts

A reading from the Acts of our fathers the pure apostles, who were invested with the grace of the Holy Spirit. May their blessing be with us all. Amen.

Do you remember last week that the Jewish High Priest arrested the Apostles and put them in jail? And remember how an angel let them out to everyone's surprise, and they were arrested again? Now the Apostles were defending themselves in front of the High Priest. St Peter and the other Apostles said: Jesus was sent by our God to save Israel and the whole wide world. You hung him on the Cross, but now He sits at the right hand of the Father! Why are you so angry with us when we are just telling you what the Holy Spirit taught us? But the High Priest and his friends were angry. They wanted to kill the Apostles! But one of Jews stood up to speak. His name was Gamaliel [Ga-ma-lee-el], and he was a Pharisee and he had studied the Bible very carefully. He said, "Take the Apostles outside for a minute. I have something important to say." So they took them outside, and everyone else listened very carefully to Gamaliel. "Hey, everyone, let's just stop and think carefully about this whole 'Christians' thing. Let's be sensible and wise about how we handle them." "Remember a while ago, a guy called Theudas made himself a leader, and gathered 400 followers? What happened to him? He was killed, and now, no one even remembers him." "And remember another guy— Judas of Galilee? He also gathered followers, and he also died, and now no one remembers him either." "So I reckon, let's just leave these 'Christian' guys alone. If they are just like the others, then in time, they will be forgotten too." "But if they really are from God, well, we don't want to fight against God, do we!?" Well, everyone thought that Gamaliel made an awful lot of sense. So they called the Apostles back, and got the soldiers to just give them one more beating for good measure. Then they told them they were free to go, and to stop talking about Jesus. And the Apostles thought they were very, very blessed to have suffered for the name of Jesus. But do you think they stopped telling people about their beloved Jesus? Nope! In fact, in the temple and in people's homes, every day, day after day, they taught and preached about Jesus the Christ of God. (Chapter 5:30-42)

The word of the Lord shall grow, multiply, be mighty and be confirmed in the holy Church of God. Amen.

Holy Gospel

Stand up in the fear of God and listen to the Holy Gospel,A chapter from the Holy Gospel according to Saint Luke, May his blessings be with us all, Amen

From the psalms of our teacher David the prophet and king,May his blessings be with us all, Amen

> But You, O Lord, are compassionate and merciful, Longsuffering and very merciful and truthful. Look upon me and have mercy; Give Your strength to Your servant, And save the son of Your handmaid. Alleluia.
> - Psalm 86:15-16

Blessed is He who comes in the Name of the Lord Our Lord, God and Saviour and the King of us all, Jesus Christ, the Son of the living God. Glory be to You forever more, Amen

Now great multitudes went with Him. And He turned and said to them, If anyone comes to Me and does not hate his father and mother, wife and children, brothers and sisters, yes, and his own life also, he cannot be My disciple. And whoever does not bear his cross and come after Me cannot be My disciple. For which of you, intending to build a tower, does not sit down first and count the cost, whether he has enough to finish it— lest, after he has laid the foundation, and is not able to finish, all who see it begin to mock him, saying `This man began to build and was not able to finish.' Or what king, going to make war against another king, does not sit down first and consider whether he is able with ten thousand to meet him who comes against him with twenty thousand? Or else, while the other is still a great way off, he sends a delegation and asks conditions of peace. So likewise, whoever of you does not forsake all that he has cannot be My disciple. Salt is good; but if the salt has lost its flavour, how shall it be seasoned? It is neither fit for the land nor for the dunghill, but men throw it out. He who has ears to hear, let him hear!
Luke 14:25-35

Glory be to God Forever, Amen

FOURTH SUNDAY OF HATHOR

Holy Gospel

MATINS

Stand up in the fear of God and listen to the Holy Gospel, A chapter from the Holy Gospel according to Saint John, May his blessings be with us all, Amen

From the psalms of our teacher David the prophet and king, May his blessings be with us all, Amen

> Cause me to hear Your lovingkindness in the morning, For in You do I trust; Cause me to know the way in which I should walk, For I lift up my soul to You. Alleluia. - Psalm 143:8

Blessed is He who comes in the Name of the Lord Our Lord, God and Saviour and the King of us all, Jesus Christ, the Son of the living God. Glory be to You forever more, Amen

Now the first day of the week Mary Magdalene went to the tomb early, while it was still dark, and saw that the stone had been taken away from the tomb. Then she ran and came to Simon Peter, and to the other disciple, whom Jesus loved, and said to them, "They have taken away the Lord out of the tomb, and we do not know where they have laid Him." Peter therefore went out, and the other disciple, and were going to the tomb. So they both ran together, and the other disciple outran Peter and came to the tomb first. And he, stooping down and looking in, saw the linen cloths lying there; yet he did not go in. Then Simon Peter came, following him, and went into the tomb; and he saw the linen cloths lying there, and the handkerchief that had been around His head, not lying with the linen cloths, but folded together in a place by itself. Then the other disciple, who came to the tomb first, went in also; and he saw and believed. For as yet they did not know the Scripture, that He must rise again from the dead. Then the disciples went away again to their own homes. But Mary stood outside by the tomb weeping, and as she wept she stooped down and looked into the tomb. And she saw two angels in white sitting, one at the head and the other at the feet, where the body of Jesus had lain. Then they said to her, "Woman, why are you weeping?" She said to them, "Because they have taken away my Lord, and I do not know where they have laid

Him." Now when she had said this, she turned around and saw Jesus standing there, and did not know that it was Jesus. Jesus said to her, "Woman, why are you weeping? Whom are you seeking?" She, supposing Him to be the gardener, said to Him, "Sir, if You have carried Him away, tell me where You have laid Him, and I will take Him away." Jesus said to her, "Mary!" She turned and said to Him, "Rabboni!" (which is to say, Teacher). Jesus said to her, "Do not cling to Me, for I have not yet ascended to My Father; but go to My brethren and say to them, 'I am ascending to My Father and your Father, and to My God and your God.' "Mary Magdalene came and told the disciples that she had seen the Lord, and that He had spoken these things to her. John 20: 1-18

Glory be to God Forever, Amen

Pauline LITURGY

Paul, the servant of our Lord Jesus Christ, called to be an apostle, appointed to the Gospel of God. A reading from First Epistle of our teacher Paul to the Corinthians. May his holy blessings be with us. Amen.

St Paul the Apostle was writing a letter to the Christians who lived in the rich city of Corinth. Dear Corinthians, I know some people have been grumbling about me, and my fellow servants who serve you (like Apollos). But I want you to know that God is the one who called us to be responsible for you, and we always do our best to take care of you. Actually, it doesn't worry me if you judge me. It wouldn't even worry me if a judge in court judged me! I know we are doing the right thing. But what really matters is what God thinks of us—not any human being. So it's best for us not to judge others—because we are just human beings. When the time comes, God knows everything (even secrets) and He will judge the right way. This is important, because I don't want you to be proud and try to boss each other around. Do you think you are better than everyone else? Why on earth would you think that?! If there's anything good about you, isn't it a gift from God? So why do you act as if it wasn't, as if it is all just your own cleverness? You are rich! You act like kings and queens! I wish you really knew what that means! Actually, I think God made us apostles to be an example for everyone else. Not because we are rich or powerful, but because we are poor and humble. We are fools for Christ's sake, but you are wise in Christ! We look weak, but you are strong! You are important, but we are kicked around! Every day, we are hungry and thirsty. Our clothes are poor. We are beaten and homeless. And we work with our own hands to make a living. Why do we put up with this? Because humbly serving and loving others is what really, really matters. When someone curses us, we bless them. When they harm us, we are patient. When they say nasty things, we pray. You are the children born from my preaching! Like a father who loves you and cares for you, I want you to learn from my example how to love and serve. You can have 10,000 teachers but not many fathers. (1 Corinthians 4:1-16)

Signed, Paul

The grace of God the Father be with you all, Amen.

Catholicon

The Catholic Epistle from the Second Epistle of our teacher St Peter. May his holy blessings be with us.

My little children, This is the Apostle, Simon Peter, who really loves Jesus and loves serving Him, I am writing to those who also love our precious Jesus and believe in Him like me. When we love Jesus, we find grace and peace— that means we feel happy and safe, because we know how very much He loves us and looks after us. When we know the power of God in Jesus, we have everything we need to live a really good life of godliness— being good, like God. We get to share in the good nature of God, and this helps us run away from temptations, so we do good things, not bad things. So be very careful to grow more and more in your love for Jesus. If you have faith (you trust God), then learn to have virtue (to be a good person deep inside). If you have virtue, then learn to have knowledge (to know God). If you have knowledge, then learn to have self-control. If you have self-control, then learn to have perseverance (to be really patient and never give up). If you have perseverance, then learn to have godliness (to be good like God). If you have godliness, then learn to have brotherly kindness (always be kind to others). And if you have brotherly kindness, then learn to have agape love (love others the way God loves us). If you learn all these things, you will truly know Jesus, and your life will be full of goodness! Amen. (2 Peter 1:1-8)

Bye for now!

Signed, Peter the Apostle

Do not love the world, nor the things which are in the world. The world shall pass away and all its desires; but he who does the will of God shall abide forever. Amen.

The Acts

A reading from the Acts of our fathers the pure apostles, who were invested with the grace of the Holy Spirit. May their blessing be with us all. Amen.

Do you remember the Apostle St Paul? He and his friend Silas were in jail in a city called Philippi. But finally, they got out. Then Paul and Silas went to stay with their friend, Lydia. After a little while, they travelled to another city called Thessalonica, where the Thessalonians live. As he always did, Paul went to the synagogue—the place where Jewish people went to pray and read the Bible together. For three weeks in row, Paul read the Bible with them, and showed them how it tells us about Jesus, who died and rose again from the dead, because Jesus is God's chosen Christ. Some of the Jews from the synagogue believed Paul and Silas. And heaps of the Greeks, men and women, believed Paul and Silas. But the Jews who did not believe got really cranky. They wanted to get rid of Paul and Silas from their city of Thessalonica. So guess what they did? They went to the market place and they found some big bullies to help them then, they all went shouting and screaming to the house of Jason, where Paul and Silas were staying. But Paul and Silas weren't there! They were out! So instead, the mob grabbed poor Jason, and dragged him in front of the rulers of Thessalonica. And they began to accuse poor Jason, saying, "Jason has been helping troublemakers! They have turned everything upside down!" "They say there is another king, instead of the Emperor, Caesar! They call this king, Jesus. You'd better do something, or Caesar will be angry!" Oh dear, whatever will happen to poor Jason? And will the Jews manage to find Paul and Silas? I'm afraid that's another story. (Chapter 16:40-17:7)

The word of the Lord shall grow, multiply, be mighty and be confirmed in the holy Church of God. Amen.

Holy Gospel

Stand up in the fear of God and listen to the Holy Gospel, A chapter from the Holy Gospel according to Saint Mark, May his blessings be with us all, Amen

From the psalms of our teacher David the prophet and king, May his blessings be with us all, Amen

Know this: the Lord, He is God; He made us, and not we ourselves; We are His people and the sheep of His pasture. Alleluia. - Psalm 100:3

Blessed is He who comes in the Name of the Lord Our Lord, God and Saviour and the King of us all, Jesus Christ, the Son of the living God. Glory be to You forever more, Amen

Now as He was going out on the road, one came running, knelt before Him, and asked Him, Good Teacher, what shall I do that I may inherit eternal life? So Jesus said to him, Why do you call Me good? No one is good but One, that is, God. You know the commandments: `Do not commit adultery,' `Do not murder,' `Do not steal,' `Do not bear false witness,' `Do not defraud,' `Honour your father and your mother.' And he answered and said to Him, Teacher, all these things I have kept from my youth. Then Jesus, looking at him, loved him, and said to him, one thing you lack: Go your way, sell whatever you have and give to the poor, and you will have treasure in heaven; and come, take up the cross, and follow Me. But he was sad at this word, and went away sorrowful, for he had great possessions. Then Jesus looked around and said to His disciples, How hard it is for those who have riches to enter the kingdom of God! And the disciples were astonished at His words. But Jesus answered again and said to them, Children, how hard it is for those who trust in riches to enter the kingdom of God! It is easier for a camel to go through the eye of a needle than for a rich man to enter the kingdom of God. And they were greatly astonished, saying among themselves, Who then can be saved? But Jesus looked at them and said, With men it is impossible, but not with God; for with God all things are possible. Then Peter began to say to Him, See, we have left all and followed You. So Jesus answered and said assuredly, I say to you, there is no one who has left house or brothers or sisters or father or mother or wife or children or lands, for My sake and the gospel's, who shall not receive a hundredfold now in this time— houses and brothers and sisters and mothers and children and lands, with persecutions and in the age to come, eternal life. But many who are first will be last, and the last first. Mark 10:17-31

Glory be to God Forever, Amen

FIRST SUNDAY OF KIAHK

Holy Gospel

MATINS

Stand up in the fear of God and listen to the Holy Gospel, A chapter from the Holy Gospel according to Saint Mark, May his blessings be with us all, Amen

From the psalms of our teacher David the prophet and king, May his blessings be with us all, Amen

> For He looked down from the height of His sanctuary; From heaven the Lord viewed the earth, To hear the groaning of the prisoner, To release those appointed to death, To declare the name of the Lord in Zion, And His praise in Jerusalem Alleluia. - Psalm 102: 19-21

Blessed is He who comes in the Name of the Lord Our Lord, God and Saviour and the King of us all, Jesus Christ, the Son of the living God. Glory be to You forever more, Amen

Now Jesus sat opposite the treasury and saw how the people put money into the treasury. And many who were rich put in much. Then one poor widow came and threw in two mites, which make a quadrans. So He called His disciples to Himself and said to them, "Assuredly, I say to you that this poor widow has put in more than all those who have given to the treasury; for they all put in out of their abundance, but she out of her poverty put in all that she had, her whole livelihood." Mark 12:41-44

Glory be to God Forever, Amen

Pauline

Paul, the servant of our Lord Jesus Christ, called to be an apostle, appointed to the Gospel of God. A reading from Epistle of our teacher Paul to the Romans. May his holy blessings be with us. Amen.

St Paul the Apostle was writing a letter to the Christians who lived in the great city of Rome. Dear Romans, This is Paul, the Apostle of Jesus Christ, the Son of God, whose power was revealed by the Holy Spirit, and who rose from the dead. Jesus gave us the special giftof knowing and obeying God, and of sharing this wonderful gift with the whole world. I always pray for you, dear Romans, and thank God for you and for your strong faith. I also pray that God will find a way for me to come to visit you one day soon, so we can help and encourage each other to grow in our love and faith in Jesus. I've wanted to visit you for a long time now, but something always got in the way. You know I love to tell people about Jesus and His Gospel, especially, people like you, dear Romans, who are Gentiles, who are not Jewish. For I am not ashamed of the gospel of Christ, for it is the power of God to salvation for everyone who believes, for the Jew first and also for the Greek. It is in the Gospel of Jesus that we learn about the goodness of God, and we come to love Him, and have faith in Him, as it is written: "The just shall live by faith." (Romans 1:1-17)

Signed, Paul

The grace of God the Father be with you all, Amen.

Catholicon

The Catholic Epistle from the Epistle of our teacher St James. May his holy blessings be with us. Amen.

Hello Everyone Out There! This is James, the servant of God, and the servant of our Lord Jesus Christ. I know this sounds a little weird, but I think we should actually be happy when things don't go our way. Why, you ask? Because, when things are tough, your faith is tested and you learn how to be patient. We all need to learn patience! And we all need wisdom! If you feel that you are not wise, ask God for wisdom. And be confident that God will generously give it you. If you are poor, be happy that God loves you, and will lift you up!! But if you are rich, be humble, because riches quickly fade like a flower in the hot sun. God has prepared a beautiful crown of life for everyone who is patient and keeps loving God, even when things are tough. Never think that God is the one who makes things tough! It is not God, but our own sins that make things tough. Desire leads to sin and sin leads to death. But God's love and goodness never, ever change. Every good and perfect gift comes down to us from God, the Father of Lights. Out of His own loving will He made us through His word, and He made us to be the most important of all His creatures. That is how precious and so, so special you are to God! (James 1:1-18)

Bye for now!

Signed, James the Apostle

Do not love the world, nor the things which are in the world. The world shall pass away and all its desires; but he who does the will of God shall abide forever. Amen.

The Acts

A reading from the Acts of our fathers the pure apostles, who were invested with the grace of the Holy Spirit. May their blessing be with us all. Amen.

The Book of Acts in the Bible was written by St Luke the apostle, to his friend Theophilus [Thee-OFF-ill-us]. In it, Luke continues the story of what happened to the followers of Jesus, after He had suffered on the Cross, risen from the dead, and spent forty days with them. Jesus gathered His followers and told them not to leave Jerusalem, because He was going to send them the Holy Spirit! They asked Jesus if He was going to bring back the Kingdom of Israel. But Jesus told them to be patient. The Holy Spirit would soon come upon them and fill them with

His power, so that they would go all over the world to tell everyone about Jesus. When Jesus finished speaking, something amazing happened, Jesus was taken up into the sky, until He disappeared into a cloud! And as His followers stood there looking up, two men in white clothes appeared and said to them, Don't worry! This same Jesus, who was taken up from you into heaven, will come back to you in the same way from heaven. So the followers of Jesus left the Mountain of Olives and went back home to Jerusalem, just like Jesus had asked them to. The Disciples were there: Peter, James, John, and Andrew; Philip and Thomas; Bartholomew and Matthew; James the son of Alphaeus and Simon the Zealot; and Judas the son of James. And St Mary, the Mother of Jesus was there, and His women followers, and His relatives. They all prayed together and waited and waited And waited. (Chapter 1:1-14)

The word of the Lord shall grow, multiply, be mighty and be confirmed in the holy Church of God. Amen.

Holy Gospel

Stand up in the fear of God and listen to the Holy Gospel, A chapter from the Holy Gospel according to Saint Luke, May his blessings be with us all, Amen

From the psalms of our teacher David the prophet and king, May his blessings be with us all, Amen

> When You rise up, You shall have compassion on Zion, For it is time to have compassion on her, because the time is come; For the Lord shall build Zion, And He shall be seen in His glory. Alleluia. - Psalm 102:13,16

Blessed is He who comes in the Name of the Lord Our Lord, God and Saviour and the King of us all, Jesus Christ, the Son of the living God. Glory be to You forever more, Amen

It seemed good to me also, having had perfect understanding of all things from the very first, to write to you an orderly account, most excellent Theophilus, There was in the days of Herod, the king of Judea, a certain priest named Zacharias. His wife was of the daughters of Aaron, and her name was Elizabeth. And they were both righteous before God, But they had no child, because Elizabeth was barren, and they were both well advanced in years. So it was, that while he was serving as priest before God, his lot fell to burn incense when he went into the temple of the Lord. Then an angel of the Lord appeared to him, standing on the right side of the altar of incense. And when Zacharias saw him, he was troubled, and fear fell upon him. But the angel said to him, Do not be afraid, Zacharias, for your prayer is heard; and your wife Elizabeth will bear you a son, and you shall call his name John. And you will have joy and gladness, and many will rejoice at his birth. For he will be great in the sight of the Lord, and shall drink neither wine nor strong drink. He will also be filled with the Holy Spirit, even from his mother's womb. And he will turn many of the children of Israel to the Lord their God. He will also go before Him in the spirit and power of Elijah, `to turn the hearts of the fathers to the children,' and the disobedient to the wisdom of the just, to make ready a people prepared for the Lord. And Zacharias said to the angel, How shall I know this? For I am an |old man, and my wife is well advanced in years. And the angel answered and said to him, I am Gabriel, who stands in the presence of God, and was sent to speak to you and bring you these glad tidings. But behold, you will be mute and not able to speak until the day these things take place, because you did not believe my words which will be fulfilled in their own time. And the people waited for Zacharias, but when he came out, he could not speak to them; and they perceived that he had seen a vision in the temple. And so it was, as soon as the days of his service were completed, that he departed to his own house. Now after those days his wife Elizabeth conceived; and she hid herself five months, saying, Thus the Lord has dealt with me, in the days when He looked on me, to take away my reproach among people. Luke 1: 1-25

Glory be to God Forever, Amen

SECOND SUNDAY OF KIAHK

Holy Gospel

MATINS

Stand up in the fear of God and listen to the Holy Gospel, A chapter from the Holy Gospel according to Saint Luke, May his blessings be with us all, Amen

From the psalms of our teacher David the prophet and king, May his blessings be with us all, Amen

> He shall come down like rain upon the grass before mowing, Like showers that water the earth. In His days the righteous shall flourish, And abundance of peace, Until the moon is no more. Alleluia. - Psalm 72:6-7

Blessed is He who comes in the Name of the Lord Our Lord, God and Saviour and the King of us all, Jesus Christ, the Son of the living God. Glory be to You forever more, Amen

But if I cast out demons with the finger of God, surely the kingdom of God has come upon you. When a strong man, fully armed, guards his own palace, his goods are in peace. But when a stronger than he comes upon him and overcomes him, he takes from him all his armor in which he trusted, and divides his spoils. He who is not with Me is against Me, and he who does not gather with Me scatters. "When an unclean spirit goes out of a man, he goes through dry places, seeking rest; and finding none, he says, 'I will return to my house from which I came.' And when he comes, he finds it swept and put in order. Then he goes and takes with him seven other spirits more wicked than himself, and they enter and dwell there; and the last state of that man is worse than the first." And it happened, as He spoke these things, that a certain woman from the crowd raised her voice and said to Him, "Blessed is the womb that bore You, and the breasts which nursed You!" But He said, "More than that, blessed are those who hear the word of God and keep it!" Luke 11:20-28

Glory be to God Forever, Amen

Pauline LITURGY

Paul, the servant of our Lord Jesus Christ, called to be an apostle, appointed to the Gospel of God. A reading from Epistle of our teacher Paul to the Romans. May his holy blessings be with us. Amen.

St Paul the Apostle was writing a letter to the Christians who lived in the great city of Rome! Dear Romans, You know that there are some people called the Jews or Hebrews? These were God's people in the Old Testament, in the time of Abraham, and Moses, and David the King. And everyone else who is not Jewish is called a Gentile. So is it better to be a Jew or a Gentile? What do you think? On the one hand, God gave the Jews His own Law, and sent them His own prophets. That's pretty special! But on the other hand, the Jews were quite naughty, and they often didn't listen to God. That's pretty bad! But do you know what? Everybody is bad sometimes. Everybody needs God to help them to be good, whether they are a Jew or a Gentile. In fact, "all have sinned and fall short of the glory of God". So did the Jews do better, because they knew the Law of God? Actually, no! They were more guilty, because they knew what they were doing was wrong; the Law told them so but they still did it anyway! So here is a very important question: What is it that really, really makes us into good people who love God? Does the Law of Moses make us good? Not by itself! The Jews had the Law, but they were still pretty bad! Does doing good things make us good? Not by itself! All the bad things we do cancel out all the good things! No, what really, really makes us good is when we know how much God loves us, and we love Him back. This is called "faith". So whether you are a Jew or a Gentile, it doesn't really matter. God loves absolutely, positively, everyone! And whether you have God's Law (like the Jews), Or whether you don't have God's law (like the Gentiles) It doesn't really matter, because loving God is what really matters. What was it that made Abraham such a good person in God's eyes? Was it just because Abraham obeyed every little bit of the law? If that was it, then Abraham could show off and tell everyone just how clever he was— impressing God with his actions! But that wasn't it, God loved Abraham because Abraham believed in God, trusted God, and his heart was good, like God. (Romans 3:1-4:3)

Bye for now!

Signed, Paul

The grace of God the Father be with you all, Amen.

Catholicon

The Catholic Epistle from the First Epistle of our teacher St John. May his holy blessings be with us. Amen.

Hello everyone, this is John the Disciple of Jesus Christ. I was so, so blessed to actually see Jesus with my very own eyes, and touch Him with my very own hands! So you really can believe me when I tell you that God the Father gave us a beautiful eternal life through His Son, Jesus. When we are friends with God, through Jesus, we are so, so, so happy! Here is what I learned from Jesus: "God is light and in Him is no darkness at all". If we say we are Jesus' friends, but we walk in darkness by doing bad things, do you think we are really Jesus' friends? No! We would be lying! Jesus' real friends walk in the light, because, remember "God is light and in Him is no darkness at all". And if we do walk in the light of Jesus, we are friends with each other too, And Jesus forgives us any bad things we did. Have you ever done something wrong? Don't pretend like you haven't, because everybody has done something wrong sometime! But don't worry. Jesus loves you very much indeed. He wants to make everything better. So when we are very brave and honest, and tell the truth about the bad things we did, Jesus forgives us, and cleans our hearts, and makes us good again. He is always Standing up for us, Saving us, Protecting us, Forgiving us. And He does this for the whole wide world! (1 John 1:1-2:2)

Bye for now!

Signed, John the Beloved

Do not love the world, nor the things which are in the world. The world shall pass away and all its desires; but he who does the will of God shall abide forever. Amen.

The Acts

A reading from the Acts of our fathers the pure apostles, who were invested with the grace of the Holy Spirit. May their blessing be with us all. Amen.

Do you remember the story of Moses the prophet? When Moses was about 80 years old, something really odd happened to him. Moses was walking on a mountain called Sinai, when he saw a big bush on fire, but it wasn't burning up! And that's not the oddest thing yet, the burning bush spoke to Moses! Yes, it said words! Do you know what the burning bush said? It said: "I am the God of your fathers—the God of Abraham, the God of Isaac, and the God of Jacob" It was God talking to Moses! Moses was scared! Moses was frightened! Moses was trembling! Then God spoke again "Take your sandals off your feet, for the place where you stand is holy ground", and Moses took off his sandals right away! And God continued: "Moses, I am sending you back to Egypt, to save my people from suffering as slaves". Did Moses go to Egypt? Well, that's a story for another day. Or, you can go home today and read it in your own Bible! (Chapter 7:30-34)

The word of the Lord shall grow, multiply, be mighty and be confirmed in the holy Church of God. Amen.

Holy Gospel

Stand up in the fear of God and listen to the Holy Gospel, A chapter from the Holy Gospel according to Saint Luke, May his blessings be with us all, Amen

From the psalms of our teacher David the prophet and king, May his blessings be with us all, Amen

> Listen, O daughter, behold and incline your ear, And forget your people and your father's house; For the King desired your beauty, For He is your Lord. Alleluia. - Psalm 45:10-11

Blessed is He who comes in the Name of the Lord Our Lord, God and Saviour and the King of us all, Jesus Christ, the Son of the living God. Glory be to You forever more, Amen

Now in the sixth month the angel Gabriel was sent by God to a city of Galilee named Nazareth, to a virgin betrothed to a man whose name was Joseph, of the house of David. The virgin's name was Mary. And having come in, the angel said to her, Rejoice, highly favoured one, the Lord is with you; blessed are you among women! But when she saw him, she was troubled at his saying, and considered what manner of greeting this was. Then the angel said to her, Do not be afraid, Mary, for you have found favour with God. And behold, you will conceive in your womb and bring forth a Son, and shall call His name Jesus. He will be great, and will be called the Son of the Highest; and the Lord God will give Him the throne of His father David. And He will reign over the house of Jacob forever, and of His kingdom there will be no end. Then Mary said to the angel, How can this be, since I do not know a man? And the angel answered and said to her, The Holy Spirit will come upon you, and the power of the Highest will overshadow you; therefore, also, that Holy One who is to be born will be called the Son of God. Now indeed, Elizabeth your relative has also conceived a son in her old age; and this is now the sixth month for her who was called barren. For with God nothing will be impossible. Then Mary said "Behold the maidservant of the Lord! Let it be to me according to your word." And the angel departed from her. Luke 1:26-38

Glory be to God Forever, Amen

THIRD SUNDAY OF KIAHK

Holy Gospel

Stand up in the fear of God and listen to the Holy Gospel, A chapter from the Holy Gospel according to Saint Matthew, May his blessings be with us all, Amen

From the psalms of our teacher David the prophet and king, May his blessings be with us all, Amen

> Show us Your mercy, Lord, And grant us Your salvation. I will hear what God the Lord will speak, For He will speak peace To His people and to His saints; But let them not turn back to folly. Alleluia. - Psalm 85:7-8

Blessed is He who comes in the Name of the Lord Our Lord, God and Saviour and the King of us all, Jesus Christ, the Son of the living God. Glory be to You forever more, Amen

Then Jesus went out from there and departed to the region of Tyre and Sidon. And behold, a woman of Canaan came from that region and cried out to Him, saying, "Have mercy on me, O Lord, Son of David! My daughter is severely demon-possessed." But He answered her not a word. And His disciples came and urged Him, saying, "Send her away, for she cries out after us." But He answered and said, "I was not sent except to the lost sheep of the house of Israel." Then she came and worshiped Him, saying, "Lord, help me!" But He answered and said, "It is not good to take the children's bread and throw it to the little dogs. And she said, "Yes, Lord, yet even the little dogs eat the crumbs which fall from their masters' table." Then Jesus answered and said to her, "O woman, great is your faith! Let it be to you as you desire." And her daughter was healed from that very hour. Jesus departed from there, skirted the Sea of Galilee, and went up on the mountain and sat down there. Then great multitudes came to Him, having with them the lame, blind, mute, maimed, and many others; and they laid them down at Jesus' feet, and He healed them. So the multitude marveled when they saw the mute speaking, the maimed made whole, the lame walking, and the blind seeing; and they glorified the God of Israel. Matthew 15: 21-31

Glory be to God Forever, Amen

Pauline

Paul, the servant of our Lord Jesus Christ, called to be an apostle, appointed to the Gospel of God. A reading from Epistle of our teacher Paul to the Romans. May his holy blessings be with us. Amen.

St Paul the Apostle was writing a letter to the Christians who lived in the great city of Rome. Dear Romans, What do you think makes a person a good person in God's eyes? Do you think it is enough to do a few good things, and that makes you a good person? But wait—we all do bad things too. So, to really be a good person we also need God to be kind to us, and forgive us, and accept us. The Bible tells us that God told Abraham that he should be circumcised. That's a kind of mark on his body, that shows that He belongs to God. Was Abraham a good person just because he had the mark of circumcision? No! God said Abraham was good before he was circumcised. That's because Abraham believed in God and loved God before he was circumcised. That's what made Abraham a good person. And God promised to bless Abraham and everyone who is like Abraham. But that doesn't mean "circumcised like Abraham." That means God will bless those who believe in God and love God just like Abraham. That's what makes a person good. And that's how we become the children of Abraham. Abraham has many children from all over the world! Because Abraham believed and loved God, he believed God when He told him that he would have a son, even though he and his wife Sarah were very, very old. Because Abraham believed what God told him, he was a good person in the eyes of God. But that's not just about Abraham; you know, it's also about us! If we believe in and love God, if we believe that God raised Jesus from the dead. We will be good people too, just like our father, Abraham!   (Romans 4:4-24)

Bye for now!

Signed, Paul

The grace of God the Father be with you all, Amen.

Catholicon

The Catholic Epistle from the First Epistle of our teacher St John. May his holy blessings be with us. Amen.

From John, My beloved brothers and sisters, Do you remember the most important commandment God has given us? It has been around for a long, long time! When Jesus came, He reminded us of this important commandment. Do you know what it is? Of course, it's LOVE! When we love God and love each other, it's like we came out of a dark, dark cave and into the beautiful sunlight. The light of God! So if you hate someone, how can you say you are in the light? You are in darkness if you hate. But if you love instead of hating, then you are in the light, not the darkness. You will never have to worry about the dark. I wanted to write these things to you, O little children Because God has forgiven your sins. I wanted to write these things to you, O parents Because you have known God very well. I wanted to write these things to you, O young people Because you have beaten the devil. I wanted to write these things to you, O little children Because you are friends with the Father. I wanted to write these things to you, O parents Because you are friends with God. I wanted to write these things to you, O young people Because you are strong, and God's word lives in you, and you have beaten the devil. Don't love the world. If you love the world, you won't be able to love God. The things you might love in the world are all selfish things. But God does not teach us to be selfish! God teaches us to be free! We won't let ourselves be tied up to anything in this world! Because one day, sooner or later, all those things in the world are going to disappear. But if you do God's will you will go on forever and ever and ever and ever!   (1 John 2:7-17)

God loves you!

Signed, John the Beloved

Do not love the world, nor the things which are in the world. The world shall pass away and all its desires; but he who does the will of God shall abide forever. Amen.

The Acts

A reading from the Acts of our fathers the pure apostles, who were invested with the grace of the Holy Spirit. May their blessing be with us all. Amen.

St Stephen the First Deacon was defending himself. Some evil people accused him of stirring up trouble and saying bad things about Moses! So Stephen told them, God chose Moses to save the Israelites from being slaves in Egypt. And Moses told them that God would send another Great Prophet, One that everyone should listen carefully to. (Can you guess who Moses was talking about?) But the Israelites didn't want to listen to Moses. How sad. They wanted to go back to being slaves in Egypt! They wanted to worship idols like they did in Egypt, instead of worshipping the True God! So what do you think God did with them? God left them to do whatever they want. But when enemies came and fought them, and hurt them, and took them away as slaves, do you think their idols could save them? No they could not! Instead of making idols, they should have paid more attention to God, and to the tabernacle— the great tent—that God told Moses to make for Him. The great King David wanted to build a stone temple to pray to God in, instead of a tent. But God asked David's son, King Solomon, to build His temple. And he did. But do you think that God needs a tent or a temple to live in? Don't you know who God is? God said, "Heaven is My throne, And earth is My footstool, "What house will you build for Me? says the Lord, Or what is the place of My rest? Has My hand not made all these things?" (Chapter 7:35-50)

The word of the Lord shall grow, multiply, be mighty and be confirmed in the holy Church of God. Amen.

Holy Gospel

Stand up in the fear of God and listen to the Holy Gospel, A chapter from the Holy Gospel according to Saint Luke, May his blessings be with us all, Amen

From the psalms of our teacher David the prophet and king, May his blessings be with us all, Amen

> Mercy and truth met together; Righteousness and peace kissed each other; Truth arose from the earth, And righteousness looked down from heaven.   Alleluia. - Psalm 85:10,11

Blessed is He who comes in the Name of the Lord Our Lord, God and Saviour and the King of us all, Jesus Christ, the Son of the living God. Glory be to You forever more, Amen

Now Mary arose in those days and went into the hill country with haste, to a city of Judah, and entered the house of Zacharias and greeted Elizabeth. And it happened, when Elizabeth heard the greeting of Mary, that the babe leaped in her womb; and Elizabeth was filled with the Holy Spirit. Then she spoke out with a loud voice and said, Blessed are you among women, and blessed is the fruit of your womb! But why is this granted to me, that the mother of my Lord should come to me? For indeed, as soon as the voice of your greeting sounded in my ears, the babe leaped in my womb for joy. Blessed is she who believed, for there will be a fulfilment of those things which were told her from the Lord. And Mary said: My soul magnifies the Lord, And my spirit has rejoiced in God my Saviour. For He has regarded the lowly state of His maidservant; For behold, henceforth all generations will call me blessed. For He who is mighty has done great things for me, And holy is His name. And His mercy is on those who fear Him From generation to generation. He has shown strength with His arm; He has scattered the proud in the imagination of their hearts. He has put down the mighty from their thrones, And exalted the lowly. He has filled the hungry with good things, And the rich, He has sent away empty. He has helped His servant Israel, In remembrance of His mercy, As He spoke to our fathers, To Abraham and to his seed forever. And Mary remained with her about three months, and returned to her house. Luke 1:39-56

Glory be to God Forever, Amen

FOURTH SUNDAY OF KIAHK

Holy Gospel

Stand up in the fear of God and listen to the Holy Gospel, A chapter from the Holy Gospel according to Saint Mark, May his blessings be with us all, Amen

From the psalms of our teacher David the prophet and king, May his blessings be with us all, Amen

> Let the heavens rejoice, and let the earth be glad; Let the sea roar, and all its fullness; Let the field be joyful, and all that is in it. Then all the trees of the woods will rejoice before the Lord. For He is coming, for He is coming to judge the earth. He shall judge the world with righteousness, And the peoples with His truth Alleluia. - Psalm 96: 11-13

Blessed is He who comes in the Name of the Lord Our Lord, God and Saviour and the King of us all, Jesus Christ, the Son of the living God. Glory be to You forever more, Amen

"Assuredly, I say to you, all sins will be forgiven the sons of men, and whatever blasphemies they may utter; but he who blasphemes against the Holy Spirit never has forgiveness, but is subject to eternal condemnation"— because they said, "He has an unclean spirit." Then His brothers and His mother came, and standing outside they sent to Him, calling Him. And a multitude was sitting around Him; and they said to Him, "Look, Your mother and Your brothers are outside seeking You." But He answered them, saying, "Who is My mother, or My brothers?" And He looked around in a circle at those who sat about Him, and said, "Here are My mother and My brothers! For whoever does the will of God is My brother and My sister and mother." Mark 3: 28-35

Glory be to God Forever, Amen

Pauline

Paul, the servant of our Lord Jesus Christ, called to be an apostle, appointed to the Gospel of God. A reading from Epistle of our teacher Paul to the Romans. May his holy blessings be with us. Amen.

Dear Romans, A long, long time ago, God chose a group of people to be His special people. They were the children of a very good man called Abraham. But God did not make His promises to all of Abraham's children. He only chose one of them: Isaac. And then, the promise was not for all of Isaac's children, but only for the one called Jacob. Do you think this means that God is not fair? Do you think the brothers of Isaac and Jacob should have been upset, because they were not chosen? Hmmm, let's think about this! We have to remember that God is the BOSS. He is the Boss of the whole wide world! He is the One who made everything. He is the one who made Abraham, Isaac and Jacob and their brothers. He is the One who made Pharaoh strong in the time of Moses. And He is the One who made Pharaoh give in and let Moses and the Israelites go free. So if God is the Boss and if God is the One who made everyone; shouldn't God be able to do whatever He wants? Imagine if a potter made a water jar out of clay. Should the jar say to the potter, "Hey, you can't use me for that! I don't want to be a water jar!" But that's what you were made for, you silly water jar! You didn't make yourself! The potter who made you is the one who should say how you are used, not you! So in the same way, God is the One who gets to say what should happen to us. He is the Big Potter! He is the Boss of the whole world! (and us). So if God decided that people who are not the children of Abraham also should be God's special people, why should anyone complain? He is the Boss! If God decides He wants to share His promise with lots of people (like you and me) who are not Israelites who can say no? He is the Boss! So the Israelites should not complain about others becoming God's special people. They should not grumble and say, "But WE are His special people, no one else!" God is the Boss, and He is a kind and loving Boss. He wants all kinds of people to be His special people. Even you and me! (Romans 9:6-33)

Bye for now!

Signed, Paul

The grace of God the Father be with you all, Amen.

Catholicon

The Catholic Epistle from the First Epistle of our teacher St John. May his holy blessings be with us. Amen.

Hello Everyone! I want to warn you about something very important today, some people will try to tell you things that are not true. They will try to make you believe things about God that are just not right! Don't listen to them! From the beginning, you have learned the truth about God, about Jesus His Son, and about eternal life— living forever. Also, you were filled with the Holy Spirit when you were baptised, and the Holy Spirit who lives in you helps you to feel when you hear something that's not true about God. So if you let God's truth live inside you, you will also live in God! And when Jesus comes back at the end of the world, you will be so happy, not scared at all! If you do good things, you are God's child because He is good. Isn't it amazing how much God loves us? He loves us so much He even called us His own children! Because we are His children, then we have to be just like Him. We have to be just as good as He is, because children always look like their father! Some people in the world don't like God. So don't be surprised if they don't like you either, because you are good like God. That doesn't matter! What really matters is that we should work hard to make ourselves good just like God our Father. (1 John 2:24-3:3)

God loves you!

Signed, John the Beloved

Do not love the world, nor the things which are in the world. The world shall pass away and all its desires; but he who does the will of God shall abide forever. Amen

The Acts

A reading from the Acts of our fathers the pure apostles, who were invested with the grace of the Holy Spirit. May their blessing be with us all. Amen.

St Stephen the first Archdeacon had been arrested by the soldiers! Some evil people accused him of stirring up trouble and saying bad things about Moses!

They said that this 'Jesus' he spoke about was going to spoil everything! Could this really be true? This is what St Stephen told the Jews who were questioning him. Listen everyone, he said, I know all about Abraham, and how he trusted God. And God promised to bless Abraham's son Isaac, and Isaac's son Jacob, and the twelve sons of Jacob. And God helped one of those twelve sons, Joseph, when he was a slave in Egypt. God got him out of prison and made him ruler over all the land of Egypt! And Joseph's father and brothers had to come and beg him for food when there was a famine, and they were starving. So Joseph called his whole family— 75 people altogether— to come and live with him in Egypt so he could care for them. And Joseph's father, Jacob, died in Egypt, and they took his body back to Israel to bury it there with his grandfather Abraham. But many years later, long after Joseph and his brothers had died, a new pharaoh made these people of Abraham and Joseph into slaves! He was really mean to the Israelites. He even ordered that they had to kill any boy babies that were born, so they would not have anyone to fight for them! But one boy baby escaped! The daughter of the mean Pharaoh found him in a basket on the River Nile, and felt sorry for him, so she took him home to the palace and brought him up as if he were her own son. And so Moses became a wise and learned prince of Egypt! Oh dear! We've run out of time! If you want to know what happened next, you can read all about it in your Bible. (Chapter 7:8-22)

The word of the Lord shall grow, multiply, be mighty and be confirmed in the holy Church of God. Amen.

Holy Gospel

Stand up in the fear of God and listen to the Holy Gospel, A chapter from the Holy Gospel according to Saint Luke, May his blessings be with us all, Amen

From the psalms of our teacher David the prophet and king, May his blessings be with us all, Amen

> Give heed, O You who shepherd Israel; Reveal Yourself, O You who lead Joseph like a flock, Who sit upon the cherubim. Raise up Your power before Ephraim, Benjamin, and Manasseh, And come for our salvation. Alleluia. - Psalm 80:1-3

Blessed is He who comes in the Name of the Lord Our Lord, God and Saviour and the King of us all, Jesus Christ, the Son of the living God. Glory be to You forever more, Amen

Now Elizabeth's full time came for her to be delivered, and she brought forth a son. So it was, on the eighth day, that they came to circumcise the child; and they would have called him by the name of his father, Zacharias. His mother answered and said, No; he shall be called John. But they said to her, There is no one among your relatives who is called by this name. So they made signs to his father— what he would have him called. And he asked for a writing tablet, and wrote, saying, His name is John. So they all marvelled. Immediately his mouth was opened and his tongue loosed, and he spoke, praising God. Blessed is the Lord God of Israel, For He has visited and redeemed His people, And has raised up a horn of salvation for us In the house of His servant David, As He spoke by the mouth of His holy prophets, Who have been since the world began, That we should be saved from our enemies And from the hand of all who hate us, To perform the mercy promised to our fathers And to remember His holy covenant, The oath which He swore to our father Abraham: To grant us that we, Being delivered from the hand of our enemies, Might serve Him without fear, In holiness and righteousness before Him all the days of our life. And you, child, will be called the prophet of the Highest; For you will go before the face of the Lord to prepare His ways, To give knowledge of salvation to His people By the remission of their sins, Through the tender mercy of our God, With which the Dayspring from on high has visited us; To give light to those who sit in darkness and the shadow of death, To guide our feet into the way of peace. So the child grew and became strong in spirit, and was in the deserts till the day of his manifestation to Israel. Luke 1:57-80

Glory be to God Forever, Amen

FIRST SUNDAY OF TOUBAH

Holy Gospel

MATINS

Stand up in the fear of God and listen to the Holy Gospel, A chapter from the Holy Gospel according to Saint Luke, May his blessings be with us all, Amen

From the psalms of our teacher David the prophet and king, May his blessings be with us all, Amen

> The Lord reigns, He is clothed with majesty; The Lord is clothed, He has girded Himself with strength. Surely the world is established, so that it cannot be moved. Your throne is established from of old; You are from everlasting. Alleluia. - Psalm 93:1-2

Blessed is He who comes in the Name of the Lord Our Lord, God and Saviour and the King of us all, Jesus Christ, the Son of the living God. Glory be to You forever more, Amen

Then He went down to Capernaum, a city of Galilee, and was teaching them on the Sabbaths. And they were astonished at His teaching, for His word was with authority. Now in the synagogue there was a man who had a spirit of an unclean demon. And he cried out with a loud voice, saying, "Let us alone! What have we to do with You, Jesus of Nazareth? Did You come to destroy us? I know who You are— the Holy One of God!" But Jesus rebuked him, saying, "Be quiet, and come out of him!" And when the demon had thrown him in their midst, it came out of him and did not hurt him. Then they were all amazed and spoke among themselves, saying, "What a word this is! For with authority and power He commands the unclean spirits, and they come out." And the report about Him went out into every place in the surrounding region. Luke 4:31-37

Glory be to God Forever, Amen

Pauline

Paul, the servant of our Lord Jesus Christ, called to be an apostle, appointed to the Gospel of God. A reading from Epistle of our teacher Paul to the Romans. May his holy blessings be with us. Amen.

Dear Romans, Did you know that God speaks to us through His Bible? His words teach us and give us hope! So I pray that God gives you comfort and patience. I pray that God helps you to think the like each other and praise Him with one voice together! Take care of each other, just as Jesus takes care of each of us. In the olden days, God made some big promises to the Fathers (like Abraham). And Jesus came to fulfil those promises to the children of those Fathers— I mean the Jewish people. But those promises can now also be for people who are NOT Jewish— the "Gentiles". A Gentile is someone who is not Jewish. That's you! Even in the Old Testament it says things like: "Rejoice O Gentiles, with His people" And: "Praise the Lord all you Gentiles." And also: "The Son of David will rule over the Gentiles and give them hope." May God fill your hearts with joy and peace, because you believe in Him. The Holy Spirit will make you strong, because He gives us hope. Now, I know that you Roman Christians are good people. You know lots about God and you are able to teach one another. But I still felt I should write to you because Jesus has given me this job: to teach the Gentiles about Him and to make them like a holy, beautiful present to give to God. I am so happy that God has given me the chance to teach you about Jesus, and to show you how to behave the right way and to even do mighty miracles so I could convince you Gentiles to believe in Him. But all of that comes from the power of the Holy Spirit of God. (Romans 15:4-19)

Bye for now!

Signed, Paul

> *The grace of God the Father be with you all, Amen.*

Catholicon

The Catholic Epistle from the First Epistle of our teacher St John. May his holy blessings be with us. Amen.

Hello Everyone! Isn't it amazing how much God loves us?!!! He loves us so much that He calls us His Children!!! But those who are far from God don't understand this. My beloved, we know now that we are God's Children, but we don't know yet just how incredibly great this is! But when He comes back at the end of the world, then we shall know— because we will see Him as He really is and we shall become just like Him! So if you are looking forward to that day, then keep your heart pure and clean, just as Jesus is pure and clean. If you do a sin, you are breaking God's rules. But Jesus came to take away all our sins. In Him there is no sin at all. So if you really, truly love Jesus— don't do any sins! Don't let anyone trick you: Doing good comes from God. Doing sins comes from the devil. But Jesus came to beat the devil and to destroy his works. So, if you really are Children of God, Do not sin! This is how we can tell who is really a child of God, and who is not: A person who always keeps doing the wrong thing is not a child of God. And a person who does not love others is not a child of God either. Because this is the message you heard from the start: "Love one another." (1 John 3:1-11)

God loves you!

Signed, John the Beloved

Do not love the world, nor the things which are in the world. The world shall pass away and all its desires; but he who does the will of God shall abide forever. Amen.

The Acts

St Paul and St Barnabas were travelling all over the world to tell people about Jesus. They came to a city called Antioch [Ann-tee-yok] and they got all the Christians there together in the Church, and told them about their great adventures. They told them how God was using them to bring many Gentiles to become Christians. They rested in Antioch for many days. While they were there, some Jewish Christians came from Judea. But these men were trouble-makers! They started to tell everyone that you couldn't be a Christian unless you became Jewish first!!! But St Paul and St Barnabas said, "NO!" Jesus accepts people from any country and any race. But sadly, they couldn't convince these trouble-makers, so they all agreed on a plan: St Paul, St Barnabas and some other men would go to Jerusalem and ask the Disciples to settle this question, once and for all! So off they went to Jerusalem. And all along the way they met many Christians. They told them stories about how so many Gentiles were becoming Christians, which made them so happy (Chapter 14:24 - 15:3)

Holy Gospel

Stand up in the fear of God and listen to the Holy Gospel, A chapter from the Holy Gospel according to Saint Matthew, May his blessings be with us all, Amen

From the psalms of our teacher David the prophet and king, May his blessings be with us all, Amen

> The Lord made known His salvation; He revealed His righteousness in the sight of the Gentiles. He remembered His mercy to Jacob And His truth to the house of Israel.   Alleluia. - Psalm 98:2,3

Blessed is He who comes in the Name of the Lord Our Lord, God and Saviour and the King of us all, Jesus Christ, the Son of the living God. Glory be to You forever more, Amen

Now when they had departed, behold, an angel of the Lord appeared to Joseph in a dream, saying "Arise, take the young Child and His mother, flee to Egypt, and stay there until I bring you word; for Herod will seek the young Child to destroy Him." When he arose, he took the young Child and His mother by night and departed for Egypt, and was there until the death of Herod, that it might be fulfilled which was spoken by the Lord through the prophet, saying, "Out of Egypt I called My Son." Then Herod, when he saw that he was deceived by the wise men, was exceedingly angry; and he sent forth and put to death all the male children who were in Bethlehem and in all its districts, from two years old and under, according to the time which he had determined from the wise men. Then was fulfilled what was spoken by Jeremiah the prophet, saying: "A voice was heard in Ramah, Lamentation, weeping, and great mourning, Rachel weeping for her children, Refusing to be comforted, Because they are no more." Now when Herod was dead, behold, an angel of the Lord appeared in a dream to Joseph in Egypt, saying "Arise, take the young Child and His mother, and go to the land of Israel, for those who sought the young Child's life are dead." Then he arose, took the young Child and His mother, and came into the land of Israel. But when he heard that Archelaus was reigning over Judea instead of his father Herod, he was afraid to go there. And being warned by God in a dream, he turned aside into the region of Galilee. And he came and dwelt in a city called Nazareth, that it might be fulfilled which was spoken by the prophets, "He shall be called a Nazarene." Matthew 2:13-23

Glory be to God Forever, Amen

SECOND SUNDAY OF TOUBAH

Holy Gospel

Stand up in the fear of God and listen to the Holy Gospel, A chapter from the Holy Gospel according to Saint Mark, May his blessings be with us all, Amen

From the psalms of our teacher David the prophet and king, May his blessings be with us all, Amen

> The Lord reigns; Let the earth rejoice; Let the multitude of isles be glad! Clouds and darkness surround Him; Righteousness and justice are the foundation of His throne Alleluia. - Psalm 97:1-2

Blessed is He who comes in the Name of the Lord Our Lord, God and Saviour and the King of us all, Jesus Christ, the Son of the living God. Glory be to You forever more, Amen

But Jesus withdrew with His disciples to the sea. And a great multitude from Galilee followed Him, and from Judea and Jerusalem and Idumea and beyond the Jordan; and those from Tyre and Sidon, a great multitude, when they heard how many things He was doing, came to Him. So He told His disciples that a small boat should be kept ready for Him because of the multitude, lest they should crush Him. For He healed many, so that as many as had afflictions pressed about Him to touch Him. And the unclean spirits, whenever they saw Him, fell down before Him and cried out, saying, "You are the Son of God." But He sternly warned them that they should not make Him known. Mark 3:7-12

Glory be to God Forever, Amen

Pauline

Paul, the servant of our Lord Jesus Christ, called to be an apostle, appointed to the Gospel of God. A reading from Epistle of our teacher Paul to the Galatians. May his holy blessings be with us. Amen.

St Paul the Apostle was writing a letter to the Christians who lived in a land called Galatia. Dear Galatians, I have to say, I am a little surprised by you! Don't waste your time trying to do the same things that the Jews did in the olden days! Don't worry about following every little law from the time of Moses, things like being circumcised (that means getting a kind of mark on your body). It won't help you to love Jesus more. Loving Jesus is not just about following rules. Just following rules doesn't make you a good person. Jesus taught us what makes a person good: Believe in Jesus! Trust in Jesus! Open your heart to the Holy Spirit! Jesus gives you a good heart full of the Holy Spirit. And this good heart means you will follow Jesus, and be just like Jesus Full of love. I don't know who it is who has confused you and made you forget this. Whoever it is, I am sure he will get what he deserves. But I don't want you to be lost. I want you to know the Truth and to live in the Truth, the Truth that comes from God himself. The God who truly loves you and called you to follow Him. (Galatians 5:2–10)

Bye for now!

Signed, Paul

The grace of God the Father be with you all, Amen.

Catholicon

The Catholic Epistle from the First Epistle of our teacher St John. May his holy blessings be with us. Amen.

My little children, Let's not just SAY that we love each other. Let's SHOW that we love each other in everything we SAY and everything we THINK and everything we DO. If we really love like this, then our hearts won't ever be worried. And even when we feel guilty, we know that God will never stop loving us! We know that God answers our prayers, especially if we keep His commandments and do what makes Him happy. Do you know what His commandment is? That we should believe in the name of His Son Jesus Christ and that we should love one another. Whoever keeps God's commandments is living in God and God lives in him. That's how we know that God is living inside us— because His Holy Spirit inside us helps us to obey Him! (1 John 3:18–24)

Signed, John the Beloved

Do not love the world, nor the things which are in the world. The world shall pass away and all its desires; but he who does the will of God shall abide forever. Amen.

The Acts

A reading from the Acts of our fathers the pure apostles, who were invested with the grace of the Holy Spirit. May their blessing be with us all. Amen.

The Apostles of Jesus had just finished a big meeting where they made some big decisions. Now they needed to let everyone know just what they had decided. So they chose some messengers: Paul and Barnabas, Silas and Judas Barsabas. And they wrote a letter for the messengers to take to all the Churches. And this is what the letter said:

The apostles, the elders, and all the Christian brothers and sisters. To the Christians who are Gentiles (that means, not Jewish) who live in Antioch, Syria, and Cilicia, Greetings! We have heard that some Christians have been telling you that you have to become Jewish, and keep all the laws of the Jews, like circumcision (a kind of mark on the body). But WE never asked them to tell you any such thing! That's why we are sending you these messengers now: Paul, and Barnabas, and the others — good men who truly love God, and have even risked their lives for Jesus. Please listen to them. Because when we all got together, and we talked about this, the Holy Spirit guided us to tell you that you don't have to worry about doing all the things that Moses taught the Jews to do. You don't have to follow hundreds of very picky rules. God wants you to be good because you love Him, and because you love Goodness. So, the only rules we will give you are these: Don't worship idols that aren't the True God. And don't do bad things. If you can stay away from doing those things you will be doing pretty well! Farewell. (Chapter 15:22–29)

The word of the Lord shall grow, multiply, be mighty and be confirmed in the holy Church of God. Amen.

Holy Gospel

Stand up in the fear of God and listen to the Holy Gospel, A chapter from the Holy Gospel according to Saint Luke, May his blessings be with us all, Amen

From the psalms of our teacher David the prophet and king, May his blessings be with us all, Amen

> In the valley of weeping, into the place he appointed; For there the lawgiver shall give blessings. They shall go from strength to strength Hear my prayer; To You all flesh shall come. Alleluia. - Psalm 84:6-7, 65:2

Blessed is He who comes in the Name of the Lord Our Lord, God and Saviour and the King of us all, Jesus Christ, the Son of the living God. Glory be to You forever more, Amen

And it happened, as He spoke these things, that a certain woman from the crowd raised her voice and said to Him, Blessed is the womb that bore You, and the breasts which nursed You! But He said, More than that, blessed are those who hear the word of God and keep it! And while the crowds were thickly gathered together, He began to say, This is an evil generation. It seeks a sign, and no sign will be given to it except the sign of Jonah the prophet. For as Jonah became a sign to the Ninevites, so also the Son of Man will be to this generation. The queen of the South will rise up in the judgment with the men of this generation and condemn them for she came from the ends of the earth to hear the wisdom of Solomon; and indeed a greater than Solomon is here. The men of Nineveh will rise up in the judgment with this generation and condemn it for they repented at the preaching of Jonah; and indeed a greater than Jonah is here. No one, when he has lit a lamp, puts it in a secret place or under a basket, but on a lampstand, that those who come in may see the light. The lamp of the body is the eye. Therefore, when your eye is good, your whole body also is full of light. But when your eye is bad, your body also is full of darkness. Therefore take heed that the light which is in you is not darkness. If then your whole body is full of light, having no part dark, the whole body will be full of light, as when the bright shining of a lamp gives you light. Luke 11:27-36

Glory be to God Forever, Amen

THIRD SUNDAY OF TOUBAH

Holy Gospel

MATINS

Stand up in the fear of God and listen to the Holy Gospel, A chapter from the Holy Gospel according to Saint John, May his blessings be with us all, Amen

From the psalms of our teacher David the prophet and king, May his blessings be with us all, Amen

The heavens declare His righteousness, And all the peoples see His glory. His lightnings light the world; The earth sees and trembles. Alleluia. - Psalm 97:6,4

Blessed is He who comes in the Name of the Lord Our Lord, God and Saviour and the King of us all, Jesus Christ, the Son of the living God. Glory be to You forever more, Amen

There was a man of the Pharisees named Nicodemus, a ruler of the Jews. This man came to Jesus by night and said to Him, "Rabbi, we know that You are a teacher come from God; for no one can do these signs that You do unless God is with him." Jesus answered and said to him, "Most assuredly, I say to you, unless one is born again, he cannot see the kingdom of God." Nicodemus said to Him, "How can a man be born when he is old? Can he enter a second time into his mother's womb and be born?" Jesus answered, "Most assuredly, I say to you, unless one is born of water and the Spirit, he cannot enter the kingdom of God. That which is born of the flesh is flesh, and that which is born of the Spirit is spirit. Do not marvel that I said to you, 'You must be born again.' The wind blows where it wishes, and you hear the sound of it, but cannot tell where it comes from and where it goes. So is everyone who is born of the Spirit." Nicodemus answered and said to Him, "How can these things be?" Jesus answered and said to him, "Are you the teacher of Israel, and do not know these things? Most assuredly, I say to you, We speak what We know and testify what We have seen, and you do not receive Our witness. If I have told you earthly things and you do not believe, how will you believe if I tell you heavenly things? No one has ascended to heaven but He who came down from heaven, that is, the Son of Man who is in heaven. And as Moses lifted up the serpent in the wilderness, even so must the Son of Man be lifted up, that whoever believes in Him should not perish but have eternal life. For God so loved the world that He gave His only begotten Son, that whoever believes in Him should not perish but have everlasting life. For God did not send His Son into the world to condemn the world, but that the world through Him might be saved. "He who believes in Him is not condemned; but he who does not believe is condemned already, because he has not believed in the name of the only begotten Son of God. And this is the condemnation, that the light has come into the world, and men loved darkness rather than light, because their deeds were evil. For everyone practicing evil hates the light and does not come to the light, lest his deeds should be exposed. But he who does the truth comes to the light, that his deeds may be clearly seen, that they have been done in God." John 3:1-21

Glory be to God Forever, Amen

Pauline

Paul, the servant of our Lord Jesus Christ, called to be an apostle, appointed to the Gospel of God. A reading from Epistle of our teacher Paul to the Hebrews. May his holy blessings be with us. Amen.

St Paul the Apostle was writing a letter to the Jewish Christians (Who are also called "Hebrews"). Dear Hebrews, Do you remember the beautiful Temple King Solomon built to pray to God? The High Priest used to go through its door, past the curtain and into the Holy of Holies room to pray for the people.

Well now, Jesus has found a better way to meet God: HE is our High Priest and instead of a curtain, we go in through eating His Body and drinking His Blood and instead of the Holy of Holies room, we can go into Heaven! Wow!!!! If you want to go in, you have to have a nice clean heart— wash all that nasty sin and evil away! And if you want to go in, you have to trust in God, and always hope in Him. And if you want to go in, we have to all love one another, encourage each other and we have to come together every Sunday to pray together. Back in the Old Testament, in the time of Moses, naughty people were punished really badly for not obeying God's Commandments, so what do you think will happen to someone who doesn't listen to Jesus, or who doesn't respect His Precious Blood which He shed for us? But remember those old days when you first became Christians— how people treated you so badly! And how they even stole your things! And you saw how they locked me up in prison! But you got through all this with a smile, because you knew that you have a better treasure in Heaven! So long as you remember that; So long as you keep doing God's will; and so long as you are patient— you will be sure to receive your reward from God! So long as you remember that; So long as you keep doing God's will; and so long as you are patient— you will be sure to receive your reward from God! And when He comes, anyone He finds doing the right thing because they love Him and believe in Him, they will live with Him forever! But I will be so sad if any of you go back to being naughty again. That's not US!!! We're not the naughty ones who deserve to be punished! We are God's children! We believe in Him and He will save us! (Hebrews 10:19-39)

Bye for now!

Signed, Paul

The grace of God the Father be with you all, Amen.

Catholicon

The Catholic Epistle from the First Epistle of our teacher St John. May his holy blessings be with us. Amen.

My little children, If God loves us SO much then we also should love each other! Nobody has ever actually seen God, but if we truly love each other, God truly lives inside us! Do you want to know how you can tell if you are a good follower of God? Well, if you have the Holy Spirit living in you, you are a good Jesus Follower. And if you believe that Jesus is the Son of God, and that He came to save us, you are a good Jesus Follower. And if you know just how much God loves you, you are a good Jesus Follower. God is Love. Whoever lives in love, lives in God and God lives in Him. God's perfect love inside us makes us ready to face the scary Judgement Day. No way! WE won't be scared! That's because when your heart is full of love, there's no room left for being afraid! Say it with me: "Perfect love casts out fear." And do you know WHY we love God? Because He loved us first! But what about if someone says that he loves God, but at the same time, he hates other people? Do you think he truly loves God? No way! You can't truly love God (who you can't see), But hate other people (who you can see very well)! So God taught us that if we truly love Him, we must truly love others too. (1 John 4:11-21)

God loves you!

Signed, John the Beloved

Do not love the world, nor the things which are in the world. The world shall pass away and all its desires; but he who does the will of God shall abide forever. Amen.

The Acts

A reading from the Acts of our fathers the pure apostles, who were invested with the grace of the Holy Spirit. May their blessing be with us all. Amen.

The Apostles of Jesus had just finished a big meeting where they made some big decisions. Now they needed to let everyone know just what they had decided. So they chose some messengers: Paul and Barnabas, Silas and Judas Barsabas. And they wrote a letter for the messengers to take to all the Churches. And this is what the letter said:

On the day of Pentecost, when the Holy Spirit came down like tongues of fire and filled the Apostles. Some people asked St Peter, "What do we have to do to follow Jesus? Please tell us!" Peter answered, "First you have to repent. That means, you have to feel really sorry for any sins or naughty things you have done. "Then, you must get baptised in the Name of Jesus Christ, so your sins can be washed away, and you can be filled with the Holy Spirit. "Because God's wonderful promise wasn't just for us— it's for you, and your children, and people who live in other countries, absolutely EVERYONE!" And Peter told them lots of other things, about how they should not just copy any naughty people they met. So many people were baptised that day— about 3,000! Imagine your school class. Now imagine a 100 classes. That's how many people were baptised that day! Phew! And all those people loved each other, and learned from the Apostles, and prayed together and had Holy Communion together. The Apostles kept on doing lots of miracles, like healing sick people. Everyone was amazed at their powers! But all the Christians shared what they had among them equally, so there was no longer anyone rich or poor and because they shared, everyone had everything they could possibly need. (Chapter 2:38-45)

The word of the Lord shall grow, multiply, be mighty and be confirmed in the holy Church of God. Amen

Holy Gospel

Stand up in the fear of God and listen to the Holy Gospel, A chapter from the Holy Gospel according to Saint John, May his blessings be with us all, Amen

From the psalms of our teacher David the prophet and king, May his blessings be with us all, Amen

> You have caused men to ride over our heads; We went through fire and through water; But You brought us out to rich fulfillment. Oh, bless our God, you peoples! And make the voice of His praise to be heard. Alleluia. - Psalm 66: 12,8

Blessed is He who comes in the Name of the Lord Our Lord, God and Saviour and the King of us all, Jesus Christ, the Son of the living God. Glory be to You forever more, Amen

After these things Jesus and His disciples came into the land of Judea, and there He remained with them and baptized. Now John also was baptizing in Aenon near Salim, because there was much water there. And they came and were baptized. For John had not yet been thrown into prison. Then there arose a dispute between some of John's disciples and the Jews about purification. And they came to John and said to him, "Rabbi, He who was with you beyond the Jordan, to whom you have testified—behold, He is baptizing, and all are coming to Him!" John answered and said, "A man can receive nothing unless it has been given to him from heaven. You yourselves bear me witness, that I said, 'I am not the Christ,' but, 'I have been sent before Him.' He who has the bride is the bridegroom; but the friend of the bridegroom, who stands and hears him, rejoices greatly because of the bridegroom's voice. Therefore this joy of mine is fulfilled. He must increase, but I must decrease. He who comes from above is above all; he who is of the earth is earthly and speaks of the earth. He who comes from heaven is above all. And what He has seen and heard, that He testifies; and no one receives His testimony. He who has received His testimony has certified that God is true. For He whom God has sent speaks the words of God, for God does not give the Spirit by measure. The Father loves the Son, and has given all things into His hand. He who believes in the Son has everlasting life; and he who does not believe the Son shall not see life, but the wrath of God abides on him." John 3:22-36

Glory be to God Forever, Amen

FOURTH SUNDAY OF TOUBAH

Holy Gospel

MATINS

Stand up in the fear of God and listen to the Holy Gospel, A chapter from the Holy Gospel according to Saint John, May his blessings be with us all, Amen

From the psalms of our teacher David the prophet and king, May his blessings be with us all, Amen

> Restore us, O God of hosts; Cause Your face to shine, And we shall be saved! You have brought a vine out of Egypt; You have cast out the nations, and planted it. Alleluia. - Psalm 80:7-8

Blessed is He who comes in the Name of the Lord Our Lord, God and Saviour and the King of us all, Jesus Christ, the Son of the living God. Glory be to You forever more, Amen

A Most assuredly, I say to you, he who believes in Me has everlasting life. I am the bread of life. Your fathers ate the manna in the wilderness, and are dead. This is the bread which comes down from heaven, that one may eat of it and not die. I am the living bread which came down from heaven. If anyone eats of this bread, he will live forever; and the bread that I shall give is My flesh, which I shall give for the life of the world." The Jews therefore quarreled among themselves, saying, "How can this Man give us His flesh to eat?" Then Jesus said to them, "Most assuredly, I say to you, unless you eat the flesh of the Son of Man and drink His blood, you have no life in you. Whoever eats My flesh and drinks My blood has eternal life, and I will raise him up at the last day. For My flesh is food indeed, and My blood is drink indeed. He who eats My flesh and drinks My blood abides in Me, and I in him. As the living Father sent Me, and I live because of the Father, so he who feeds on Me will live because of Me. This is the bread which came down from heaven—not as your fathers ate the manna, and are dead. He who eats this bread will live forever." John 6: 47-58

Glory be to God Forever, Amen

Pauline

Paul, the servant of our Lord Jesus Christ, called to be an apostle, appointed to the Gospel of God. A reading from Epistle of our teacher Paul to the Romans. May his holy blessings be with us. Amen.

St Paul the Apostle was writing a letter to the Christians who lived in the great city of Rome. Dear Romans, You are Gentiles. That means you are not Jewish, like me and the other Apostles. But that doesn't matter to Jesus. The Jews are like a tree that God made holy. Sure, some of the branches of that Jewish tree turned bad, and God chopped them off. You Gentiles are like new branches that God grafted on— stuck on to the tree. But don't ever think that the branches don't need the roots! That's how they stay alive! So Gentiles should appreciate the Jews and be kind to them. A long, long time ago, God chose the Jews to be His special people. But sadly, they went bad. But don't think you are better than them. If they could go bad and be chopped off, so could you! And God will save the Jews and bring them back to Him one day. God will be kind and save EVERYONE who turns to Him. So remember, we are all in this together! "Oh, the depth of the riches both of the wisdom and knowledge of God! How unsearchable are His judgements and His ways past finding out!" "For who has known the mind of the Lord? Or who has become his counsellor?" "For of Him and through Him and to Him are all things, to whom be the glory forever, amen." (Romans 11:13-36)

Bye for now!

Signed, Paul

The grace of God the Father be with you all, Amen.

Catholicon

The Catholic Epistle from the First Epistle of our teacher St John. May his holy blessings be with us. Amen.

From John,

My beloved brothers and sisters, Did you know that you and I share a very special secret? But it's the kind of secret that God wants us to tell everybody about! And here it is are you ready? God has given us eternal life! That means that we can live forever with Him in Heaven! So if you know about Jesus and believe in Him and love Him and if Jesus lives inside you, You will get to live forever with Jesus in Heaven! So keep believing in Jesus. Keep loving Him more and more. Because He gives us more and more

Jesus hears every word we say to Him when we pray. Jesus answers our prayers. Especially when we pray for a brother or sister who is doing something wrong. They really need someone to pray for them! So they can stop being naughty! When you really love God, you just don't want to do anything wrong. And even though the devil might trick the whole world to do the wrong thing, he can never trick us — if we really, really love God. For God is true And Jesus is true And He protects us every day of our lives. (1 John 5:9-21)

God loves you!

Signed, John the Beloved

Do not love the world, nor the things which are in the world. The world shall pass away and all its desires; but he who does the will of God shall abide forever. Amen.

The Acts

A reading from the Acts of our fathers the pure apostles, who were invested with the grace of the Holy Spirit. May their blessing be with us all. Amen.

St Peter the Disciple came to Jerusalem. Some of the Christians who were Jewish wanted to pick a fight with him! "Hey, Peter," they said, "we heard a rumour that you sat down and ate with Gentiles! They're not Jews, man! How can you eat with them?" Peter asked the Jewish Christians to calm down and listen to his side of the story. He began to tell them about something amazing, "When I was in a city called Joppa," he began, "God showed me a VISION. I saw a big sheet—like the one on your bed—coming down from the sky! And on this sheet I saw all kinds of food; pork from pigs, and all kinds of birds, and wild animals. Some of them were the kinds of food that Jews are not allowed to eat. The a voice said: "Go ahead and eat, Peter." But I said, "I can't Lord! I am Jewish, and we're not allowed to eat that kind of food." But the voice answered, "Everything God made is good and clean and pure." And just as I was in shock about all this, someone knocked on my door! There were three men, who had come to call me and my friends to go to the house of a Gentile in Caesarea. He wasn't a Christian. When we got there, the man told us that an angel had come to him, and told him to send for me by name, even though he had never heard of me! So I talked to them about Jesus. And then, the Holy Spirit came down upon them, just like He had come upon us on the Day of Pentecost! That's when it hit me! God doesn't care if you are a Jew or a Gentile! God loves us all! If God wants Gentiles to be Christians, and gives them the same gifts He gave to us Jewish Christians, who am I to say no?" When the Jewish Christians heard this, they realised they had been wrong to stay away from the Gentiles. They realised that God loves EVERYBODY and He wants to save EVERYBODY, wherever they come from.. (Chapter 11:2-18)

The word of the Lord shall grow, multiply, be mighty and be confirmed in the holy Church of God. Amen

Holy Gospel

Stand up in the fear of God and listen to the Holy Gospel, A chapter from the Holy Gospel according to Saint John, May his blessings be with us all, Amen

From the psalms of our teacher David the prophet and king, May his blessings be with us all, Amen

> For with You is the fountain of life; In Your light we shall see light.
> Extend Your mercy to those who know You, And Your righteousness to
> the upright in heart.   Alleluia. - Psalm 36:9-10

Blessed is He who comes in the Name of the Lord Our Lord, God and Saviour and the King of us all, Jesus Christ, the Son of the living God. Glory be to You forever more, Amen

Now as Jesus passed by, He saw a man who was blind from birth. And His disciples asked Him, saying, "Rabbi, who sinned, this man or his parents, that he was born blind?" Jesus answered, "Neither this man nor his parents sinned, but that the works of God should be revealed in him. I " As long as I am in the world, I am the light of the world." When He had said these things, He spat on the ground and made clay with the saliva; and He anointed the eyes of the blind man with the clay. And He said to him, "Go, wash in the pool of Siloam" (which is translated, Sent). So he went and washed, and came back seeing.

Therefore the neighbours and those who previously had seen that he was blind said, "Is not this he who sat and begged?" Some said, "This is he." Others said, "He is like him." He said, "I am he." Therefore they said to him, "How were your eyes opened?" He answered and said, "A Man called Jesus made clay and anointed my eyes and said to me, 'Go to the pool of Then they said to him, "Where is He?" He said, "I do not know."

They brought him who formerly was blind to the Pharisees. Now it was a Sabbath when Jesus made the clay and opened his eyes. Then the Pharisees also asked him again how he had received his sight. He said to them, "He put clay on my eyes, and I washed, and I see." Therefore some of the Pharisees said, "This Man is not from God, because He does not keep the Sabbath." Others said, "How can a man who is a sinner do such signs?" And there was a division among them. They said to the blind man again, "What do you say about Him because He opened your eyes?" He said, "He is a prophet." But the Jews did not believe concerning him, that he had been blind and received his sight, until they called the parents of him who had received his sight. And they asked them, saying, "Is this your son, who you say was born blind? How then does he now see?" His parents answered them and said, "We know that this is our son, and that he was born blind; but by what means he now sees we do not know, or who opened his eyes we do not know. He is of age; ask him. He will speak for himself." His parents said these things because they feared the Jews, for the Jews had agreed already that if anyone confessed that He was Christ, he would be put out of the synagogue. Therefore his parents said, "He is of age; ask him." So they again called the man who was blind, and said to him, "Give God the glory! We know that this Man is a sinner." He answered and said, "Whether He is a sinner or not I do not know. One thing I know: that though I was blind, now I see." Then they said to him again, "What did He do to you? How did He open your eyes?" He answered them, "I told you already, and you did not listen. Why do you want to hear it again? Do you also want to become His disciples?" Then they reviled him and said, "You are His disciple, but we are Moses' disciples. We know that God spoke to Moses; as for this fellow, we do not know where He is from." The man answered and said to them, "Why, this is a marvellous thing, that you do not know where He is from; yet He has opened my eyes! Now we know that God does not hear sinners; but if anyone is a worshiper of God and does His will, He hears him. Since the world began it has been unheard of that anyone opened the eyes of one who was born blind. If this Man were not from God, He could do nothing." They answered and said to him, "You were completely born in sins, and are you teaching us?" And they cast him out.

Jesus heard that they had cast him out; and when He had found him, He said to him, "Do you believe in the Son of God?" He answered and said, "Who is He, Lord, that I may believe in Him?" And Jesus said to him, "You have both seen Him and it is He who is talking with you." Then he said, "Lord, I believe!" And he worshiped Him. John 9:1-38

Glory be to God Forever, Amen

FIRST SUNDAY OF AMSHIR

Holy Gospel

MATINS

Stand up in the fear of God and listen to the Holy Gospel, A chapter from the Holy Gospel according to Saint John, May his blessings be with us all, Amen

From the psalms of our teacher David the prophet and king, May his blessings be with us all, Amen

> Your word is a lamp to my feet And a light to my path. Make Your face shine upon Your servant, And teach me Your statutes. Alleluia. - Psalm 119:105,135

Blessed is He who comes in the Name of the Lord Our Lord, God and Saviour and the King of us all, Jesus Christ, the Son of the living God. Glory be to You forever more, Amen

Most assuredly, I say to you, if anyone keeps My word he shall never see death." Then the Jews said to Him, "Now we know that You have a demon! Abraham is dead, and the prophets; and You say, 'If anyone keeps My word he shall never taste death.' Are You greater than our father Abraham, who is dead? And the prophets are dead. Who do You make Yourself out to be?" Jesus answered, "If I honor Myself, My honor is nothing. It is My Father who honors Me, of whom you say that He is your God. Yet you have not known Him, but I know Him. And if I say, 'I do not know Him,' I shall be a liar like you; but I do know Him and keep His word. Your father Abraham rejoiced to see My day, and he saw it and was glad." Then the Jews said to Him, "You are not yet fifty years old, and have You seen Abraham?" Jesus said to them, "Most assuredly, I say to you, before Abraham was, I AM." Then they took up stones to throw at Him; but Jesus hid Himself and went out of the temple, going through the midst of them, and so passed by. John 8:51-59

Glory be to God Forever, Amen

Pauline

LITURGY

Paul, the servant of our Lord Jesus Christ, called to be an apostle, appointed to the Gospel of God. A reading from the First Epistle of our teacher Paul to the Corinthians. May his holy blessings be with us. Amen.

Dear Corinthians, Sometimes, people who are not Christians do the wrong thing. We can't really judge them, though: maybe they really don't know any better. But what about a CHRISTIAN person who does naughty things? Shouldn't they know better? What should we do if a Christian person steals, or is a bully, or if they get drunk or if they want everything for themselves? What should we do with them? We should tell them they have to stop! But if they just won't listen, then keep right away from them! What if two Christians have a big argument and they can't decide who is right and who is wrong? What should they do? Should they go to a judge to tell them who's right? Or should they go to the wise Christian people at Church to tell them who's right? Do you know when Jesus comes back, the Christians will help Him to judge the world! So don't you think they would be able to judge your little problems of this life? If you can't work out your own problems with each other, maybe you don't really have Jesus in your hearts. How sad! I have heard that some of you actually try to cheat each other! Oh my! Don't you understand? Do you want to miss out on being in heaven? Don't you know that anyone who keeps on stealing, or being jealous of others, or making fun of others, or bullying others doesn't belong Heaven? I know that some of you used to do lots of bad stuff like that BEFORE you became a Christian. But now, Jesus has washed you clean through the Holy Spirit, and He has made you good and holy. So please, don't go back to doing the wrong things again! (1 Corinthians 5:11-6:11)

Bye for now!

Signed, Paul

The grace of God the Father be with you all, Amen.

Catholicon

The Catholic Epistle from the Second Epistle of our teacher St Peter. May his holy blessings be with us. Amen.

From Peter,

My dear friends, remember that Jesus is going to come back one day. Are you ready? Being ready means being good like God in everything we do. Being ready means not fighting with others. Being ready means being a peaceful person. Remember, God is being patient so we can have enough time to get ready. So start getting ready!!! My friend Paul has also written to you about the end of the world, Although his letters are a bit hard to understand sometimes, and some naughty people tried to use them to confuse you. So, I am making sure that you are not confused, so that no one can trick you: Keep doing what is right and good! No one knows when our Lord Jesus will come back to us. So always be ready. Keep growing in God's grace. Keep knowing Him better. Keep praising Him with joy. Glory be to Him, now and forever, Amen. (2 Peter 3:14-18)

Bye for now!

Signed, Peter the Apostle

Do not love the world, nor the things which are in the world. The world shall pass away and all its desires; but he who does the will of God shall abide forever. Amen.

The Acts

A Jewish man named Saul hated the Christians and wandered about arresting them, so they could be tortured and killed. One day, he was travelling to a city called Damascus, looking for more Christians to arrest. Something AMAZING happened! Suddenly, a bright light shone all around him from heaven! He was so surprised that he fell of his horse! And he was blinded! Then he heard a great voice saying to him: "Saul, Saul, why are you doing this to Me?" Whose voice was that? The people who were travelling with Saul were very frightened indeed. They could hear a voice, but they couldn't see anyone! "Who are you, Lord?" Saul answered while all his body was absolutely shaking and shivering with fright. "I am Jesus whom you are fighting against" said the Voice. "Aren't you tired of fighting Me?" Saul was shocked! Saul was muddled! Saul was befuddled! Saul was shaking all over! "Wha-, wha- what do you want me to do, Lord?" he asked. "Get up", said the Voice. "Go into the city and there you will find out what I want you to do". So Saul got up, but when he tried to open his eyes, he discovered that he had gone blind! His friends had to lead him by the hand into Damascus. And he stayed in Damascus waiting for God's instructions. For three days he waited and he fasted too, having nothing at all to eat or drink. Later, God made Saul see again, and Saul changed his name, and became an Apostle. Do you know his new name? It was Paul. (Chapter 9:3-9)

Holy Gospel

Stand up in the fear of God and listen to the Holy Gospel,A chapter from the Holy Gospel according to Saint John, May his blessings be with us all, Amen

From the psalms of our teacher David the prophet and king,May his blessings be with us all, Amen

> Thanksgiving and beauty are before Him; Holiness and majesty are in His holy place. For the Lord is great, and is greatly to be praised; And He is to be feared above all the gods.   Alleluia. - Psalm 96:6,4

Blessed is He who comes in the Name of the Lord Our Lord, God and Saviour and the King of us all, Jesus Christ, the Son of the living God. Glory be to You forever more, Amen

On the following day, when the people who were standing on the other side of the sea saw that there was no other boat there, except that one which His disciples had entered and that Jesus had not entered the boat with His disciples, but His disciples had gone away alone— however, other boats came from Tiberias, near the place where they ate bread after the Lord had given thanks— when the people therefore saw that Jesus was not there, nor His disciples, they also got into boats and came to Capernaum, seeking Jesus. And when they found Him on the other side of the sea, they said to Him, "Rabbi, when did You come here?" Jesus answered them and said, "Most assuredly, I say to you, you seek Me, not because you saw the signs, but because you ate of the loaves and were filled. Do not labour for the food which perishes, but for the food which endures to everlasting life, which the Son of Man will give you, because God the Father has set His seal on Him." John 6:22-27

Glory be to God Forever, Amen

SECOND SUNDAY OF AMSHIR

Holy Gospel

MATINS

Stand up in the fear of God and listen to the Holy Gospel, A chapter from the Holy Gospel according to Saint John, May his blessings be with us all, Amen

From the psalms of our teacher David the prophet and king, May his blessings be with us all, Amen

> Who may ascend into the hill of the Lord? Or who may stand in His holy place? He who has clean hands and a pure heart, Who has not lifted up his soul to an idol, Nor sworn deceitfully. Alleluia. - Psalm 24:3-4

Blessed is He who comes in the Name of the Lord Our Lord, God and Saviour and the King of us all, Jesus Christ, the Son of the living God. Glory be to You forever more, Amen

For God did not send His Son into the world to condemn the world, but that the world through Him might be saved. "He who believes in Him is not condemned; but he who does not believe is condemned already, because he has not believed in the name of the only begotten Son of God. And this is the condemnation, that the light has come into the world, and men loved darkness rather than light, because their deeds were evil. For everyone practicing evil hates the light and does not come to the light, lest his deeds should be exposed. But he who does the truth comes to the light, that his deeds may be clearly seen, that they have been done in God." John 3: 17-21

Glory be to God Forever, Amen

Pauline

Paul, the servant of our Lord Jesus Christ, called to be an apostle, appointed to the Gospel of God. A reading from the Epistle of our teacher Paul to the Hebrews. May his holy blessings be with us. Amen.

St Paul the Apostle was writing a letter to the Christians who were Jewish. We also call them Israelites or Hebrews.

Dear Hebrews, Along time ago, there was a very famous King of SALEM (which means "peace") who was also a priest. His name was Melchizedek. Can you say it with me? "Mell - cheese - eh - deck". One day, Melchizedek met old father Abraham. And Abraham knew that Melchizedek was a holy priest of God. So Abraham asked Melchizedek to bless him and he gave Melchizedek one tenth of what he had. Melchizedek is a bit like Jesus. Can you guess how? What makes Jesus like Melchizedek? Well, Melchizedek was the King of Salem which means "peace" and we call Jesus the "King of Peace"! Melchizedek blessed Abraham, the father of all Hebrews. And Jesus blessed the whole world, including the Hebrews! Jesus is OUR Melchizedek. Jesus is the One who blesses us, just like Melchizedek blessed Abraham. And Jesus is our High Priest mysterious, and very great and holy, just like Melchizedek. That's why the Psalms spoke about Jesus and said: "You are a priest forever According to the order of Melchizedek." Jesus is our Melchizedek! (Hebrews 7:1-17)

Bye for now!

Signed, Paul the Apostle

The grace of God the Father be with you all, Amen.

Catholicon

The Catholic Epistle from the Second Epistle of our teacher St John. May his holy blessings be with us. Amen.

From John the Elder, My Dear Lady, and her dear children, I truly love you! And everyone who knows the truth of God loves you too! May God our Father and His beloved Son, Jesus grant you grace, mercy and peace in truth and love. You made me so happy when I heard that some of you always tell the truth, just as the Father told us to! But I beg of you, dear lady, always remember what Jesus taught us right from the beginning, to love one another. How can we love one another? By keeping God's commandments! I am sad to say that some people have gone around telling everyone that Jesus never became a human being just like us! They're not telling the truth! They are the enemies of Jesus Christ! Please, don't listen to them and lose the beautiful truth of Jesus, which takes us to heaven. If someone sins or does naughty things all the time, they don't really have God in their heart. But if someone follows Jesus and lives the way that Jesus taught us to live, they have both God the Father and the Son in their heart. So if anyone tries to tell you anything bad about Jesus, don't listen to them, don't welcome them and don't hang around with them. I have a lot more I want to tell you, but I want to tell you face to face, not just with a letter. Hopefully, I will see you soon. (2 John 1-13)

Bye for now!

Signed, John the Beloved

PS. The children of your sister say hello.

Do not love the world, nor the things which are in the world. The world shall pass away and all its desires; but he who does the will of God shall abide forever. Amen.

The Acts

St Paul came to a big city called Corinth. He stayed there for a long time, telling people about Jesus, and lots of people were being baptised and becoming Christians. And God told Paul not be scared of anyone, but to keep telling everyone he could the Good News about Jesus. But some of the Jewish people of Corinth grew very jealous of St Paul. "Look how he steals people away from our synagogue!" they complained. Some of them got so angry that they went and grabbed St Paul and dragged him in front of the Roman Governor, named Gallio. But when he had heard them out, Gallio said, "This has nothing to do with me! Go and work out your own religious problems and stop bugging me!" So St Paul got to stay a bit longer in Corinth, to help the new Church there to grow and to be brave and strong. When he was done, he set off to visit other cities with new Churches. Wherever he went, the Christians asked him to stay with them, but he had somewhere to go "I must go to Jerusalem to celebrate the Feast," he told them, "but I will come and visit you again, God willing". And every place he went, he helped the Christians there and made their faith stronger. (Chapter 18:9-21)

Holy Gospel

Stand up in the fear of God and listen to the Holy Gospel,A chapter from the Holy Gospel according to Saint John, May his blessings be with us all, Amen

From the psalms of our teacher David the prophet and king,May his blessings be with us all, Amen

> Bring to the Lord, O families of the Gentiles, Bring to the Lord glory and honour; Bring to the Lord the glory of His name; Take up sacrifices and enter into His courts; Worship the Lord in His holy court. Alleluia.
> - Psalm 96:7-9

Blessed is He who comes in the Name of the Lord Our Lord, God and Saviour and the King of us all, Jesus Christ, the Son of the living God. Glory be to You forever more, Amen

Then Jesus lifted up His eyes, and seeing a great multitude coming toward Him, He said to Philip, "Where shall we buy bread, that these may eat?" But this He said to test him, for He Himself knew what He would do. Philip answered Him, "Two hundred denarii worth of bread is not sufficient for them, that every one of them may have a little." One of His disciples, Andrew, Simon Peter's brother, said to Him, "There is a lad here who has five barley loaves and two small fish, but what are they among so many?" Then Jesus said, "Make the people sit down." Now there was much grass in the place. So the men sat down, in number about five thousand. And Jesus took the loaves, and when He had given thanks He distributed them to the disciples, and the disciples to those sitting down; and likewise of the fish, as much as they wanted. So when they were filled, He said to His disciples, "Gather up the fragments that remain, so that nothing is lost." Therefore they gathered them up, and filled twelve baskets with the fragments of the five barley loaves which were left over by those who had eaten. Then those men, when they had seen the sign that Jesus did, said, "This is truly the Prophet who is to come into the world."   John 6:5-14

Glory be to God Forever, Amen

THIRD SUNDAY OF AMSHIR

Holy Gospel

MATINS

Stand up in the fear of God and listen to the Holy Gospel, A chapter from the Holy Gospel according to Saint John, May his blessings be with us all, Amen

From the psalms of our teacher David the prophet and king, May his blessings be with us all, Amen

> Blessed be the Lord forevermore! Amen and Amen. Lord, where are Your former lovingkindnesses, Which You swore to David in Your truth? Alleluia. - Psalm 89:52,49

Blessed is He who comes in the Name of the Lord Our Lord, God and Saviour and the King of us all, Jesus Christ, the Son of the living God. Glory be to You forever more, Amen

Then Jesus cried out and said, "He who believes in Me, believes not in Me but in Him who sent Me. And he who sees Me sees Him who sent Me. I have come as a light into the world, that whoever believes in Me should not abide in darkness. And if anyone hears My words and does not believe, I do not judge him; for I did not come to judge the world but to save the world. He who rejects Me, and does not receive My words, has that which judges him—the word that I have spoken will judge him in the last day. For I have not spoken on My own authority; but the Father who sent Me gave Me a command, what I should say and what I should speak. And I know that His command is everlasting life. Therefore, whatever I speak, just as the Father has told Me, so I speak." John 12:44-50

Glory be to God Forever, Amen

Pauline

Paul, the servant of our Lord Jesus Christ, called to be an apostle, appointed to the Gospel of God. A reading from the Epistle of our teacher Paul to the Hebrews. May his holy blessings be with us. Amen.

St Paul the Apostle was writing a letter to the Christians who were Jewish. We also call them Israelites or Hebrews.

Dear Hebrews, Do you remember the great prophet Moses? Moses loved God and obeyed God. So, Moses saved God's people (the Hebrews) from being slaves in Egypt. He started them off in their new life in their own kingdom under God's care. Moses SERVED God faithfully. But Jesus IS the Son of God! So we Hebrews really should listen to Jesus' voice, even more than to Moses' voice. And remember, sometimes the Hebrews DIDN'T listen to Moses, when they were wandering in the desert for 40 years. The ones who didn't listen to Moses are the ones who never made it to the beautiful new kingdom, the Promised Land. They heard the words that God spoke to them through Moses, but they didn't listen. They didn't learn anything from him. Please, let's not be like them! We've got someone so much better than Moses. We've got Jesus! So let's help each other and remind each other every day. Don't wait till tomorrow to be close to Jesus. Do it right now! Today! (Hebrews 3:1-4:2)

Bye for now!

Signed, Paul

> *The grace of God the Father be with you all, Amen.*

Catholicon

The Catholic Epistle from the Epistle of our teacher St Jude. May his holy blessings be with us. Amen.

My little children, This is the Apostle Jude writing to warn you about false teachers, You have to be very careful about these people, the ones who try to confuse you about Jesus. The prophets long ago warned us that false teachers would come and teach the wrong things about Jesus, and about how we should follow Him. They warned us that the false teachers will be judged by God, when He comes back with His angels! These false teachers are not nice at all! They like to grumble and complain about everything. They like to boast and show off, they like to make people turn against each other, they like to crawl and suck up to people so that they can get what they want for themselves. But I don't want you to be tricked by them, my beloved. Remember how Jesus warned us that evil people like these would come. So make sure that you stick to the true faith, remembering the love and kindness of God, and always praying for the Holy Spirit to guard you. Be gentle with those who go wrong, but with some people you have to be really tough to save them from the fire! God is able to keep you from stumbling, until you stand happily in front of His Throne at the end. To God our Saviour, Who alone is wise, be glory and majesty, dominion and power, Both now and forever. Amen (Jude 14-25)

Bye for now!

Signed Jude the Apostle

Do not love the world, nor the things which are in the world. The world shall pass away and all its desires; but he who does the will of God shall abide forever. Amen.

The Acts

A reading from the Acts of our fathers the pure apostles, who were invested with the grace of the Holy Spirit. May their blessing be with us all. Amen.

One day, the Apostle St Paul was in a big house where lots of people had come to listen to him tell them about Jesus. Paul spoke and spoke and they listened and listened, so happy to learn more about Jesus' love. Before anyone realised, it was already midnight! It was way past the bedtime of a boy called Eutychus [Yoo-tie-kuss]. They were on the third floor and Eutychus was sitting somewhere that was not very clever. Eutychus was sitting on the window sill. And the window was open. And Eutychus fell asleep! OH! Be careful Eutychus! Oh no! Eutychus fell out the window! How awful! Everyone rushed downstairs. Is he hurt? Is he alive? Oh no!

Oh no! Eutychus was dead. But Paul went through all the people, and he picked up Eutychus. Paul hugged him. Paul prayed for him. Then, a miracle happened! Eutychus came back to life! He was alive again! Everyone was so happy! Then they all went back inside, and had something to eat, which they needed after a shock like that! And they kept listening to Paul all through the night, all the way to morning. The things he was telling them about Jesus were just so beautiful. They didn't want him to stop! And in the morning, Paul left to get on a ship to continue his adventures. He visited lots more places, but he was in hurry. He wanted to get to Jerusalem in time for Pentecost, the great and happy feast. And as for Eutychus well, I don't think sat on a window sill on the third floor again! (Chapter 20:7-16)

The word of the Lord shall grow, multiply, be mighty and be confirmed in the holy Church of God. Amen.

Holy Gospel

Stand up in the fear of God and listen to the Holy Gospel,A chapter from the Holy Gospel according to Saint John, May his blessings be with us all, Amen

From the psalms of our teacher David the prophet and king,May his blessings be with us all, Amen

> O Lord, I will sing of Your mercies forever; I will proclaim Your truth with my mouth For who in the clouds shall be compared to the Lord, And who among the sons of God shall be compared to the Lord? Alleluia. - Psalm 89:1,6

Blessed is He who comes in the Name of the Lord Our Lord, God and Saviour and the King of us all, Jesus Christ, the Son of the living God. Glory be to You forever more, Amen

Do not labour for the food which perishes, but for the food which endures to everlasting life, which the Son of Man will give you, because God the Father has set His seal on Him." Then they said to Him, "What shall we do, that we may work the works of God?" Jesus answered and said to them, "This is the work of God, that you believe in Him whom He sent". Then Jesus said to them, "Most assuredly,

I say to you, Moses did not give you the bread from heaven, but My Father gives you the true bread from heaven. For the bread of God is He who comes down from heaven and gives life to the world." Then they said to Him, "Lord, give us this bread always." And Jesus said to them, "I am the bread of life. He who comes to Me shall never hunger, and he who believes in Me shall never thirst. But I said to you that you have seen Me and yet do not believe. All that the Father gives Me will come to Me, and the one who comes to Me I will by no means cast out. For I have come down from heaven, not to do My own will, but the will of Him who sent Me. This is the will of the Father who sent Me, that of all He has given Me I should lose nothing, but should raise it up at the last day.

The Jews then complained about Him, because He said, "I am the bread which came down from heaven." And they said, "Is not this Jesus, the son of Joseph, whose father and mother we know? How is it then that He says, 'I have come down from heaven'?" Jesus therefore answered and said to them, "Do not murmur among yourselves. No one can come to Me unless the Father who sent Me draws him; and I will raise him up at the last day. It is written in the prophets, 'And they shall all be taught by God.' Therefore everyone who has heard and learned from the Father comes to Me. Not that anyone has seen the Father, except He who is from God; He has seen the Father."   John 6:27-46

Glory be to God Forever, Amen

FOURTH SUNDAY OF AMSHIR

Holy Gospel

MATINS

Stand up in the fear of God and listen to the Holy Gospel, A chapter from the Holy Gospel according to Saint Luke, May his blessings be with us all, Amen

From the psalms of our teacher David the prophet and king, May his blessings be with us all, Amen

> The heavens are Yours, the earth also is Yours; The world and all its fullness, You have founded them. I will sing of the mercies of the Lord forever; With my mouth will I make known Your faithfulness to all generations.   Alleluia. - Psalm 89:11,1

Blessed is He who comes in the Name of the Lord Our Lord, God and Saviour and the King of us all, Jesus Christ, the Son of the living God. Glory be to You forever more, Amen

Now it happened, the day after, that He went into a city called Nain; and many of His disciples went with Him, and a large crowd. And when He came near the gate of the city, behold, a dead man was being carried out, the only son of his mother; and she was a widow. And a large crowd from the city was with her. When the Lord saw her, He had compassion on her and said to her, "Do not weep." Then He came and touched the open coffin, and those who carried him stood still. And He said, "Young man, I say to you, arise." So he who was dead sat up and began to speak. And He presented him to his mother.

Then fear came upon all, and they glorified God, saying, "A great prophet has risen up among us"; and, "God has visited His people." And this report about Him went throughout all Judea and all the surrounding region. Then the disciples of John reported to him concerning all these things. And John, calling two of his disciples to him, sent them to Jesus, saying, "Are You the Coming One, or do we look for another?" Luke 7:11-19

Glory be to God Forever, Amen

Pauline

Paul, the servant of our Lord Jesus Christ, called to be an apostle, appointed to the Gospel of God. A reading from the First Epistle of our teacher Paul to the Corinthians. May his holy blessings be with us. Amen.

St Paul the Apostle was writing a letter to the Christians who lived in the rich city of Corinth. To my dear friends in the Church of Corinth, who always pray to our Lord Jesus Christ. Grace and peace to you. I always thank God that God has given you the gift of knowing Jesus really well, and being able to speak about Jesus. Even the way you live your life shows the world how beautiful Jesus is. What a lovely gift from God! I want you to know that God will always be with you, even to the last day. But there is something else I really need to say to you; I have heard that you sometimes argue and fight with each other! Christians should all be following Jesus TOGETHER. I've even heard that some of you say things like this: "I'm on Paul's team!" Or "No, I am on Apollos' team, not Paul!" Or "I don't like either! I'm on Cephas' team!" Oh my goodness! What is wrong with you??? Don't you know that we are all on just ONE team together? We are all on Jesus' team! Were you baptised in the name of "Paul" or in the name of Jesus? Jesus, of course! So let's forget this "team" silliness that makes us argue with each other, And remember that ALL of us are following Jesus, not anyone else. (1 Corinthians 1:1-16)

Bye for now!

Signed, Paul

The grace of God the Father be with you all, Amen.

Catholicon

The Catholic Epistle from the Epistle of our teacher St James. May his holy blessings be with us. Amen.

Hello Everyone! Have you ever had the feeling that you wanted to do something that you knew was naughty? That happens to all of us some time or other. It's called "temptation." Where do you think temptation comes from? Do you think God is the one who makes us want to be naughty? Of course not! God is perfectly good and He always helps people to be good, not naughty. Never naughty! So what tempts us to be naughty? Temptation comes from inside us. It comes from our own feelings. I don't want you to be tricked my brothers and sisters. Doing the wrong thing just NEVER leads to anything good in the end. But every good thing comes down to us from our Heavenly Father, the Father of Lights, who never changes but is always good. Out of His goodness, He made us, the most special of all His creatures. So, my beloved, I want you all to be Quick to listen, Slow to speak, Slow to anger. Don't let yourself get angry too easily, because when a human being gets angry, they almost never do what our good God wants them to do. So, say "NO!" to naughtiness! Say "NO!" to doing bad things. And instead, say "YES!" to Jesus and to the things Jesus teaches you deep in your heart. (James 1:13-21)

Be good!

Signed, James the Apostle

Do not love the world, nor the things which are in the world. The world shall pass away and all its desires; but he who does the will of God shall abide forever. Amen.

The Acts

A reading from the Acts of our fathers the pure apostles, who were invested with the grace of the Holy Spirit. May their blessing be with us all. Amen.

St Philip the Deacon travelled all the way to a place called Samaria to tell the people there about Jesus and His Good News. Lots of people believed in Jesus, because of what Philip told them, but also because Philip had the gift of doing miracles. Philip healed lots of sick people! People who couldn't walk suddenly found they were healed—they could walk! Now in that place, there was a man called Simon the Sorcerer. For a long time, Simon had amazed everyone with his tricks. Simon was curious so he came to listen to what Philip had to say. This time, it was Simon's turn to be amazed! Simon the Sorcerer had never heard such beautiful words. And for all his tricks, Simon had never seen such miracles as those that Philip did! So, when Simon saw that Philip was baptising the people who believed in Jesus, he wanted to be baptised too. And that is exactly what happened. Not only was Simon the Sorcerer baptised—he also followed Philip, and saw him do even more amazing miracles! (Chapter 8:5-13)

The word of the Lord shall grow, multiply, be mighty and be confirmed in the holy Church of God. Amen.

Holy Gospel

Stand up in the fear of God and listen to the Holy Gospel, A chapter from the Holy Gospel according to Saint Luke , May his blessings be with us all, Amen

From the psalms of our teacher David the prophet and king, May his blessings be with us all, Amen

> The earth is the Lord's, and its fullness, The world and all who dwell therein. For He founded it upon the seas And prepared it upon the rivers Alleluia. - Psalm 24: 1-2

Blessed is He who comes in the Name of the Lord Our Lord, God and Saviour and the King of us all, Jesus Christ, the Son of the living God. Glory be to You forever more, Amen

Then Jesus entered and passed through Jericho. Now behold, there was a man named Zacchaeus who was a chief tax collector, and he was rich. And he sought to see who Jesus was, but could not because of the crowd, for he was of short stature. So he ran ahead and climbed up into a sycamore tree to see Him, for He was going to pass that way. And when Jesus came to the place, He looked up and saw him, and said to him Zacchaeus, make haste and come down, for today I must stay at your house. So he made haste and came down, and received Him joyfully. But when they saw it, they all complained, saying, He has gone to be a guest with a man who is a sinner. Then Zacchaeus stood and said to the Lord, Look, Lord, I give half of my goods to the poor; and if I have taken anything from anyone by false accusation, I restore fourfold. And Jesus said to him, Today salvation has come to this house, because he also is a son of Abraham; for the Son of Man has come to seek and to save that which was lost. Luke 19:1-10

Glory be to God Forever, Amen

THIRD SUNDAY OF BASHANS

Holy Gospel

MATINS

Stand up in the fear of God and listen to the Holy Gospel, A chapter from the Holy Gospel according to Saint Luke, May his blessings be with us all, Amen

From the psalms of our teacher David the prophet and king, May his blessings be with us all, Amen

> For God is my King from of old, Working salvation in the midst of the earth. Remember Your congregation, which You have purchased of old, The tribe of Your inheritance, which You have redeemed— This Mount Zion where You have dwelt Alleluia. - Psalm 74: 12,2

Blessed is He who comes in the Name of the Lord Our Lord, God and Saviour and the King of us all, Jesus Christ, the Son of the living God. Glory be to You forever more, Amen

Now on the first day of the week, very early in the morning, they, and certain other women with them, came to the tomb bringing the spices which they had prepared. But they found the stone rolled away from the tomb. Then they went in and did not find the body of the Lord Jesus. And it happened, as they were greatly perplexed about this, that behold, two men stood by them in shining garments. Then, as they were afraid and bowed their faces to the earth, they said to them, "Why do you seek the living among the dead? He is not here, but is risen! Remember how He spoke to you when He was still in Galilee, saying, 'The Son of Man must be delivered into the hands of sinful men, and be crucified, and the third day rise again.' " And they remembered His words. Then they returned from the tomb and told all these things to the eleven and to all the rest. It was Mary Magdalene, Joanna, Mary the mother of James, and the other women with them, who told these things to the apostles. And their words seemed to them like idle tales, and they did not believe them. But Peter arose and ran to the tomb; and stooping down, he saw the linen cloths lying by themselves; and he departed, marveling to himself at what had happened. Luke 24:1-12

Glory be to God Forever, Amen

Pauline

Paul, the servant of our Lord Jesus Christ, called to be an apostle, appointed to the Gospel of God. A reading from the Epistle of our teacher Paul to the Hebrews. May his holy blessings be with us. Amen.

Dear Hebrews,

Do you know what the word "faith" means? It means that we believe in God; we trust God. If you have faith in God, you trust Him, even when you are not sure what is going to happen! We have faith in God because He made the whole wide world! And He made it out of nothing! Even in the Old Testament, a long, long time ago, there were good people who had faith in God. Let me remind you about some of them, remember Cain and Abel? Abel had faith in God. Cain didn't.That's why God accepted the sacrifice of Abel, but He didn't accept Cain's. Remember Enoch? Enoch had faith. And because Enoch trusted God, God took Enoch to be with Him in Heaven. Remember Noah and his ark? Noah had faith. And because Noah trusted God, God saved Noah and his family from the flood. Remember Abraham? Abraham had faith. And because Abraham trusted God, he obeyed God and left his home to go wherever God told him. Abraham was looking for the Land of God—the Kingdom of Heaven. And God even gave Abraham a beautiful land here on earth, too! All these people had FAITH. They believed in God. They trusted God. (Hebrews 11:1–10)

Bye for now!

Signed, Paul

The grace of God the Father be with you all, Amen.

Catholicon

The Catholic Epistle from the First Epistle of our teacher St John. May his holy blessings be with us. Amen.

Jesus is the Son of God. If you love Jesus, then that means that God lives in you, and you live in God. God is Love. Whoever lives in love, lives in God and God lives in Him. God's perfect love inside us makes us ready to face the scary Judgement Day. No way! We won't be scared! That's because when your heart is full of love. There's no room left for being afraid! Say it with me: "Perfect love casts out fear." And do you know WHY we love God? Because He loved us first! But what about if someone says that he loves God, but at the same time, he hates other people? Do you think he truly loves God? No way! You can't truly love God (who you can't see), But hate other people (who you can see very well)! So God taught us that if we truly love Him, we must truly love others too. If you believe that Jesus is God's Son, then you love God; and you love God's Son, Jesus; and you obey God. It's really not that hard to obey God. His rules are nice! God's rules teach us how to love God, and how to love other people. And this makes us SO strong! Nothing in the world is stronger than a person who has faith in God and loves God. (1 John 4:15–5:4)

Signed, John the Beloved

Do not love the world, nor the things which are in the world. The world shall pass away and all its desires; but he who does the will of God shall abide forever. Amen.

The Acts

St Paul and his friend St Barnabas were visiting a city called Antioch. The Jewish people there asked them to teach them something about God. Paul told them such wonderful, marvellous things about Jesus that the next week, almost the whole city came to listen to him! They wanted to know all about Jesus. When some of the Jewish people saw such a big crowd of Gentiles (that means people who are not Jewish), they were a bit jealous! "Paul doesn't know what he's talking about!" they started to say. "Don't listen to him! Do you think this made Paul angry with the Jews? No! Paul wasn't angry. He knew they were just being jealous. So Paul said to the Jews, "Since you don't want to hear about Jesus, I will tell the Gentiles about Jesus. "Long ago, the prophet Isaiah said that Jesus is like a light for the Gentiles. He came to save everyone, all over the world." Lots and lots of the Gentiles loved what Paul was teaching them about Jesus, and they became Christians. But the jealous Jews still weren't happy. They stirred up trouble. They made life hard for Paul. Until finally, Paul and Barnabas were kicked out of Antioch. Do you think THIS made Paul angry with the Jews? No No! Paul still wasn't angry with the Jews. His heart was still full of joy. The Holy Spirit made him quite calm. Paul. Paul and his friends just went on to the next town. There were still lots and lots more people who needed to hear how much Jesus loves them! (Chapter 13:44–52)

Holy Gospel

Stand up in the fear of God and listen to the Holy Gospel, A chapter from the Holy Gospel according to Saint Luke, May his blessings be with us all, Amen

From the psalms of our teacher David the prophet and king, May his blessings be with us all, Amen

> Bless God in the churches, The Lord from the fountains of Israel. Blessed is the Lord from day to day; The God of our salvation will bring prosperity upon us. Alleluia. -Psalm 68:26, 19

Blessed is He who comes in the Name of the Lord Our Lord, God and Saviour and the King of us all, Jesus Christ, the Son of the living God. Glory be to You forever more, Amen

And behold, a certain lawyer stood up and tested Him, saying, "Teacher, what shall I do to inherit eternal life?" He said to him, "What is written in the law? What is your reading of it?" So he answered and said, "'You shall love the Lord your God with all your heart, with all your soul, with all your strength, and with all your mind,' and 'your neighbour as yourself.'" And He said to him, "You have answered rightly; do this and you will live." But he, wanting to justify himself, said to Jesus, "And who is my neighbour?" Then Jesus answered and said: "A certain man went down from Jerusalem to Jericho, and fell among thieves, who stripped him of his clothing, wounded him, and departed, leaving him half dead. Now by chance a certain priest came down that road. And when he saw him, he passed by on the other side. Likewise a Levite, when he arrived at the place, came and looked, and passed by on the other side. But a certain Samaritan, as he journeyed, came where he was. And when he saw him, he had compassion. So he went to him and bandaged his wounds, pouring on oil and wine; and he set him on his own animal, brought him to an inn, and took care of him. On the next day, when he departed, he took out two denarii, gave them to the innkeeper, and said to him, 'Take care of him; and whatever more you spend, when I come again, I will repay you.' So which of these three do you think was neighbour to him who fell among the thieves?" And he said, "He who showed mercy on him." Then Jesus said to him, "Go and do likewise." Luke 10:25–37

Glory be to God Forever, Amen

FOURTH SUNDAY OF BASHANS

Holy Gospel

Stand up in the fear of God and listen to the Holy Gospel, A chapter from the Holy Gospel according to Saint John, May his blessings be with us all, Amen

From the psalms of our teacher David the prophet and king, May his blessings be with us all, Amen

> Sing praises to God, sing praises! Sing praises to our King, sing praises!
> For God is the King of all the earth; Sing praises with understanding.
> Alleluia. -Psalm 47:6-7

Blessed is He who comes in the Name of the Lord Our Lord, God and Saviour and the King of us all, Jesus Christ, the Son of the living God. Glory be to You forever more, Amen

Now the first day of the week Mary Magdalene went to the tomb early, while it was still dark, and saw that the stone had been taken away from the tomb. Then she ran and came to Simon Peter, and to the other disciple, whom Jesus loved, and said to them, "They have taken away the Lord out of the tomb, and we do not know where they have laid Him." Peter therefore went out, and the other disciple, and were going to the tomb. So they both ran together, and the other disciple outran Peter and came to the tomb first. And he, stooping down and looking in, saw the linen cloths lying there; yet he did not go in. Then Simon Peter came, following him, and went into the tomb; and he saw the linen cloths lying there, and the handkerchief that had been around His head, not lying with the linen cloths, but folded together in a place by itself. Then the other disciple, who came to the tomb first, went in also; and he saw and believed. For as yet they did not know the Scripture, that He must rise again from the dead. Then the disciples went away again to their own homes. But Mary stood outside by the tomb weeping, and as she wept she stooped down and looked into the tomb. And she saw two angels in white sitting, one at the head and the other at the feet, where the body of Jesus had lain. Then they said to her, "Woman, why are you weeping?"

She said to them, "Because they have taken away my Lord, and I do not know where they have laid Him." Now when she had said this, she turned around and saw Jesus standing there, and did not know that it was Jesus. Jesus said to her, "Woman, why are you weeping? Whom are you seeking?" She, supposing Him to be the gardener, said to Him, "Sir, if You have carried Him away, tell me where You have laid Him, and I will take Him away."

Jesus said to her, "Mary!" She turned and said to Him, "Rabboni!" (which is to say, Teacher). Jesus said to her, "Do not cling to Me, for I have not yet ascended to My Father; but go to My brethren and say to them, 'I am ascending to My Father and your Father, and to My God and your God.' " Mary Magdalene came and told the disciples that she had seen the Lord, and that He had spoken these things to her. John 20:1-18

Glory be to God Forever, Amen

Pauline

Paul, the servant of our Lord Jesus Christ, called to be an apostle, appointed to the Gospel of God. A reading from the First Epistle of our teacher Paul to the Corinthians. May his holy blessings be with us. Amen.

Dear Corinthians,

You know how God gives some people the special gift of being able to pray in different languages? Well, God has given me that gift, more than anyone! But we all have to use these gifts very carefully and wisely. Even though I can pray in different languages, when I am in the Church, I would rather speak 5 words we all understand, instead of 10,000 words that no one understands! My brothers and sisters, be innocent like children, but also be wise and understanding. In the Bible, God says, "I will speak to people in languages, but they will not hear me." So languages are meant to help those who are not Christian to come to God, not for those who are already Christians. If you are all praying with different languages in the Church, and a non-Christian walks in won't they think you are crazy? But if everyone is speaking the Truth of God in a language you do understand, and a non-Christian walks in that non-Christian's heart will be touched, and he will begin to understand, and to worship God, and know that God is truly with you. So let's do things properly. Each person has their own gift from God. Some people are good at singing, or teaching, or helping others to understand. Whatever you do in Church, do it to help others. Don't go on and on! Don't say things that no one understands! Listen to each other, and be kind to each other. Our God is not a messy God! He is peaceful. So the Churches that really do follow God are the Churches that are well-organised and peaceful. Please try to do that in your Church. (1 Corinthians 14:18–33)

Bye for now!

Signed, Paul

The grace of God the Father be with you all, Amen.

Catholicon

The Catholic Epistle from the Third Epistle of our teacher St John. May his holy blessings be with us. Amen.

To my beloved Gaius, whom I love in truth:

My beloved, I pray that you are well, in your body and in your soul. Nothing makes me happier than to hear that my children are walking in truth, just like you are. Lots of people have told me, Gaius, how kind you are both to Christians and to strangers. When you take someone in and care for them, and send them safely on their way, you are doing a really good thing. Especially, if the people you care for are Christians who are travelling to share Jesus with others. When you help them, Gaius, you are sharing in their good work. (3 John 1–8)

Signed, John the Beloved

Do not love the world, nor the things which are in the world. The world shall pass away and all its desires; but he who does the will of God shall abide forever. Amen.

The Acts

In the days when the Christian Church was still young, most of the Christians were Jewish, just like Jesus and like His apostles. But soon, lots of people who were not Jewish began to know about Jesus and to become Christian. Some of the Jewish Christians didn't think letting them in was a very good idea. This is how St Peter answered them. He said: "I don't think God agrees with you. I think God wants everyone to be Christian, even if they are not Jewish. And here's why "One day, I was praying to God, when suddenly, I saw something so strange a great big sheet came down from heaven! And the great big sheet was full of stuff, "There were all kinds of animals and food; even the kinds of food that Jewish people are not allowed to eat. But just then, I heard a voice. And do you know what the voice said to me? "The voice said, 'Get up and and eat, Peter.''No!' I said, 'I can't eat that! I'm Jewish, and those kinds of food are not clean for us. We're not allowed to eat them.' "But the voice answered me and said: 'Didn't God make this food? How can you say it is not allowed? Of course it is clean.' "And just then, three men knocked on my door. They had come to take me to see a Gentile man—he isn't Jewish—called Cornelius. The Holy Spirit told me I should go with them. "So I went with them. And when I met Cornelius, he told me how an angel had come to him, and told him to send for a man called Peter (that's me, of course!) And this man would tell him how he could be saved. "So I started to tell Cornelius about Jesus Christ our Saviour. But as I was speaking, something really amazing happened right before our very own eyes. "The Holy Spirit came down upon Cornelius! Just like the Holy Spirit once came down upon the Apostles on Pentecost! Right away, I realised something very important, "God Himself had chosen Cornelius and his friends to be Christians! God Himself was baptising them with the Holy Spirit! Even though they are Gentiles, not Jews! "So who are we to say 'no' to God? How can we say that Gentiles can't become Christians, when it is God Himself who is making them become Christians?" And when the Jewish Christians heard this, they went very quiet indeed. "Wow!" they said, "So God DOES want everyone to be Christian. You DON'T have to be Jewish." (Chapter 11:2–18)

Holy Gospel

Stand up in the fear of God and listen to the Holy Gospel, A chapter from the Holy Gospel according to Saint Luke , May his blessings be with us all, Amen

From the psalms of our teacher David the prophet and king, May his blessings be with us all, Amen

> Let all the earth worship You and sing to You; Let them sing to Your name. Shout to God, all the earth; Sing now to His name; Give glory to His praise. Alleluia. -Psalm 66:4, 1–2

Blessed is He who comes in the Name of the Lord Our Lord, God and Saviour and the King of us all, Jesus Christ, the Son of the living God. Glory be to You forever more, Amen

Then Jesus, being filled with the Holy Spirit, returned from the Jordan and was led by the Spirit into the wilderness, being tempted for forty days by the devil. And in those days He ate nothing, and afterward, when they had ended, He was hungry. And the devil said to Him, "If You are the Son of God, command this stone to become bread." But Jesus answered him, saying, "It is written, 'Man shall not live by bread alone, but by every word of God.' " Then the devil, taking Him up on a high mountain, showed Him all the kingdoms of the world in a moment of time. And the devil said to Him "All this authority I will give You, and their glory; for this has been delivered to me, and I give it to whomever I wish. Therefore, if You will worship before me, all will be Yours." And Jesus answered and said to him, "Get behind Me, Satan! For it is written, 'You shall worship the Lord your God, and Him only you shall serve.' " Then he brought Him to Jerusalem, set Him on the pinnacle of the temple, and said to Him, "If You are the Son of God, throw Yourself down from here. For it is written: 'He shall give His angels charge over you, to keep you,' and, 'In their hands they shall bear you up, lest you dash your foot against a stone.'" And Jesus answered and said to him, "It has been said, 'You shall not tempt the Lord your God.' " Now when the devil had ended every temptation, he departed from Him until an opportune time. Luke 4:1–13

Glory be to God Forever, Amen

FIRST SUNDAY OF BAOUNA

Holy Gospel

MATINS

Stand up in the fear of God and listen to the Holy Gospel,A chapter from the Holy Gospel according to Saint Matthew , May his blessings be with us all, Amen

From the psalms of our teacher David the prophet and king, May his blessings be with us all, Amen

> In Judah God is known; His name is great in Israel. In Salem also is His tabernacle, And His dwelling place in Zion.   Alleluia. -Psalm 76:1-2

Blessed is He who comes in the Name of the Lord Our Lord, God and Saviour and the King of us all, Jesus Christ, the Son of the living God. Glory be to You forever more, Amen

Now after the Sabbath, as the first day of the week began to dawn, Mary Magdalene and the other Mary came to see the tomb. And behold, there was a great earthquake; for an angel of the Lord descended from heaven, and came and rolled back the stone from the door, and sat on it. His countenance was like lightning, and his clothing as white as snow. And the guards shook for fear of him, and became like dead men. But the angel answered and said to the women, "Do not be afraid, for I know that you seek Jesus who was crucified. He is not here; for He is risen, as He said. Come, see the place where the Lord lay. And go quickly and tell His disciples that He is risen from the dead, and indeed He is going before you into Galilee; there you will see Him. Behold, I have told you."

So they went out quickly from the tomb with fear and great joy, and ran to bring His disciples word. And as they went to tell His disciples, behold, Jesus met them, saying, "Rejoice!" So they came and held Him by the feet and worshiped Him. Then Jesus said to them, "Do not be afraid. Go and tell My brethren to go to Galilee, and there they will see Me." Now while they were going, behold, some of the guard came into the city and reported to the chief priests all the things that had happened. When they had assembled with the elders and consulted together, they gave a large sum of money to the soldiers, saying, "Tell them, 'His disciples came at night and stole Him away while we slept.' And if this comes to the governor's ears, we will appease him and make you secure." So they took the money and did as they were instructed; and this saying is commonly reported among the Jews until this day.

Then the eleven disciples went away into Galilee, to the mountain which Jesus had appointed for them. When they saw Him, they worshiped Him; but some doubted. And Jesus came and spoke to them, saying, "All authority has been given to Me in heaven and on earth. Go therefore and make disciples of all the nations, baptizing them in the name of the Father and of the Son and of the Holy Spirit, teaching them to observe all things that I have commanded you; and lo, I am with you always, even to the end of the age." Amen. Matthew 28:1-20

Glory be to God Forever, Amen

Pauline LITURGY

Paul, the servant of our Lord Jesus Christ, called to be an apostle, appointed to the Gospel of God. A reading from the Epistle of our teacher Paul to the Romans. May his holy blessings be with us. Amen.

St Paul the Apostle was writing a letter to the Christians who lived in the great city of Rome. Dear Romans, I know that Holy Spirit lives in you, and that you know what is right and what is wrong, and that you know how to teach each other. But since Jesus gave me the job of serving the Gentiles, the people who are not Jewish, I have to tell you a few more things. I will only tell you the things Jesus taught me, as I went around the world, telling people about Him. I didn't just go to people who already knew about Jesus. I especially tried to go to people who had never heard about Jesus! But now, I think I am ready to come to visit you Romans, who already know about Jesus, because you are on my way to Spain. I am looking forward to seeing you, so we can talk about Jesus together, and so you can help me on my way to Spain. Other people have been so kind! The Gentile people from Macedonia and Achaia gave me lots of donations to give to the poor Jewish people in Jerusalem. The Gentiles (who are not Jewish) took the Bible from the Jewish people, and in return, they gave money to the poor Jewish people. That's a good deal! The Jews were generous to the Gentiles by giving them holy things, and the Gentiles were generous to the Jews by giving them donations! So, I am really looking forward to seeing you, so we can all be generous together, just like Jesus taught us! (Romans 15:13-29)

Bye for now!

Signed, Paul

The grace of God the Father be with you all, Amen.

Catholicon

The Catholic Epistle from the First Epistle of our teacher St Peter. May his holy blessings be with us. Amen.

My little children, This is the Apostle Peter writing to all of you who love God. We have a lot to thank God for – He gave us hope when Jesus rose from the dead and He opened the way for us to go to Heaven and to live there forever and ever and ever; And His power protects us all our lives. Even when things go a bit wrong for us. Now I've heard that you have been having a hard time lately. I have heard that some evil people are attacking you because you are Christian. Don't be sad about this but Be HAPPY! All these attacks will only make your faith stronger, just like gold is made stronger by being heated in the flames of fire. Even though you have never met Jesus yourselves, you have believed in Him. And this has given you so much JOY! And that joy means that Jesus has saved us! (1 Peter 1:1-9)

Signed, Peter the Apostle

Do not love the world, nor the things which are in the world. The world shall pass away and all its desires; but he who does the will of God shall abide forever. Amen.

The Acts

A reading from the Acts of our fathers the pure apostles, who were invested with the grace of the Holy Spirit. May their blessing be with us all. Amen.

In a place called Antioch, there were some very good apostles of Jesus. Their names were Barnabas, and John Mark, Simon Niger, Lucius of Cyrene, a man called Manaen (whose childhood friend was King Herod!) and Saul. One day, when everyone was fasting and praying, they felt the Holy Spirit was asking for something. God especially wanted Barnabas and Saul to go and tell some people far away all about Jesus. So the rest of the apostles in Antioch laid their hands on the heads of Barnabas and Saul. They fasted and prayed for them. Then they sent them off on their great adventure! Barnabas and Saul took a young man called John Mark with them (we just call him St Mark now!) And they sailed all over the place! What an adventure! Everywhere they went, they told people all about Jesus, and how much He loves everyone! When they came to an island called Paphos, a sorcerer was there, who was good friends with the ruler of the island. He was very interested in the apostles! When they came to an island called Paphos, the ruler of the island, Sergius Paulus, was curious. He called the apostles and wanted to hear what they had to say. But there was an evil sorcerer on that island, whose name was Elymas. Do you think he wanted Sergius the Ruler to listen to the apostles? No he did not! He tried to stop them! He didn't want people following Jesus! But Saul wasn't afraid of any sorcerer! He knew That Jesus is much stronger than any sorcerer! So Saul (we call him St Paul now) looked Elymas the sorcerer right in the eye, and said: "You are a liar, Elymas!" "When will you stop doing the work of the devil?" "How dare you twist the beautiful words of God?" "From now on, you will be blind!" And from that very moment, evil Elymas was blind! He couldn't see anymore, and needed someone to lead him around everywhere! But Sergius the ruler believed in Jesus! (Chapter 12:25-13:12)

The word of the Lord shall grow, multiply, be mighty and be confirmed in the holy Church of God. Amen.

Holy Gospel

Stand up in the fear of God and listen to the Holy Gospel, A chapter from the Holy Gospel according to Saint Luke , May his blessings be with us all, Amen

From the psalms of our teacher David the prophet and king, May his blessings be with us all, Amen

> Your good Spirit shall guide me in the land of uprightness. Cause me to hear Your mercy in the morning, For I hope in You. Alleluia. -Psalm 143:10,8

Blessed is He who comes in the Name of the Lord Our Lord, God and Saviour and the King of us all, Jesus Christ, the Son of the living God. Glory be to You forever more, Amen

Now it came to pass, as He was praying in a certain place, when He ceased, that one of His disciples said to Him, Lord, teach us to pray, as John also taught his disciples. So He said to them, When you pray, say: Our Father in heaven, Hallowed be Your name. Your kingdom come. Your will be done On earth as it is in heaven. Give us day by day our daily bread. And forgive us our sins, For we also forgive everyone who is indebted to us. And do not lead us into temptation, But deliver us from the evil one. And He said to them, Which of you shall have a friend, and go to him at midnight and say to him, `Friend, lend me three loaves; `for a friend of mine has come to me on his journey, and I have nothing to set before him'; and he will answer from within and say, `Do not trouble me; the door is now shut, and my children are with me in bed; I cannot rise and give to you'? I say to you, though he will not rise and give to him because he is his friend, yet because of his persistence he will rise and give him as many as he needs. So I say to you, ask, and it will be given to you; seek, and you will find; knock, and it will be opened to you. For everyone who asks receives, and he who seeks finds, and to him who knocks it will be opened. If a son asks for bread from any father among you, will he give him a stone? Or if he asks for a fish, will he give him a serpent instead of a fish? Or if he asks for an egg, will he offer him a scorpion? If you then, being evil, know how to give good gifts to your children, how much more will your heavenly Father give the Holy Spirit to those who ask Him! Luke 11:1-13

Glory be to God Forever, Amen

SECOND SUNDAY OF BAOUNA

Holy Gospel

Stand up in the fear of God and listen to the Holy Gospel, A chapter from the Holy Gospel according to Saint Mark , May his blessings be with us all, Amen

From the psalms of our teacher David the prophet and king, May his blessings be with us all, Amen

> I will bless the Lord at all times; His praise shall continually be in my mouth. My soul shall make its boast in the Lord; The humble shall hear of it and be glad. Alleluia. -Psalm 34:1-2

Blessed is He who comes in the Name of the Lord Our Lord, God and Saviour and the King of us all, Jesus Christ, the Son of the living God. Glory be to You forever more, Amen

Very early in the morning, on the first day of the week, they came to the tomb when the sun had risen. And they said among themselves, "Who will roll away the stone from the door of the tomb for us?" But when they looked up, they saw that the stone had been rolled away—for it was very large. And entering the tomb, they saw a young man clothed in a long white robe sitting on the right side; and they were alarmed. But he said to them, "Do not be alarmed. You seek Jesus of Nazareth, who was crucified. He is risen! He is not here. See the place where they laid Him. But go, tell His disciples—and Peter—that He is going before you into Galilee; there you will see Him, as He said to you." So they went out quickly and fled from the tomb, for they trembled and were amazed. And they said nothing to anyone, for they were afraid. Mark 16:2-8

Glory be to God Forever, Amen

Pauline

Paul, the servant of our Lord Jesus Christ, called to be an apostle, appointed to the Gospel of God. A reading from the First Epistle of our teacher Paul to the Corinthians. May his holy blessings be with us. Amen.

St Paul the Apostle was writing a letter to the Christians who lived in the rich city of Corinth. Dear Corinthians, I want you to be wise. That means being able to understand things really well. But I want you to know that God's wisdom is much, much wiser than the wisdom of any human being, even a king! If they were really wise, do you think they would have crucified Jesus on the cross? Of course not! But God's wisdom and understanding is so deep, sometimes it is hard for human beings to really understand it. We call this "mystery". What is heaven like? It is a mystery. That's why the Bible says, "Eye has not seen, nor ear heard, Nor have entered into the heart of man The things which God has prepared for those who love Him." But God gave us a way to understand these mysteries. Just as the spirit of a human understands humans, so the Holy Spirit of God understands the mysteries of God. And we have the Holy Spirit in us! And the Holy Spirit in us is happy to teach us about these deep, wise mysteries! This teaching of the Holy Spirit is not like the teaching of human beings, the teaching of the world. Other people hear it but they don't want to listen to the Holy Spirit, so they just don't get it. They think it makes no sense! But we know just how beautiful and true the spiritual wisdom of God is. We learn, little by little, to think and understand just like Jesus did. We have the mind of Christ. (1 Corinthians 2:6-16)

Bye for now!

Signed, Paul

The grace of God the Father be with you all, Amen.

Catholicon

The Catholic Epistle from the Second Epistle of our teacher St Peter. May his holy blessings be with us. Amen.

My little children, This is the Apostle, Simon Peter, who really loves Jesus and loves serving Him. I am writing to those who also love our precious Jesus and believe in Him like me. When we love Jesus, we find grace and peace—that means we feel happy and safe, because we know how very much He loves us and looks after us. When we know the power of God in Jesus, we have everything we need to live a really good life of godliness—being good, like God. We get to share in the good nature of God, and this helps us run away from temptations, so we do good things, not bad things. So be very careful to grow more and more in your love for Jesus. If you have faith (you trust God), then learn to have virtue (to be a good person deep inside). If you have virtue, then learn to have knowledge (to know God). If you have knowledge, then learn to have self-control. If you have self-control, then learn to have perseverance (to be really patient and never give up). If you have perseverance, then learn to have godliness (to be good like God). If you have godliness, then learn to have brotherly kindness (always be kind to others). And if you have brotherly kindness, then learn to have agape love (love others the way God loves us). If you learn all these things, you will truly know Jesus, and your life will be full of goodness! (2 Peter 1:1-8)

Signed, Peter the Apostle

Do not love the world, nor the things which are in the world. The world shall pass away and all its desires; but he who does the will of God shall abide forever. Amen.

The Acts

One day, in a city called Lystra, Paul was preaching to a large group of people, telling them all about Jesus. As he was speaking, he noticed something very sad indeed! There was a crippled man who had never been able to walk, even when he was a little boy! And this man was listening oh so carefully to Paul! So Paul looked at him very hard, and said loudly, "Stand up straight on your feet!" And guess what happened next; The crippled man jumped up suddenly and walked on this feet! He was healed! His feet were normal and healthy! Now the people Paul was talking to weren't Christians. They got a funny idea when they saw him heal the crippled man. They thought Paul was a god! Oh dear! They thought Paul was the Greek god Hermes (Her-mees), because he was a clever speaker! And they thought that the apostle Barnabas was Zeus (Zoos), the king of the gods! Oh dear, oh dear! And the pagan priest of Zeus even brought some cows and flowers to sacrifice to Paul and Barnabas! Oh dear, oh dear, oh dear! Well, Paul had to do something, and pretty quick! So he started to speak to the people saying, "Hey everybody, listen to me. We are just men like you! We are not gods! "There is just One True God—not Zeus or Hermes—but the God who made heaven, earth, sea, and everything in them." "And God shows everyone in the world just how much He loves us all, by giving us rain from heaven so the fruits will grow, and filling our hearts with food and gladness." Then some Jews came along, and convinced the crowd to let them take Paul away. But they wanted to hurt Paul. They threw stones at him, until he was almost dead! Poor, poor Paul! They left him lying on the ground outside the city. But when the other Christians found him, he got up! He was OK! Hooray! And he went to more cities to tell people about Jesus. And one day, he even came back to Lystra again. He was so brave. He said, "Don't be afraid. Even if things go wrong for us, we know we are heading for the kingdom of God". (Chapter 14:8-22)

Holy Gospel

Stand up in the fear of God and listen to the Holy Gospel,A chapter from the Holy Gospel according to Saint Luke, May his blessings be with us all, Amen

From the psalms of our teacher David the prophet and king, May his blessings be with us all, Amen

> I will sing to the Lord, who shows kindness to me; But I hope in Your mercy; My heart shall greatly rejoice in Your salvation. Alleluia. -Psalm 13:6,5

Blessed is He who comes in the Name of the Lord Our Lord, God and Saviour and the King of us all, Jesus Christ, the Son of the living God. Glory be to You forever more, Amen

Now it happened on a certain day, as He was teaching, that there were Pharisees and teachers of the law sitting by, who had come out of every town of Galilee, Judea, and Jerusalem. And the power of the Lord was present to heal them. Then behold, men brought on a bed a man who was paralysed, whom they sought to bring in and lay before Him. And when they could not find how they might bring him in, because of the crowd, they went up on the housetop and let him down with his bed through the tiling into the midst before Jesus. When He saw their faith, He said to him, Man, your sins are forgiven you. And the scribes and the Pharisees began to reason, saying, Who is this who speaks blasphemies? Who can forgive sins but God alone? And the scribes and the Pharisees began to reason, saying, Who is this who speaks blasphemies? Who can forgive sins but God alone? But when Jesus perceived their thoughts, He answered and said to them, Why are you reasoning in your hearts? Which is easier, to say, 'Your sins are forgiven you,' or to say, 'Rise up and walk'? But that you may know that the Son of Man has power on earth to forgive sins— He said to the man who was paralysed, I say to you, arise, take up your bed, and go to your house. Immediately he rose up before them, took up what he had been lying on, and departed to his own house, glorifying God. And they were all amazed, and they glorified God and were filled with fear, saying, We have seen strange things today! Luke 5:17-26

Glory be to God Forever, Amen

THIRD SUNDAY OF BAOUNA

Holy Gospel

MATINS

Stand up in the fear of God and listen to the Holy Gospel, A chapter from the Holy Gospel according to Saint Luke , May his blessings be with us all, Amen

From the psalms of our teacher David the prophet and king, May his blessings be with us all, Amen

> Do not forsake me, O Lord; O my God, be not far from me! Make haste to help me, O Lord, my salvation! Alleluia. -Psalm 38:21-22

Blessed is He who comes in the Name of the Lord Our Lord, God and Saviour and the King of us all, Jesus Christ, the Son of the living God. Glory be to You forever more, Amen

Now on the first day of the week, very early in the morning, they, and certain other women with them, came to the tomb bringing the spices which they had prepared. But they found the stone rolled away from the tomb. Then they went in and did not find the body of the Lord Jesus. And it happened, as they were greatly perplexed about this, that behold, two men stood by them in shining garments. Then, as they were afraid and bowed their faces to the earth, they said to them, "Why do you seek the living among the dead? He is not here, but is risen! Remember how He spoke to you when He was still in Galilee, saying, 'The Son of Man must be delivered into the hands of sinful men, and be crucified, and the third day rise again.' " And they remembered His words. Then they returned from the tomb and told all these things to the eleven and to all the rest. It was Mary Magdalene, Joanna, Mary the mother of James, and the other women with them, who told these things to the apostles. And their words seemed to them like idle tales, and they did not believe them. But Peter arose and ran to the tomb; and stooping down, he saw the linen cloths lying by themselves; and he departed, marveling to himself at what had happened. Luke 24:1-12

Glory be to God Forever, Amen

Pauline

Paul, the servant of our Lord Jesus Christ, called to be an apostle, appointed to the Gospel of God. A reading from the First Epistle of our teacher Paul to the Corinthians. May his holy blessings be with us. Amen.

Dear Corinthians, I know some people have been grumbling about me, and my fellow servants who serve you (like Apollos). But I want you to know that God is the one who called us to be responsible for you, and we always do our best to take care of you. Actually, it doesn't worry me if you judge me. It wouldn't even worry me if a judge in court judged me! I know we are doing the right thing. But what really matters is what God thinks of us—not any human being. So it's best for us not to judge others—because we are just human beings. When the time comes, God knows everything (even secrets) and He will judge the right way. This is important, because I don't want you to be proud and try to boss each other around. Do you think you are better than everyone else? Why on earth would you think that?! If there's anything good about you, isn't it a gift from God? So why do you act as if it wasn't, as if it is all just your own cleverness? You are rich! You act like kings and queens! I wish you really knew what that means! Actually, I think God made us apostles to be an example for everyone else. Not because we are rich or powerful, but because we are poor and humble. We are fools for Christ's sake, but you are wise in Christ! We look weak, but you are strong! You are important, but we are kicked around! Every day, we are hungry and thirsty. Our clothes are poor. We are beaten and homeless. And we work with our own hands to make a living. Why do we put up with this? Because humbly serving and loving others is what really, really matters. When someone curses us, we bless them. When they harm us, we are patient. When they say nasty things, we pray. You are the children born from my preaching! Like a father who loves you and cares for you, I want you to learn from my example how to love and serve. You can have 10,000 teachers but not many fathers. (1 Corinthians 4:1-16)

Bye for now!

Signed, Paul

The grace of God the Father be with you all, Amen

Catholicon

The Catholic Epistle from the Second Epistle of our teacher St Peter. May his holy blessings be with us. Amen.

My little children, The Bible is like a light that shines in the darkness and helps us to see the world as it really is. But remember that the people who wrote the Bible were moved by the Holy Spirit. So we have to be careful not to just pick and choose what we want its words to mean! Even back then, there were false prophets—people who pretended to speak God's words, but they were really just their own words. And even now, false prophets will appear and cause all kinds of mischief. Selfishly, they will speak smooth words to trick you. But don't worry, they will get what they deserve. Remember how God cast the devil out of heaven when he sinned? Remember the flood of Noah, and how God destroyed evil Sodom and Gomorrah, but saved Lot? God knows how to save those who are good, and how to make sure those who are evil get exactly what they deserve. Isn't it better to be one of the good people? (2 Peter 1:19-2:9)

Signed, Peter the Apostle

Do not love the world, nor the things which are in the world. The world shall pass away and all its desires; but he who does the will of God shall abide forever. Amen.

The Acts

A reading from the Acts of our fathers the pure apostles, who were invested with the grace of the Holy Spirit. May their blessing be with us all. Amen.

Paul and his friends were passing through a city called Thessalonica on their long, long journey. Paul found a Jewish synagogue there, where the Jews of the city would pray and read the Bible. So he went in, and guess what he spoke to them about? He told them about Jesus, of course! And how Jesus suffered, died and rose from the dead. The Jews were waiting for a Saviour, a Messiah, a Christ to save them. That Saviour is Jesus!, Paul told them. Now the funny thing is that most of the Jews didn't listen to Paul. But lots of the pagan Greek men and women did!

Even some very important ones. So the Jews were angry with Paul. A big angry group of them went to the house of Jason, where Paul was staying, but Paul wasn't there. So instead, they dragged Jason out and took him to the rulers of the city. They wanted to get them all in really big trouble! "Paul and his friends have turned the world upside down!" they complained. "They say Jesus is the real king instead of the Emperor, Caesar! "And Jason has been helping them!" The rulers of Thessalonica were worried when they heard this. So they made Jason pay a fine and warned him to stop helping Paul and his friends. But when Paul heard about all this trouble, he and Silas decided it was best to leave Thessalonica quietly. They didn't want poor Jason to be in trouble. Next they went to a city called Berea, and told the people there about Jesus. But the people in Berea were much more sensible and reasonable than the Thessalonians! The Jews in the synagogue believed in Jesus! And the Greeks believed in Jesus. Men and women all believed in Jesus! They spent a long time reading the Bible together, finding out more and more about God's love for us, through Jesus Christ. (Chapter 17:1-12)

The word of the Lord shall grow, multiply, be mighty and be confirmed in the holy Church of God. Amen.

Holy Gospel

Stand up in the fear of God and listen to the Holy Gospel, A chapter from the Holy Gospel according to Saint Matthew, May his blessings be with us all, Amen

From the psalms of our teacher David the prophet and king, May his blessings be with us all, Amen

> For You, O God, hear my prayers; You give an inheritance to those who
> fear Your name. So I will sing praise to Your name unto ages of ages,
> That I may pay my vows day to day. Alleluia. - Psalm 61:5,8

Blessed is He who comes in the Name of the Lord Our Lord, God and Saviour and the King of us all, Jesus Christ, the Son of the living God. Glory be to You forever more, Amen

Then one was brought to Him who was demon-possessed, blind and mute; and He healed him, so that the blind and mute man both spoke and saw. And all the multitudes were amazed and said, Could this be the Son of David? Now when the Pharisees heard it they said, This fellow does not cast out demons except by Beelzebub (Bee-el-zeh-bub), the ruler of the demons. But Jesus knew their thoughts, and said to them: Every kingdom divided against itself is brought to desolation, and every city or house divided against itself will not stand. If Satan casts out Satan, he is divided against himself. How then will his kingdom stand? And if I cast out demons by Beelzebub, by whom do your sons cast them out? Therefore they shall be your judges. But if I cast out demons by the Spirit of God, surely the kingdom of God has come upon you. Or how can one enter a strong man's house and plunder his goods, unless he first binds the strong man? And then he will plunder his house. He who is not with Me is against Me, and he who does not gather with Me scatters abroad. Therefore I say to you, every sin and blasphemy will be forgiven men, but the blasphemy against the Spirit will not be forgiven men. Anyone who speaks a word against the Son of Man, it will be forgiven him; but whoever speaks against the Holy Spirit, it will not be forgiven him, either in this age or in the age to come. Either make the tree good and its fruit good, or else make the tree bad and its fruit bad; for a tree is known by its fruit. Brood of vipers! How can you, being evil, speak good things? For out of the abundance of the heart the mouth speaks. A good man out of the good treasure of his heart brings forth good things, and an evil man out of the evil treasure brings forth evil things. But I say to you that for every idle word men may speak, they will give account of it in the day of judgment. For by your words you will be justified, and by your words you will be condemned. Matthew 12:22-37

Glory be to God Forever, Amen

FOURTH SUNDAY OF BAOUNA

Holy Gospel

MATINS

Stand up in the fear of God and listen to the Holy Gospel, A chapter from the Holy Gospel according to Saint John, May his blessings be with us all, Amen

From the psalms of our teacher David the prophet and king, May his blessings be with us all, Amen

> For You, O God, have heard my vows; You have given me the heritage of those who fear Your name. You will prolong the king's life, His years as many generations Alleluia. - Psalm 61:5-6

Blessed is He who comes in the Name of the Lord Our Lord, God and Saviour and the King of us all, Jesus Christ, the Son of the living God. Glory be to You forever more, Amen

Now the first day of the week Mary Magdalene went to the tomb early, while it was still dark, and saw that the stone had been taken away from the tomb. Then she ran and came to Simon Peter, and to the other disciple, whom Jesus loved, and said to them, "They have taken away the Lord out of the tomb, and we do not know where they have laid Him." Peter therefore went out, and the other disciple, and were going to the tomb. So they both ran together, and the other disciple outran Peter and came to the tomb first. And he, stooping down and looking in, saw the linen cloths lying there; yet he did not go in. Then Simon Peter came, following him, and went into the tomb; and he saw the linen cloths lying there, and the handkerchief that had been around His head, not lying with the linen cloths, but folded together in a place by itself. Then the other disciple, who came to the tomb first, went in also; and he saw and believed. For as yet they did not know the Scripture, that He must rise again from the dead. Then the disciples went away again to their own homes. But Mary stood outside by the tomb weeping, and as she wept she stooped down and looked into the tomb. And she saw two angels in white sitting, one at the head and the other at the feet, where the body of Jesus had lain. Then they said to her, "Woman, why are you weeping?"

She said to them, "Because they have taken away my Lord, and I do not know where they have laid Him." Now when she had said this, she turned around and saw Jesus standing there, and did not know that it was Jesus. Jesus said to her, "Woman, why are you weeping? Whom are you seeking?" She, supposing Him to be the gardener, said to Him, "Sir, if You have carried Him away, tell me where You have laid Him, and I will take Him away." Jesus said to her, "Mary!" She turned and said to Him, "Rabboni!" (which is to say, Teacher). Jesus said to her, "Do not cling to Me, for I have not yet ascended to My Father; but go to My brethren and say to them, 'I am ascending to My Father and your Father, and to My God and your God.' " Mary Magdalene came and told the disciples that she had seen the Lord, and that He had spoken these things to her. John 20:1-18

Glory be to God Forever, Amen

Pauline LITURGY

Paul, the servant of our Lord Jesus Christ, called to be an apostle, appointed to the Gospel of God. A reading from the Epistle of our teacher Paul to the Colossians. May his holy blessings be with us. Amen.

St Paul the Apostle was writing a letter to the Christians who lived in the town of Colossae. Dear Colossians, I have some very important advice for you, about how to live as true Christians. Always pray from your heart, and remember to say thank You to God for everything. (And please pray for me and my friends too! Pray that God helps us to find the right words to tell more people about the mystery of Jesus.) Always speak nicely and wisely with people who are not Christian. Let them see God's grace in your lovely words. Now I want to tell you some news about my friends, who are serving God with me; I'm sending Tychicus (Tie-ki-kus) to you, to comfort your hearts, and find out how you are all going. Together with Onesimus (Oh-ness-ee-muss), who is from Colossae, your town. They will also tell you more of our news, and all the adventures we have had. Some of the Jewish servants who are with me are Mark, the cousin of Barnabas, and Justus (whose other name is Jesus, like our Lord Jesus), and Aristarchus, (Arr-iss-tar-kus) who is here in jail with me. Then of course, there's Epaphras (Ep-aff-rass), who is also from Colossae. He says a huge hello, and has been praying for you all so much. Finally, Doctor Luke and Demas also say hello. And could you please do some things for me? Say hi to the Christians in the town next you, Laodicea (Layo-diss-ee-uh), and especially to the Church in the house of Nymphas. Could you please share this letter with them, so they can read it too? And I'd like you to read the letter I sent to them as well. And finally, I have a message for Archippus (Arr-kip-us): Tell him to carry out the service that God has given him as well as he can. That's all! I got someone to write down this letter for me, but here is my own signature in my own handwriting: (Colossians 4:2-18)

Bye for now!

Signed, Paul

The grace of God the Father be with you all, Amen.

Catholicon

The Catholic Epistle from our teacher St James. May his holy blessings be with us. Amen.

My brothers and sisters, Please don't grumble against each other, or else you will get yourself in big trouble! Remember the prophets in the Old Testament? Remember how patient Job was? Try to be patient with other like them. Remember that God is so very kind. He will make sure things end up just as they should! And most important, never say "I swear it's true!" about anything. Yes means yes, And no means no. That's it. You don't need to swear! Is anyone among you suffering? He should pray. Is anyone among you cheerful? She should sing hymns and psalms. Is anyone among you sick? They should call for Abouna, so that Abouna can pray for the sick person, and anoint them with Holy Oil. And the prayer of faith will save the sick, And the Lord will raise him up. And if he has done anything wrong, God will forgive him. Confess your sins to each other. And pray for each other. When a good person prays, God hears. Remember Elijah the prophet? He was a man just like you and me, but he was a very good man. Once, he prayed for the rain to stop, and it didn't rain for three and a half years! Then he prayed again, and it started to rain again! If someone goes wrong, and another person brings them back to the right way, they are doing a wonderful thing. They have saved a soul, and made up for so many sins. (*James* 5:9-20)

Signed, James the Apostle

Do not love the world, nor the things which are in the world. The world shall pass away and all its desires; but he who does the will of God shall abide forever. Amen.

157

The Acts

A reading from the Acts of our fathers the pure apostles, who were invested with the grace of the Holy Spirit. May their blessing be with us all. Amen.

Would you like to know how the Corinthians became Christians? Here is the story. Paul left Athens and came to the big, rich city of Corinth. There he found a husband and wife, Aquila and Priscilla, who had to leave Italy because all the Jews were kicked out from there. Now Aquila and Priscilla's job was to make tents. And guess what Paul's job was? He made tents too! So they became good friends, and Paul stayed at their house in Corinth. And he preached about Jesus every week at the synagogue, the place where the Jewish people would meet to pray. But even though Paul's friends, Timothy and Silas helped him, the Jewish people in the synagogue didn't want to listen to him. So Paul said to these stubborn people, "I have done my best with you, but you just won't listen! From now on, I will go and preach to the Greek people in Corinth." But some of the Jews did listen to Paul, including the leader of the synagogue, Crispus, with all his family. And they were all baptised. Wasn't that nice! And they weren't the only ones. Lots of the Greek Corinthians also believed in Jesus through Paul's words. And they were baptised too! But there were people who were angry with Paul and wanted to hurt him and kick him out of town. Do you think Paul was scared? Do you think he stopped telling people about Jesus? One night, God spoke to Paul in a vision. God said, "Don't be afraid, Paul. Don't stop telling people about Me. I am with you, and there are lots of good people in this city. I won't let anyone hurt you." So Paul stayed in Corinth, teaching them about Jesus, and how to be a real Christian, for a whole year and a half. And that's the story of how the Church in Corinth began. (Chapter 18:1-11)

The word of the Lord shall grow, multiply, be mighty and be confirmed in the holy Church of God. Amen.

Holy Gospel

Stand up in the fear of God and listen to the Holy Gospel,A chapter from the Holy Gospel according to Saint Luke, May his blessings be with us all, Amen

From the psalms of our teacher David the prophet and king,May his blessings be with us all, Amen

> Seek God, and your soul shall live, For the Lord hears the poor. I will praise God's name with a song; I will magnify Him in praise. Alleluia.
> - Psalm 69:32-33, 30

Blessed is He who comes in the Name of the Lord Our Lord, God and Saviour and the King of us all, Jesus Christ, the Son of the living God. Glory be to You forever more, Amen

But I say to you who hear: Love your enemies, do good to those who hate you, bless those who curse you, and pray for those who spitefully use you. To him who strikes you on the one cheek, offer the other also. And from him who takes away your cloak, do not withhold your tunic either. Give to everyone who asks of you. And from him who takes away your goods do not ask them back. And just as you want men to do to you, you also do to them likewise. But if you love those who love you, what credit is that to you? For even sinners love those who love them. And if you do good to those who do good to you, what credit is that to you? For even sinners do the same. And if you lend to those from whom you hope to receive back, what credit is that to you? For even sinners lend to sinners to receive as much back. But love your enemies, do good, and lend, hoping for nothing in return; and your reward will be great, and you will be sons of the Most High. For He is kind to the unthankful and evil. Therefore be merciful, just as your Father also is merciful. Judge not, and you shall not be judged. Condemn not, and you shall not be condemned. Forgive, and you will be forgiven. Give, and it will be given to you: good measure, pressed down, shaken together, and running over will be put into your bosom. For with the same measure that you use, it will be measured back to you. Luke 6:27-38

Glory be to God Forever, Amen

FIRST SUNDAY OF ABIB

Holy Gospel

MATINS

Stand up in the fear of God and listen to the Holy Gospel, A chapter from the Holy Gospel according to Saint Matthew, May his blessings be with us all, Amen

From the psalms of our teacher David the prophet and king, May his blessings be with us all, Amen

> Oh, love the Lord, all you His saints! For the Lord preserves the faithful, And fully repays the proud person. Oh, how great is Your goodness, Which You have laid up for those who fear You, Which You have prepared for those who trust in You In the presence of the sons of men! Alleluia. - Psalm 31:23, 19

Blessed is He who comes in the Name of the Lord Our Lord, God and Saviour and the King of us all, Jesus Christ, the Son of the living God. Glory be to You forever more, Amen

Now after the Sabbath, as the first day of the week began to dawn, Mary Magdalene and the other Mary came to see the tomb. And behold, there was a great earthquake; for an angel of the Lord descended from heaven, and came and rolled back the stone from the door, and sat on it. His countenance was like lightning, and his clothing as white as snow. And the guards shook for fear of him, and became like dead men. But the angel answered and said to the women, "Do not be afraid, for I know that you seek Jesus who was crucified. He is not here; for He is risen, as He said. Come, see the place where the Lord lay. And go quickly and tell His disciples that He is risen from the dead, and indeed He is going before you into Galilee; there you will see Him. Behold, I have told you."

So they went out quickly from the tomb with fear and great joy, and ran to bring His disciples word. And as they went to tell His disciples, behold, Jesus met them, saying, "Rejoice!" So they came and held Him by the feet and worshiped Him. Then Jesus said to them, "Do not be afraid. Go and tell My brethren to go to Galilee, and there they will see Me."

Now while they were going, behold, some of the guard came into the city and reported to the chief priests all the things that had happened. When they had assembled with the elders and consulted together, they gave a large sum of money to the soldiers, saying, "Tell them, 'His disciples came at night and stole Him away while we slept.' And if this comes to the governor's ears, we will appease him and make you secure." So they took the money and did as they were instructed; and this saying is commonly reported among the Jews until this day. Then the eleven disciples went away into Galilee, to the mountain which Jesus had appointed for them. When they saw Him, they worshiped Him; but some doubted. And Jesus came and spoke to them, saying, "All authority has been given to Me in heaven and on earth. Go therefore and make disciples of all the nations, baptizing them in the name of the Father and of the Son and of the Holy Spirit, teaching them to observe all things that I have commanded you; and lo, I am with you always, even to the end of the age." Amen. Matthew 28: 1-20

Glory be to God Forever, Amen

Pauline

Paul, the servant of our Lord Jesus Christ, called to be an apostle, appointed to the Gospel of God. A reading from the Epistle of our teacher Paul to First Epistle of our teacher Paul to the Corinthians. May his holy blessings be with us. Amen.

St Paul the Apostle was writing a letter to the Christians who lived in a big, rich city called Corinth.

Dear Corinthians, I have some very important advice for you, about how to live as true Christians. Aren't I an Apostle? Didn't I see Jesus Christ our Lord? Didn't I teach you how to be Christians? Some of you say I am greedy. But am I really greedy? I chose not to have a wife, so I could serve God better; Was that greedy? Moses said that it is only fair for an ox to eat some of the grain it is grinding. He deserves to eat some of the food he is making for others! So, if someone serves you and tells you about God, It is only fair that you should look after him and give him food to eat. But my friend Barnabas and I have never asked for anything from anyone. Was that greedy? We have told you about God for free! We never asked you for anything in return. I am not saying this so I can show off! I love Jesus.

All I want to do is just work for Jesus. I don't want anything from you except that you love Jesus too. I don't want anything from you except that you love Jesus too. You might forget about loving Jesus! That would really be sad! Look how much I love Jesus, and how hard I try to tell everyone about Him. Even though I am a free man, I have made myself like a faithful slave to everyone, so I could get more people to love Jesus. When I find someone who is weak, I speak to them as if I was weak too, so that they listen to me when I tell them about Jesus. When I meet a Jewish person, I tell them that I am Jewish too, so that they listen to me when I tell them about Jesus. When I meet someone who never heard of God, I talk like someone who never heard of God too, so that they listen to me when I tell them about Jesus. I made friends with lots of different kinds of people, because I want everyone to know Jesus and to be saved. I have worked so hard because I believe in the Gospel, just like you do. I want to share the Gospel with you! Now, when you are running in a race, don't you do your best to win? After all, only one person can win the gold medal! Do your best to win the heavenly prize; not just a gold medal. Don't run like someone who's not sure where the finish line is! Don't fight like someone who can't see anything and keeps punching the air! Do your best to win the heavenly prize. That's what I am doing, I control my body. I stop it from being naughty. I teach it to serve God. If I didn't do these things, do you know what could happen? Something awful! Even though I am one of the Apostles, Even though I have taught others what to do to get to heaven; I might miss out on heaven myself! So let's all be very careful to obey God, Every day of our lives. (1 Corinthians 9:1-27)

Bye for now!

Signed, Paul

The grace of God the Father be with you all, Amen.

Catholicon

The Catholic Epistle from the First Epistle of our teacher St Peter. May his holy blessings be with us. Amen.

My little children, This is the Apostle Peter writing to all of you who love God, We have a lot to thank God for – He gave us hope when Jesus rose from the dead and He opened the way for us to go to Heaven and to live there forever and ever and ever, And His power protects us all our lives. Even when things go a bit wrong for us. Now I've heard that you have been having a hard time lately. I have heard that some evil people are attacking you because you are Christian. Don't be sad about this but Be HAPPY! All these attacks will only make your faith stronger, just like gold is made stronger by being heated in the flames of fire. Even though you have never met Jesus yourselves, you have believed in Him. And this has given you so much JOY! Because the prophets from olden times really wanted to see the Saviour – but they couldn't and the Angels really wanted to know about the Saviour – but they couldn't! But now, we get to know Him, because we have heard the Gospel, the story of Jesus Christ. (1 Peter 1:1-12)

Signed, *Peter the Apostle*

Do not love the world, nor the things which are in the world. The world shall pass away and all its desires; but he who does the will of God shall abide forever. Amen.

The Acts

A reading from the Acts of our fathers the pure apostles, who were invested with the grace of the Holy Spirit. May their blessing be with us all. Amen.

Now the Apostles were doing lots of amazing miracles even so, every day, more and more men and women and children were becoming Christian. And everyone would bring those who were sick to the Apostles, hoping they might heal them. And guess what? They DID heal them! But someone was getting a bit JEALOUS. That someone was the High Priest of the Temple. "How dare these men talk about God?" he shouted. "That's my job!" So he got the soldiers to arrest the Apostles

163

and throw them into jail. Oh no! Now what were they to do? But God had the answer. That night, God sent an angel to the jail, and he opened the doors for them! And the angel said: "Don't be scared – God wants you to keep on telling people about Him" "Go to the Temple and tell everyone about Jesus and the new life He brings to those who believe in Him." So the Apostles went early the next morning and began to tell people about Jesus again. Guess who was going to get the surprise of is life? Meanwhile, the High Priest called a meeting of the elders and the leaders to judge the Apostles, thinking they were still locked up in jail. And they sent some soldiers to the jail, to bring the Apostles to be judged. But when they got there would you like to know what happened? (Chapter 5:12-21)

We'll find out next Sunday!

The word of the Lord shall grow, multiply, be mighty and be confirmed in the holy Church of God. Amen.

Holy Gospel

Stand up in the fear of God and listen to the Holy Gospel, A chapter from the Holy Gospel according to Saint Luke, May his blessings be with us all, Amen

From the psalms of our teacher David the prophet and king, May his blessings be with us all, Amen

> God is greatly to be feared in the assembly of the saints, And to be held in reverence by all those around Him Alleluia. - Psalm 89:7

Blessed is He who comes in the Name of the Lord Our Lord, God and Saviour and the King of us all, Jesus Christ, the Son of the living God. Glory be to You forever more, Amen

After these things the Lord appointed seventy others also, and sent them two by two before His face into every city and place where He Himself was about to go. "Then He said to them, "The harvest truly is great, but the labourers are few; therefore pray the Lord of the harvest to send out labourers into His harvest. Go your way; behold, I send you out as lambs among wolves. Carry neither money bag, knapsack, nor sandals; and greet no one along the road. But whatever house you enter, first say, 'Peace to this house.' And if a son of peace is there, your peace will rest on it; if not, it will return to you. And remain in the same house, eating and drinking such things as they give, for the labourer is worthy of his wages. Do not go from house to house. Whatever city you enter, and they receive you, eat such things as are set before you. And heal the sick there, and say to them, 'The kingdom of God has come near to you.' But whatever city you enter, and they do not receive you, go out into its streets and say, 'The very dust of your city which clings to us But " "Woe to you, Chorazin! Woe to you, Bethsaida! For if the mighty works which were done in you had been done in Tyre and Sidon, they would have repented long ago, sitting in sackcloth and ashes. But it will be more tolerable for Tyre and Sidon at the judgment than for you. And you, Capernaum, who are exalted to heaven, will be brought down to Hades. "He who hears you hears Me, he who rejects you rejects Me, and he who rejects Me rejects Him who sent Me. "Then the seventy "And He said to them, "I saw Satan fall like lightning from heaven. Behold, I give you the authority to trample on serpents and scorpions, and over all the power of the enemy, and nothing shall by any means hurt you. Nevertheless do not rejoice in this, that the spirits are subject to you, but rather rejoice because your names are written in heaven." Luke 10:1-20

Glory be to God Forever, Amen

SECOND SUNDAY OF ABIB

Holy Gospel

Stand up in the fear of God and listen to the Holy Gospel, A chapter from the Holy Gospel according to Saint Mark, May his blessings be with us all, Amen

From the psalms of our teacher David the prophet and king, May his blessings be with us all, Amen

> Blessed is he who considers the poor; The Lord will deliver him in time of trouble. The Lord will preserve him and keep him alive, And he will be blessed on the earth; You will not deliver him to the will of his enemies. Alleluia. - Psalm 41:1-2

Blessed is He who comes in the Name of the Lord Our Lord, God and Saviour and the King of us all, Jesus Christ, the Son of the living God. Glory be to You forever more, Amen

Very early in the morning, on the first day of the week, they came to the tomb when the sun had risen. And they said among themselves, "Who will roll away the stone from the door of the tomb for us?" But when they looked up, they saw that the stone had been rolled away—for it was very large. And entering the tomb, they saw a young man clothed in a long white robe sitting on the right side; and they were alarmed. But he said to them, "Do not be alarmed. You seek Jesus of Nazareth, who was crucified. He is risen! He is not here. See the place where they laid Him. But go, tell His disciples—and Peter—that He is going before you into Galilee; there you will see Him, as He said to you." So they went out quickly and fled from the tomb, for they trembled and were amazed. And they said nothing to anyone, for they were afraid. Mark 16:2-8

Glory be to God Forever, Amen

Pauline

Paul, the servant of our Lord Jesus Christ, called to be an apostle, appointed to the Gospel of God. A reading from the Epistle of our teacher Paul to the Galatians. May his holy blessings be with us. Amen.

St Paul the Apostle was writing a letter to the Christians who lived in a place called Galatia.

Dear Galatians, I hope you are all well and happy in the care of God who loves us and saved us. I have heard some news that has got me really worried. Is it true that you have been listening to people who are telling you the wrong thing? Now you know how I came to you and taught you the truth about Jesus, and how to follow His Way. But now I hear you have left my teachings and followed what other people have been telling you. This is awful! Even if I come to you and try to confuse you about Jesus, DON'T LISTEN TO ME! Even if an ANGEL came to you and tried to confuse you about Jesus: DON'T LISTEN TO HIM! I know some people will get upset about what I am saying, but I don't want to please people, I want to please God. You have to know that all I told you about Jesus wasn't told to me by people, it was told to me by God Himself. You remember how I was so good at arresting Christians before and throwing them in jail? But then Jesus appeared to me, and changed my life! Well the first thing I did after that was to go to Arabia, where I lived in the desert to be alone with God for three years. And after that, I went to Jerusalem, but I only met Peter, and James and I only spent a few days with them. But I did not meet any other Apostles. So when I went to visit the churches in Israel, no one knew who I was. There was just the rumour going around that I was the one who used to arrest Christians so they could be killed, and that now I was a Christian myself! And when people heard about how I had changed, they glorified God and praised Him! (Galatians 1:1-24)

Bye for now!

Signed, Paul

> *The grace of God the Father be with you all, Amen.*

Catholicon

The Catholic Epistle from the First Epistle of our teacher St Jude. May his holy blessings be with us. Amen.

My little children, This is the Apostle Jude writing to warn you about false teachers. You have to be very careful about these people, the ones who try to confuse you about Jesus. The prophets long ago warned us that false teachers would come and teach the wrong things about Jesus, and about how we should follow Him. They warned us that the false teachers will be judged by God, when He comes back with His angels! These false teachers are not nice at all! They like to grumble and complain about everything. They like to boast and show off, they like to make people turn against each other, they like to crawl and suck up to people so that they can get what they want for themselves. But I don't want you to be tricked by them, my beloved. Remember how Jesus warned us that evil people like these would come. So make sure that you stick to the true faith, remembering the love and kindness of God, and always praying for the Holy Spirit to guard you. Be gentle with those who go wrong, but with some people you have to be really tough to save them from the fire! God is able to keep you from stumbling, until you stand happily in front of His Throne at the end. To God our Saviour, Who alone is wise, be glory and majesty, dominion and power, Both now and forever. Amen (Jude 14-25)

Bye for now!

Signed, *Jude the Apostle*

Do not love the world, nor the things which are in the world. The world shall pass away and all its desires; but he who does the will of God shall abide forever. Amen.

The Acts

Do you remember what had happened to the Apostles in our story from last Sunday? That's right! The High Priest of the Temple had them arrested and thrown in jail. But then, God had the answer to their problems. That night, God sent an angel to the jail, and he opened the doors for them! And the angel said: "Don't be scared – God wants you to keep on telling people about Him" "Go to the Temple and tell everyone about Jesus and the new life He brings to those who believe in Him." So the Apostles went early the next morning and began to tell people about Jesus again. Guess who was going to get the surprise of is life? Meanwhile, the High Priest called a meeting of the elders and the leaders to judge the Apostles, thinking they were still locked up in jail. And they sent some soldiers to the jail, to bring the Apostles to be judged. But when they got there the jail was empty! There was no one there! What? How? The surprised soldiers ran back to the High Priest as quick as they could. He would never believe them "You won't believe this!" they said. "We got to the jail, and the guards were standing guard as usual outside the door of the jail" "and the door of the jail was locked, nice and safe, as usual" "And the guards said everything was fine" "But when we opened the door to get the prisoners "It was empty! "There was no one inside! "It's impossible! How could they possibly have got out without anyone seeing anything?" They were all absolutely shocked. But YOU know how the Apostles got out don't you? (Chapter 5:19-23)

Holy Gospel

Stand up in the fear of God and listen to the Holy Gospel, A chapter from the Holy Gospel according to Saint Matthew, May his blessings be with us all, Amen

From the psalms of our teacher David the prophet and king, May his blessings be with us all, Amen

> Blessed are the undefiled in the way, Who walk in the law of the Lord! Blessed are those who keep His testimonies, Who seek Him with the whole heart! Alleluia. - Psalm 119:1-2

Blessed is He who comes in the Name of the Lord Our Lord, God and Saviour and the King of us all, Jesus Christ, the Son of the living God. Glory be to You forever more, Amen

Jesus' friends came to Him with a question: Who is the greatest in the Kingdom of Heaven? Jesus looked at them for a little while. And then, instead of answering them, He did something they did not expect, He called over a little child, and asked him to sit down with all the grown ups! "You see this child?" He asked them. "Unless you become like him, you will never enter the Kingdom of Heaven!" "Whoever is humble like this little child will be the greatest in the Kingdom of Heaven." "Whoever cares for a little child like this is actually caring for Me." "But if anyone makes one of these little ones to sin well, it would have been better for him to have had a big stone tied around his neck and thrown into the sea!" "It is very sad that evil has to come into this world, but the one who brings that evil – he's in big, big trouble!" "So do whatever it takes for you to be sure that you do not sin, that you do not practice evil." "It is better for you to lose something very precious and be good, rather than keep everything but end up down in horrible Hades!" "So always do what is right and good, no matter what it costs you." Matthew 18:1-9

Glory be to God Forever, Amen

THIRD SUNDAY OF ABIB

Holy Gospel

MATINS

Stand up in the fear of God and listen to the Holy Gospel,A chapter from the Holy Gospel according to Saint Luke, May his blessings be with us all, Amen

From the psalms of our teacher David the prophet and king,May his blessings be with us all, Amen

> Praise the Lord! Praise the name of the Lord; Praise Him, O you servants of the Lord! You who stand in the house of the Lord, In the courts of the house of our God Alleluia. - Psalm 135:1-3

Blessed is He who comes in the Name of the Lord Our Lord, God and Saviour and the King of us all, Jesus Christ, the Son of the living God. Glory be to You forever more, Amen

Now on the first day of the week, very early in the morning, they, and certain other women with them, came to the tomb bringing the spices which they had prepared. But they found the stone rolled away from the tomb. Then they went in and did not find the body of the Lord Jesus. And it happened, as they were greatly perplexed about this, that behold, two men stood by them in shining garments. Then, as they were afraid and bowed their faces to the earth, they said to them, "Why do you seek the living among the dead? He is not here, but is risen! Remember how He spoke to you when He was still in Galilee, saying, 'The Son of Man must be delivered into the hands of sinful men, and be crucified, and the third day rise again.' " And they remembered His words. Then they returned from the tomb and told all these things to the eleven and to all the rest. It was Mary Magdalene, Joanna, Mary the mother of James, and the other women with them, who told these things to the apostles. And their words seemed to them like idle tales, and they did not believe them. But Peter arose and ran to the tomb; and stooping down, he saw the linen cloths lying by themselves; and he departed, marveling to himself at what had happened. Luke 24:1-12

Glory be to God Forever, Amen

Pauline

Paul, the servant of our Lord Jesus Christ, called to be an apostle, appointed to the Gospel of God. A reading from First Epistle of our teacher Paul to Timothy. May his holy blessings be with us. Amen.

St Paul the Apostle was writing a letter to his good friend Timothy. Dear Timothy, I am very concerned that there are some people in church who don't follow what Jesus taught us. These people think that THEY know everything, and love nothing better than arguing and arguing for hours over nothing. They blame everyone else and make friends become enemies. They that church is a place for them to become rich and popular! They just want to boss everyone around. You really should just stay right away from people like this. The best thing in life is to do good things and to be happy with what you have. We were born owning nothing, weren't we! And when we die, can we take our riches with us? But some people love money instead of God, and this has made them greedy and sad and really nasty to other people. So if you really love God, don't be like that. Try to be kind, and generous, and patient and gentle instead. Fight the good fight of faith which you believe in, and have shared with others. Remember always that Jesus is with us and He can see everything we do.   (1 Timothy 6:3-16)

Bye for now!

Signed, Paul

The grace of God the Father be with you all, Amen.

Catholicon

The Catholic Epistle from the Epistle of our teacher St James. May his holy blessings be with us. Amen.

My little children, This is the Apostle James writing to tell you about something that is little, but very, very dangerous. I wonder if you can guess what it is? When you ride a horse, you put a little tiny 'bit' in the horse's mouth so you can make him go wherever you wish. And big huge ships can be steered by the tiny little rudder that pokes out from the back. A little tiny match can set a whole forest on fire! Well, this dangerous little thing can change the whole life of a big strong human being. Have you guessed what it is yet? It's the tongue! You see, we use our tongues to speak, and our little words can do so much damage! We use our tongues to pray to God, yet we use the same tongue to tease people who are made in the image of God! We use our tongue to say kind things, Yet we use the same tongue to say mean, hurtful things! My little children, this should not be so. Does a spring pour out sweet water and bitter water from the same place? Does a fig tree bear olives? Can a grapevine bear figs? That's just crazy! But people find it so hard to control their tongues! We have tamed every kind of animal, or bird, or reptile, or even sea creatures! But we still seem to have so much trouble taming our tongue! Please, please, please be careful about what you say! (James 3:1-12)

Signed, James the Apostle

Do not love the world, nor the things which are in the world. The world shall pass away and all its desires; but he who does the will of God shall abide forever. Amen.

The Acts

A reading from the Acts of our fathers the pure apostles, who were invested with the grace of the Holy Spirit. May their blessing be with us all. Amen.

St Paul came to a big city called Corinth. He stayed there for a long time, telling people about Jesus, and lots of people were being baptised and becoming Christians. But some of the Jewish people of Corinth grew very jealous of St Paul. "Look how he steals people away from our synagogue!" they complained. Some of them got so angry that they went and grabbed St Paul and dragged him in front of the Roman Governor, named Gallio. But when he had heard them out, Gallio said, "This has nothing to do with me! Go and work out your own religious problems and stop bugging me!" So St Paul got to stay a bit longer in Corinth, to help the new Church there to grow and to be brave and strong. When he was done, he set off to visit other cities with new Churches. Wherever he went, the Christians asked him to stay with them, but he had somewhere to go "I must go to Jerusalem to celebrate the Feast", he told them, "but I will come and visit you again, God willing". So he travelled on through places like Caesarea and Antioch and Galatia and Phrygia. And every place he went, he helped the Christians there and made their faith stronger. (Chapter 18:12-23)

The word of the Lord shall grow, multiply, be mighty and be confirmed in the holy Church of God. Amen.

Holy Gospel

Stand up in the fear of God and listen to the Holy Gospel, A chapter from the Holy Gospel according to Saint Luke, May his blessings be with us all, Amen

From the psalms of our teacher David the prophet and king, May his blessings be with us all, Amen

> The Lord is righteous in all His ways, Gracious in all His works. The Lord is near to all who call upon Him, To all who call upon Him in truth. Alleluia. - Psalm 145:17-18

Blessed is He who comes in the Name of the Lord Our Lord, God and Saviour and the King of us all, Jesus Christ, the Son of the living God. Glory be to You forever more, Amen

And the apostles, when they had returned, told Him all that they had done. Then He took them and went aside privately into a deserted place belonging to the city called Bethsaida. But when the multitudes knew it, they followed Him; and He received them and spoke to them about the kingdom of God, and healed those who had need of healing. When the day began to wear away, the twelve came and said to Him, "Send the multitude away, that they may go into the surrounding towns and country, and lodge and get provisions; for we are in a deserted place here." But He said to them, "You give them something to eat." And they said, "We have no more than five loaves and two fish, unless we go and buy food for all these people." For there were about five thousand men. Then He said to His disciples, "Make them sit down in groups of fifty." And they did so, and made them all sit down. Then He took the five loaves and the two fish, and looking up to heaven, He blessed and broke them, and gave them to the disciples to set before the multitude. So they all ate and were filled, and twelve baskets of the leftover fragments were taken up by them. Luke 9:10-17

Glory be to God Forever, Amen

FOURTH SUNDAY OF ABIB

Holy Gospel

Stand up in the fear of God and listen to the Holy Gospel, A chapter from the Holy Gospel according to Saint John, May his blessings be with us all, Amen

From the psalms of our teacher David the prophet and king, May his blessings be with us all, Amen

> I will praise You, O Lord my God, with all my heart, And I will glorify Your name forevermore. For great is Your mercy toward me, And You have delivered my soul from the depths of Sheol. Alleluia. - Psalm 86:12-13

Blessed is He who comes in the Name of the Lord Our Lord, God and Saviour and the King of us all, Jesus Christ, the Son of the living God. Glory be to You forever more, Amen

Now the first day of the week Mary Magdalene went to the tomb early, while it was still dark, and saw that the stone had been taken away from the tomb. Then she ran and came to Simon Peter, and to the other disciple, whom Jesus loved, and said to them, "They have taken away the Lord out of the tomb, and we do not know where they have laid Him." Peter therefore went out, and the other disciple, and were going to the tomb. So they both ran together, and the other disciple outran Peter and came to the tomb first. And he, stooping down and looking in, saw the linen cloths lying there; yet he did not go in. Then Simon Peter came, following him, and went into the tomb; and he saw the linen cloths lying there, and the handkerchief that had been around His head, not lying with the linen cloths, but folded together in a place by itself. Then the other disciple, who came to the tomb first, went in also; and he saw and believed. For as yet they did not know the Scripture, that He must rise again from the dead. Then the disciples went away again to their own homes. But Mary stood outside by the tomb weeping, and as she wept she stooped down and looked into the tomb. And she saw two angels in white sitting, one at the head and the other at the feet, where the body of Jesus had lain. Then they said to her, "Woman, why are you weeping?"

She said to them, "Because they have taken away my Lord, and I do not know where they have laid Him." Now when she had said this, she turned around and saw Jesus standing there, and did not know that it was Jesus. Jesus said to her, "Woman, why are you weeping? Whom are you seeking?" She, supposing Him to be the gardener, said to Him, "Sir, if You have carried Him away, tell me where You have laid Him, and I will take Him away."

Jesus said to her, "Mary!" She turned and said to Him, "Rabboni!" (which is to say, Teacher). Jesus said to her, "Do not cling to Me, for I have not yet ascended to My Father; but go to My brethren and say to them, 'I am ascending to My Father and your Father, and to My God and your God.' " Mary Magdalene came and told the disciples that she had seen the Lord, and that He had spoken these things to her. John 20:1-18

Glory be to God Forever, Amen

Pauline

Paul, the servant of our Lord Jesus Christ, called to be an apostle, appointed to the Gospel of God. A reading from the Epistle of our teacher Paul to Philippians. May his holy blessings be with us. Amen.

St Paul the Apostle was writing a letter to the Christians who lived in a city called Philippi.

Dear Philippians, It is very important that we always follow the teachings of our Lord Jesus Christ. It shouldn't matter whether I'm there with you or travelling far away – you should always be working together for the glory of God. And never be scared of your enemies! God has allowed you a special gift! He has allowed you to suffer for His sake, just as I often have. SO let us always be united together as one. Let us always comfort each other, let us always share things together let us always be kind and forgive each other And let us never fight with each other. Don't be selfish, but instead, try to always put others before yourself. Try to think like Jesus: Even though He is God, He did not hold on to His Heavenly Throne but instead, He chose to humble Himself, to come down to the earth, and become nothing more than a poor baby in a manger! And then, instead of thinking of Himself, He humbled Himself even more by dying on the Cross to save us! That's what love really means – to put the happiness of others ahead of your own happiness. And that's why everybody in heaven and on earth kneels and bows to Jesus. Because of His great love, they all cry out that Jesus Christ is Lord! Glory to God His Father! (Philippians 1:27-2:11)

Bye for now!

Signed, Paul

The grace of God the Father be with you all, Amen.

Catholicon

The Catholic Epistle from the First Epistle of our teacher St Peter. May his holy blessings be with us. Amen.

My little children, This is the Apostle Peter writing to tell you about a very important stone. Which stone am I talking about? I'll tell you in a little while. But first I want to remind you all that if you have got to know Jesus, and you really, really love Him, then you will not do any of these things: You won't HATE anyone, you won't LIE to anyone, you won't be TWO-FACED, you won't be JEALOUS of anyone, And, you won't SAY BAD THINGS about anyone. For you see: if you don't do any of these evil things, you will be like a precious stone to God. Jesus Himself was like a very special stone. In any building made of stone, there is one very, very special stone: The Cornerstone. The Cornerstone is so important because the rest of the building gets built around it. Now Jesus is the Cornerstone of our lives – our lives, everything we say or do – is built around Jesus. But when Jesus was on Earth, His own people didn't want Him to be their Cornerstone. They tried to get rid of Him. But instead of being thrown out, He died and rose from the dead, and became the Cornerstones in the lives of billions of people! So it was as if they had stubbed their toes on the very stone they tried to get rid of! Have you ever stubbed your toe? It hurts! It hurts a lot!! So don't you be like them. Jesus loves you very much! You are all so special to Him. You, and everyone else in your Church. Everyone of you is a part of His special people. He has forgiven your sins, and He has saved you from the darkness and brought you into the light. So don't stub your toe on Jesus, the Cornerstone. Instead, build your life around Him! (1 Peter 1:25-2:10)

Bye for now!

Signed, Peter the Apostle

Do not love the world, nor the things which are in the world. The world shall pass away and all its desires; but he who does the will of God shall abide forever. Amen.

The Acts

A reading from the Acts of our fathers the pure apostles, who were invested with the grace of the Holy Spirit. May their blessing be with us all. Amen.

Do you remember St Paul? He was the man who used to arrest Christians and throw them in jail. But then Jesus appeared to Him and he changed. He changed a lot. He changed so much that God did lots of miracles through him. For example, people used to take his old handkerchiefs and clothes and put them on the sick. And then, the sick would be healed! Those were miracles. And they put them on people who were troubled by the demons and the demons ran away! They were miracles too. Now some other very tricky men who were not very honest heard about all these miracles. They got an idea! "Hmmmmm," they thought, "We could make a lot of money using this power that Paul has. All we have to do is copy him!" Do you think this would work? Well, they tried. They found a man who had an evil demon. "Come out of him, in the name of the Jesus that Paul uses!" they shouted at him. But the evil demon did not come out. He answered them instead "Yes, I know Jesus." said the demon. "And I know Paul. And I am very afraid of them, but who are you? I'm not afraid of you!" And the demon made the man he was in jump up and start to hit them, really hard! "Ouch!" they yelped. "Stop it!" they cried. They ran away, with lots of bruises! Now this story became well known, for people told each other what had happened. So everybody praised God whose power was so clear in St Paul. And everyone who had magic books or tried to do magic Realised how dangerous it is! So they brought all their books and their equipment and they burned them, promising never ever to go back to magic again. This was how the Word of God spread and more and more people believed the Apostles and became Christian. But St Paul wasn't finished yet. "I must go to Jerusalem" he said, "And then I must go to Rome." (Chapter 19:11-22)

The word of the Lord shall grow, multiply, be mighty and be confirmed in the holy Church of God. Amen.

Holy Gospel

Stand up in the fear of God and listen to the Holy Gospel, A chapter from the Holy Gospel according to Saint John, May his blessings be with us all, Amen

From the psalms of our teacher David the prophet and king, May his blessings be with us all, Amen

> The Lord is righteous in all His ways, Gracious in all His works. The Lord is near to all who call upon Him, To all who call upon Him in truth. Alleluia. - Psalm 40:5,16

Blessed is He who comes in the Name of the Lord Our Lord, God and Saviour and the King of us all, Jesus Christ, the Son of the living God. Glory be to You forever more, Amen

Now a certain man was sick, Lazarus of Bethany, the town of Mary and her sister Martha. It was that Mary who anointed the Lord with fragrant oil and wiped His feet with her hair, whose brother Lazarus was sick. Therefore the sisters sent to Him, saying, "Lord, behold, he whom You love is sick." When Jesus heard that, He said, "This sickness is not unto death, but for the glory of God, that the Son of God may be glorified through it." Now Jesus loved Martha and her sister and Lazarus. So, when He heard that he was sick, He stayed two more days in the place where He was. Then after this He said to the disciples, "Let us go to Judea again." The disciples said to Him, "Rabbi, lately the Jews sought to stone You, and are You going there again?" "Jesus answered, "Are there not twelve hours in the day? If anyone walks in the day, he does not stumble, because he sees the light of this world. But if one walks in the night, he stumbles, because the light is not in him." These things He said, and after that He said to them, "Our friend Lazarus sleeps, but I go that I may wake him up." Then His disciples said, "Lord, if he sleeps he will get well." However, Jesus spoke of his death, but they thought that He was speaking about taking rest in sleep. Then Jesus said to them plainly, "Lazarus is dead. And I am glad for your sakes that I was not there, that you may believe. Nevertheless let us go to him." Then Thomas, who is called the Twin, said to his fellow disciples, "Let us also go, that we may die with Him."

So when Jesus came, He found that he had already been in the tomb four days. Now Bethany was near Jerusalem, about two miles away. And many of the Jews had joined the women around Martha and Mary, to comfort them concerning their brother. Then Martha, as soon as she heard that Jesus was coming, went and met Him, but Mary was sitting in the house. Then Martha said to Jesus, "Lord, if You had been here, my brother would not have died. But even now I know that whatever You ask of God, God will give You." Jesus said to her, "Your brother will rise again." Martha said to Him, "I know that he will rise again in the resurrection at the last day." Jesus said to her, "I am the resurrection and the life. He who believes in Me, though he may die, he shall live. And whoever lives and believes in Me shall never die. Do you believe this?" She said to Him, "Yes, Lord, I believe that You are the Christ, the Son of God, who is to come into the world." And when she had said these things, she went her way and secretly called Mary her sister, saying, "The Teacher has come and is calling for you." As soon as she heard that, she arose quickly and came to Him. Now Jesus had not yet come into the town, but was in the place where Martha met Him. Then the Jews who were with her in the house, and comforting her, when they saw that Mary rose up quickly and went out, followed her, saying, "She is going to the tomb to weep there." Then, when Mary came where Jesus was, and saw Him, she fell down at His feet, saying to Him, "Lord, if You had been here, my brother would not have died."

Therefore, when Jesus saw her weeping, and the Jews who came with her weeping, He groaned in the spirit and was troubled. And He said, "Where have you laid him?" They said to Him, "Lord, come and see." Jesus wept. Then the Jews said, "See how

He loved him!" And some of them said, "Could not this Man, who opened the eyes of the blind, also have kept this man from dying?" Then Jesus, again groaning in Himself, came to the tomb. It was a cave, and a stone lay against it. Jesus said, "Take away the stone." Martha, the sister of him who was dead, said to Him, "Lord, by this time there is a stench, for he has been dead four days." Jesus said to her, "Did I not say to you that if you would believe you would see the glory of God?" Then they took away the stone from the place where the dead man was lying. And Jesus lifted up His eyes and said, "Father, I thank You that You have heard Me. And I know that You always hear Me, but because of the people who are standing by I said this, that they may believe that You sent Me." Now when He had said these things, He cried with a loud voice, "Lazarus, come forth!" And he who had died came out bound hand and foot with graveclothes, and his face was wrapped with a cloth. Jesus said to them, "Loose him, and let him go." Then many of the Jews who had come to Mary, and had seen the things Jesus did, believed in Him. John 11:1-45

Glory be to God Forever, Amen

FIRST SUNDAY OF MISRA

Holy Gospel

MATINS

Stand up in the fear of God and listen to the Holy Gospel, A chapter from the Holy Gospel according to Saint Matthew, May his blessings be with us all, Amen

From the psalms of our teacher David the prophet and king, May his blessings be with us all, Amen

> Our soul waits for the Lord; He is our help and our shield. For our heart shall rejoice in Him, Because we have trusted in His holy name. Alleluia. - Psalm 33:20-21

Blessed is He who comes in the Name of the Lord Our Lord, God and Saviour and the King of us all, Jesus Christ, the Son of the living God. Glory be to You forever more, Amen

Now after the Sabbath, as the first day of the week began to dawn, Mary Magdalene and the other Mary came to see the tomb. And behold, there was a great earthquake; for an angel of the Lord descended from heaven, and came and rolled back the stone from the door, and sat on it. His countenance was like lightning, and his clothing as white as snow. And the guards shook for fear of him, and became like dead men. But the angel answered and said to the women, "Do not be afraid, for I know that you seek Jesus who was crucified. He is not here; for He is risen, as He said. Come, see the place where the Lord lay. And go quickly and tell His disciples that He is risen from the dead, and indeed He is going before you into Galilee; there you will see Him. Behold, I have told you."

 So they went out quickly from the tomb with fear and great joy, and ran to bring His disciples word. And as they went to tell His disciples, behold, Jesus met them, saying, "Rejoice!" So they came and held Him by the feet and worshiped Him. Then Jesus said to them, "Do not be afraid. Go and tell My brethren to go to Galilee, and there they will see Me."

Now while they were going, behold, some of the guard came into the city and reported to the chief priests all the things that had happened. When they had assembled with the elders and consulted together, they gave a large sum of money to the soldiers, saying, "Tell them, 'His disciples came at night and stole Him away while we slept.' And if this comes to the governor's ears, we will appease him and make you secure." So they took the money and did as they were instructed; and this saying is commonly reported among the Jews until this day. Then the eleven disciples went away into Galilee, to the mountain which Jesus had appointed for them. When they saw Him, they worshiped Him; but some doubted. And Jesus came and spoke to them, saying, "All authority has been given to Me in heaven and on earth. Go therefore and make disciples of all the nations, baptizing them in the name of the Father and of the Son and of the Holy Spirit, teaching them to observe all things that I have commanded you; and lo, I am with you always, even to the end of the age." Amen. Matthew 28: 1-20

Glory be to God Forever, Amen

Pauline

Paul, the servant of our Lord Jesus Christ, called to be an apostle, appointed to the Gospel of God. A reading from the First Epistle of our teacher Paul to Corinthians. May his holy blessings be with us. Amen.

St Paul the Apostle was writing a letter to the Christians who lived in a big, rich city called Corinth. Dear Corinthians, You have made me a little bit sad. Why do some of you think and say bad things about me? Aren't I an Apostle? Didn't I see Jesus Christ our Lord? Didn't I teach you how to be Christians? Some of you say I am greedy. But am I really greedy? I chose not to have a wife, so I could serve God better, was that greedy?

Moses said that it is only fair for an ox to eat some of the grain it is grinding. He deserves to eat some of the food he is making for others! So, if someone serves you and tells you about God, It is only fair that you should look after him and give him food to eat. But my friend Barnabas and I have never asked for anything from anyone. Was that greedy? We have told you about God for free! We never asked you for anything in return. Was that greedy? I am not saying this so I can show off! I love Jesus. All I want to do is just work for Jesus. I don't want anything from you except that you love Jesus too. If you waste all you time calling me greedy

You might forget about loving Jesus! That would really be sad! Look how much I love Jesus, and how hard I try to tell everyone about Him. Even though I am a free man, I have made myself like a faithful slave to everyone, so I could get more people to love Jesus. When I find someone who is weak, I speak to them as if I was weak too, so that they listen to me when I tell them about Jesus. When I meet a Jewish person, I tell them that I am Jewish too, so that they listen to me when I tell them about Jesus. When I meet someone who never heard of God, I talk like someone who never heard of God too, so that they listen to me when I tell them about Jesus. I made friends with lots of different kinds of people, because I want everyone to know Jesus and to be saved. I have worked so hard because I believe in the Gospel, just like you do. I want to share the Gospel with you! Now, when you are running in a race, don't you do your best to win? After all, only one person can win the gold medal! Do your best to win the heavenly prize; not just a gold medal. Don't run like someone who's not sure where the finish line is! Don't fight like someone who can't see anything and keeps punching the air! Do your best to win the heavenly prize. That's what I am doing, I control my body. I stop it from being naughty. I teach it to serve God. If I didn't do these things, do you know what could happen? Something awful! Even though I am one of the Apostles, Even though I have taught others what to do to get to heaven; If I didn't always do my best to do the right thing, I might miss out on heaven myself! So let's all be very careful to obey God, Every day of our lives. (1 Corinthians 9:1-27)

Bye for now!

Signed, Paul

> *The grace of God the Father be with you all, Amen.*

Catholicon

The Catholic Epistle from the First Epistle of our teacher St Peter. May his holy blessings be with us. Amen.

Hello Everyone!

Today, I have some very important advice to give you, I want you all to be one together. Be kind to each other. Love everyone as if they were your brother or sister. Don't be cruel. Use good manners with everyone. If someone calls you names, don't do it back to them. Instead, bless them, for this is what God called us to do: He said: "If you want to have a good life, stop your tongue from saying bad things, and don't let a lie come out of your lips." So turn away from evil, and do good instead. Try as hard as you can to make peace with everyone. Remember that God is always watching us and He always hears our prayers. He's on our side. But God is not on the side of those who do naughty things. And if God is on our side, then who could possibly hurt us when we do good? And even if you suffer a little, God will turn it into a blessing for you. So don't be afraid of anything, Don't let anything scare you. God lives in your hearts. (*1 Peter 3:8-15*)

Signed, Peter the Apostle

Do not love the world, nor the things which are in the world. The world shall pass away and all its desires; but he who does the will of God shall abide forever. Amen.

The Acts

A reading from the Acts of our fathers the pure apostles, who were invested with the grace of the Holy Spirit. May their blessing be with us all. Amen.

There was a man called Demetrius the Silversmith who lived in a city called Ephesus. Demetrius was very clever at making things out of precious, shiny silver. He made statues of an idol called Diana. He sold these statues of Diana to the idol worshippers who came to Ephesus. This made lots of money for him! But one day, Saint Paul came to Ephesus. HE did not come to worship the statue of Diana! He came to tell the people about the true God. Lots of people started to listen to St Paul. Lots of people started to leave Diana, and worship the true God. But this made Demetrius the Silversmith very, very angry! Can you guess why he was so angry? No one wanted to buy his silver statues of Diana anymore! He was going out of business! But he wasn't going to go without a fight! He called all the idol worshippers of Ephesus together and told them: "This man Paul is going to make everyone forget the great Diana. "What's worse, he is going to put us out of business!" "We've got to do something!" He got all the idol worshippers as angry as he was. They started to shout, "Great is Diana of the Ephesians!" They ran and found two men who were St Paul's friends and they grabbed them, shouting, "Great is Diana of the Ephesians!" They took St Paul's friends to the theatre and threatened them, shouting, "Great is Diana of the Ephesians!" When St Paul heard what was happening, he started to go out to try to talk to the idol worshippers and rescue his two friends. But the Christians stopped him. They knew that the idol worshippers would not listen. They would only want to hurt St Paul, they were so angry. A man called Alexander tried to calm the crowd down, but they wouldn't listen to him, because he was a Jew. For two hours they kept shouting, "Great is Diana of the Ephesians!" Finally, the Town Clerk managed to get the crowd to listen to him. He said: "Men of Ephesus! "Everyone in the world knows how great Ephesus is" "Everyone knows that we have the great temple of Diana. "We have the image of Diana that fell from heaven—no one else in the world has that!" "So control your temper and don't be silly. "These two men haven't stolen anything or broken any laws. If you think they have, then take them to court!" "But let's stop this silly behaviour! Why, if anyone saw you shouting like that, they would think you were crazy!" And then he told everyone to go home and calm down. And finally, that was exactly what they did. Thank you God! St Paul and his friends were safe! God had kept them safe from Demetrius and his friends. (Chapter 19:23-41)

The word of the Lord shall grow, multiply, be mighty and be confirmed in the holy Church of God. Amen.

Holy Gospel

Stand up in the fear of God and listen to the Holy Gospel, A chapter from the Holy Gospel according to Saint Luke, May his blessings be with us all, Amen

From the psalms of our teacher David the prophet and king, May his blessings be with us all, Amen

O God of hosts, convert us now; Look down from heaven and behold, And visit this vineyard, which Your right hand planted, and perfect it. And visit the son of man, whom You strengthened for Yourself. Alleluia. -Psalm 80:14,15

Blessed is He who comes in the Name of the Lord Our Lord, God and Saviour and the King of us all, Jesus Christ, the Son of the living God. Glory be to You forever more, Amen

Then He began to tell the people this parable: "A certain man planted a vineyard, leased it to vinedressers, and went into a far country for a long time. Now at vintage-time he sent a servant to the vinedressers, that they might give him some of the fruit of the vineyard. But the vinedressers beat him and sent him away empty-handed. Again he sent another servant; and they beat him also, treated him shamefully, and sent him away empty-handed. And again he sent a third; and they wounded him also and cast him out. Then the owner of the vineyard said, 'What shall I do? I will send my beloved son. Probably they will respect him when they see him.' But when the vinedressers saw him, they reasoned among themselves, saying, 'This is the heir. Come, let us kill him, that the inheritance may be ours.' So they cast him out of the vineyard and killed him. Therefore what will the owner of the vineyard do to them? " He will come and destroy those vinedressers and give the vineyard to others." And when they heard it they said, "Certainly not!" " Then He looked at them and said, "What then is this that is written: 'The stone which the builders rejected Has become the chief cornerstone'? "Whoever falls on that stone will be broken; but on whomever it falls, it will grind him to powder." And the chief priests and the scribes that very hour sought to lay hands on Him, but they feared the people*--for they knew He had spoken this parable against them. Luke 20:9-19

Glory be to God Forever, Amen

SECOND SUNDAY OF MISRA

Holy Gospel

MATINS

Stand up in the fear of God and listen to the Holy Gospel, A chapter from the Holy Gospel according to Saint Mark, May his blessings be with us all, Amen

From the psalms of our teacher David the prophet and king, May his blessings be with us all, Amen

> I will sing of the mercies of the Lord forever; With my mouth will I make known Your faithfulness to all generations. For I have said, "Mercy shall be built up forever; Your faithfulness You shall establish in the very heavens." Alleluia. -Psalm 89:1-2

Blessed is He who comes in the Name of the Lord Our Lord, God and Saviour and the King of us all, Jesus Christ, the Son of the living God. Glory be to You forever more, Amen

Very early in the morning, on the first day of the week, they came to the tomb when the sun had risen. And they said among themselves, "Who will roll away the stone from the door of the tomb for us?" But when they looked up, they saw that the stone had been rolled away—for it was very large. And entering the tomb, they saw a young man clothed in a long white robe sitting on the right side; and they were alarmed. But he said to them, "Do not be alarmed. You seek Jesus of Nazareth, who was crucified. He is risen! He is not here. See the place where they laid Him. But go, tell His disciples—and Peter—that He is going before you into Galilee; there you will see Him, as He said to you." So they went out quickly and fled from the tomb, for they trembled and were amazed. And they said nothing to anyone, for they were afraid. Mark 16:2-8

Glory be to God Forever, Amen

Pauline

Paul, the servant of our Lord Jesus Christ, called to be an apostle, appointed to the Gospel of God. A reading from our teacher Paul to Ephesians. May his holy blessings be with us. Amen.

Dear Ephesians, I have some really important advice for each of you today. Please listen very carefully! CHILDREN: Listen to your parents. God gave them to you so they can look after you and help you. Remember: "Honour your father and your mother" PARENTS: Be nice and kind to your children. Don't annoy them or make them angry. SERVANTS and WORKERS: Obey your bosses, not by crawling to them but by being honest, just as if you were serving God instead of people. And BOSSES: Do the same thing with your workers. Remember that you too have a very Big Boss, the One who is in Heaven! Finally, I want you all to be STRONG, for our Lord is very STRONG! But I don't mean strong in the muscles of your body. I mean strong in your heart and in your thinking. God makes us strong inside. He is like our armour, the armour that a soldier wears to battle. This armour of God helps us to fight against the devil and all his evil, and to win the battle! What is our armour? Put on the Belt of Truth. Jesus always told the Truth, and the Truth makes us strong. And the Breastplate of Righteousness. Jesus always did what was right and good. Doing good makes us strong. And the Boots of the Gospel of Peace. Jesus taught us His Gospel—His Good News—so we could have peace, and that makes us strong. And the Shield of Faith. When we believe in Jesus, and trust Him with our lives, nothing can ever really hurt us, so we are strong. And the Helmet of Salvation. Jesus saved us! This salvation protects our thoughts and our minds and makes us strong. And finally, the Sword of the Spirit. Jesus gave us His Holy Spirit, who fights our enemy, the devil for us, and makes us strong. Now you have the whole Armour of God! Now you are ready to fight against evil! Are you ready? But first, remember you are not fighting alone. We must always remember to pray for each other, for all our fellow soldiers of Christ. And that includes me, your friend Paul! Pray that God will always send us all the the right words to say. Pray that God will help me to be bold and brave, and to tell people how much Jesus loves them. Sometimes, people don't want to hear this. Sometimes, they get really angry when I tell them about Jesus. That is why they put me in jail! But I don't mind. I love Jesus and will always tell people how much He loves them. Because I know Jesus loves me, I am STRONG! Peace to all my brothers and sisters, and love with faith, from God the Father and the Lord Jesus Christ. God be with all those who love our Lord Jesus Christ from all their hearts. (Ephesians 6:1-23)

Bye for now!

Signed, Paul

The grace of God the Father be with you all, Amen.

Catholicon

The Catholic Epistle from the First Epistle of our teacher St John. May his holy blessings be with us. Amen.

Hello Everyone!

From John, My beloved brothers and sisters, do you remember the most important commandment God has given us? The most important commandment, from long ago, and forevermore, is LOVE! We must love God, and love one another. That is what Jesus taught us. If you don't love other people, you are like a person who lives in darkness. You will always stumble and fall. But if you love other people, you are like a person who lives in the light. You will never stumble or fall! The light of Jesus is much stronger than the darkness. I wanted to write these things to you, O little children Because God has forgiven your sins. I wanted to write these things to you, O parents because you have known God very well. I wanted to write these things to you, O young people because you have beaten the devil. I wanted to write these things to you, O little children because you are friends with the Father. I wanted to write these things to you, O parents because you are friends with God. I wanted to write these things to you, O young people because you are strong, and God's word lives in you, and you have beaten the devil. If you are selfish, and just love the things in the world, you won't be able to truly love God. God teaches us to NOT be selfish. So we don't really care that much about those selfish things everyone else goes crazy about. This world is going to end one day. But our love for God is forever! God loves you! Signed, John Everyone together: Do not love the world, nor the things which are in the world. The world shall pass away and all its desires; but he who does the will of God shall abide forever. Amen. (1 John 2:7-17)

Signed,   John the Beloved

Do not love the world, nor the things which are in the world. The world shall pass away and all its desires; but he who does the will of God shall abide forever. Amen.

190

The Acts

A reading from the Acts of our fathers the pure apostles, who were invested with the grace of the Holy Spirit. May their blessing be with us all. Amen.

Remember last week, how St Paul and his friends were in Ephesus, and Demetrius stirred up a crowd against them, shouting "Great is Diana of the Ephesians!"? Well, when all that trouble had finally died down, Paul decided it was time to leave Ephesus and go to Greece. And from Greece, Paul travelled to lots of other places: Macedonia, and Greece, and Philippi, and Troas. Let's let St Luke tell us what happened next.

Hello everyone. My name is St Luke, and I am the one who wrote the Book of Acts. Today, I want to tell you a little more of the story of St Paul. One Sunday, we were in Troas, and we came together to pray, have communion, and talk. Paul spoke and spoke and they listened and listened, so happy to learn more about Jesus' love. Before anyone realised, it was already midnight! It was way past the bedtime of a boy called Eutychus [Yoo-tie-kuss].They were on the third floor and Eutychus was sitting somewhere that was not very clever. Eutychus was sitting on the window sill. And the window was open. And Eutychus fell asleep! OH! Be careful Eutychus! Oh no! Eutychus fell out the window! How awful! Everyone rushed downstairs. Is he hurt? Is he alive? Oh no! Oh no! Eutychus was dead. But Paul went through all the people, and he picked up Eutychus. Paul hugged him. Paul prayed for him. Then, a miracle happened! Eutychus came back to life! He was alive again! Everyone was so happy! Then we all went back inside, and had something to eat, which we needed after a shock like that! And we kept listening to Paul all through the night, all the way to morning. The things he was telling us about Jesus were just so beautiful. We didn't want him to stop! And in the morning, Paul left to get on a ship to continue his adventures. (Chapter 20:1–12)

The word of the Lord shall grow, multiply, be mighty and be confirmed in the holy Church of God. Amen

Holy Gospel

Stand up in the fear of God and listen to the Holy Gospel, A chapter from the Holy Gospel according to Saint Luke, May his blessings be with us all, Amen

From the psalms of our teacher David the prophet and king, May his blessings be with us all, Amen

The heavens shall confess Your wonders, O Lord, And Your truth in the church of the saints. Blessed are the people who know glad shouting; O Lord, they shall walk in the light of Your face Alleluia. -Psalm 89:5,15

Blessed is He who comes in the Name of the Lord Our Lord, God and Saviour and the King of us all, Jesus Christ, the Son of the living God. Glory be to You forever more, Amen

After these things He went out and saw a tax collector named Levi, sitting at the tax office. And He said to him, "Follow Me." So he left all, rose up, and followed Him. Then Levi gave Him a great feast in his own house. And there were a great number of tax collectors and others who sat down with them. And their scribes and the Pharisees " Jesus answered and said to them, "Those who are well have no need of a physician, but those who are sick. " I have not come to call the righteous, but sinners, to repentance." Then they said to Him, "Why do " And He said to them, "Can you make the friends of the bridegroom fast while the bridegroom is with them? " But the days will come when the bridegroom will be taken away from them; then they will fast in those days." " Then He spoke a parable to them: "No one puts a piece from a new garment on an old one; And no one puts new wine into old wineskins; or else the new wine will burst the wineskins and be spilled, and the wineskins will be ruined. But new wine must be put into new wineskins, and both are preserved. " And no one, having drunk old wine, immediately. Luke 5:27–39

Glory be to God Forever, Amen

THIRD SUNDAY OF MISRA

Holy Gospel

MATINS

Stand up in the fear of God and listen to the Holy Gospel, A chapter from the Holy Gospel according to Saint Luke, May his blessings be with us all, Amen

From the psalms of our teacher David the prophet and king, May his blessings be with us all, Amen

> Lord, who may abide in Your tabernacle? Who may dwell in Your holy hill? He who walks uprightly, And works righteousness, And speaks the truth in his heart;   Alleluia. -Psalm 15:1-2

Blessed is He who comes in the Name of the Lord Our Lord, God and Saviour and the King of us all, Jesus Christ, the Son of the living God. Glory be to You forever more, Amen

Now on the first day of the week, very early in the morning, they, and certain other women with them, came to the tomb bringing the spices which they had prepared. But they found the stone rolled away from the tomb. Then they went in and did not find the body of the Lord Jesus. And it happened, as they were greatly perplexed about this, that behold, two men stood by them in shining garments. Then, as they were afraid and bowed their faces to the earth, they said to them, "Why do you seek the living among the dead? He is not here, but is risen! Remember how He spoke to you when He was still in Galilee, saying, 'The Son of Man must be delivered into the hands of sinful men, and be crucified, and the third day rise again.' " And they remembered His words. Then they returned from the tomb and told all these things to the eleven and to all the rest. It was Mary Magdalene, Joanna, Mary the mother of James, and the other women with them, who told these things to the apostles. And their words seemed to them like idle tales, and they did not believe them. But Peter arose and ran to the tomb; and stooping down, he saw the linen cloths lying by themselves; and he departed, marveling to himself at what had happened. Luke 24:1-12

Glory be to God Forever, Amen

Pauline

Paul, the servant of our Lord Jesus Christ, called to be an apostle, appointed to the Gospel of God. A reading from Epistle of our teacher Paul to Romans. May his holy blessings be with us. Amen.

St Paul the Apostle was writing a letter to the Christians who lived in the great city of Rome. Dear Romans, Be careful, my brothers and sisters, because there are some people in your Church who like to make problems. Instead of obeying what Jesus taught us, they try to make you get upset with each other or they try to split you up into groups that don't like each other. Do you know what you should do with such people? Stay right away from them! They are not serving God. They are serving themselves! They trick people by talking so cleverly. Don't listen to them! Don't let them spoil the good name you have for always being obedient to the words of God. I really want you to be so wise in good things but I don't want you to be good at evil things! And God will give you peace, and He will quickly crush the devil under your feet! The grace of our Lord Jesus Christ be with you, amen (Romans 16:17-20)

Bye for now!

Signed, Paul

The grace of God the Father be with you all, Amen.

Catholicon

The Catholic Epistle from the First Epistle of our teacher St Peter. May his holy blessings be with us. Amen.

Hello Everyone! From Peter, I have some very important advice to give you all today; If you have a master (like your teacher, for example, or your parents) you must do what they tell you to, even if you think they are being a bit too strict. Let me tell you why: Sometimes, when you really have done something wrong, you get in trouble; Well that's OK, Then, it's fair for you to get in trouble! You should take the punishment that you deserve. But sometimes, you get in trouble when you haven't really done anything wrong, Should you just "take it" then? That's exactly what happened to Jesus! He NEVER did anything wrong, but they arrested Him and said He did things that weren't true. And even though He was innocent, He never talked back to the rulers or the soldiers. He never got angry with them. He never argued with them. He put up with all that horrible stuff they did to Him, and trusted in His Father to look after Him. Do you know why? Because He wanted to save us from OUR sins. That's right, He died the death WE were going to die, when He died for us on the Cross so that we could live. We were like sheep who had gone astray and gotten lost and He is our Good Shepherd, who gave His life to save His sheep. So if you truly love Jesus, be like Him: Be obedient to the people that God gave you, to look after you. Are there any Mums there? OK, this is the advice I have for you, Mums and Dads should always try to get along with each other nicely, and to work together. If the Dad gets a bit too cranky sometimes, the Mum can calm him down by being a good example, and by treating him with love. Girls and ladies: don't worry too much about how you look - you know what I mean; clothes and hair-styles and make-up. That's not what makes you beautiful! What really makes you beautiful is if you have a gentle and quiet spirit deep in your heart; this is so, so beautiful! This is so, so precious to God! This is what made the ladies in the Bible so beautiful, like Sarah, who trusted in God, and dealt with her husband Abraham so calmly. She loved Abraham SO much - do you know what she used to call him? She used to call him, "my lord Abraham"! And she always tried to work nicely with him, because he was her husband. If you want to be the daughters of the great Sarah, you must also love and get along with your husbands. And Daddies also have to love the Mummies and look after them really well. Daddies must honour their wives: that means they have to treat them like a queen! They should always do their best to understand their wives and to give them whatever they need. After all, aren't they both working together to try to get to Heaven?   (1 Peter 2:18-3:7)

Bye for now!

Signed,   Peter the Apostle

Do not love the world, nor the things which are in the world. The world shall pass away and all its desires; but he who does the will of God shall abide forever. Amen.

The Acts

St Paul and his friends were visiting a city called "Caesaria", and they were staying at the house of Phillip, one of the Seven Archdeacons. Phillip had four daughters, and all four of them could prophesy – God would sometimes tell them to say things that everybody needed to hear! While they were staying at Phillip's house, something really strange and unexpected happened. Another man came to visit Phillip - a prophet called Agabus. As soon as he saw St Paul, he went and took his belt. That was strange! What would he do with his belt? Then he tied the belt around his own hands and feet, and then he began to speak "The Holy Spirit says that the man who owns this belt is going to be tied up just like this by the Jews at Jerusalem" "And they will give him up to the Roman soldiers". Everyone was shocked and frightened for Paul. They didn't want him to go to gaol! They begged and pleaded and cried and argued with Paul. "Please, please don't go to Jerusalem! It's too dangerous!" they cried. But Paul was the only one who wasn't scared! "Why are you breaking my heart like this?" he asked them, "Don't you know that I love Jesus so much, that I would do anything for Him? Not only am I ready to go to gaol - I am ready to die for Him!" he said bravely. So when his friends saw that they could not change his mind, they stopped trying to convince him. Instead they said, "May God's will be done". And they let him go. (Chapter 21:8-14)

Holy Gospel

Stand up in the fear of God and listen to the Holy Gospel,A chapter from the Holy Gospel according to Saint Mark , May his blessings be with us all, Amen

From the psalms of our teacher David the prophet and king,May his blessings be with us all, Amen

> Hear the voice of my supplication. The Lord is my helper and my champion. Blessed is the Lord, Because He heard the voice of my supplication Alleluia. -Psalm 28:2,7,6

Blessed is He who comes in the Name of the Lord Our Lord, God and Saviour and the King of us all, Jesus Christ, the Son of the living God. Glory be to You forever more, Amen

A And the scribes who came down from Jerusalem said, "He has Beelzebub," and, "By the ruler of the demons He casts out demons." So He called them to Himself and said to them in parables: "How can Satan cast out Satan? If a kingdom is divided against itself, that kingdom cannot stand. And if a house is divided against itself, that house cannot stand. And if Satan has risen up against himself, and is divided, he cannot stand, but has an end. No one can enter a strong man's house and plunder his goods, unless he first binds the strong man. And then he will plunder his house. "Assuredly, I say to you, all sins will be forgiven the sons of men, and whatever blasphemies they may utter; but he who blasphemes against the Holy Spirit never has forgiveness, but is subject to eternal condemnation"-- because they said, "He has an unclean spirit."

Then His brothers and His mother came, and standing outside they sent to Him, calling Him. And a multitude was sitting around Him; and they said to Him, "Look, Your mother and Your brothers are outside seeking You." But He answered them, saying, "Who is My mother, or My brothers?" And He looked around in a circle at those who sat about Him, and said, "Here are My mother and My brothers! For whoever does the will of God is My brother and My sister and mother." Mark 3:22-35

Glory be to God Forever, Amen

FOURTH SUNDAY OF MISRA

Holy Gospel

MATINS

Stand up in the fear of God and listen to the Holy Gospel, A chapter from the Holy Gospel according to Saint John, May his blessings be with us all, Amen

From the psalms of our teacher David the prophet and king, May his blessings be with us all, Amen

> Lord, You have been our dwelling place in all generations. Before the mountains were brought forth, Or ever You had formed the earth and the world, Even from everlasting to everlasting, You are God. Alleluia. -Psalm 90:1-2

Blessed is He who comes in the Name of the Lord Our Lord, God and Saviour and the King of us all, Jesus Christ, the Son of the living God. Glory be to You forever more, Amen

Now the first day of the week Mary Magdalene went to the tomb early, while it was still dark, and saw that the stone had been taken away from the tomb. Then she ran and came to Simon Peter, and to the other disciple, whom Jesus loved, and said to them, "They have taken away the Lord out of the tomb, and we do not know where they have laid Him." Peter therefore went out, and the other disciple, and were going to the tomb. So they both ran together, and the other disciple outran Peter and came to the tomb first. And he, stooping down and looking in, saw the linen cloths lying there; yet he did not go in. Then Simon Peter came, following him, and went into the tomb; and he saw the linen cloths lying there, and the handkerchief that had been around His head, not lying with the linen cloths, but folded together in a place by itself. Then the other disciple, who came to the tomb first, went in also; and he saw and believed. For as yet they did not know the Scripture, that He must rise again from the dead. Then the disciples went away again to their own homes. But Mary stood outside by the tomb weeping, and as she wept she stooped down and looked into the tomb. And she saw two angels in white sitting, one at the head and the other at the feet, where the body of Jesus had lain. Then they said to her, "Woman, why are you weeping?"

She said to them, "Because they have taken away my Lord, and I do not know where they have laid Him." Now when she had said this, she turned around and saw Jesus standing there, and did not know that it was Jesus. Jesus said to her, "Woman, why are you weeping? Whom are you seeking?" She, supposing Him to be the gardener, said to Him, "Sir, if You have carried Him away, tell me where You have laid Him, and I will take Him away."

Jesus said to her, "Mary!" She turned and said to Him, "Rabboni!" (which is to say, Teacher). Jesus said to her, "Do not cling to Me, for I have not yet ascended to My Father; but go to My brethren and say to them, 'I am ascending to My Father and your Father, and to My God and your God.' " Mary Magdalene came and told the disciples that she had seen the Lord, and that He had spoken these things to her. John 20:1-18

Glory be to God Forever, Amen

Pauline

Paul, the servant of our Lord Jesus Christ, called to be an apostle, appointed to the Gospel of God. A reading from the First Epistle of our teacher Paul to Thessalonians. May his holy blessings be with us. Amen.

St Paul the Apostle was writing a letter to the Christians who lived in the big city called Thessalonica

Dear Thessalonians, I thank God for you every day. You understand that when we tell you about God, we're not making things up! We are just telling you exactly what God told us. You have been just like your brothers and sisters who live in Judea, where Jesus lived. The Judeans gave them a hard time for being Christian. And the Thessalonicans give you a hard time for being Christian! The Jews in Judea killed the prophets, And then they killed Jesus, And now they try to kill us! But don't worry, God sees the evil things they do, and He will deal with them. They can't stop us from telling people about Jesus! I miss you all so much and I have tried to come to see you many times. You fill our hearts with joy! When I imagine you standing before Jesus when He comes again, I feel such hope and rejoicing. So, when I couldn't stand being away from you any longer, I sent you my helper, Timothy to encourage you and make you strong and to keep you going through the hard and the sad times, since I knew that it is so, so hard for you. Remember, last time I saw you, I warned you this was coming? But when Timothy came back to me, he told me how strong your faith and love still are. He told me how you have resisted your enemies, and that you miss me too. This good news made me feel so much better, even in the middle of my own suffering. Even though we are in different countries, let us both stand firm together for Jesus! How can I thank God enough for you? You have made us so happy! And we pray for you, night and day, that we might see you soon to help you and support you in your struggles. May God lead us to you soon, may God make you grow in loving each other and in loving everyone. May God prepare you to meet Him when He comes again with all His saints. (1 Thessalonians 2:13–3:13)

Bye for now!

Signed, Paul

The grace of God the Father be with you all, Amen.

Catholicon

The Catholic Epistle from the Epistle of our teacher St James. May his holy blessings be with us. Amen.

From James, Give in to God! Stand up to the devil, and he will run away from you! Come closer to God and He will come closer to you. If you have done the wrong thing, tell God that you are sorry. Don't be all mixed up! Don't try to get away with doing the wrong thing! That's crazy! It is so much better to own up and confess before God. Be sad for your sins, so God can forgive you and make you happy again. He will lift you up high! Don't say bad things about each other - who made you the Judge??? There is only one true Judge - so leave the judging to Him. And don't be so proud as to say "I will do this", or "I am certainly going to do that". Our life is only short, and we are weak, like smoke that soon blows away in the wind. So it's better to say, "If God wills, I will do this or that". If you know how to do the right thing, and you still don't do it, that's bad: that's a sin. You who are rich— I feel so sorry for you! You should cry and weep for yourselves too! Do you know why? Because you thought your gold and your silver were going to protect you. But when Jesus comes, your money isn't going to do you any good at all! In fact, because you got your money by cheating and stealing and lying. Because you were selfish and didn't share your riches with anyone else. Boy, are you going to be in BIG trouble! (James 4:7-5:5)

Bye for now!

Signed, James, the Apostle

Do not love the world, nor the things which are in the world. The world shall pass away and all its desires; but he who does the will of God shall abide forever. Amen.

The Acts

A reading from the Acts of our fathers the pure apostles, who were invested with the grace of the Holy Spirit. May their blessing be with us all. Amen.

After the Stephen the Archdeacon was killed, many Christians left Jerusalem and travelled to Syria and Lebanon and Cyprus Mostly they preached about Jesus to other Jews, but some of them were very brave and preached to the Gentiles too (Gentiles are all those people who are not Jews - like us). And the Lord was with them. Heaps and heaps of people believed their words and became Christians! When the Church in Jerusalem heard about what was happening, they sent out a very good and holy man called Barnabas to help them and encourage them. He was so happy with all that he saw God doing there. Barnabas went to Tarsus and brought back St Paul with him, and together, they stayed with this new Church for a whole year. And in Antioch in Syria, they were the first ones to come up with the name "Christians". Now all of us are called Christians! Now, while they were there, a prophet called Agabus made a prediction: A great famine was coming on all the world—there wouldn't be enough food for people to eat! So the Christians all decided to get ready. But they also decided to help their poor brothers and sisters in Judea too. They weren't selfish! So they all made donations and gave them to Paul and Barnabas to take back to the elders in Jerusalem. (Chapter 11:19-30)

The word of the Lord shall grow, multiply, be mighty and be confirmed in the holy Church of God. Amen.

Holy Gospel

Stand up in the fear of God and listen to the Holy Gospel,A chapter from the Holy Gospel according to Saint Mark, May his blessings be with us all, Amen

From the psalms of our teacher David the prophet and king,May his blessings be with us all, Amen

> The heavens belong to You, and the earth is Yours; You founded the world and all its fullness. You created the north wind and the seas; Tabor and Hermon shall greatly rejoice in Your name. Your arm rules with power; Let Your hand be strengthened; let Your right hand be exalted Alleluia. -Psalm 89:11-12,13

Blessed is He who comes in the Name of the Lord Our Lord, God and Saviour and the King of us all, Jesus Christ, the Son of the living God. Glory be to You forever more, Amen

Now as He sat on the Mount of Olives opposite the temple, Peter, James, John, and Andrew asked Him privately, Tell us, when will these things be? And what will be the sign when all these things will be fulfilled? And Jesus, answering them, began to say: Take heed that no one deceives you. For many will come in My name, saying, 'I am He,' and will deceive many. But when you hear of wars and rumours of wars, do not be troubled; for such things must happen, but the end is not yet. For nation will rise against nation, and kingdom against kingdom. And there will be earthquakes in various places, and there will be famines and troubles. These are the beginnings of sorrows. And the gospel must first be preached to all the nations. Then if anyone says to you, 'Look, here is the Christ!' or, 'Look, He is there!' do not believe it. For false christs and false prophets will rise and show signs and wonders to deceive, if possible, even the elect. But take heed; see, I have told you all things beforehand. But in those days, after that tribulation, the sun will be darkened, and the moon will not give its light; the stars of heaven will fall, and the powers in the heavens will be shaken. Then they will see the Son of Man coming in the clouds with great power and glory. And then He will send His angels, and gather together His elect from the four winds, from the farthest part of earth to the farthest part of heaven. Heaven and earth will pass away, but My words will by no means pass away. Watch therefore, for you do not know when the master of the house is coming— in the evening, at midnight, at the crowing of the rooster, or in the morning— lest, coming suddenly, he find you sleeping. And what I say to you, I say to all: Watch! Mark 13:3-37

Glory be to God Forever, Amen

FIRST SUNDAY OF NASI

Holy Gospel

MATINS

Stand up in the fear of God and listen to the Holy Gospel, A chapter from the Holy Gospel according to Saint Mark, May his blessings be with us all, Amen

From the psalms of our teacher David the prophet and king, May his blessings be with us all, Amen

> But You, O Lord, shall endure forever, And the remembrance of Your name to all generations. I said, "O my God, Do not take me away in the midst of my days; Your years are throughout all generations. Alleluia. -Psalm 102:12,24

Blessed is He who comes in the Name of the Lord Our Lord, God and Saviour and the King of us all, Jesus Christ, the Son of the living God. Glory be to You forever more, Amen

"But of that day and hour no one knows, not even the angels in heaven, nor the Son, but only the Father. Take heed, watch and pray; for you do not know when the time is. It is like a man going to a far country, who left his house and gave authority to his servants, and to each his work, and commanded the doorkeeper to watch. Watch therefore, for you do not know when the master of the house is coming—in the evening, at midnight, at the crowing of the rooster, or in the morning— lest, coming suddenly, he find you sleeping. And what I say to you, I say to all: Watch!" Mark 13:32-37)

Pauline

Paul, the servant of our Lord Jesus Christ, called to be an apostle, appointed to the Gospel of God. A reading from the Second Epistle of our teacher Paul to Thessalonians. May his holy blessings be with us. Amen.

St Paul the Apostle was writing a letter to the Christians who lived in the big city called Thessalonica. Dear Thessalonian Today I want to tell you about the time when Jesus will come back to the world; when He will gather us all together with Him— what an exciting day that will be! But I have heard that some people are spreading a rumour that Jesus has already come back. Don't believe them! Before Jesus comes back, some other things have to happen first: Before Jesus comes, lots of people in the world will stop loving Jesus! Before Jesus comes, the Bad Man will try to trick people to pray to him as if he was God! This Bad Man is the exact opposite of Jesus Christ. He is the Antichrist. That means the opposite of Christ. Don't you remember that when I was with you I told you all this? But the right time has not yet come. For now, God is stopping the Antichrist from doing whatever he wants. But one day, God will let go, and then Satan, will give the Antichrist the power to do miracles and wonders and amazing things! And then anyone who doesn't love God will be tricked by the Antichrist's lies, and follow him. Because they love to do what is wrong, they will all be punished with the Antichrist. But don't worry, because after that, God will destroy our enemy, the Antichrist as easily as blowing away a dandelion! So I say "Thank You God!" because from the beginning you have believed in Jesus and you have loved doing good. So be strong! Be steady! Hold on to the traditions and everything I taught you about God. Now, may our Lord Jesus Christ Himself, and His Heavenly Father, comfort your heart and help you to do and to say everything that is good, because, do you know what? He loves us!   (2 Thessalonians 2:1-17)

Bye for now!

Signed, Paul

The grace of God the Father be with you all, Amen.

Catholicon

The Catholic Epistle from the Second Epistle of our teacher St Peter. May his holy blessings be with us. Amen.

From Peter, Hello my beloved friends! I want to remind you about some very important things that will happen at the end of the world. Before the end, people will make fun of us and say things like, "Where is your Jesus? How come He hasn't come back yet? "See," they will say, "the world goes on like it always has; nothing changes. I bet He's never going to come back!" But they forget that God is in control of the whole world. In Noah's time, He flooded the whole world by His power, and all the evil men who made fun of Him suddenly died. Time is nothing to God. For God, one day is like a thousand years, and a thousand years are like one day! So Jesus has not forgotten to come back to the world! He wants to give everyone a chance to come back to Him and be good. Then, He will come back, all of a sudden! And this whole world will be quickly taken away. And He will make a new Heaven and a new Earth for those who are ready to meet Him. So if God is going to take away this world, don't you think we should try to be ready for Him when He comes? How can we get ready? Being ready means being good like God in everything we do. Being ready means not fighting with others. Being ready means being a peaceful person. Remember, God is being patient so we can have enough time to get ready. So start getting ready!!! My friend Paul has also written to you about the end of the world, Although his letters are a bit hard to understand sometimes, and some naughty people tried to use them to confuse you. So, I am making sure that you are not confused, so that no one can trick you: Keep doing what is right and good! No one knows when our Lord Jesus will come back to us. So always be ready. Keep growing in God's grace. Keep knowing Him better. Keep praising Him with joy. Glory be to Him, now and forever, amen. (2 Peter 3:1-18)

Bye for now!

Signed,   Peter the Apostle

Do not love the world, nor the things which are in the world. The world shall pass away and all its desires; but he who does the will of God shall abide forever. Amen.

The Acts

A reading from the Acts of our fathers the pure apostles, who were invested with the grace of the Holy Spirit. May their blessing be with us all. Amen.

The Disciples of Jesus had just been filled by the Holy Spirit. He appeared on their heads like tongues of fire! He made them so brave. St Peter heard the people gathering outside to see what all the fuss was about, so he went outside to tell them. And this is what he said: "In olden days, Joel the prophet delivered the words of God. This is what Joel said: "In the last days, at the end, God will pour out His Spirit on all. Your sons and daughters will speak God's words "Your young men shall see beautiful visions And your old men shall have beautiful dreams. "God will show signs and miracles of blood and fire and smoke, in the sky above and on the earth below. "The sun will turn dark. The moon will turn the colour of blood. "And then, the awesome Day of the coming of the Lord will be here. And whoever prays to God will be saved!" (Chapter 2:14-21)

The word of the Lord shall grow, multiply, be mighty and be confirmed in the holy Church of God. Amen.

Holy Gospel

Stand up in the fear of God and listen to the Holy Gospel, A chapter from the Holy Gospel according to Saint Matthew, May his blessings be with us all, Amen

From the psalms of our teacher David the prophet and king, May his blessings be with us all, Amen

> Your years are throughout all generations. In the beginning, O Lord,
> You founded the earth, And the heavens are the works of Your hands.
> They shall perish, but You shall remain Alleluia. -Psalm 102:24-26

Blessed is He who comes in the Name of the Lord Our Lord, God and Saviour and the King of us all, Jesus Christ, the Son of the living God. Glory be to You forever more, Amen

Now as He sat on the Mount of Olives, the disciples came to Him privately, saying, Tell us, when will these things be? And what will be the sign of Your coming, and of the end of the age? And Jesus answered and said to them: Take heed that no one deceives you. For many will come in My name, saying, `I am the Christ,' and will deceive many And then many will be offended, will betray one another, and will hate one another. And because lawlessness will abound, the love of many will grow cold. But he who endures to the end shall be saved. And this gospel of the kingdom will be preached in all the world as a witness to all the nations, and then the end will come. For then there will be great tribulation, such as has not been since the beginning of the world until this time, no, nor ever shall be. And unless those days were shortened, no flesh would be saved; but for the elect's sake those days will be shortened. Then if anyone says to you, `Look, here is the Christ!' or `There!' do not believe it. For false christs and false prophets will rise and show great signs and wonders to deceive, if possible, even the elect. See, I have told you beforehand. Therefore if they say to you, `Look, He is in the desert!' do not go out; or `Look, He is in the inner rooms!' do not believe it. For as the lightning comes from the east and flashes to the west, so also will the coming of the Son of Man be. For wherever the carcass is, there the eagles will be gathered together. Immediately after the tribulation of those days the sun will be darkened, and the moon will not give its light; the stars will fall from heaven, and the powers of the heavens will be shaken. Then the sign of the Son of Man will appear in heaven, and then all the tribes of the earth will mourn, and they will see the Son of Man coming on the clouds of heaven with power and great glory. And He will send His angels with a great sound of a trumpet, and they will gather together His elect from the four winds, from one end of heaven to the other. So you also, when you see all these things, know that it is near— at the doors! Assuredly, I say to you, this generation will by no means pass away till all these things take place. Heaven and earth will pass away, but My words will by no means pass away Matthew 24:3-35

Glory be to God Forever, Amen

FIFITH SUNDAY

Holy Gospel

Stand up in the fear of God and listen to the Holy Gospel, A chapter from the Holy Gospel according to Saint Mark, May his blessings be with us all, Amen

From the psalms of our teacher David the prophet and king, May his blessings be with us all, Amen

> Light is sown for the righteous, And gladness for the upright in heart. Rejoice in the Lord, you righteous, And give thanks at the remembrance of His holy name. Alleluia. -Psalm 97:11-12

Blessed is He who comes in the Name of the Lord Our Lord, God and Saviour and the King of us all, Jesus Christ, the Son of the living God. Glory be to You forever more, Amen

When the day was now far spent, His disciples came to Him and said, "This is a deserted place, and already the hour is late. Send them away, that they may go into the surrounding country and villages and buy themselves bread; for they have nothing to eat." But He answered and said to them, "You give them something to eat." And they said to Him, "Shall we go and buy two hundred denarii worth of bread and give them something to eat?" But He said to them, "How many loaves do you have? Go and see." And when they found out they said, "Five, and two fish."

Then He commanded them to make them all sit down in groups on the green grass. So they sat down in ranks, in hundreds and in fifties. And when He had taken the five loaves and the two fish, He looked up to heaven, blessed and broke the loaves, and gave them to His disciples to set before them; and the two fish He divided among them all. So they all ate and were filled. And they took up twelve baskets full of fragments and of the fish. Now those who had eaten the loaves were about five thousand men. Mark 6:35-44

Glory be to God Forever, Amen

Pauline

Paul, the servant of our Lord Jesus Christ, called to be an apostle, appointed to the Gospel of God. A reading from the First Epistle of our teacher Paul to Corinthians. May his holy blessings be with us. Amen.

St Paul the Apostle was writing a letter to the Christians who lived in the rich city of Corinth. Dear Corinthians, You know how God gives some people the special gift of being able to pray in different languages? Well, God has given me that gift, more than anyone! But we all have to use these gifts very carefully and wisely. Even though I can pray in different languages, when I am in the Church, I would rather speak 5 words we all understand, instead of 10,000 words that no one understands! My brothers and sisters, be innocent like children, but also be wise and understanding. In the Bible God says,"I will speak to people in languages, but they will not hear me." So languages are meant to help those who are not Christian to come to God, not for those who are already Christians. If people are all praying with different languages in the Church, and a non-Christian walks in, won't they think you are crazy? But if everyone is speaking the Truth of God in a language you do understand, and a non-Christian walks in, that non-Christian's heart will be touched, and he will begin to understand, and to worship God, and know that God is truly with you. Wouldn't that be much better? (1 Corinthians 14:18–25)

Bye for now!

Signed, Paul

The grace of God the Father be with you all, Amen.

Catholicon

The Catholic Epistle from the Epistle of our teacher St James. May his holy blessings be with us. Amen.

Hello Everyone! I have some more very important advice for you. You who are rich— I feel so sorry for you! You should cry and weep for yourselves too! Do you know why? Because you thought your gold and your silver were going to protect you. But when Jesus comes, your money isn't going to do you any good at all! In fact, because you got your money by cheating and stealing and lying. Because you were selfish and didn't share your riches with anyone else. Boy, are you going to be in BIG trouble, on that Last Day, when Jesus comes back! So, my brothers and sisters, all of us should get ready for the coming of the Lord. You know how farmers sow their seeds, then they wait for the early rain. And then they wait the late rain. They are very patient, waiting and waiting, but always ready to gather the precious fruit as soon as it is ready. So we also should be patient and always ready, until Jesus comes. Be strong, for the Lord is near. (James 5:1–8)

Bye for now!

Signed, James the Apostle

Do not love the world, nor the things which are in the world. The world shall pass away and all its desires; but he who does the will of God shall abide forever. Amen.

The Acts

A reading from the Acts of our fathers the pure apostles, who were invested with the grace of the Holy Spirit. May their blessing be with us all. Amen.

St Paul the Apostle was in jail again! People were accusing him of being a trouble-maker. Ananias, the Jewish High Priest, got his clever friend, Tertullus [Ter-too-luss] to make a big speech to the Governor against Paul. This is what Tertullus said: "Oh noble and great Governor Felix, you are truly the best! You have kept us all safe and happy. What a great Governor you are! But I don't want to waste your time, so let's get down to business. This fellow, Paul is, to be frank, a big pest. He makes Jews argue with each other. He is one of the ringleaders of those pesky Christians. He was even going to not respect our Temple! We wanted to teach him the lesson he deserves! But your Roman soldiers stopped us and took him away, and told us we have to explain the whole thing to you, O wise, noble, clever Governor." And the other Jews also agreed with what Tertullus said. What did Governor Felix do next? You'll have to read that at home in your Bible! (Chapter 24:1–9)

The word of the Lord shall grow, multiply, be mighty and be confirmed in the holy Church of God. Amen.

Holy Gospel

Stand up in the fear of God and listen to the Holy Gospel,A chapter from the Holy Gospel according to Saint Luke, May his blessings be with us all, Amen

From the psalms of our teacher David the prophet and king,May his blessings be with us all, Amen

> I spread out my hands to You; My soul thirsts for You like a waterless land. Hear me speedily, O Lord; My spirit faints within me Alleluia. -Psalm 142:6–7

Blessed is He who comes in the Name of the Lord Our Lord, God and Saviour and the King of us all, Jesus Christ, the Son of the living God. Glory be to You forever more, Amen

When the day began to wear away, the twelve came and said to Him, "Send the multitude away, that they may go into the surrounding towns and country, and lodge and get provisions; for we are in a deserted place here." But He said to them, "You give them something to eat." And they said, "We have no more than five loaves and two fish, unless we go and buy food for all these people." For there were about five thousand men. Then He said to His disciples, "Make them sit down in groups of fifty." And they did so, and made them all sit down. Then He took the five loaves and the two fish, and looking up to heaven, He blessed and broke them, and gave them to the disciples to set before the multitude. So they all ate and were filled, and twelve baskets of the leftover fragments were taken up by them. Luke 9:12–17

Glory be to God Forever, Amen

FEATS OF THE LORD

Holy Gospel

MATINS

Stand up in the fear of God and listen to the Holy Gospel, A chapter from the Holy Gospel according to Saint Mark, May his blessings be with us all, Amen

From the psalms of our teacher David the prophet and king, May his blessings be with us all, Amen

> Oh, sing to the Lord a new song! For He has done marvelous things; His right hand and His holy arm have gained Him the victory -Psalm 98:1

Blessed is He who comes in the Name of the Lord Our Lord, God and Saviour and the King of us all, Jesus Christ, the Son of the living God. Glory be to You forever more, Amen

The disciples of John and of the Pharisees were fasting. Then they came and said to Him, "Why do the disciples of John and of the Pharisees fast, but Your disciples do not fast?" And Jesus said to them, "Can the friends of the bridegroom fast while the bridegroom is with them? As long as they have the bridegroom with them they cannot fast. But the days will come when the bridegroom will be taken away from them, and then they will fast in those days. No one sews a piece of unshrunk cloth on an old garment; or else the new piece pulls away from the old, and the tear is made worse. And no one puts new wine into old wineskins; or else the new wine bursts the wineskins, the wine is spilled, and the wineskins are ruined. But new wine must be put into new wineskins." Mark 2: 18-22

Glory be to God Forever, Amen

Pauline LITURGY

St Paul the Apostle was writing a letter to the Christians who lived in the rich city of Corinth.

Dear Corinthians, I want to tell you something very important indeed about Jesus. Jesus died for us! So we should all live for Jesus! Then, we will also rise with Jesus! When Jesus rose, He made the whole world new. And that includes you and me. In Jesus, we are a new creation In olden times, God comforted His people. He said to them "Do not worry! It is time for Me to hear you and to help you. This is the day I will save you." And guess what? Those words are for us too! This is the day that God will save us! My friends and I have tried to serve you the best we can. But it has not been easy. We have had to be really patient through all kinds of troubles. Sometimes, bad people hit us, or put us in jail without a reason. But we continued to have pure hearts, to be patient and kind, and to love them. God is our strength. He is like a suit of armour that protects us from any evil or danger. Because He is with us, we are not worried by anything. When people say bad things about us, we don't care. They say we are liars, yet all our words are true! They say no one knows us, but you (and others) listen to us! They say they will kill us, yet here we still are! They say we are sad, yet look at how happy Jesus makes us! They say we are poor, yet we have made lots of people rich because we gave them Jesus! They say we have nothing, yet all the world belongs to our Lord Jesus! Oh, people of Corinth— we have been really open and honest with you! We haven't tried to tie you up with too many rules. Now, do you think you can be open and honest with us? (2 Corinthians 5:11–6:13)

Bye for now!

Signed, Paul

Catholicon

The Catholic Epistle from the First Epistle of our teacher St John. May his holy blessings be with us. Amen.

From John to my beloved brothers and sisters, do you remember the most important commandment God has given us? The most important commandment, from long ago, and forevermore, is LOVE! We must love God, and love one another. That is what Jesus taught us. If you don't love other people, you are like a person who lives in darkness. You will always stumble and fall. But if you love other people, you are like a person who lives in the light. You will never stumble or fall! The light of Jesus is much stronger than the darkness. I wanted to write these things to you, O little children Because God has forgiven your sins. I wanted to write these things to you, O parents Because you have known God very well. I wanted to write these things to you, O young people Because you have beaten the devil. I wanted to write these things to you, O little children Because you are friends with the Father. I wanted to write these things to you, O parents Because you are friends with God. I wanted to write these things to you, O young people Because you are strong, and God's word lives in you, and you have beaten the devil. If you are selfish, and just love the things in the world, you won't be able to truly love God. God teaches us to NOT be selfish. So we don't really care that much about those selfish things everyone else goes crazy about. This world is going to end one day. But our love for God is forever! (1 John 2:7–17)

Bye for now!

Signed, John the Beloved

Do not love the world, nor the things which are in the world. The world shall pass away and all its desires; but he who does the will of God shall abide forever. Amen

The Acts

St Paul was waiting for his friends from overseas to join him in the great city of Athens, the capital of the country called Greece. While he was there he would go down to the marketplace of Athens and talk to whomever he might find there. Some were Jews, like him. Some were Greeks. The Greeks worshipped their own gods in their own temples, with statues. But some of them were really curious about the things that Paul was saying. So they invited Paul to a public place called the Areopagus [aer-ee-oh-pay-guss] for a discussion. They loved talking about new ideas! This is what Paul said to them: "Men of Athens! I noticed you have many altars to all your gods. But one of them caught my eye. On this altar is written: To the Unknown God. Let me tell you about the real God you don't know yet. The real God is the One who made the whole world and everything in it. Including all of us, wherever we come from! We are all His children. So we should all look for Him, try to know Him better. But actually, He is not very far from us at all. Your own poets said: "In Him we live, and move, and have our being." He is all around us! God is not made of gold or silver, like your statues. He is bigger than the whole world, and He loves us all. Don't you want to love Him back? Don't you want to stop all your sins? One day, we will rise from the dead like Jesus, and Jesus will come back and judge the whole world." Some of the Greeks laughed at Paul. But some of them believed what he told them, including Dionysius the Areopagite and a lady called Damaris. (Chapter 17:16–34)

Holy Gospel

Stand up in the fear of God and listen to the Holy Gospel,A chapter from the Holy Gospel according to Saint Luke, May his blessings be with us all, Amen

From the psalms of our teacher David the prophet and king,May his blessings be with us all, Amen

> You will bless the crown of the year with Your goodness, And Your fields will be filled with fatness .. Sing aloud to God our strength; Make a joyful shout to the God of Jacob. Alleluia. Psalm 65:11 & 81:1

Blessed is He who comes in the Name of the Lord Our Lord, God and Saviour and the King of us all, Jesus Christ, the Son of the living God. Glory be to You forever more, Amen

Then Jesus returned in the power of the Spirit to Galilee, and news of Him went out through all the surrounding region. And He taught in their synagogues, being glorified by all. So He came to Nazareth, where He had been brought up. And as His custom was, He went into the synagogue on the Sabbath day, and stood up to read. "The Spirit of the Lord is upon Me, Because He has anointed Me To preach the gospel to the poor; He has sent Me to heal the brokenhearted " To proclaim liberty to the captives And recovery of sight to the blind, To set at liberty those who are oppressed; To proclaim the acceptable year of the Lord." Then He closed the book, and gave it back to the attendant and sat down. And the eyes of all who were in the synagogue were fixed on Him. And He began to say to them, "Today this Scripture is fulfilled in your hearing." So all bore witness to Him, and marvelled at the gracious words which proceeded out of His mouth. And they said, "Is this not Joseph's son?" He said to them, "You will surely say this proverb to Me, 'Physician, heal yourself! Whatever we have heard done in Capernaum, do also here in Your country.' "Then He said, "Assuredly, I say to you, no prophet is accepted in his own country. "But I tell you truly, many widows were in Israel in the days of Elijah, when the heaven was shut up three years and six months, and there was a great famine throughout all the land; but to none of them was Elijah sent except to Zarephath and many lepers were in Israel in the time of Elisha the prophet, and none of them was cleansed except Naaman the Syrian." So all those in the synagogue, when they heard these things, were filled with wrath, and rose up and thrust Him out of the city; and they led Him to the brow of the hill on which their city was built, that they might throw Him down over the cliff. Then passing through the midst of them, He went His way. Luke Luke 4:14–30

Glory be to God Forever, Amen

FIRST DAY OF THE FEAST OF THE CROSS

Holy Gospel

MATINS

Stand up in the fear of God and listen to the Holy Gospel, A chapter from the Holy Gospel according to Saint John, May his blessings be with us all, Amen

From the psalms of our teacher David the prophet and king, May his blessings be with us all, Amen

> You have given a banner to those who fear You, That it may be displayed because of the truth. Selah That Your beloved may be delivered, Save with Your right hand, and hear me. Alleluia. Psalm 60:4-5

Blessed is He who comes in the Name of the Lord Our Lord, God and Saviour and the King of us all, Jesus Christ, the Son of the living God. Glory be to You forever more, Amen

If anyone serves Me, let him follow Me; and where I am, there My servant will be also. If anyone serves Me, him My Father will honor. "Now My soul is troubled, and what shall I say? 'Father, save Me from this hour'? But for this purpose I came to this hour. Father, glorify Your name." Then a voice came from heaven, saying, "I have both glorified it and will glorify it again." Therefore the people who stood by and heard it said that it had thundered. Others said, "An angel has spoken to Him." Jesus answered and said, "This voice did not come because of Me, but for your sake. Now is the judgment of this world; now the ruler of this world will be cast out. And I, if I am lifted up from the earth, will draw all peoples to Myself." This He said, signifying by what death He would die. The people answered Him, "We have heard from the law that the Christ remains forever; and how can You say, 'The Son of Man must be lifted up'? Who is this Son of Man?" Then Jesus said to them, "A little while longer the light is with you. Walk while you have the light, lest darkness overtake you; he who walks in darkness does not know where he is going. While you have the light, believe in the light, that you may become sons of light." These things Jesus spoke, and departed, and was hidden from them. John 12:26-36

Glory be to God Forever, Amen

Pauline

Paul, the servant of our Lord Jesus Christ, called to be an apostle, appointed to the Gospel of God. A reading from First Epistle of our teacher Paul to the Corinthians. May his holy blessings be with us. Amen.

St Paul the Apostle was writing a letter to the Christians who lived in the rich city of Corinth.

Dear Corinthians, Jesus Christ our Lord died on the Cross because He loves us. That's how Jesus saved us, and saved the whole wide world. We depend on Jesus. But some people don't depend on Jesus and His Cross. Instead, some people depend on their OWN cleverness! They think Jesus wasn't very clever, because He let people kill Him on the Cross. But Jesus was being much more clever than they can realise! Because when Jesus died on the Cross, He knew He would rise again! And Jesus knew He would save the world! That is VERY clever indeed! That's How God works. He doesn't need to prove Himself to anyone. God does things that don't SEEM very clever; but they are very, very clever! God works through people who don't SEEM very strong; but they are very, very strong! God works through people who don't SEEM very important; But they are very, very important! That way, no one can show off and say, "Look at me! I am so clever! I am so strong! I am so important!" So, we should never show off like that. We can only be clever, and strong, and important because God helps us, through His Son, Jesus Christ. Jesus is the One who makes us clever. Jesus is the One who makes us good. Jesus is the One who saves us. Jesus is the One who deserves all the credit! (1 Corinthians 1:17–31)

Bye for now!

Signed, Paul

> *The grace of God the Father be with you all, Amen.*

Catholicon

The Catholic Epistle from the First Epistle of our teacher St Peter. May his holy blessings be with us. Amen.

Hello Everyone! Sometimes, you might meet someone who doesn't like you very much. But you might make them your friend just by being kind to them. When you are a Christian, you are free! But that doesn't mean free to be naughty! It means you are free to be kind, and helpful, and happy and to serve God. So, Treat everyone with respect. Love your friends. Listen to God. Follow the law. If you have a master (like your teacher, for example, or your parents) you must do what they tell you to, even if you think they are being a bit too strict. Let me tell you why: Sometimes, when you really have done something wrong, you get in trouble, Well that's OK, Then, it's fair for you to get in trouble! You should take the punishment that you deserve. But sometimes, you get in trouble when you haven't really done anything wrong. Should you just "take it" then? That's exactly what happened to Jesus! He NEVER did anything wrong, but they arrested Him and said He did things that weren't true. And even though He was innocent, He never talked back to the rulers or the soldiers. He never got angry with them. He never argued with them. He put up with all that horrible stuff they did to Him, and trusted in His Father to look after Him. Do you know why? Because He wanted to save us from OUR sins. That's right, He died the death WE were going to die, when He died for us on the Cross so that we could live. We were like sheep who had gone astray and gotten lost, and He is our Good Shepherd, who gave His life to save His sheep. So if you truly love Jesus,   be like Him: Be obedient to the people that God gave you, to look after you. (1 Peter 2:11–25)

Bye for now!

Signed,   Peter the Apostle

Do not love the world, nor the things which are in the world. The world shall pass away and all its desires; but he who does the will of God shall abide forever. Amen.

The Acts

A reading from the Acts of our fathers the pure apostles, who were invested with the grace of the Holy Spirit. May their blessing be with us all. Amen.

God had sent St Peter the Apostle to talk to a very kind Roman soldier, a centurion, whose name was Cornelius. Peter said: Wow! God really does love EVERYONE in the world! God doesn't just like Jewish people. He loves everyone! It doesn't matter where you live. It doesn't matter who you are. If you love God, God accepts you. So, it doesn't matter that you're not Jewish, Cornelius. You are a good man. God loves you! God accepts you! It seems, Cornelius, that you have heard what is being said about Jesus of Nazareth. How he was baptised by John the Baptist, and how the Holy Spirit appeared above Him, and how He helped people, and healed them. We saw all this with our own eyes! And we saw how they crucified Him on the Cross, and we saw Him when He came back to life again on the third day! He even ate and drank with us, after he rose from the dead! He told us that we must preach about Him— we must tell everyone that Jesus is the Lord of all the world, the living and the dead. As the old prophets said, whoever believes in Him will have their sins forgiven. (Chapter 10:34–43)

The word of the Lord shall grow, multiply, be mighty and be confirmed in the holy Church of God. Amen.

Holy Gospel

Stand up in the fear of God and listen to the Holy Gospel, A chapter from the Holy Gospel according to Saint John, May his blessings be with us all, Amen

From the psalms of our teacher David the prophet and king, May his blessings be with us all, Amen

> It is fitting to sing a hymn to You in Zion, O God, And a vow shall be rendered to You in Jerusalem. Hear my prayer; To You all flesh shall come. Alleluia. Psalm 65:1–2

Blessed is He who comes in the Name of the Lord Our Lord, God and Saviour and the King of us all, Jesus Christ, the Son of the living God. Glory be to You forever more, Amen

Now it was the Feast of Dedication in Jerusalem, and it was winter. And Jesus walked in the temple, in Solomon's porch. Then the Jews surrounded Him and said to Him, "How long do You keep us in doubt? If You are the Christ, tell us plainly." Jesus answered them, "I told you, and you do not believe. The works that I do in My Father's name, they bear witness of Me. "But you do not believe, because you are not of My sheep, as I said to you. My sheep hear My voice, and I know them, and they follow Me. "And I give them eternal life, and they shall never perish; neither shall anyone snatch them out of My hand. "My Father, who has given them to Me, is greater than all; and no one is able to snatch them out of My Father's hand. "I and My Father are one." Then the Jews took up stones again to stone Him. Jesus answered them, "Many good works I have shown you from My Father. For which of those works do you stone Me?" The Jews answered Him, saying, "For a good work we do not stone You, but for blasphemy, and because You, being a Man, make Yourself God." Jesus answered them, "Is it not written in your law, 'I said, "You are gods" '? "If He called them gods, to whom the word of God came (and the Scripture cannot be broken), "do you say of Him whom the Father sanctified and sent into the world, 'You are blaspheming,' because I said, 'I am the Son of God'? "If I do not do the works of My Father, do not believe Me; but if I do, though you do not believe Me, believe the works, "that you may know and believe that the Father is in Me, and I in Him." John 10:22–38

Glory be to God Forever, Amen

SECOND DAY OF THE FEAST OF CROSS

Holy Gospel

Stand up in the fear of God and listen to the Holy Gospel, A chapter from the Holy Gospel according to Saint John, May his blessings be with us all, Amen

From the psalms of our teacher David the prophet and king, May his blessings be with us all, Amen

> You are my God, and I will praise You; You are my God, I will exalt You. The right hand of the Lord is exalted; The right hand of the Lord does valiantly.   Alleluia. Psalm 118: 28,16

Blessed is He who comes in the Name of the Lord Our Lord, God and Saviour and the King of us all, Jesus Christ, the Son of the living God. Glory be to You forever more, Amen

And as Moses lifted up the serpent in the wilderness, even so must the Son of Man be lifted up, that whoever believes in Him should not perish but have eternal life. For God so loved the world that He gave His only begotten Son, that whoever believes in Him should not perish but have everlasting life. For God did not send His Son into the world to condemn the world, but that the world through Him might be saved.

"He who believes in Him is not condemned; but he who does not believe is condemned already, because he has not believed in the name of the only begotten Son of God. And this is the condemnation, that the light has come into the world, and men loved darkness rather than light, because their deeds were evil. For everyone practicing evil hates the light and does not come to the light, lest his deeds should be exposed. But he who does the truth comes to the light, that his deeds may be clearly seen, that they have been done in God." John 4: 14-21

Glory be to God Forever, Amen

Pauline

Paul, the servant of our Lord Jesus Christ, called to be an apostle, appointed to the Gospel of God. A reading from the Epistle of our teacher Paul to Galatians. May his holy blessings be with us. Amen.

St Paul the Apostle was writing a letter to the Christians who lived in the land of Galatia. Dear Galatians, See what a long letter I have written to you? I want to make sure you follow Jesus properly. Some people want you to be circumcised, just like a Jewish person, so that the Jews don't give us Christians a hard time. But they don't get it. They want to boast about belonging to God's people. But they don't even obey God's laws themselves! But God forbid that I should boast except in the Cross of our Lord Jesus Christ, by whom the world has been crucified to me, and I to the world. God doesn't care if I have a mark on my body or not. What matters is that He makes me new on the INSIDE. Those who are new on the INSIDE always walk in God's peace and mercy. They are the REAL Israel, the real chosen people of God. From now on, don't give me a hard time. My wounded body shows you how much I have suffered for my Lord Jesus. My brothers and sisters, the grace of our Lord Jesus Christ be with your spirit, Amen.   (Galatians 6:11–18)

Bye for now!

Signed, Paul

> *The grace of God the Father be with you all, Amen.*

Catholicon

The Catholic Epistle from the First Epistle of our teacher St Peter. May his holy blessings be with us. Amen.

My little children, This is the Apostle Peter writing to all of you who love God and who are the special children of God the Father, made holy by the Holy Spirit, and washed clean by the Blood of Jesus Christ. We have a lot to thank God for— He gave us hope when Jesus rose from the dead. He opened the way for us to go to

Heaven and to live there forever and ever and ever. His power protects us all our lives, Even when things go a bit wrong for us. Now I've heard that you have been having a hard time lately. I have heard that some evil people are attacking you because you are Christian. Don't be sad about this but Be HAPPY! All these attacks will only make your faith stronger, just like gold is made stronger by being heated in the flames of fire. Even though you have never met Jesus yourselves, you have believed in Him. And this has given you so much JOY! Because the prophets from olden times really wanted to see the Saviour—but they couldn't and the Angels really wanted to know about the Saviour—but they couldn't! But now, we get to know Him, because we have heard the Gospel, the story of Jesus Christ.   (1 Peter 1:3-12)

Bye for now!

Signed, Peter the Apostle

Do not love the world, nor the things which are in the world. The world shall pass away and all its desires; but he who does the will of God shall abide forever. Amen.

The Acts

A reading from the Acts of our fathers the pure apostles, who were invested with the grace of the Holy Spirit. May their blessing be with us all. Amen.

St Peter and St John had healed a poor lame man and made him able to walk normally again. You would think everyone would be thrilled! But some people were certainly NOT thrilled. The Jewish High Priest and the rulers of the Temple arrested Peter and John, and they put them on trial. Here's what Peter said: Why are you judging us for healing a sick man? Do you want to know how we made him well? I will tell you—listen very carefully now! We healed the sick man by the Name of Jesus Christ. That's right, Jesus is the One that you crucified on the cross! But Jesus rose from the dead! And Jesus made this man well! You rejected Him, but He is the only way that all of us can be saved. The High Priest and the rulers suddenly recognised that these were Disciples of Jesus. But there was the healed man standing in front of everyone. What could they say? What could they do? They had to let Peter and John go. They had done nothing wrong, after all. But then the High Priest and the rulers had a big meeting. "These men are working miracles, and everyone has seen them. But we have to stop them! What can we do?" So they called Peter and John back, and they told them: "Now listen here. You had better stop talking about this Jesus of yours. "If you don't stop, you will be in BIG trouble! Got it?!?" But do you think Peter and John stopped talking about Jesus? (Chapter 4:8–18)

The word of the Lord shall grow, multiply, be mighty and be confirmed in the holy Church of God. Amen.

Holy Gospel

Stand up in the fear of God and listen to the Holy Gospel, A chapter from the Holy Gospel according to Saint John, May his blessings be with us all, Amen

From the psalms of our teacher David the prophet and king, May his blessings be with us all, Amen

> I shall exalt You, my God and my King, And I shall bless Your name forever and unto ages of ages. Every day I shall bless You And praise Your name forever and unto ages of ages. Alleluia. -Psalm 145:1–2

Blessed is He who comes in the Name of the Lord Our Lord, God and Saviour and the King of us all, Jesus Christ, the Son of the living God. Glory be to You forever more, Amen

And Jesus said to them, "I am the bread of life. He who comes to Me shall never hunger, and he who believes in Me shall never thirst. But I said to you that you have seen Me and yet do not believe. All that the Father gives Me will come to Me, and the one who comes to Me I will by no means cast out. For I have come down from heaven, not to do My own will, but the will of Him who sent Me. This is the will of the Father who sent Me, that of all He has given Me I should lose nothing, but should raise it up at the last day. And this is the will of Him who sent Me, that everyone who sees the Son and believes in Him may have everlasting life; and I will raise him up at the last day." The Jews then complained about Him, because He said, "I am the bread which came down from heaven." And they said, "Is not this Jesus, the son of Joseph, whose father and mother we know? How is it then that He says, 'I have come down from heaven'?" Jesus therefore answered and said to them, "Do not murmur among yourselves, no one can come to Me unless the Father who sent Me draws him; and I will raise him up at the last day. It is written in the prophets, 'And they shall all be taught by God.' Therefore everyone who has heard and learned from the Father comes to Me. Not that anyone has seen the Father, except He who is from God; He has seen the Father. John 6:35–46

Glory be to God Forever, Amen

THIRD DAY OF THE FEAST OF CROSS

Holy Gospel MATINS

Stand up in the fear of God and listen to the Holy Gospel, A chapter from the Holy Gospel according to Saint Mark, May his blessings be with us all, Amen

From the psalms of our teacher David the prophet and king, May his blessings be with us all, Amen

> Remember Your congregation, which You have purchased of old, The tribe of Your inheritance, which You have redeemed— This Mount Zion where You have dwelt. For God is my King from of old, Working salvation in the midst of the earth. Alleluia. -Psalm 74:2,12

Blessed is He who comes in the Name of the Lord Our Lord, God and Saviour and the King of us all, Jesus Christ, the Son of the living God. Glory be to You forever more, Amen

When He had called the people to Himself, with His disciples also, He said to them, "Whoever desires to come after Me, let him deny himself, and take up his cross, and follow Me. For whoever desires to save his life will lose it, but whoever loses his life for My sake and the gospel's will save it. For what will it profit a man if he gains the whole world, and loses his own soul? Or what will a man give in exchange for his soul? For whoever is ashamed of Me and My words in this adulterous and sinful generation, of him the Son of Man also will be ashamed when He comes in the glory of His Father with the holy angels." And He said to them, "Assuredly, I say to you that there are some standing here who will not taste death till they see the kingdom of God present with power." Mark 8:34-9:1

Glory be to God Forever, Amen

Pauline

Paul, the servant of our Lord Jesus Christ, called to be an apostle, appointed to the Gospel of God. A reading from the Epistle of our teacher Paul to Colossians. May his holy blessings be with us. Amen.

St Paul the Apostle was writing a letter to the Christians who lived in the old city called Colossae.

Dear Colossians,

We should build our lives on Jesus Christ, our Lord, and always be thankful that we get to know Jesus. Don't try to be too clever about everything! Don't let people trick you by saying things that sound good, but really, they are not true at all. Our Lord, Jesus Christ is the Truth. In Him, in His Body, that is where we can find God. Jesus is the one who helps us to become exactly what we should be. He buried us with Him when we were baptised in the water of baptism and then He lifted us up again, to start a new life with Him; just like He died on the Cross, then rose again from the dead. Even though we were guilty because of all the wrong things we've done, Jesus saved us, and took away our guilt and our punishment. On the Cross, Jesus killed evil itself! He beat the devil and all his armies! And He beat the evil that was inside us too! So please don't get all caught up in things that don't really matter so much. Don't listen to people who tell you that exactly what food you eat, or exactly which day you celebrate, is what will make you a really good person. These things are just like shadows. But Jesus is the Real Thing Hold onto Jesus! That's what makes you a really good person! Jesus is like the Head of the Body. And you and I are the rest of the Body. So, let's listen to our Head! (Colossians 2:6–19)

Bye for now!

Signed, Paul

The grace of God the Father be with you all, Amen.

Catholicon

The Catholic Epistle from the First Epistle of our teacher St John. May his holy blessings be with us. Amen.

From John,

My beloved brothers and sisters, did you know that you and I share a very special secret? But it's the kind of secret that God wants us to tell everybody about! And here it is, are you ready? God has given us eternal life! That means that we can live forever with Him in Heaven! So if you know about Jesus; And believe in Him; And love Him; And if Jesus lives inside you, You will get to live forever with Jesus in Heaven! So keep believing in Jesus. Keep loving Him more and more. Because He gives us more and more. Jesus hears every word we say to Him when we pray. Jesus answers our prayers. Especially when we pray for a brother or sister who is doing something wrong. They really need someone to pray for them! So they can stop being naughty! When you really love God, you just don't want to do anything wrong. And even though the devil might trick the whole world to do the wrong thing he can never trick us — if we really, really love God. For God is true And Jesus is true And He protects us every day of our lives. (1 John 5:13–21)

God loves you!

Signed, John the Beloved

Do not love the world, nor the things which are in the world. The world shall pass away and all its desires; but he who does the will of God shall abide forever. Amen.

The Acts

Two of the Apostles, St Peter and St John, had just healed a man who couldn't walk. They prayed for him, and all of a sudden—He got up and walked! Wow! What an amazing miracle! All the people who saw it couldn't believe their eyes! How on earth could anyone do something like that? So Peter began to explain.

Peter said: "Hey, do you think that John and I have the power to heal a man like that? Of course not! It was God who healed him. "The same God who healed this man, is the God who sent His Son, Jesus Christ into the world to teach us, and to heal us. Jesus is the Prince of Life, who came to give us life. "But what did you do to Jesus? Did you love Him and follow Him? No! You had Jesus killed! What an awful thing to do! "But hey, I know that you didn't really know what you were doing. I know you didn't really understand what a terrible thing it was that you did. "But now, you can see how loving and kind and strong Jesus is. Don't you think it is time for you to say sorry for killing Jesus, and start to follow Jesus, so that He can heal you too? "After all, it is Jesus that your own prophets spoke about in the Bible. And it is Jesus who went up to heaven, until He comes back to make everything right again. "Why not just say, 'sorry'? Jesus loves you, and He wants to be your friend." (Chapter 3:12–21)

Holy Gospel

Stand up in the fear of God and listen to the Holy Gospel,A chapter from the Holy Gospel according to Saint Luke, May his blessings be with us all, Amen

From the psalms of our teacher David the prophet and king,May his blessings be with us all, Amen

> You lifted me high on a rock. You guided me, for You became my hope, A tower of strength from the face of the enemy. For You, O God, hear my prayers; You give an inheritance to those who fear Your name. Alleluia. Psalm 61:2–3,5

Blessed is He who comes in the Name of the Lord Our Lord, God and Saviour and the King of us all, Jesus Christ, the Son of the living God. Glory be to You forever more, Amen

Now great multitudes went with Him. And He turned and said to them, "If anyone comes to Me and does not hate his father and mother, wife and children, brothers and sisters, yes, and his own life also, he cannot be My disciple. "And whoever does not bear his cross and come after Me cannot be My disciple. "For which of you, intending to build a tower, does not sit down first and count the cost, whether he has enough to finish it—"lest, after he has laid the foundation, and is not able to finish, all who see it begin to mock him, saying, 'This man began to build and was not able to finish.' "Or what king, going to make war against another king, does not sit down first and consider whether he is able with ten thousand to meet him who comes against him with twenty thousand? "Or else, while the other is still a great way off, he sends a delegation and asks conditions of peace. "So likewise, whoever of you does not forsake all that he has cannot be My disciple. "Salt is good; but if the salt has lost its flavour, how shall it be seasoned? "It is neither fit for the land nor for the dunghill, but men throw it out. He who has ears to hear, let him hear!" Luke 14:25–35

Glory be to God Forever, Amen

PARAMOUN OF THE CHRISTMAS FEAST

Holy Gospel

MATINS

Stand up in the fear of God and listen to the Holy Gospel, A chapter from the Holy Gospel according to Saint Matthew, May his blessings be with us all, Amen

From the psalms of our teacher David the prophet and king, May his blessings be with us all, Amen

> In Judah God is known; His name is great in Israel. In Salem also is His tabernacle, And His dwelling place in Zion. Alleluia. Psalm 76:1-2

Blessed is He who comes in the Name of the Lord Our Lord, God and Saviour and the King of us all, Jesus Christ, the Son of the living God. Glory be to You forever more, Amen

Now the birth of Jesus Christ was as follows: After His mother Mary was betrothed to Joseph, before they came together, she was found with child of the Holy Spirit. Then Joseph her husband, being a just man, and not wanting to make her a public example, was minded to put her away secretly. But while he thought about these things, behold, an angel of the Lord appeared to him in a dream, saying, "Joseph, son of David, do not be afraid to take to you Mary your wife, for that which is conceived in her is of the Holy Spirit. And she will bring forth a Son, and you shall call His name Jesus, for He will save His people from their sins."

So all this was done that it might be fulfilled which was spoken by the Lord through the prophet, saying: "Behold, the virgin shall be with child, and bear a Son, and they shall call His name Immanuel," which is translated, "God with us." Then Joseph, being aroused from sleep, did as the angel of the Lord commanded him and took to him his wife, and did not know her till she had brought forth her firstborn Son. And he called His name Jesus. Matthew 1:18-25

Glory be to God Forever, Amen

Pauline

Paul, the servant of our Lord Jesus Christ, called to be an apostle, appointed to the Gospel of God. A reading from the Epistle of our teacher Paul to Galatians. May his holy blessings be with us. Amen.

Dear Galatians,

Do you remember the story of old father Abraham? How God promised that Abraham would have children, even though he was 100 years old? Well, what God actually promised Abraham was that God would give Abraham a SON. And Abraham's great great great great great great great [take a breath!] great great grandSON was Jesus! But God also gave the children of Abraham the Law of Moses.Why did God do that? Why did they need it? The Law of Moses (that's in the Old Testament) was like a teacher for when we were still little; when didn't know about Jesus yet. But now Jesus has come. We don't need that teacher anymore! We've finished school! Now we have faith in Jesus Himself. So don't be jealous of the Jewish people because they have the Law of Moses. God doesn't care if you are Jewish or Greek, God doesn't care if you are a slave or a free person. God doesn't care if you area man or a woman. We are ALL one in Jesus Christ. In Jesus, we are ALL Abraham's children. In Jesus, we are ALL God's children. God adopted us as His children, and made us the brothers and sisters of Jesus. He filled us with His Holy Spirit, so now we call God: "Abba! Daddy! Father!" So, don't go back to the bad old days before you got to know God; when you worried so much about: "What day are we celebrating today? Oh dear, we have to get it right!" Is that all that matters to God? I hope that all that time and effort I spent with you, to teachyou about God wasn't wasted! You know I love you so much; I would give you my eyes if you asked for them! So please don't be upset with me when I tell you the truth. It's good to try hard but please remember; Loving God means so much more than just following rules! (Galatians 3:15–4:18)

Bye for now!

Signed, Paul

> *The grace of God the Father be with you all, Amen.*

Catholicon

The Catholic Epistle from the First Epistle of our teacher St John. May his holy blessings be with us. Amen.

Hello, I need to warn you; don't just believe everything that anyone tells you! Here is how you can tell if someone is telling you the truth about God: If they say that Jesus really is God—that's the Holy Spirit speaking. But, if they say that Jesus is not really God— that's a lying spirit. Don't believe them! You belong to God, little children. God lives in you. And no one can beat you, because He who is in you is stronger than anyone else in the whole world. Some Christians speak like the rest of the world. But we speak the way God taught us. Anyone who really knows God understands us. My Beloved, Let us love one another for love is of God and everyone who loves is born of God. Anyone who does not love, Does not know God. For God is love. Say it with me now: God is love. And how do we know that God loves us so? Because God sent to us His Only-Begotten Son, Jesus Christ, to give us life. Where does love come from? We love God, because He first loved us, and sent His Son Jesus Christ to save us from our sins. My little children, If God loves us SO much then we also should love each other! Nobody has ever actually seen God, but if we truly love each other, God truly lives inside us! Do you want to know how you can tell if you are a good follower of God? Well, if you have the Holy Spirit living in you, you are a good Jesus Follower. (1 John 4:1–14)

Bye for now!

Signed,   John the Beloved

Do not love the world, nor the things which are in the world. The world shall pass away and all its desires; but he who does the will of God shall abide forever. Amen

The Acts

A reading from the Acts of our fathers the pure apostles, who were invested with the grace of the Holy Spirit. May their blessing be with us all. Amen.

St Paul and his friends were on an adventure. One of his friends was St Mark, but he had to leave and go back to Jerusalem. The rest of them came to a city called Antioch, and they went into the Jewish synagogue, and they sat down, and listened to all the readings (just like you're doing now!) When they had finished reading from the Old Testament, from the Books of Moses and the prophets, the elders asked the visitors—St Paul and his friends—if they would like to say something. So St Paul, said, "Yes, please." "Men of Israel," he said, "you know the story of our people. You know that God chose Abraham; and saved his children from being slaves in Egypt and God led them 40 years in the desert; and gave them the Promised Land to live in. And when they asked for a king, God gave them King Saul, and then King David. God said that David had a heart just like the heart of God. From David's children, after a very, very long time, a Saviour was born:Jesus "And God sent a man called John the Baptist to get everyone ready for Jesus. John told everyone to stop doing bad things, and to be baptised, washing away their awful sins but John was very honest with everyone. He told them that he was not the Saviour. Instead, he said: 'There is One who will come after me, and I am not even worthy to take off His sandals!'" St Paul said lots more than this to the people in the synagogue at Antioch. And they were very interested indeed! In fact, they asked him and his friends to come every week! (Chapter 13:13–25)

The word of the Lord shall grow, multiply, be mighty and be confirmed in the holy Church of God. Amen

Holy Gospel

Stand up in the fear of God and listen to the Holy Gospel, A chapter from the Holy Gospel according to Saint Luke, May his blessings be with us all, Amen

From the psalms of our teacher David the prophet and king, May his blessings be with us all, Amen

> With You is the beginning in the day of Your power, In the brightness of Your saints; "I have begotten You from the womb before the morning star." Alleluia. Psalm 110:3

Blessed is He who comes in the Name of the Lord Our Lord, God and Saviour and the King of us all, Jesus Christ, the Son of the living God. Glory be to You forever more, Amen

And it came to pass in those days that a decree went out from Caesar Augustus that all the world should be registered Joseph also went up from Nazareth to the city of David, which is called Bethlehem, because he was of the house and lineage of David, to be registered with Mary, his betrothed wife, who was with child. So it was, that while they were there, the days were completed for her to be delivered. And she brought forth her firstborn Son and wrapped Him in swaddling cloths, and laid Him in a manger, because there was no room for them in the inn. Now there were in the same country shepherds living out in the fields, keeping watch over their flock by night. And behold, an angel of the Lord stood before them, and the glory of the Lord shone around them, and they were greatly afraid. Then the angel said to them, "Do not be afraid, for behold, I bring you good tidings of great joy which will be to all people. "For there is born to you this day in the city of David a Saviour, who is Christ the Lord. And this will be the sign to you: You will find a Babe wrapped in swaddling cloths, lying in a manger." And suddenly there was with the angel a multitude of the heavenly host praising God and saying: "Glory to God in the highest, And on earth peace, goodwill toward men!" So it was, when the angels had gone away from them into heaven they came with haste and found Mary and Joseph, and the Babe lying in a manger And all those who heard it marvelled at those things which were told them by the shepherds. But Mary kept all these things and pondered them in her heart. Then the shepherds returned, glorifying and praising God for all the things that they had heard and seen, as it was told them. Luke 2:1–20

Glory be to God Forever, Amen

THE CHRISTMAS FEAST

Holy Gospel

Stand up in the fear of God and listen to the Holy Gospel, A chapter from the Holy Gospel according to Saint John, May his blessings be with us all, Amen

From the psalms of our teacher David the prophet and king, May his blessings be with us all, Amen

> And He shall live; And the gold of Sheba will be given to Him; Prayer also will be made for Him continually, And daily He shall be praised Alleluia. Psalm 72:15

Blessed is He who comes in the Name of the Lord Our Lord, God and Saviour and the King of us all, Jesus Christ, the Son of the living God. Glory be to You forever more, Amen

And the Word became flesh and dwelt among us, and we beheld His glory, the glory as of the only begotten of the Father, full of grace and truth. John bore witness of Him and cried out, saying, "This was He of whom I said, 'He who comes after me is preferred before me, for He was before me.' " And of His fullness we have all received, and grace for grace. For the law was given through Moses, but grace and truth came through Jesus Christ. John 1:14-17

Glory be to God Forever, Amen

Pauline

Paul, the servant of our Lord Jesus Christ, called to be an apostle, appointed to the Gospel of God. A reading from the Epistle of our teacher Paul to Hebrews. May his holy blessings be with us. Amen.

St Paul the Apostle was writing a letter to the Christians who were Jewish, that is, the Hebrews.

Dear Hebrews, In the olden days, God would speak to His people through some special people called the Prophets. But now, God has spoken to us through His own Son — Jesus — the One who made all the worlds, and who keeps everything going! Jesus is the exact image of God the Father. Jesus is the glorious bright Light of God the Father. Jesus is the One who took away our sins, and sits at the right hand of God the Father in heaven. So, Jesus is so much higher than the angels. God the Father never said to any angel: "You are My Son, Today I have begotten You." Or "Your throne O God, is for ever and ever; A royal staff of righteousness is the royal staff of Your kingdom." But He did say those things about Jesus, His Son, through His holy Prophets. The angels serve Jesus, for they know who Jesus really is. As the Prophets said about Jesus, "You, Lord, in the beginning laid the foundation of the earth, and made the heavens with Your hands. They will end one day, but You will always remain." So we need to learn from these words of the Prophets! We need to know just who Jesus is. Or what shall happen to us if we don't pay attention? Whenever we do wrong sooner or later, we get just what we deserve. Let us not ignore what God has told us, through His Prophets, His angels and lately, through His own Son, Jesus, who did such great miracles and wonders, and through the gift of His Holy Spirit working in us. Let us listen to these words and learn about Jesus who made us and saved us. (Hebrews 1:1–2:4)

Bye for now!

Signed, Paul

The grace of God the Father be with you all, Amen.

Catholicon

The Catholic Epistle from the Second Letter written by St Peter . May his holy blessings be with us. Amen.

Hello everyone! This is your old friend Peter the Apostle.

I am getting rather old these days, and I will soon be going to heaven, But before I do, I want to make really sure that you know right from wrong, And that you know the truth about Jesus. We didn't make up stories, you know! We were actually there when Jesus was on the mountain. And we heard the voice of God the Father speak from heaven! Remember what He said? "This is My beloved Son, in whom I am well pleased." That Beloved Son is Jesus! (the One who was born on this day). (2 Peter 1:12-17)

Bye for now!

Signed, Peter the Apostle

Do not love the world, nor the things which are in the world. The world shall pass away and all its desires; but he who does the will of God shall abide forever. Amen.

The Acts

A reading from the Acts of our fathers the pure apostles, who were invested with the grace of the Holy Spirit. May their blessing be with us all. Amen.

St Paul the Apostle was travelling, and stopped at a place where there was a Jewish synagogue, a place where the Jews gathered to pray and read the Bible. And after they had read the Scriptures, they asked if anyone wanted to say something. St Paul certainly had something to say! So he got up and started to tell everyone about how the Old Testament Scriptures (the Bible) tell us all about Jesus! "You, my brothers, being Jews and children of Abraham, you need to understand the words of your own prophets, which you read every Sabbath (which is Saturday). "But instead, you asked Pontius Pilate to kill Jesus on the Cross, even though Jesus never did anything wrong. "And Jesus died, just as the prophets in the Scripture said, and He was buried in a tomb, but then something really amazing happened, "God raised Jesus from the dead! Jesus was alive again! "We know this, because lots and lots of people saw Him. "So that's why I'm telling you all this Good News. "Jesus died and rose for you and me. That's what the Scriptures of the Old Testament were telling you, all this time. That's why the second Psalm says, 'You are My Son, Today I have begotten You' "We are the children of Abraham and the prophets, Jesus rose for you and for me and for everyone!" (Chapter 13:25-33)

The word of the Lord shall grow, multiply, be mighty and be confirmed in the holy Church of God. Amen.

Holy Gospel

Stand up in the fear of God and listen to the Holy Gospel, A chapter from the Holy Gospel according to Saint Matthew, May his blessings be with us all, Amen

From the psalms of our teacher David the prophet and king, May his blessings be with us all, Amen

> The Lord said to Me, 'You are My Son, Today I have begotten You; Ask of Me, and I will give You The nations for Your inheritance And the ends of the earth for Your possession.' Alleluia. Psalm 2:7-8

Blessed is He who comes in the Name of the Lord Our Lord, God and Saviour and the King of us all, Jesus Christ, the Son of the living God. Glory be to You forever more, Amen

Now after Jesus was born in Bethlehem of Judea in the days of Herod the king, behold, wise men from the East came to Jerusalem, saying: "Where is He who has been born King of the Jews? For we have seen His star in the East and have come to worship Him." When Herod the king heard this, he was troubled, and all Jerusalem with him. And when he had gathered all the chief priests and scribes of the people together, he inquired of them where the Christ was to be born. So they said to him, "In Bethlehem of Judea, for thus it is written by the prophet: 'But you, Bethlehem, in the land of Judah, Are not the least among the rulers of Judah; For out of you shall come a Ruler Who will shepherd My people Israel.' " Then Herod, when he had secretly called the wise men, determined from them what time the star appeared. And he sent them to Bethlehem and said, "Go and search carefully for the young Child, and when you have found Him, bring back word to me, that I may come and worship Him also." When they heard the king, they departed; and behold, the star which they had seen in the East went before them, till it came and stood over where the young Child was. When they saw the star, they rejoiced with exceedingly great joy. And when they had come into the house, they saw the young Child with Mary His mother, and fell down and worshiped Him. And when they had opened their treasures, they presented gifts to Him: gold, frankincense, and myrrh. Then, being divinely warned in a dream that they should not return to Herod, they departed for their own country another way. Matthew 2:1-12

Glory be to God Forever, Amen

SECOND DAY THE CHRISTMAS FEAST

Holy Gospel

Stand up in the fear of God and listen to the Holy Gospel, A chapter from the Holy Gospel according to Saint Matthew, May his blessings be with us all, Amen

From the psalms of our teacher David the prophet and king, May his blessings be with us all, Amen

> Yes, all kings shall fall down before Him; All nations shall serve Him. And blessed be His glorious name forever! And let the whole earth be filled with His glory. Amen and Amen. Alleluia. Psalm 72:11,19

Blessed is He who comes in the Name of the Lord Our Lord, God and Saviour and the King of us all, Jesus Christ, the Son of the living God. Glory be to You forever more, Amen

While the Pharisees were gathered together, Jesus asked them, saying, "What do you think about the Christ? Whose Son is He?" They said to Him, "The Son of David." He said to them, "How then does David in the Spirit call Him 'Lord,' saying: 'The Lord said to my Lord, "Sit at My right hand, Till I make Your enemies Your footstool" '? If David then calls Him 'Lord,' how is He his Son?" And no one was able to answer Him a word, nor from that day on did anyone dare question Him anymore. Matthew 22:41-46

Glory be to God Forever, Amen

Pauline

Paul, the servant of our Lord Jesus Christ, called to be an apostle, appointed to the Gospel of God. A reading from the Epistle of our teacher Paul to Galatians . May his holy blessings be with us. Amen.

St Paul the Apostle was writing a letter to the Christians who were Jewish, that is, the Hebrews.

Dear Galatians, How I wish I could be with you now, because I am working hard to see Jesus born in your hearts. But sometimes, you worry me. Some of you want to go back and be Jewish again, and follow all those laws of Moses that the Jews still follow till today. Why do you want to make yourselves like slaves? Don't you realise that when you follow Jesus, you are free? You are no longer a slave! Let me tell you a little story. A long time ago, Abraham had two wives. One of them was called Sarah, she was his real wife. The other wife was called Hagar. She was a slave. Now Abraham had son from Sarah whose name was Isaac. God made a promise with Abraham and Isaac. Abraham, Sarah, and their son Isaac were free. But Abraham also had a son from Hagar the slave. His name was Ishmael, and he was always just the son of the slave woman. So which of Abraham's sons would you want to be? Isaac, the free man? Or Ishmael the slave? Christians are like Isaac: Jesus makes us free! But the Jews are like Ishmael: they are still slaves to the Law of Moses. And even today, the children of the slave (that's the Jews) are being mean to the children who are free (that's the Christians). So my dear Galatians, please don't give up your freedom in Jesus. Please don't go back to being slaves of the law of Moses Jesus makes us free! (Galatians 4:19-5:1)

Bye for now!

Signed, Paul

The grace of God the Father be with you all, Amen.

Catholicon

The Catholic Epistle from the First Epistle of our teacher St John. May his holy blessings be with us. Amen.

Jesus is the Son of God. If you love Jesus, then that means that God lives in you, and you live in God. God is Love. Whoever lives in love, lives in God and God lives in Him. God's perfect love inside us makes us ready to face the scary Judgement Day. No way! WE won't be scared! That's because when your heart is full of love there's no room left for being afraid! Say it with me: "Perfect love casts out fear." And do you know WHY we love God? Because He loved us first! But what about if someone says that he loves God, but at the same time, he hates other people? Do you think he truly loves God? No way! You can't truly love God (who you can't see), But hate other people (who you can see very well)! So God taught us that if we truly love Him, we must truly love others too. If you believe that Jesus is God's Son, then you love God; and you love God's Son, Jesus; and you obey God. It's really not that hard to obey God. His rules are nice! God's rules teach us how to love God, and how to love other people. And this makes us SO strong! Nothing in the world is stronger than a person who has faith in God and loves God. (1 John 4:15-5:4)

God loves you!

Signed,   John the Beloved

Do not love the world, nor the things which are in the world. The world shall pass away and all its desires; but he who does the will of God shall abide forever. Amen.

The Acts

One day, St Paul was preaching about Jesus in the synagogue, the meeting place where all the Jewish people came to pray. After telling them the story of how God has helped human beings from the very beginning, Paul was up to the bit about King David: You all know, said Paul, That after King David had served his people well, he grew old and died. But Jesus served His people, died, and rose again from the dead! This is why Jesus can do something that no one else could ever do. Moses couldn't do it, king David couldn't do it! Do you know what it is? Yes! Jesus can forgive sins! Even Moses and King David made prophecies about Him. They believed in Him, even though they hadn't seen Him yet. So, if YOU don't believe in Jesus, be careful, be very, very careful, because your own prophets warned you about the punishments of those who don't believe in God, and now, God has done an amazing miracle when He sent His Son to earth and you have heard all about Him. So, what are you going to do? After the service was finished, they all went out, and lots of the Jewscame out and asked St Paul to tell them more about this wonderful Jesus. And even their friends who were not even Jewish, they said to St Paul: "Can you PLEASE speak to us next week? We want to hear about this Jesus too!" (Chapter 13:36–43)

Holy Gospel

Stand up in the fear of God and listen to the Holy Gospel,A chapter from the Holy Gospel according to Saint John, May his blessings be with us all, Amen

From the psalms of our teacher David the prophet and king,May his blessings be with us all, Amen

> Let His name be blessed unto the ages; His name shall remain before the sun, And all the tribes of the earth shall be blessed in Him; All the Gentiles shall bless Him. Alleluia. Psalm 72:17

Blessed is He who comes in the Name of the Lord Our Lord, God and Saviour and the King of us all, Jesus Christ, the Son of the living God. Glory be to You forever more, Amen

In the beginning was the Word, and the Word was with God, and the Word was God.All things were made through Him, and without Him nothing was made that was made. In Him was life, and the life was the light of men. And the light shines in the darkness, and the darkness did not comprehend it. There was a man sent from God, whose name was John. This man came for a witness, to bear witness of the Light, that all through him might believe. He was not that Light, but was sent to bear witness of that Light. That was the true Light which gives light to every man coming into the world. He was in the world, and the world was made through Him, and the world did not know Him. But as many as received Him, to them He gave the right to become children of God, to those who believe in His name: who were born, not of blood, nor of the will of the flesh, nor of the will of man, but of God. John 1:1–13

Glory be to God Forever, Amen

THE FEAST OF CIRCUMCISION

Holy Gospel

Stand up in the fear of God and listen to the Holy Gospel, A chapter from the Holy Gospel according to Saint Luke, May his blessings be with us all, Amen

From the psalms of our teacher David the prophet and king, May his blessings be with us all, Amen

> I will go into Your house with burnt offerings; I will pay You my vows, Which my lips have uttered And my mouth has spoken when I was in trouble. I will offer You burnt sacrifices of fat animals, With the sweet aroma of rams; I will offer bulls with goats. Selah Alleluia. Psalm 66: 13-15

Blessed is He who comes in the Name of the Lord Our Lord, God and Saviour and the King of us all, Jesus Christ, the Son of the living God. Glory be to You forever more, Amen

And the Child grew and became strong in spirit, filled with wisdom; and the grace of God was upon Him. His parents went to Jerusalem every year at the Feast of the Passover. And when He was twelve years old, they went up to Jerusalem according to the custom of the feast. When they had finished the days, as they returned, the Boy Jesus lingered behind in Jerusalem. And Joseph and His mother did not know it; but supposing Him to have been in the company, they went a day's journey, and sought Him among their relatives and acquaintances. So when they did not find Him, they returned to Jerusalem, seeking Him. Now so it was that after three days they found Him in the temple, sitting in the midst of the teachers, both listening to them and asking them questions. And all who heard Him were astonished at His understanding and answers. So when they saw Him, they were amazed; and His mother said to Him, "Son, why have You done this to us? Look, Your father and I have sought You anxiously."

And He said to them, "Why did you seek Me? Did you not know that I must be about My Father's business?" But they did not understand the statement which He spoke to them. Then He went down with them and came to Nazareth, and was subject to them, but His mother kept all these things in her heart. And Jesus increased in wisdom and stature, and in favor with God and men. Luke 2:40-52

Glory be to God Forever, Amen

Pauline

Paul, the servant of our Lord Jesus Christ, called to be an apostle, appointed to the Gospel of God. A reading from the Epistle of our teacher Paul to Philippians. May his holy blessings be with us. Amen.

St Paul the Apostle was writing a letter to the Christians who lived in the busy city of Philippi. Dear Philippians, Rejoice in the Lord! I hope you don't mind my saying some things over and over to you. I just want to make sure that you've really got it. Especially, I want to remind you about circumcision. This is that mark that Jewish people make on a baby's body when he is just eight days old. Jesus was Jewish, and He got circumcised. I am Jewish, and I got circumcised. But I want to be sure that you understand— That was a JEWISH thing. It is not a CHRISTIAN thing! Let me explain why Christians don't need to be circumcised: The Jewish people thought that a mark on their bodies made them good people, special people, the people of God. But Jesus taught us that it is not marks on the outside of your body that make you good or special. The people of God are the ones whose heart like God. So it's not what you have on the OUTSIDE of your body that matters; it's what you are like on the INSIDE that matters. I was a very famous Jew! But I gave all that up, because I found something so, so much better: I found Jesus! Now, all that fame is like rubbish to me. Anything at all that used to make me think I was special— now it is just like rubbish to me. Because Jesus is my real Treasure. I know I can't be a truly good person without Jesus. So I try to think about His resurrection; And share with Him in His suffering; And be like Him when He was on the Cross so that I can rise from the dead with Him too! That is much more important than a mark on your body like circumcision! (Philippians 3:1–12)

Bye for now!

Signed, Paul

The grace of God the Father be with you all, Amen.

Catholicon

The Catholic Epistle from the Second Epistle of our teacher St Peter. May his holy blessings be with us. Amen.

Hello everyone! This is your old friend Peter the Apostle. I am getting rather old these days, and I will soon be going to heaven, But before I do, I want to make really sure that you know right from wrong, And that you know the truth about Jesus. We didn't make up stories, you know! We were actually there when Jesus was on the mountain. And we heard the voice of God the Father speak from heaven! Remember what He said? "This is My beloved Son, in whom I am well pleased." That's what the prophets in the Old Testament said would happen! They weren't making up stories either. The prophets just spoke exactly what the Holy Spirit told them to speak. Their words were like turning on the light in a dark room. Or like a bright morning star that tells you that the sun will rise soon. When we read the words of the prophets in the Bible, and we let the Holy Spirit teach us what they really meant, it's like the morning star is rising in our hearts, preparing them for the coming of Jesus. (2 Peter 1:12-21)

Be good!

Signed, Peter the Apostle

Do not love the world, nor the things which are in the world. The world shall pass away and all its desires; but he who does the will of God shall abide forever. Amen.

The Acts

The Disciples of Jesus had gathered together in the city of Jerusalem to discuss a very tough question. When a person who is not Jewish becomes a Christian, do they have to do all the things that Jewish people do? Some Jewish Christians said, "YES! Of course you can't be Christian without following all of Moses' Laws!" But other Christians said, "NO! Jesus set us free from all those Jewish laws." And when everyone had finished saying what they thought, James the Elder said: "OK, listen to me, please Peter told us that God has shown Him that He loves everyone, and it doesn't matter if they are Jewish of not. Everyone can be a Christian. And this is what God said a long time ago, in the time of the prophet Amos— that ALL people will want to find God. So it looks to me like the answer is clear, here: We should not expect people who are not Jewish to do all the Jewish stuff. You can seek the Lord, and love Jesus, and follow Jesus, and be a Christian, WITHOUT doing all that Jewish stuff. All we should ask of them is not to worship the idols that they used to worship before they became Christians. That's all." And everyone saw that James was right. And they all agreed with him. (Chapter 15:13–21)

Holy Gospel

Stand up in the fear of God and listen to the Holy Gospel, A chapter from the Holy Gospel according to Saint Luke, May his blessings be with us all, Amen

From the psalms of our teacher David the prophet and king, May his blessings be with us all, Amen

> Offer to God a sacrifice of praise, And pay your vows to the Most High.
> A sacrifice of praise shall glorify Me, And there is the way whereby I
> will show him the salvation of God. Alleluia. -Psalm 50:14, 23

Blessed is He who comes in the Name of the Lord Our Lord, God and Saviour and the King of us all, Jesus Christ, the Son of the living God. Glory be to You forever more, Amen

And when eight days were completed for the circumcision of the Child, His name was called JESUS, the name given by the angel before He was conceived in the womb. Now when the days of her purification according to the law of Moses were completed, they brought Him to Jerusalem to present Him to the Lord and behold, there was a man in Jerusalem whose name was Simeon, and this man was just and devout and it had been revealed to him by the Holy Spirit that he would not see So he came by the Spirit into the temple and he took the Child Jesus up in his arms and blessed God and said: "Lord, now You are letting Your servant depart in peace, According to Your word; For my eyes have seen Your salvation Which You have prepared before the face of all peoples, A light to bring revelation to the Gentiles, And the glory of Your people Israel." And Joseph and His mother marvelled at those things which were spoken of Him. Then Simeon blessed them, and said to Mary His mother "Behold, this Child is destined for the fall and rising of many in Israel, and for a sign which will be spoken against (yes, a sword will pierce through your own soul also), that the thoughts of many hearts may be revealed." Now there was one, Anna, a prophetess she was of a great age, a widow of about eighty-four years who did not depart from the temple, but served God with fastings and prayers night and day. And coming in that instant she gave thanks to the Lord, and spoke of Him to all those who looked for redemption in Jerusalem. So when they had performed all things according to the law of the Lord, they returned to Galilee, to their own city, Nazareth. Luke 2:21–39

Glory be to God Forever, Amen

PARAMOUN OF THE EPIPHANY FEAST

Holy Gospel MATINS

Stand up in the fear of God and listen to the Holy Gospel, A chapter from the Holy Gospel according to Saint John, May his blessings be with us all, Amen

From the psalms of our teacher David the prophet and king, May his blessings be with us all, Amen

> Deep calls unto deep at the noise of Your waterfalls; All Your waves and billows have gone over me. The Lord will command His lovingkindness in the daytime, And in the night His song shall be with me— A prayer to the God of my life. Alleluia. -Psalm 42:7-8

Blessed is He who comes in the Name of the Lord Our Lord, God and Saviour and the King of us all, Jesus Christ, the Son of the living God. Glory be to You forever more, Amen

After these things Jesus and His disciples came into the land of Judea, and there He remained with them and baptized. Now John also was baptizing in Aenon near Salim, because there was much water there. And they came and were baptized. For John had not yet been thrown into prison. Then there arose a dispute between some of John's disciples and the Jews about purification. And they came to John and said to him, "Rabbi, He who was with you beyond the Jordan, to whom you have testified—behold, He is baptizing, and all are coming to Him!" John answered and said, "A man can receive nothing unless it has been given to him from heaven. You yourselves bear me witness, that I said, 'I am not the Christ,' but, 'I have been sent before Him.' He who has the bride is the bridegroom; but the friend of the bridegroom, who stands and hears him, rejoices greatly because of the bridegroom's voice. Therefore this joy of mine is fulfilled. John 3:22-29

Glory be to God Forever, Amen

Pauline

Paul, the servant of our Lord Jesus Christ, called to be an apostle, appointed to the Gospel of God. A reading from the First Epistle of our teacher Paul to the Corinthians. May his holy blessings be with us. Amen.

To my dear friends in the Church of Corinth, who always pray to our Lord Jesus Christ Grace and peace to you. I always thank God that God has given you the gift of knowing Jesus really well, and being able to speak about Jesus. Even the way you live your life shows the world how beautiful Jesus is. What a lovely gift from God! I want you to know that God will always be with you, even to the last day. But there is something else I really need to say to you, I have heard that you sometimes argue and fight with each other! Christians should all be following Jesus TOGETHER. I've even heard that some of you say things like this: "I'm on Paul's team!" Or "No, I am on Apollos' team, not Paul!" Or "I don't like either! I'm on Cephas' team!" Oh my goodness! What is wrong with you??? Don't you know that we are all on just ONE team together? We are all on Jesus' team! Were you baptised in the name of "Paul" or in the name of Jesus? Jesus, of course! So let's forget this "team" silliness that makes us argue with each other, And remember that ALL of us are following Jesus, not anyone else. (1 Corinthians 1:1–17)

Bye for now!

Signed, Paul

The grace of God the Father be with you all, Amen.

Catholicon

The Catholic Epistle from the Second Epistle of our teacher St Peter. May his holy blessings be with us. Amen.

Hello everyone! This is your old friend Peter the Apostle. I am getting rather old these days, and I will soon be going to heaven, But before I do, I want to make really sure that you know right from wrong, And that you know the truth about Jesus. We didn't make up stories, you know! We were actually there when Jesus was on the mountain. And we heard the voice of God the Father speak from heaven! Remember what He said? "This is My beloved Son, in whom I am well pleased." That's what the prophets in the Old Testament said would happen! They weren't making up stories either. The prophets just spoke exactly what the Holy Spirit told them to speak. Their words were like turning on the light in a dark room. Or like a bright morning star that tells you that the sun will rise soon. When we read the words of the prophets in the Bible, and we let the Holy Spirit teach us what they really meant, it's like the morning star is rising in our hearts, preparing them for the coming of Jesus. (2 Peter 1:12-19)

Bye for now!

Signed,   Peter the Apostle

Do not love the world, nor the things which are in the world. The world shall pass away and all its desires; but he who does the will of God shall abide forever. Amen.

The Acts

A reading from the Acts of our fathers the pure apostles, who were invested with the grace of the Holy Spirit. May their blessing be with us all. Amen.

One day, St Paul the Apostle and his friend St Silas the Apostle were stuck in a jail in Philippi. Would you be sad if you were stuck in jail? Do you think Paul and Silas were sad in jail? Paul and Silas were NOT sad in jail! They knew Jesus was with them, so do you know what they were doing in their jail cell? They were singing happy hymns! They were praying! And all the other prisoners were listening to them. Just then; a great earthquake shook the whole jail! All the doors of the cells fell open! All the chains on the prisoners fell off! It was a miracle! When the guard came to see what was happening, he saw all the open doors. "Oh no! I'm going to be in very big trouble indeed!" he said to himself. "I let the prisoners escape!" But Paul came up to him and said, "Please don't be worried. Don't look so sad. See, we haven't escaped at all. We're still here." The guard was amazed! He didn't know what was going on! But he did know one thing: Paul and Silas were very special people indeed. So the guard asked Paul and Silas, "What do I need to do to be saved?" And they answered: "Believe in Jesus, and you and your family will be saved." So the guard took Paul and Silas home to his own house. Paul and Silas told the guard and his whole family about Jesus our loving Saviour. They were so happy to hear about Jesus! And the guard and his family took care of Paul and Silas. They washed their ouchies and made them better. They gave them nice food to eat. And then Paul and Silas got lots of water, and they baptised the guard and his whole family, right there in their house. They had become Christians! Hooray! (Chapter 16:25–34)

The word of the Lord shall grow, multiply, be mighty and be confirmed in the holy Church of God. Amen.

Holy Gospel

Stand up in the fear of God and listen to the Holy Gospel, A chapter from the Holy Gospel according to Saint Luke, May his blessings be with us all, Amen

From the psalms of our teacher David the prophet and king, May his blessings be with us all, Amen

> You are more beautiful than the sons of men; Grace was poured out
> on Your lips; Therefore God blessed You forever. Alleluia. -Psalm 45:2

Blessed is He who comes in the Name of the Lord Our Lord, God and Saviour and the King of us all, Jesus Christ, the Son of the living God. Glory be to You forever more, Amen

Now in the fifteenth year of the reign of Tiberius Caesar, Pontius Pilate being governor of Judea, Herod being tetrarch of Galilee. The word of God came to John the son of Zacharias in the wilderness. And he went into all the region around the Jordan, preaching a baptism of repentance for the remission of sins, as it is written in the book of the words of Isaiah the prophet, saying: "The voice of one crying in the wilderness: 'Prepare the way of the Lord; Make His paths straight" Then he said to the multitudes that came out to be baptized by him, "Brood of vipers! Who warned you to flee from the wrath to come? "Therefore bear fruits worthy of repentance, and do not begin to say to yourselves, 'We have Abraham as our father.' "For I say to you that God is able to raise up children to Abraham from these stones. And even now the axe is laid to the root of the trees. "Therefore every tree which does not bear good fruit is cut down and thrown into the fire." So the people asked him, saying, "What shall we do then?" He answered and said to them, "He who has two tunics, let him give to him who has none; and he who has food, let him do likewise." Then tax collectors also came to be baptized, and said to him, "Teacher, what shall we do?" And he said to them, "Collect no more than what is appointed for you." Likewise the soldiers asked him, saying, "And what shall we do? "So he said to them, "Do not intimidate anyone or accuse falsely, and be content with your wages." Now as the people were in expectation, and all reasoned in their hearts about John, whether he was the Christ or not, John answered, saying to all, "I indeed baptize you with water; but One mightier than I is coming, whose sandal strap I am not worthy to loose. He will baptize you with the Holy Spirit and fire. (Luke 3:1–18)

Glory be to God Forever, Amen

Holy Gospel

Stand up in the fear of God and listen to the Holy Gospel,A chapter from the Holy Gospel according to Saint Mark, May his blessings be with us all, Amen

From the psalms of our teacher David the prophet and king,May his blessings be with us all, Amen

> The voice of the Lord is over the waters; The God of glory thunders; The Lord is over many waters. The voice of the Lord is powerful; The voice of the Lord is full of majesty. Alleluia. -Psalm 29:3-4

Blessed is He who comes in the Name of the Lord Our Lord, God and Saviour and the King of us all, Jesus Christ, the Son of the living God. Glory be to You forever more, Amen

The beginning of the gospel of Jesus Christ, the Son of God. As it is written in the Prophets: "Behold, I send My messenger before Your face, Who will prepare Your way before You." "The voice of one crying in the wilderness: 'Prepare the way of the Lord; Make His paths straight.' "

John came baptizing in the wilderness and preaching a baptism of repentance for the remission of sins. Then all the land of Judea, and those from Jerusalem, went out to him and were all baptized by him in the Jordan River, confessing their sins. Now John was clothed with camel's hair and with a leather belt around his waist, and he ate locusts and wild honey. And he preached, saying, "There comes One after me who is mightier than I, whose sandal strap I am not worthy to stoop down and loose. I indeed baptized you with water, but He will baptize you with the Holy Spirit." It came to pass in those days that Jesus came from Nazareth of Galilee, and was baptized by John in the Jordan. And immediately, coming up from the water, He saw the heavens parting and the Spirit descending upon Him like a dove. Then a voice came from heaven, "You are My beloved Son, in whom I am well pleased." Mark 1: 1-11

Glory be to God Forever, Amen

Pauline

Paul, the servant of our Lord Jesus Christ, called to be an apostle, appointed to the Gospel of God. A reading from the Epistle of our teacher Paul to Titus. May his holy blessings be with us. Amen.

Dear Titus,

Please don't forget your responsibility to teach your flock to be good. Remind them always to stay away from doing bad things, and to always do the right thing. Because we are looking forward to the day when Jesus will come back. We want Jesus to find good children, not naughty ones! So remind them to: follow the rules; do good to others; not be mean, but be kind and peaceful; and be humble with everyone. Remember that all of us were once mean and rude. We used to be selfish, and we treated others very badly. But when we got to know Jesus, everything changed! He saved us by being kind to us! He forgave us! He washed us with baptism, and He poured out his Holy Spirit on us! That's how God made us His own beloved children, so we can live with Jesus forever and ever. (Titus 2:11–3:7)

Bye for now!

Signed, Paul

> *The grace of God the Father be with you all, Amen.*

Catholicon

The Catholic Epistle from the First Epistle of our teacher St John. May his holy blessings be with us. Amen.

From John,

My beloved brothers and sisters, I have something so beautiful to tell you today, If you believe that Jesus is the Son of God, nothing in this world will be stronger than you. And this is how we know: There are Three in Heaven who tell us: the Father; the Son; and the Holy Spirit. And these Three are One. And there are three on earth who tell us: the Spirit; the water; and the Blood. And these three agree as one. In fact, God has told us, you and I, a very special secret about His Son Jesus Christ. But it's the kind of secret that God wants us to tell everybody about! And here it is, are you ready? God has given us eternal life! That means that we can live forever with Him in Heaven! So if you know about Jesus, believe in Him, love Him and if Jesus lives inside you. You will get to live forever with Jesus in Heaven! So keep believing in Jesus. Keep loving Him more and more. Because He gives us more and more. Jesus hears every word we say to Him when we pray. Jesus answers our prayers. Especially when we pray for a brother or sister who is doing something wrong. They really need someone to pray for them! So they can stop being naughty! When you really love God, you just don't want to do anything wrong. And even though the devil might trick the whole world to do the wrong thing. He can never trick us — if we really, really love God. For God is true And Jesus is true And He protects us every day of our lives. (1 John 5:5–21)

God loves you!

Signed, John the Beloved

Do not love the world, nor the things which are in the world. The world shall pass away and all its desires; but he who does the will of God shall abide forever. Amen.

The Acts

A reading from the Acts of our fathers the pure apostles, who were invested with the grace of the Holy Spirit. May their blessing be with us all. Amen.

There was a good Jewish man called Apollos who came from Egypt. He believed in Jesus, but he didn't know about being baptised as Christian. One day, Paul's friends, Priscilla and Aquila, heard Apollos saying beautiful things about Jesus. So they started to chat with him. They helped Apollos understand Jesus even better. And Apollos was very, very good at talking about Jesus. Now he was able to do that even better than before! About the same time, in another place, Paul met some more people like Apollos. They believed in Jesus, but there was something important missing, Paul asked them: "Have you been baptised in the name of

Jesus? Have you received the Holy Spirit?" "No," they answered "We have never even heard of the Holy Spirit!" So Paul took them and baptised them in the name of the Lord Jesus Christ. And then Paul laid his hands on their heads and prayed for them. And something wonderful happened to them; They were filled with the Holy Spirit! They were so happy! They started to sing and praise God in different languages, just like the disciples on the Day of Pentecost! Now, they were REALLY Christians! (Chapter 18:24–19:6)

The word of the Lord shall grow, multiply, be mighty and be confirmed in the holy Church of God. Amen.

Holy Gospel

Stand up in the fear of God and listen to the Holy Gospel, A chapter from the Holy Gospel according to Saint John, May his blessings be with us all, Amen

From the psalms of our teacher David the prophet and king, May his blessings be with us all, Amen

> Blessed is he who comes in the name of the Lord; We blessed you from the house of the Lord. You are my God, and I will give thanks to You; You are my God, and I shall exalt You. Alleluia. -Psalm 118:26,28

Blessed is He who comes in the Name of the Lord Our Lord, God and Saviour and the King of us all, Jesus Christ, the Son of the living God. Glory be to You forever more, Amen

No one has seen God at any time. The only begotten Son, who is in the bosom of the Father, He has declared Him. Now this is the testimony of John, when the Jews sent priests and Levites from Jerusalem to ask him, "Who are you?" He confessed, and did not deny, but confessed, "I am not the Christ."And they asked him, "What then? Are you Elijah?" He said, "I am not." "Are you the Prophet?" And he answered, "No." He said: "I am 'The voice of one crying in the wilderness: "Make straight the way of the Lord," ' as the prophet Isaiah said." "I baptize with water, but there stands One among you whom you do not know. It is He who, coming after me, is preferred before me, whose sandal strap I am not worthy to loose."

The next day John saw Jesus coming toward him, and said, "Behold! The Lamb of God who takes away the sin of the world! "This is He of whom I said, 'After me comes a Man who is preferred before me, for He was before me.' I did not know Him; but that He should be revealed to Israel, therefore I came baptizing with water." And John bore witness, saying, "I saw the Spirit descending from heaven like a dove, and He remained upon Him. "I did not know Him, but He who sent me to baptize with water said to me, 'Upon whom you see the Spirit descending, and remaining on Him, this is He who baptizes with the Holy Spirit.' "And I have seen and testified that this is the Son of God." John 1:18–34

Glory be to God Forever, Amen

SECOND DAY OF THE FEAST OF EPIPHANY

Holy Gospel MATINS

Stand up in the fear of God and listen to the Holy Gospel, A chapter from the Holy Gospel according to Saint Matthew, May his blessings be with us all, Amen

From the psalms of our teacher David the prophet and king, May his blessings be with us all, Amen

> Come, you children, listen to me; I will teach you the fear of the Lord. They looked to Him and were radiant, And their faces were not ashamed. Alleluia. -Psalm 34:11,5

Blessed is He who comes in the Name of the Lord Our Lord, God and Saviour and the King of us all, Jesus Christ, the Son of the living God. Glory be to You forever more, Amen

Then Jesus came from Galilee to John at the Jordan to be baptized by him. And John tried to prevent Him, saying, "I need to be baptized by You, and are You coming to me?" But Jesus answered and said to him, "Permit it to be so now, for thus it is fitting for us to fulfill all righteousness." Then he allowed Him. When He had been baptized, Jesus came up immediately from the water; and behold, the heavens were opened to Him, and He saw the Spirit of God descending like a dove and alighting upon Him. And suddenly a voice came from heaven, saying, "This is My beloved Son, in whom I am well pleased. Matthew 3:13-17

Glory be to God Forever, Amen

Pauline

Paul, the servant of our Lord Jesus Christ, called to be an apostle, appointed to the Gospel of God. A reading from the Epistle of our teacher Paul to Ephesians. May his holy blessings be with us. Amen.

St Paul the Apostle was writing a letter to the Christians who lived in the city of Ephesus. Dear Ephesians, We should always be so thankful to God that He chose us— even before we were born— to be His children. This was God's gift to us. I call it "grace." God's grace to us makes us able to know Him. God's grace is what saves us through His Son Jesus Christ. God's grace brings everything together in heaven and on earth in Jesus Christ. So God— the One who does all things— has chosen us to receive His goodness, because He loves us. This is the loving God whom you trusted from the moment you first heard about Him, when you heard His Gospel. And the Holy Spirit sealed your love in your heart. And there your love will always be safe until Jesus finishes saving the world. The grace of God the Father be with you all. Amen. (Ephesians 1:1-14)

Bye for now!

Signed, Paul

> *The grace of God the Father be with you all, Amen.*

Catholicon

The Catholic Epistle from the First Epistle of our teacher St Peter. May his holy blessings be with us. Amen.

Hello Everyone! Are you keeping God's love safely sealed in your hearts? If you are, you will always be ready to politely answer anyone who asks you "Why do you trust God? Why do you depend so much on Him?" You will never be afraid of anyone. When bad people call you names, don't worry! Everyone sees your very good behaviour! Sometimes, life isn't fair. But it's so much better to be a good person than it is to be a bad person, even when things go terribly wrong. Things went very wrong indeed for Jesus. Remember how He was crucified on the

Cross? That was very unfair. But because Jesus is good He turned the Cross into something wonderful! He saved the whole wide world! Even the people who had already died! From the Cross, Jesus went down into Hades and He set free all the people who were stuck there. Do you remember Noah and his ark? And how God brought them through the water, and saved life on earth? Jesus does the same thing for us, when we are baptised. God brings us through the water of baptism and saves our lives! Baptism saves us, because of that unfair thing that happened to Jesus: After Jesus died on the Cross He Went down to Hades. Then Jesus rose from the dead and He raised us with Him! And He went up to Heaven and He will take us to be there with Him one day! Because Jesus is the King of Heaven and all its angels. Won't that be wonderful? (1 Peter 3:15-22)

Bye for now!

Signed, Peter the Apostle

Do not love the world, nor the things which are in the world. The world shall pass away and all its desires; but he who does the will of God shall abide forever. Amen.

The Acts

A reading from the Acts of our fathers the pure apostles, who were invested with the grace of the Holy Spirit. May their blessing be with us all. Amen.

Do you remember the first seven deacons, who were chosen by the Apostles? St Stephen was their leader, but there was another one, called Philip. One day, an angel told Philip the deacon to go for a trip on the desert road. So he did. And who in the world do you think he met? He met a man from Ethiopia, a very far away country indeed! This man was no less than the servant of Queen Candace of Ethiopia herself. The Ethiopian man was sitting in his royal chariot, reading something out loud (that's how everybody used to read in those days). The Holy Spirit said to Philip: "go and talk to him." As Philip came up to the chariot, he heard what it was the man was reading. Can you guess what it was? The Ethiopian man was reading from the Bible! Philip was so happy! He said to the man, "Hi. Um, do you understand what you are reading?" And the Ethiopian man said, "How can I understand if no one explains it to me? You seem nice. Why don't you come and sit with me in my chariot and explain it to me?" It was the bit in the Bible from the Book of Isaiah that says: "He was led as a sheep to be killed and like a lamb is quiet when its wool is being shorn he did not open His mouth. He was treated so unfairly, and He was taken from the earth." The Ethiopian man asked Philip the deacon, "Who is this talking about? Is Isaiah talking about himself? Or is it about someone else?" So Philip explained that these words are all about Jesus, and how He gave up His life to save us all. The Ethiopian man was very, very touched! "Wow," he said, "that is just so beautiful! How can I follow this Jesus?" So Philip explained that he should be baptised in water. Then the Ethiopian man said, "Halt! Stop the chariot! Look, here is water! Can I be baptised right now?" Philip said, "If you believe with all your heart, you can be baptised." And he answered, "Yes, yes! I do believe that Jesus Christ is the Son of God!" So they got out of the chariot and went down to the water and Philip the deacon baptised the Ethiopian man right there and then. Then suddenly, the Holy Spirit swooshed Philip away. The Ethiopian man was amazed! But he was very, very happy, because now he was a Christian. Now, he knew Jesus and his whole life had changed. (Chapter 8:26-39)

The word of the Lord shall grow, multiply, be mighty and be confirmed in the holy Church of God. Amen.

Holy Gospel

Stand up in the fear of God and listen to the Holy Gospel, A chapter from the Holy Gospel according to Saint John, May his blessings be with us all, Amen

From the psalms of our teacher David the prophet and king, May his blessings be with us all, Amen

> Bless the Lord, O my soul. O Lord my God, You are magnified exceedingly; You clothe Yourself with thanksgiving and majesty, Who cover Yourself with light as with a garment Alleluia. -Psalm 104:1-2

Blessed is He who comes in the Name of the Lord Our Lord, God and Saviour and the King of us all, Jesus Christ, the Son of the living God. Glory be to You forever more, Amen

And when eight days were completed for the circumcision of the Child, His name was called JESUS, the name given by the angel before He was conceived in the womb. Now when the days of her purification according to the law of Moses were Again, the next day, John stood with two of his disciples. And looking at Jesus as He walked, he said, "Behold the Lamb of God!" The two disciples heard him speak, and they followed Jesus. Then Jesus turned, and seeing them following, said to them, "What do you seek?" They said to Him, "Rabbi" (which is to say, when translated, Teacher), "where are You staying?" He said to them, "Come and see." They came and saw where He was staying, and remained with Him that day (now it was about the tenth hour). One of the two who heard John speak, and followed Him, was Andrew, Simon Peter's brother. He first found his own brother Simon, and said to him, "We have found the Messiah" (which is translated, the Christ). And he brought him to Jesus. Now when Jesus looked at him, He said, "You are Simon the son of Jonah. You shall be called Cephas" (which is translated, A Stone). The following day Jesus wanted to go to Galilee, and He found Philip and said to him, "Follow Me." Now Philip was from Bethsaida, the city of Andrew and Peter. Philip found Nathanael and said to him, "We have found Him of whom Moses in the law, and also the prophets, wrote— Jesus of Nazareth, the son of Joseph." And Nathanael said to him, "Can anything good come out of Nazareth?" Philip said to him, "Come and see." Jesus saw Nathanael coming toward Him, and said of him, "Behold, an Israelite indeed, in whom is no deceit!" Nathanael said to Him, "How do You know me?" Jesus answered and said to him, "Before Philip called you, when you were under the fig tree, I saw you." Nathanael answered and said to Him, "Rabbi, You are the Son of God! You are the King of Israel!" Jesus answered and said to him, "Because I said to you, 'I saw you under the fig tree,' do you believe? You will see greater things than these." And He said to him, "Most assuredly, I say to you, hereafter you shall see heaven open, and the angels of God ascending and descending upon the Son of Man." John 1:35-51

Glory be to God Forever, Amen

THE WEDDING AT CANA OF GALILEE

Holy Gospel

Stand up in the fear of God and listen to the Holy Gospel, A chapter from the Holy Gospel according to Saint John, May his blessings be with us all, Amen

From the psalms of our teacher David the prophet and king, May his blessings be with us all, Amen

> And wine that makes glad the heart of man, Oil to make his face shine, And bread which strengthens man's heart. O Lord, how manifold are Your works! In wisdom You have made them all. The earth is full of Your possessions Alleluia. -Psalm 104:15,24

Blessed is He who comes in the Name of the Lord Our Lord, God and Saviour and the King of us all, Jesus Christ, the Son of the living God. Glory be to You forever more, Amen

Now after the two days He departed from there and went to Galilee. For Jesus Himself testified that a prophet has no honor in his own country. So when He came to Galilee, the Galileans received Him, having seen all the things He did in Jerusalem at the feast; for they also had gone to the feast. So Jesus came again to Cana of Galilee where He had made the water wine. And there was a certain nobleman whose son was sick at Capernaum. When he heard that Jesus had come out of Judea into Galilee, he went to Him and implored Him to come down and heal his son, for he was at the point of death. Then Jesus said to him, "Unless you people see signs and wonders, you will by no means believe." The nobleman said to Him, "Sir, come down before my child dies!" Jesus said to him, "Go your way; your son lives." So the man believed the word that Jesus spoke to him, and he went his way. And as he was now going down, his servants met him and told him, saying, "Your son lives!" Then he inquired of them the hour when he got better. And they said to him, "Yesterday at the seventh hour the fever left him." So the father knew that it was at the same hour in which Jesus said to him, "Your son lives." And he himself believed, and his whole household. This again is the second sign Jesus did when He had come out of Judea into Galilee. John 4:43-54

Glory be to God Forever, Amen

Pauline

Paul, the servant of our Lord Jesus Christ, called to be an apostle, appointed to the Gospel of God. A reading from the Epistle of our teacher Paul to the Romans. May his holy blessings be with us. Amen.

Dear Romans,

I wonder if you remember what Jesus did? How He died on the Cross, but then, He rose from the dead again? Well, on the day that you were baptised in the water of baptism, you did the same thing! Being baptised means that you died with Jesus. Your old life of being bad died and was buried in the water with Jesus. And then you came out of the water and began a new life of being good; just like Jesus rose from the dead and began a new life, where no one ever dies again. But this means we have to live our new lives by always being good and doing good, because Jesus is good. Sometimes, your body makes you want to be bad. Don't let your body be your boss! You are the boss! You tell your body what it should do! Actually, our real Boss is Jesus! So we have to teach our bodies to obey Jesus. Then we will be good, together with Jesus, forever. (Romans 6:3–16)

Bye for now!

Signed, Paul

The grace of God the Father be with you all, Amen.

Catholicon

The Catholic Epistle from the First Epistle of our teacher St John. May his holy blessings be with us. Amen.

Hello Everyone!

We Christians have a very, very special gift from God: His Holy Spirit lives in us! The Holy Spirit helps us to know what is true and what is a lie. If anyone says that Jesus is NOT the Christ, the One who saves us all that's a lie! And if anyone doesn't believe in Jesus, They don't believe in God the Father either! If you believe in Jesus, you believe in God the Father too. You will live safely in the love of the Son and of the Father. From the beginning, you have learned the truth about God, about Jesus His Son, and about eternal life— living forever. This is what God has promised to give you and me: eternal life; living forever with Him. (1 John 2:20–25)

God loves you!

Signed, Peter the Apostle

Do not love the world, nor the things which are in the world. The world shall pass away and all its desires; but he who does the will of God shall abide forever. Amen.

The Acts

A reading from the Acts of our fathers the pure apostles, who were invested with the grace of the Holy Spirit. May their blessing be with us all. Amen.

You know how St Paul went everywhere, telling people about Jesus? Well, before he got to know and love Jesus, he used to HATE Christians! That's right! He used to go everywhere to try and stop the Christians and hurt the Christians. So, lots of Christians ran away from him. But they still told everyone all about Jesus. That's why St Philip the Deacon travelled all the way to a place called Samaria to tell the people there about Jesus and His Good News. Lots of people believed in Jesus, because of what Philip told them, but also because Philip had the gift of doing miracles. Philip healed lots of sick people! People who couldn't walk suddenly found they were healed—they could walk! Now in that place, there was a man called Simon the Sorcerer. For a long time, Simon had amazed everyone with his tricks. Simon was curious so he came to listen to what Philip had to say This time, it was Simon's turn to be amazed! Simon the Sorcerer had never heard such beautiful words. And for all his tricks, Simon had never seen such miracles as those that Philip did! So, when Simon saw that Philip was baptising the people who believed in Jesus, he wanted to be baptised too. And that is exactly what happened. Not only was Simon the Sorcerer baptised—he also followed Philip, and saw him do even more amazing miracles! (Chapter 8:3–13)

The word of the Lord shall grow, multiply, be mighty and be confirmed in the holy Church of God. Amen.

Holy Gospel

Stand up in the fear of God and listen to the Holy Gospel, A chapter from the Holy Gospel according to Saint John, May his blessings be with us all, Amen

From the psalms of our teacher David the prophet and king, May his blessings be with us all, Amen

> You are the God who does wonders; You made known Your power among the peoples; You redeemed Your people with Your arm, The waters saw You, O God; and were afraid, Alleluia. -Psalm 77:14–15,16

Blessed is He who comes in the Name of the Lord Our Lord, God and Saviour and the King of us all, Jesus Christ, the Son of the living God. Glory be to You forever more, Amen

On the third day there was a wedding in Cana of Galilee, and the mother of Jesus was there. Now both Jesus and His disciples were invited to the wedding. And when they ran out of wine, the mother of Jesus said to Him, "They have no wine." Jesus said to her, "Woman, what does your concern have to do with Me? My hour has not yet come." His mother said to the servants, "Whatever He says to you, do it." Now there were set there six waterpots of stone, according to the manner of purification of the Jews, containing twenty or thirty gallons apiece. Jesus said to them, "Fill the waterpots with water." And they filled them up to the brim. And He said to them, "Draw some out now, and take it to the master of the feast." And they took it. When the master of the feast had tasted the water that was made wine, and did not know where it came from (but the servants who had drawn the water knew), the master of the feast called the bridegroom. And he said to him, "Every man at the beginning sets out the good wine, and when the guests have well drunk, then the inferior. You have kept the good wine until now!" This beginning of signs Jesus did in Cana of Galilee, and manifested His glory; and His disciples believed in Him. John 2:1–11

Glory be to God Forever, Amen

FEAST OF THE ENTRY INTO THE TEMPLE

Holy Gospel

Stand up in the fear of God and listen to the Holy Gospel, A chapter from the Holy Gospel according to Saint Luke, May his blessings be with us all, Amen

From the psalms of our teacher David the prophet and king, May his blessings be with us all, Amen

> I will go into Your house with burnt offerings; I will pay You my vows, Which my lips have uttered And my mouth has spoken when I was in trouble. I will offer You burnt sacrifices of fat animals, With the sweet aroma of rams; I will offer bulls with goats. Selah Alleluia. -Psalm 66: 13-15

Blessed is He who comes in the Name of the Lord Our Lord, God and Saviour and the King of us all, Jesus Christ, the Son of the living God. Glory be to You forever more, Amen

And the Child grew and became strong in spirit, filled with wisdom; and the grace of God was upon Him. His parents went to Jerusalem every year at the Feast of the Passover. And when He was twelve years old, they went up to Jerusalem according to the custom of the feast. When they had finished the days, as they returned, the Boy Jesus lingered behind in Jerusalem. And Joseph and His mother did not know it; but supposing Him to have been in the company, they went a day's journey, and sought Him among their relatives and acquaintances. So when they did not find Him, they returned to Jerusalem, seeking Him. Now so it was that after three days they found Him in the temple, sitting in the midst of the teachers, both listening to them and asking them questions. And all who heard Him were astonished at His understanding and answers. So when they saw Him, they were amazed; and His mother said to Him, "Son, why have You done this to us? Look, Your father and I have sought You anxiously."

And He said to them, "Why did you seek Me? Did you not know that I must be about My Father's business?" But they did not understand the statement which

He spoke to them. Then He went down with them and came to Nazareth, and was subject to them, but His mother kept all these things in her heart. And Jesus increased in wisdom and stature, and in favor with God and men. Luke 2: 40 -52

Glory be to God Forever, Amen

Pauline

Paul, the servant of our Lord Jesus Christ, called to be an apostle, appointed to the Gospel of God. A reading from the Epistle of our teacher Paul to Philippians. May his holy blessings be with us. Amen.

St Paul the Apostle was writing a letter to the Christians who lived in the busy city of Philippi. Dear Philippians, Rejoice in the Lord! I hope you don't mind my saying some things over and over to you. I just want to make sure that you've really got it. Especially, I want to remind you about circumcision. This is that mark that Jewish people make on a baby's body when he is just eight days old. Jesus was Jewish, and He got circumcised. I am Jewish, and I got circumcised. But I want to be sure that you understand— That was a JEWISH thing. It is not a CHRISTIAN thing! Let me explain why Christians don't need to be circumcised: The Jewish people thought that a mark on their bodies made them good people, special people, the people of God. But Jesus taught us that it is not marks on the outside of your body that make you good or special. The people of God are the ones whose heart like God. So it's not what you have on the OUTSIDE of your body that matters, it's what you are like on the INSIDE that matters. I was a very famous Jew! But I gave all that up, because I found something so, so much better: I found Jesus! Now, all that fame is like rubbish to me. Anything at all that used to make me think I was special— now it is just like rubbish to me. Because Jesus is my real Treasure. I know I can't be a truly good person without Jesus. So I try to think about His resurrection; And share with Him in His suffering; And be like Him when He was on the Cross so that I can rise from the dead with Him too! That is much more important than a mark on your body like circumcision! (Philippians 3:1–12)

Bye for now!

Signed, Paul

The grace of God the Father be with you all, Amen.

Catholicon

The Catholic Epistle from the Second Epistle of our teacher St Peter. May his holy blessings be with us. Amen.

Hello everyone! This is your old friend Peter the Apostle. I am getting rather old these days, and I will soon be going to heaven, But before I do, I want to make really sure that you know right from wrong, And that you know the truth about Jesus. We didn't make up stories, you know! We were actually there when Jesus was`on the mountain. And we heard the voice of God the Father speak from heaven! Remember what He said? "This is My beloved Son, in whom I am well pleased." That's what the prophets in the Old Testament said would happen! They weren't making up stories either. The prophets just spoke exactly what the Holy Spirit told them to speak. Their words were like turning on the light in a dark room. Or like a bright morning star that tells you that the sun will rise soon. When we read the words of the prophets in the Bible, and we let the Holy Spirit teach us what they really meant, it's like the morning star is rising in our hearts, preparing them for the coming of Jesus. (2 Peter 1:12-21)

Be good!

Signed, Peter the Apostle

Do not love the world, nor the things which are in the world. The world shall pass away and all its desires; but he who does the will of God shall abide forever. Amen.

The Acts

A reading from the Acts of our fathers the pure apostles, who were invested with the grace of the Holy Spirit. May their blessing be with us all. Amen.

The Disciples of Jesus had gathered together in the city of Jerusalem to discuss a very tough question. When a person who is not Jewish becomes a Christian, do they have to do all the things that Jewish people do? Some Jewish Christians said, "YES! Of course you can't be Christian without following all of Moses' Laws!" But other Christians said, "NO! Jesus set us free from all those Jewish laws." And when everyone had finished saying what they thought, James the Elder said: "OK, listen to me, please Peter told us that God has shown Him that He loves everyone, and it doesn't matter if they are Jewish of not. Everyone can be a Christian. And this is what God said a long time ago, in the time of the prophet Amos— that ALL people will want to find God. So it looks to me like the answer is clear, here: We should not expect people who are not Jewish to do all the Jewish stuff. You can seek the Lord, and love Jesus, and follow Jesus, and be a Christian, WITHOUT doing all that Jewish stuff. All we should ask of them is not to worship the idols that they used to worship before they became Christians. That's all." And everyone saw that James was right. And they all agreed with him. (Chapter 15:13–21)

The word of the Lord shall grow, multiply, be mighty and be confirmed in the holy Church of God. Amen.

Holy Gospel

Stand up in the fear of God and listen to the Holy Gospel, A chapter from the Holy Gospel according to Saint Luke, May his blessings be with us all, Amen

From the psalms of our teacher David the prophet and king, May his blessings be with us all, Amen

> Offer to God a sacrifice of praise, And pay your vows to the Most High.
> A sacrifice of praise shall glorify Me, And there is the way whereby I
> will show him the salvation of God. Alleluia. -Psalm 50:14, 23

Blessed is He who comes in the Name of the Lord Our Lord, God and Saviour and the King of us all, Jesus Christ, the Son of the living God. Glory be to You forever more, Amen

And when eight days were completed for the circumcision of the Child, His name was called JESUS, the name given by the angel before He was conceived in the womb. Now when the days of her purification according to the law of Moses were completed, they brought Him to Jerusalem to present Him to the Lord and behold, there was a man in Jerusalem whose name was Simeon, and this man was just and devout and it had been revealed to him by the Holy Spirit that he would not see So he came by the Spirit into the temple and he took the Child Jesus up in his arms and blessed God and said: "Lord, now You are letting Your servant depart in peace, According to Your word; For my eyes have seen Your salvation Which You have prepared before the face of all peoples, A light to bring revelation to the Gentiles, And the glory of Your people Israel." And Joseph and His mother marvelled at those things which were spoken of Him. Then Simeon blessed them, and said to Mary His mother, "Behold, this Child is destined for the fall and rising of many in Israel, and for a sign which will be spoken against (yes, a sword will pierce through your own soul also), that the thoughts of many hearts may be revealed." Now there was one, Anna, a prophetess she was of a great age a widow of about eighty-four years who did not depart from the temple, but served God with fastings and prayers night and day. And coming in that instant she gave thanks to the Lord, and spoke of Him to all those who looked for redemption in Jerusalem. So when they had performed all things according to the law of the Lord, they returned to Galilee, to their own city, Nazareth. Luke 2:21–39

Glory be to God Forever, Amen

THE FEAST OF CROSS- (in March)

Holy Gospel

Stand up in the fear of God and listen to the Holy Gospel, A chapter from the Holy Gospel according to Saint John, May his blessings be with us all, Amen

From the psalms of our teacher David the prophet and king, May his blessings be with us all, Amen

> You have given a banner to those who fear You, That it may be displayed because of the truth. Selah That Your beloved may be delivered, Save with Your right hand, and hear me. Alleluia. -Psalm 60:4-5

Blessed is He who comes in the Name of the Lord Our Lord, God and Saviour and the King of us all, Jesus Christ, the Son of the living God. Glory be to You forever more, Amen

If anyone serves Me, let him follow Me; and where I am, there My servant will be also. If anyone serves Me, him My Father will honor. "Now My soul is troubled, and what shall I say? 'Father, save Me from this hour'? But for this purpose I came to this hour. Father, glorify Your name." Then a voice came from heaven, saying, "I have both glorified it and will glorify it again." Therefore the people who stood by and heard it said that it had thundered. Others said, "An angel has spoken to Him." Jesus answered and said, "This voice did not come because of Me, but for your sake. Now is the judgment of this world; now the ruler of this world will be cast out. And I, if I am lifted up from the earth, will draw all peoples to Myself." This He said, signifying by what death He would die. The people answered Him, "We have heard from the law that the Christ remains forever; and how can You say, 'The Son of Man must be lifted up'? Who is this Son of Man?" Then Jesus said to them, "A little while longer the light is with you. Walk while you have the light, lest darkness overtake you; he who walks in darkness does not know where he is going. While you have the light, believe in the light, that you may become sons of light." These things Jesus spoke, and departed, and was hidden from them. John 12: 26-36

Glory be to God Forever, Amen

Pauline

Paul, the servant of our Lord Jesus Christ, called to be an apostle, appointed to the Gospel of God. A reading from First Epistle of our teacher Paul to the Corinthians. May his holy blessings be with us. Amen.

St Paul the Apostle was writing a letter to the Christians who lived in the rich city of Corinth.

Dear Corinthians, Jesus Christ our Lord died on the Cross because He loves us. That's how Jesus saved us, and saved the whole wide world. We depend on Jesus. But some people don't depend on Jesus and His Cross. Instead, some people depend on their OWN cleverness! They think Jesus wasn't very clever, because He let people kill Him on the Cross. But Jesus was being much more clever than they can realise! Because when Jesus died on the Cross, He knew He would rise again! And Jesus knew He would save the world! That is VERY clever indeed! That's How God works. He doesn't need to prove Himself to anyone. God does things that don't SEEM very clever; but they are very, very clever! God works through people who don't SEEM very strong; but they are very, very strong! God works through people who don't SEEM very important; But they are very, very important! That way, no one can show off and say, "Look at me! I am so clever! I am so strong! I am so important!" So, we should never show off like that. We can only be clever, and strong, and important because God helps us, through His Son, Jesus Christ. Jesus is the One who makes us clever. Jesus is the One who makes us good. Jesus is the One who saves us. Jesus is the One who deserves all the credit! (1 Corinthians 1:17–31)

Bye for now!

Signed, Paul

The grace of God the Father be with you all, Amen.

Catholicon

The Catholic Epistle from the First Epistle of our teacher St Peter. May his holy blessings be with us. Amen.

Hello Everyone!

Sometimes, you might meet someone who doesn't like you very much. But you might make them your friend just by being kind to them. When you are a Christian, you are free! But that doesn't mean free to be naughty! It means you are free to be kind, and helpful, and happy and to serve God. So, Treat everyone with respect. Love your friends. Listen to God. Follow the law. If you have a master (like your teacher, for example, or your parents) you must do what they tell you to, even if you think they are being a bit too strict. Let me tell you why: Sometimes, when you really have done something wrong, you get in trouble, Well that's OK, Then, it's fair for you to get in trouble! You should take the punishment that you deserve. But sometimes, you get in trouble when you haven't really done anything wrong, should you just "take it" then? That's exactly what happened to Jesus! He NEVER did anything wrong, but they arrested Him and said He did things that weren't true. And even though He was innocent, He never talked back to the rulers or the soldiers. He never got angry with them. He never argued with them. He put up with all that horrible stuff they did to Him, and trusted in His Father to look after Him. Do you know why? Because He wanted to save us from OUR sins. That's right, He died the death WE were going to die, when He died for us on the Cross so that we could live. We were like sheep who had gone astray and gotten lost and He is our Good Shepherd, who gave His life to save His sheep. So if you truly love Jesus, be like Him: Be obedient to the people that God gave you, to look after you. (1 Peter 2:11–25)

Bye for now!

Signed, Peter the Apostle

Do not love the world, nor the things which are in the world. The world shall pass away and all its desires; but he who does the will of God shall abide forever. Amen.

The Acts

God had sent St Peter the Apostle to talk to a very kind Roman soldier, a centurion, whose name was Cornelius. Peter said: Wow! God really does love EVERYONE in the world! God doesn't just like Jewish people. He loves everyone! It doesn't matter where you live. It doesn't matter who you are. If you love God, God accepts you. So, it doesn't matter that you're not Jewish, Cornelius. You are a good man. God loves you! God accepts you! It seems, Cornelius, that you have heard what is being said about Jesus of Nazareth. How he was baptised by John the Baptist, and how the Holy Spirit appeared above Him, and how He helped people, and healed them. We saw all this with our own eyes! And we saw how they crucified Him on the Cross, and we saw Him when He came back to life again on the third day! He even ate and drank with us, after he rose from the dead! He told us that we must preach about Him— we must tell everyone! That Jesus is the Lord of all the world, the living and the dead. As the old prophets said, whoever believes in Him will have their sins forgiven. (Chapter 10:34–43)

Holy Gospel

Stand up in the fear of God and listen to the Holy Gospel, A chapter from the Holy Gospel according to Saint John, May his blessings be with us all, Amen

From the psalms of our teacher David the prophet and king, May his blessings be with us all, Amen

> It is fitting to sing a hymn to You in Zion, O God, And a vow shall be rendered to You in Jerusalem. Hear my prayer; To You all flesh shall come. Alleluia. Psalm 65:1–2

Blessed is He who comes in the Name of the Lord Our Lord, God and Saviour and the King of us all, Jesus Christ, the Son of the living God. Glory be to You forever more, Amen

Now it was the Feast of Dedication in Jerusalem, and it was winter. And Jesus walked in the temple, in Solomon's porch. Then the Jews surrounded Him and said to Him, "How long do You keep us in doubt? If You are the Christ, tell us plainly." Jesus answered them, "I told you, and you do not believe. The works that I do in My Father's name, they bear witness of Me. "But you do not believe, because you are not of My sheep, as I said to you. My sheep hear My voice, and I know them, and they follow Me. "And I give them eternal life, and they shall never perish; neither shall anyone snatch them out of My hand. "My Father, who has given them to Me, is greater than all; and no one is able to snatch them out of My Father's hand. "I and My Father are one." Then the Jews took up stones again to stone Him. Jesus answered them, "Many good works I have shown you from My Father. For which of those works do you stone Me?" The Jews answered Him, saying, "For a good work we do not stone You, but for blasphemy, and because You, being a Man, make Yourself God." Jesus answered them, "Is it not written in your law, 'I said, "You are gods" '? "If He called them gods, to whom the word of God came (and the Scripture cannot be broken), "do you say of Him whom the Father sanctified and sent into the world, 'You are blaspheming,' because I said, 'I am the Son of God'? "If I do not do the works of My Father, do not believe Me; but if I do, though you do not believe Me, believe the works, "that you may know and believe that the Father is in Me, and I in Him." *John 10:22–38*

Glory be to God Forever, Amen

THE FEAST OF ANNUNCIATION

Holy Gospel

Stand up in the fear of God and listen to the Holy Gospel,A chapter from the Holy Gospel according to Saint Luke, May his blessings be with us all, Amen

From the psalms of our teacher David the prophet and king,May his blessings be with us all, Amen

> He shall come down like rain upon the grass before mowing, Like showers that water the earth. In His days the righteous shall flourish, And abundance of peace, Until the moon is no more Alleluia. Psalm 72:6-7

Blessed is He who comes in the Name of the Lord Our Lord, God and Saviour and the King of us all, Jesus Christ, the Son of the living God. Glory be to You forever more, Amen

But if I cast out demons with the finger of God, surely the kingdom of God has come upon you. When a strong man, fully armed, guards his own palace, his goods are in peace. But when a stronger than he comes upon him and overcomes him, he takes from him all his armor in which he trusted, and divides his spoils. He who is not with Me is against Me, and he who does not gather with Me scatters.

"When an unclean spirit goes out of a man, he goes through dry places, seeking rest; and finding none, he says, 'I will return to my house from which I came.' And when he comes, he finds it swept and put in order. Then he goes and takes with him seven other spirits more wicked than himself, and they enter and dwell there; and the last state of that man is worse than the first." And it happened, as He spoke these things, that a certain woman from the crowd raised her voice and said to Him, "Blessed is the womb that bore You, and the breasts which nursed You!" But He said, "More than that, blessed are those who hear the word of God and keep it!" Luke 11:20-28

Glory be to God Forever, Amen

Pauline

Paul, the servant of our Lord Jesus Christ, called to be an apostle, appointed to the Gospel of God. A reading from the Epistle of our teacher Paul to Romans. May his holy blessings be with us. Amen.

St Paul the Apostle was writing a letter to the Christians who lived in the great city of Rome!

Dear Romans, You know that there are some people called the Jews or Hebrews? These were God's people in the Old Testament, in the time of Abraham, and Moses, and David the King. And everyone else who is not Jewish is called a Gentile. So is it better to be a Jew or a Gentile? What do you think? On the one hand, God gave the Jews His own Law, and sent them His own prophets. That's pretty special! But on the other hand, the Jews were quite naughty, and they often didn't listen to God. That's pretty bad! But do you know what? Everybody is bad sometimes. Everybody needs God to help them to be good, whether they are a Jew or a Gentile. In fact, "all have sinned and fall short of the glory of God". So did the Jews do better, because they knew the Law of God? Actually, no! They were more guilty, because they knew what they were doing was wrong, the Law told them so but they still did it anyway! So here is a very important question: What is it that really, really makes us into good people who love God? Does the Law of Moses make us good? Not by itself! The Jews had the Law, but they were still pretty bad! Does doing good things make us good? Not by itself! All the bad things we do cancel out all the good things! No, what really, really makes us good is when we know how much God loves us, and we love Him back. This is called "faith". So whether you are a Jew or a Gentile, it doesn't really matter. God loves absolutely, positively, everyone! And whether you have God's Law (like the Jews), Or whether you don't have God's law (like the Gentiles) It doesn't really matter, because loving God is what really matters. And when we love God, our hearts change, and we become good, just like Him. (Romans 3:1-31)

Bye for now!

Signed, Paul

The grace of God the Father be with you all, Amen.

Catholicon

The Catholic Epistle from the First Epistle of our teacher St John. May his holy blessings be with us. Amen.

Hello everyone, this is John the Disciple of Jesus Christ. I was so, so blessed to actually see Jesus with my very own eyes, and touch Him with my very own hands! So you really can believe me when I tell you that God the Father gave us a beautiful eternal life through His Son, Jesus. When we are friends with God, through Jesus, we are so, so, so happy! Here is what I learned from Jesus: "God is light and in Him is no darkness at all". If we say we are Jesus' friends, but we walk in darkness by doing bad things, do you think we are really Jesus' friends? No! We would be lying! Jesus' real friends walk in the light, because, remember "God is light and in Him is no darkness at all". And if we do walk in the light of Jesus, we are friends with each other too, And Jesus forgives us any bad things we did. Have you ever done something wrong? Don't pretend like you haven't, because everybody has done something wrong sometime! But don't worry. Jesus loves you very much indeed. He wants to make everything better. So when we are very brave and honest, and tell the truth about the bad things we did, Jesus forgives us, and cleans our hearts, and makes us good again. He is always Standing up for us, Saving us, Protecting us, Forgiving us. And He does this for the whole wide world! This is how you can tell if you really love Jesus and are His friend. If you're behaviour is just like Jesus' behaviour. If you really love Jesus, you will keep His commandments. (1 John 1:1-2:6)

Bye for now!

Signed, John the Beloved

Do not love the world, nor the things which are in the world. The world shall pass away and all its desires; but he who does the will of God shall abide forever. Amen.

The Acts

Do you remember the story of Moses the prophet? Remember how he became the Prince of Egypt, even though he was really a Jew? But then, one day, when he was about 40 years old, he saw an Egyptian man beating up a Jewish slave really badly. So he stepped in and fought the Egyptian, but Moses ended up killing the Egyptian! Instead of the Jews thanking him for protecting them, they threatened to tell on him! So Moses ran away, far, far away into the desert, to a place called Midian, so no one would arrest him for killing the Egyptian. And in Midian, he married a nice lady, and they had two sons. Then when Moses was about 80 years old, something really odd happened to him. Moses was walking on a mountain called Sinai, when he saw a big bush on fire, but it wasn't burning up! And that's not the oddest thing yet! The burning bush spoke to Moses! Yes, it said words! Do you know what the burning bush said? It said: "I am the God of your fathers—the God of Abraham, the God of Isaac, and the God of Jacob" It was God talking to Moses! Moses was scared! Moses was frightened! Moses was trembling! Then God spoke again saying "Take your sandals off your feet, for the place where you stand is holy ground". And Moses took off his sandals right away! And God continued: "Moses, I am sending you back to Egypt, to save my people from suffering as slaves". Did Moses go to Egypt? Well, that's a story for another day. Or, you can go home today and read it in your own Bible! (Chapter 7:23-34)

Holy Gospel

Stand up in the fear of God and listen to the Holy Gospel, A chapter from the Holy Gospel according to Saint Luke, May his blessings be with us all, Amen

From the psalms of our teacher David the prophet and king, May his blessings be with us all, Amen

> Listen, O daughter, behold and incline your ear, And forget your people and your father's house; For the King desired your beauty, For He is your Lord.. Alleluia. Psalm 45:10-11

Blessed is He who comes in the Name of the Lord Our Lord, God and Saviour and the King of us all, Jesus Christ, the Son of the living God. Glory be to You forever more, Amen

Now in the sixth month the angel Gabriel was sent by God to a city of Galilee named Nazareth, to a virgin betrothed to a man whose name was Joseph, of the house of David. The virgin's name was Mary. And having come in, the angel said to her, "Rejoice, highly favoured one, the Lord is with you; blessed are you among women!" But when she saw him, she was troubled at his saying, and considered what manner of greeting this was. Then the angel said to her, "Do not be afraid, Mary, for you have found favour with God. And behold, you will conceive in your womb and bring forth a Son, and shall call His name Jesus. He will be great, and will be called the Son of the Highest; and the Lord God will give Him the throne of His father David. "And He will reign over the house of Jacob forever, and of His kingdom there will be no end." Then Mary said to the angel, "How can this be, since I do not know a man?" And the angel answered and said to her, "The Holy Spirit will come upon you, and the power of the Highest will overshadow you; therefore, also, that Holy One who is to be born will be called the Son of God. Now indeed, Elizabeth your relative has also conceived a son in her old age; and this is now the sixth month for her who was called barren. For with God nothing will be impossible." Then Mary said, "Behold the maidservant of the Lord! Let it be to me according to your word." And the angel departed from her. Luke 1:26-38

Glory be to God Forever, Amen

THE ENTRY OF THE HOLY FAMILY INTO EGYPT

Holy Gospel

MATINS

Stand up in the fear of God and listen to the Holy Gospel, A chapter from the Holy Gospel according to Saint Matthew, May his blessings be with us all, Amen

From the psalms of our teacher David the prophet and king, May his blessings be with us all, Amen

They forgot God their Savior, Who had done great things in Egypt,
Remember me, O Lord, with the favor You have toward Your people.
Oh, visit me with Your salvation, Alleluia. Psalm 106:21,4

Blessed is He who comes in the Name of the Lord Our Lord, God and Saviour and the King of us all, Jesus Christ, the Son of the living God. Glory be to You forever more, Amen

But when Jesus knew it, He withdrew from there. And great multitudes followed Him, and He healed them all. Yet He warned them not to make Him known, that it might be fulfilled which was spoken by Isaiah the prophet, saying:

"Behold! My Servant whom I have chosen, My Beloved in whom My soul is well pleased! I will put My Spirit upon Him, And He will declare justice to the Gentiles. He will not quarrel nor cry out, Nor will anyone hear His voice in the streets. A bruised reed He will not break, And smoking flax He will not quench, Till He sends forth justice to victory; And in His name Gentiles will trust." Then one was brought to Him who was demon-possessed, blind and mute; and He healed him, so that the blind and mute man both spoke and saw. And all the multitudes were amazed and said, "Could this be the Son of David?" Matthew 12:15-23

Glory be to God Forever, Amen

Pauline

Paul, the servant of our Lord Jesus Christ, called to be an apostle, appointed to the Gospel of God. A reading from the Epistle of our teacher Paul to the Ephesians. May his holy blessings be with us. Amen.

Dear Ephesians,

God has been so kind to us! Do you remember how many of you used to be quite naughty, and not at all nice? And then, when you got to know Jesus, everything changed! Instead of belonging to the world, now you belong to Heaven! You used to be so far, far away from God, but now, you are God's own beloved children! How did this wonderful thing happen? Was it because you are extra clever? No! It is because God is so, so kind, and He loves you so, so much. This is God's gift to you. Because you believe in Jesus and you love Jesus, He broke down the big wall that kept you away from God, and made you God's friends, not God's enemies, anymore. Now, it doesn't matter how near or far you might live. Everyone can come to God and nothing can stop them. All because Jesus came to us, then sent us His Holy Spirit. So now, no matter where you live, you can never be a stranger. Now, Heaven is your home. Now, you belong to God's family, together with all the saints and the apostles and the prophets. Now, you are like the bricks that make up the Church. Each one of you a brick in God's House. And Jesus is the cornerstone that holds up all the other bricks. And together, we are God's House, and God lives in us. Isn't that amazing? (Ephesians 2:1–22)

Bye for now!

Signed, Paul

The grace of God the Father be with you all, Amen.

Catholicon

The Catholic Epistle from the First Epistle of our teacher St John. May his holy blessings be with us. Amen.

My Beloved, Let us love one another for love is of God and everyone who loves is born of God. Anyone who does not love, Does not know God. For, God is love. And how do we know that God loves us so? Because God sent to us His Only Begotten Son, Jesus Christ, to give us life. Where does love come from? We love God, because He first loved us, and sent His Son Jesus Christ to save us from our sins. My little children, If God loves us SO much then we also should love each other! Nobody has ever actually seen God, but if we truly love each other, God truly lives inside us! Do you want to know how you can tell if you are a good follower of God? Well, If you have the Holy Spirit living in you, you are a good Jesus Follower. And if you believe that Jesus is the Son of God, and that He came to save us, you are a good Jesus Follower. And if you know just how much God loves you, you are a good Jesus Follower. God is Love. Whoever lives in love, lives in God and God lives in Him. God's perfect love inside us makes us ready to face the scary Judgement Day. No way! WE won't be scared! That's because when your heart is full of love, there's no room left for being afraid! "Perfect love casts out fear." And do you know WHY we love God? Because He loved us first! (1 John 4:7–19)

God loves you!

Signed, John the Beloved

Do not love the world, nor the things which are in the world. The world shall pass away and all its desires; but he who does the will of God shall abide forever. Amen.

The Acts

St Stephen the Deacon was speaking to some people, and telling them the story of Moses. Moses' parents were Jewish, but they lived in Egypt. And it happened that Moses was adopted by Pharaoh's daughter and brought up in her house. When he grew up, he became a very important man in Egypt. One day, he was walking along, when he saw an Egyptian fighting with a Jew. Moses was angry! He stood up for his Jewish friend! But he was so angry, that he ended up killing the Egyptian. Oops. The next day, he saw two Jewish men fighting. "Don't fight," said Moses. "You should be friends." But one of them said to Moses: "This is none of your business! Are you going to kill me like you killed the Egyptian yesterday?" Moses was scared. He realised that he would get in trouble for killing the Egyptian man. So Moses ran away to live in a land far away. Many years later, Moses saw the burning bush and heard the voice of God speaking from the bush. This is what God said to Moses: "I am the God of your fathers— the God of Abraham, the God of Isaac, and the God of Jacob. Take your sandals off your feet, for the place where you stand is holy ground, "I have seen how sad my people are in Egypt. And now, I will help them by sending you to Egypt to save them." (Chapter 7:20–34)

Holy Gospel

> And He smote all the firstborn in their land, The firstling of all their labour. Egypt was gladdened by their exodus, For fear of them fell upon them. Alleluia. Psalm 105:36,38

Blessed is He who comes in the Name of the Lord Our Lord, God and Saviour and the King of us all, Jesus Christ, the Son of the living God. Glory be to You forever more, Amen

Now when they had departed, behold, an angel of the Lord appeared to Joseph in a dream, saying: "Arise, take the young Child and His mother, flee to Egypt, and stay there until I bring you word; for Herod will seek the young Child to destroy Him." When he arose, he took the young Child and His mother by night and departed for Egypt, and was there until the death of Herod, that it might be fulfilled which was spoken by the Lord through the prophet, saying, "Out of Egypt I called My Son." Then Herod, when he saw that he was deceived by the wise men, was exceedingly angry; and he sent forth and put to death all the male children who were in Bethlehem and in all its districts, from two years old and under, according to the time which he had determined from the wise men. Then was fulfilled what was spoken by Jeremiah the prophet, saying: "A voice was heard in Ramah, Lamentation, weeping, and great mourning, "Rachel weeping for her children, refusing to be comforted, Because they are no more." Now when Herod was dead, behold, an angel of the Lord appeared in a dream to Joseph in Egypt, saying, "Arise, take the young Child and His mother, and go to the land of Israel, for those who sought the young Child's life are dead." Then he arose, took the young Child and His mother, and came into the land of Israel. But when he heard that Archelaus was reigning over Judea instead of his father Herod, he was afraid to go there. And being warned by God in a dream, he turned aside into the region of Galilee. And he came and dwelt in a city called Nazareth, that it might be fulfilled which was spoken by the prophets, "He shall be called a Nazarene."
Matthew 2:13–23

Glory be to God Forever, Amen

FEAST OF THE TRANSFIGURATION

Holy Gospel

MATINS

Stand up in the fear of God and listen to the Holy Gospel, A chapter from the Holy Gospel according to Saint Matthew, May his blessings be with us all, Amen

From the psalms of our teacher David the prophet and king, May his blessings be with us all, Amen

> May the glory of the Lord endure forever; May the Lord rejoice in His works. He looks on the earth, and it trembles; He touches the hills, and they smoke. Alleluia. Psalm 104:31-32

Blessed is He who comes in the Name of the Lord Our Lord, God and Saviour and the King of us all, Jesus Christ, the Son of the living God. Glory be to You forever more, Amen

Now after six days Jesus took Peter, James, and John his brother, led them up on a high mountain by themselves; and He was transfigured before them. His face shone like the sun, and His clothes became as white as the light. And behold, Moses and Elijah appeared to them, talking with Him. Then Peter answered and said to Jesus, "Lord, it is good for us to be here; if You wish, let us make here three tabernacles: one for You, one for Moses, and one for Elijah." While he was still speaking, behold, a bright cloud overshadowed them; and suddenly a voice came out of the cloud, saying, "This is My beloved Son, in whom I am well pleased. Hear Him!" And when the disciples heard it, they fell on their faces and were greatly afraid. But Jesus came and touched them and said, "Arise, and do not be afraid." When they had lifted up their eyes, they saw no one but Jesus only.

Now as they came down from the mountain, Jesus commanded them, saying, "Tell the vision to no one until the Son of Man is risen from the dead." Matthew 17:1-9

Glory be to God Forever, Amen

Pauline

Paul, the servant of our Lord Jesus Christ, called to be an apostle, appointed to the Gospel of God. A reading from the Epistle of our teacher Paul to Colossians. May his holy blessings be with us. Amen.

St Paul the Apostle was writing a letter to the Christians who lived in the town of Colosse.

Dear Colossians, You have made my friend Timothy and I so very happy! We thank God for you every day. Do you know why? Because you love Jesus so much! And you love one another so much! Just as the Truth of the Gospel of Jesus teaches us, and just as you learned from our friend, Epaphras (Ep-aff-rass). Since Epaphras told us about you, we have been praying for you every single day. We pray that God will make you wise and help you to understand His will better. We pray that you will be strong and live a good life, just like Jesus. We pray that you will do more and more good things, and always be patient and joyful and we pray that you will always be thankful to God, for He has invited us to live with His wonderful saints in His beautiful light! Through Jesus, His Son, God saved us from the evil power of darkness, and brought us safely to His Kingdom, full of light! Because Jesus is very special indeed. Jesus is God! When God became a man, He became Jesus! Jesus is God, the One who made everything in the world (whether you can see it or not) and everything in the world exists in Jesus! And Jesus is the Head of the Church. And the Church is His Body. That's why Jesus loves the Church so much! When Jesus shed His blood and died on the Cross, He made everyone and everything His friends again. Before you Colossians knew Jesus, you were not His friends. You thought bad thoughts. You did bad things. But Jesus loved you so much that He gave up His body on the Cross to save you from evil, and make you a part of His Body, which is the Church. So now, if you keep loving Jesus, And believing in Jesus, And hoping in Jesus, You will always be holy and beautiful in His eyes. This is the Gospel (or good news) that Jesus told me to preach to you and to every creature on earth! (Colossians 1:1-23)

Bye for now!

Signed, Paul

> *The grace of God the Father be with you all, Amen.*

Catholicon

Hello everyone! This is your old friend Peter the Apostle. I am getting rather old these days, and I will soon be going to heaven, But before I do, I want to make really sure that you know right from wrong, And that you know the truth about Jesus. We didn't make up stories, you know! We were actually there when Jesus was on the mountain. And we heard the voice of God the Father speak from heaven! Remember what He said? "This is My beloved Son, in whom I am well pleased." That's what the prophets in the Old Testament said would happen! They weren't making up stories either. The prophets just spoke exactly what the Holy Spirit told them to speak. Their words were like turning on the light in a dark room. Or like a bright morning star that tells you that the sun will rise soon. When we read the words of the prophets in the Bible, and we let the Holy Spirit teach us what they really meant, it's like the morning star is rising in our hearts, preparing them for the coming of Jesus. (2 Peter 1:12-21)

Be good!

Signed, Peter the Apostle

The Acts

St Stephen the first Archdeacon was being judged by the Jewish Council and the High Priest. He was trying to explain Jesus to them. He said, Remember how God told Moses to make a big holy tent called the tabernacle when they were wandering in the desert? And remember how Joshua brought the tabernacle into the Promised Land of Israel? And remember how King Solomon replaced the tabernacle tent by building a huge stone temple in Jerusalem to take it's place? Do you really think that God needs a holy tent or a stone temple that humans made to be His house? Really? Remember what God said in the Bible: "Heaven is My throne, And earth is My footstool." How could God need us to build Him a house? But you High Priest and Council are very stubborn. You say you read the Bible and love God, but when Jesus who is God came to you, you crucified Him on the Cross! Now the High Priest and the Council did not like being called stubborn! They were so angry with Stephen, because he showed them how wrong they were about Jesus. But Stephen was so calm and peaceful. In fact, just at that moment, he saw a miracle! And he said: "Look! I see the heavens opened, and Jesus at the right hand of God His Father!" Well, this only made the crowd angrier and angrier! They shouted out loud! They blocked their ears! They ran at Stephen and grabbed him! They dragged him out and started throwing big sharp stones at poor Stephen! OUCH!!! But do you think Stephen was angry back at them? No. Stephen was calm and peaceful. Stephen was praying "Lord, receive my spirit." "Lord, please forgive them for this horrible thing they are doing." And that is how Stephen died and became the very first martyr. But there was a young man standing nearby. He was happy about what was happening to Stephen. That young man's name was Saul. Many years after Stephen died, Saul would see Jesus in a miracle, and that miracle would change Saul into St Paul! But that's another story. (Chapter 7:44 –8:1)

The word of the Lord shall grow, multiply, be mighty and be confirmed in the holy Church of God. Amen.

Holy Gospel

Stand up in the fear of God and listen to the Holy Gospel, A chapter from the Holy Gospel according to Saint Mark, May his blessings be with us all, Amen

From the psalms of our teacher David the prophet and king, May his blessings be with us all, Amen

> His foundations are in the holy mountains; The Lord loves the gates of Zion More than all the dwellings of Jacob. A man will say, "Mother Zion, "And a man was born in her; For the Most High Himself founded it. Alleluia. Psalm 87:1-2,5

Blessed is He who comes in the Name of the Lord Our Lord, God and Saviour and the King of us all, Jesus Christ, the Son of the living God. Glory be to You forever more, Amen

Now after six days Jesus took Peter, James, and John, and led them up on a high mountain apart by themselves; and He was transfigured before them. His clothes became shining, exceedingly white, like snow, such as no launderer on earth can whiten them. And Elijah appeared to them with Moses, and they were talking with Jesus. Then Peter answered and said to Jesus, "Rabbi, it is good for us to be here; and let us make three tabernacles: one for You, one for Moses, and one for Elijah"— because he did not know what to say, for they were greatly afraid. And a cloud came and overshadowed them; and a voice came out of the cloud, saying, "This is My beloved Son. Hear Him!" Suddenly, when they had looked around, they saw no one anymore, but only Jesus with themselves. Now as they came down from the mountain, He commanded them that they should tell no one the things they had seen, till the Son of Man had risen from the dead. So they kept this word to themselves, questioning what the rising from the dead meant. And they asked Him, saying, "Why do the scribes say that Elijah must come first?" Then He answered and told them, "Indeed, Elijah is coming first and restores all things and how is it written concerning the Son of Man, that He must suffer many things and be treated with contempt? But I say to you that Elijah has also come, and they did to him whatever they wished, as it is written of him." Mark 9:2-13

Glory be to God Forever, Amen

GREAT LENT

PREPARATION SUNDAY OF THE GREAT LENT

Holy Gospel

Stand up in the fear of God and listen to the Holy Gospel, A chapter from the Holy Gospel according to Saint Luke, May his blessings be with us all, Amen

From the psalms of our teacher David the prophet and king, May his blessings be with us all, Amen

> Serve the Lord with gladness; Come before His presence with singing. Know that the Lord, He is God; It is He who has made us, and not we ourselves; We are His people and the sheep of His pasture. Alleluia. Psalm 100:2-3

Blessed is He who comes in the Name of the Lord Our Lord, God and Saviour and the King of us all, Jesus Christ, the Son of the living God. Glory be to You forever more, Amen

Take heed to yourselves. If your brother sins against you, rebuke him; and if he repents, forgive him. And if he sins against you seven times in a day, and seven times in a day returns to you, saying, 'I repent,' you shall forgive him." And the apostles said to the Lord, "Increase our faith." So the Lord said, "If you have faith as a mustard seed, you can say to this mulberry tree, 'Be pulled up by the roots and be planted in the sea,' and it would obey you. And which of you, having a servant plowing or tending sheep, will say to him when he has come in from the field, 'Come at once and sit down to eat'? But will he not rather say to him, 'Prepare something for my supper, and gird yourself and serve me till I have eaten and drunk, and afterward you will eat and drink'? Does he thank that servant because he did the things that were commanded him? I think not. So likewise you, when you have done all those things which you are commanded, say, 'We are unprofitable servants. We have done what was our duty to do.' " Luke 17: 3-10

Glory be to God Forever, Amen

Pauline

Paul, the servant of our Lord Jesus Christ, called to be an apostle, appointed to the Gospel of God. A reading from the Second Epistle of our teacher Paul to Corinthians. May his holy blessings be with us. Amen.

St Paul the Apostle was writing a letter to the Christians who lived in the rich city of Corinth. Dear Corinthians, I am sorry to say that when someone shows off, you all just listen to them! Showing off is bad. I am not going to show off like those other people. I don't want to make you like me. I just want you to love God! So, I don't need to show off. I'm just going to tell you the truth about myself, because then you will see how good God is. Are you ready? Just like those show-offs, I am a Hebrew, a child of Abraham. And I have served Jesus more than any of them. Because I love Jesus, I have been in prison, I have been beaten up and almost killed many times! Because I love Jesus, People threw stones at me, I was shipwrecked three times, and once, I was in the sea for a whole night and day! Because I love Jesus, I have been on many long journeys and seen lots and lots of danger! Danger from the ocean, Danger from robbers, Danger from my own countrymen, Danger from the Gentiles and strangers, Danger in the city, Danger in the wilderness, Danger even from other and who don't really Christians who don't really love Jesus, follow Jesus. Because I love Jesus, I have often worked so hard, been so tired, hungry and thirsty, cold and naked. All of this I have done because I love Jesus so much, And I care about His Church so much! I think about it every day. (2 Corinthians 11:16-28)

Bye for now!

Signed, Paul

The grace of God the Father be with you all, Amen.

Catholicon

The Catholic Epistle from the Second Epistle of our teacher St Peter. May his holy blessings be with us. Amen.

My little children, this is the Apostle, Simon Peter, who really loves Jesus and loves serving Him. I am writing to those who also love our precious Jesus and believe in Him like me. When we love Jesus, we find grace and peace— that means we feel happy and safe, because we know how very much He loves us and looks after us. When we know the power of God in Jesus, we have everything we need to live a really good life of godliness— being good, like God. We get to share in the good nature of God, and away from temptations, so we do good things, not bad things. So be very careful to grow more and more in your love for Jesus. If you have faith (you trust God), then learn to have virtue (to be a good person deep inside). If you have virtue, then learn to have knowledge (to know God). If you have knowledge, then learn to have self-control. If you have self-control, then learn to have perseverance (to be really patient and never give up). If you have perseverance, then learn to have godliness (to be good like God). If you have godliness, then learn to have brotherly kindness (always be kind to others). And if you have brotherly kindness, then learn to have agape love (love others the way God loves us). If you learn all these know Jesus, and your things, you will truly life will be full of goodness! If you don't learn all these things, you will be like someone who can't see, and just stumbles around bumping into everything! So, work hard to learn how to do good, so you can be a part of God's Kingdom forever. (2 Peter 1:1-11)

Bye for now!

Signed, Peter the Apostle

Do not love the world, nor the things which are in the world. The world shall pass away and all its desires; but he who does the will of God shall abide forever. Amen.

The Acts

A reading from the Acts of our fathers the pure apostles, who were invested with the grace of the Holy Spirit. May their blessing be with us all. Amen.

St Paul the Apostle arrived in Jerusalem and went to say Hi to St James and the rest of the Hebrew Christians who lived there. They were very happy to hear about all of Paul's adventures, and how so, so many people came to know and love

Jesus through him. But, they told him, there is a problem. The Hebrew Christians are still worried about letting go of all the laws that Moses gave. All those laws in the Old Testament, about washing your hands, and not eating some kinds of food, and so on, they think you don't like Moses or the Old Testament! We don't want this to turn into an argument! We have an idea to fix this problem. Here are four Hebrew men who are ready to be purified, just the way that Moses taught us. Why don't you go and be purified with them, and even pay for them all? That way, the Hebrew Christians will see that you don't have anything against Moses or the Old Testament, even though we have all agreed that Christians who are not Hebrews don't need to do these things. So Paul agreed. He went with the four Hebrew Christians, and together, they went to the temple in Jerusalem, And they offered their gifts and prayed, and just like Moses had taught, they were purified. So everyone was happy! (Chapter 21:15-26)

The word of the Lord shall grow, multiply, be mighty and be confirmed in the holy Church of God. Amen.

Holy Gospel

Stand up in the fear of God and listen to the Holy Gospel,A chapter from the Holy Gospel according to Saint Matthew, May his blessings be with us all, Amen

From the psalms of our teacher David the prophet and king,May his blessings be with us all, Amen

> Serve the Lord with fear And rejoice in Him with trembling. And now, O kings, understand; Be instructed, all you judges of the earth. Alleluia. Psalm 2:11,10

Blessed is He who comes in the Name of the Lord Our Lord, God and Saviour and the King of us all, Jesus Christ, the Son of the living God. Glory be to You forever more, Amen

Take heed that you do not do your charitable deeds before men, to be seen by them. Otherwise you have no reward from your Father in heaven. Therefore, when you do a charitable deed, do not do in the synagogues and in the streets, sound a trumpet before you as the hypocrites that they may have glory from men. Assuredly, I say to you, they have their reward. But when you do a charitable deed, do not let your left hand know what your right hand is doing, that your charitable deed may be in secret; and your Father who sees in secret will Himself reward you openly. "And when you pray, you shall not be like the hypocrites. For they love to pray standing in the synagogues and on the corners of the streets, that they may be seen by men. Assuredly, I say to you, they have their reward. But you, when you pray, go into your room, and when you have shut your door, pray to your Father who is in the secret place; and your Father who sees in secret will reward you openly. And when you pray, do not use vain repetitions as the heathen do. For they think that they will be heard for their many words. "Therefore do not be things like them. For your Father knows the you have need of before you ask Him. In this manner, therefore, pray: Our Father in heaven, Hallowed be Your name. Your kingdom come. Your will be done On earth as it is in heaven. Give us this day our daily bread. And forgive us our debts, As we forgive our debtors. And do not lead us into temptation, But deliver us from the evil one. For Yours is the kingdom and the power and the glory forever. Amen. "For if you forgive men their trespasses, your heavenly Father will also forgive you. But if you do not forgive men their trespasses, neither will your Father forgive your trespasses. "Moreover, when you fast, do not be like the hypocrites, with a sad countenance. For they disfigure their faces that they may appear to men to be fasting. Assuredly, I say to you, they have their reward. But you, when you fast, anoint your head and wash your face, so that you do not appear to men to be fasting, but to your Father who is in the secret place; and your Father who sees in secret will reward you openly. Matthew 6:1-18

Glory be to God Forever, Amen

FIRST SUNDAY OF THE GREAT LENT

Holy Gospel

MATINS

Stand up in the fear of God and listen to the Holy Gospel, A chapter from the Holy Gospel according to Saint Matthew, May his blessings be with us all, Amen

From the psalms of our teacher David the prophet and king, May his blessings be with us all, Amen

> I will love You, O Lord, my strength. The Lord is my rock and my fortress and my deliverer; My God, my strength, in whom I will trust; My shield and the horn of my salvation, my stronghold. Alleluia. Psalm 18:1-2

Blessed is He who comes in the Name of the Lord Our Lord, God and Saviour and the King of us all, Jesus Christ, the Son of the living God. Glory be to You forever more, Amen

Many will say to Me in that day, 'Lord, Lord, have we not prophesied in Your name, cast out demons in Your name, and done many wonders in Your name?' And then I will declare to them, 'I never knew you; depart from Me, you who practice lawlessness!' "Therefore whoever hears these sayings of Mine, and does them, I will liken him to a wise man who built his house on the rock: and the rain descended, the floods came, and the winds blew and beat on that house; and it did not fall, for it was founded on the rock. "But everyone who hears these sayings of Mine, and does not do them, will be like a foolish man who built his house on the sand: and the rain descended, the floods came, and the winds blew and beat on that house; and it fell. And great was its fall." And so it was, when Jesus had ended these sayings, that the people were astonished at His teaching, for He taught them as one having authority, and not as the scribes. Matthew 7:22-29

Glory be to God Forever, Amen

Pauline

St Paul the Apostle was writing a letter to the Christians who lived in the great city of Rome. Dear Romans, Did you know that it is God who puts people in charge? That means that we have to obey the people in behave to charge. Their job is make everyone nicely. They make sure everyone obeys the rules. Since God gave them that job, if you don't obey them, you are not obeying God! If you do the right thing, you have nothing to be afraid of. But if you do the wrong thing, watch out! They have the right to punish you! So please be sure to obey those who are in charge if only because of you; Not they will punish you do wrong, but also because you will be obeying God. Give to everyone what is due to them: Pay your taxes to the government, obey the law keepers, respect your elders don't owe anyone anything and give everyone what they are due. You only owe people love. Remember the 10 Commandments? "Do not kill" "Do not steal" "Do not lie" and all the rest. Well, we can sum them sentence: all up in just one "Love your neighbour as you love yourself". If you love your neighbour, you will never, ever harm them. It is time to wake up!!! I don't mean "Get out of bed", I mean wake up and stop doing the wrong thing! Let's not walk in darkness anymore, Let's put on the Armour of Light. Let's walk with Jesus, and behave like He did. Let's not be silly or naughty or selfish or fight anymore. (Romans 13:1-14)

Bye for now!

Signed, Paul

The grace of God the Father be with you all, Amen.

Catholicon

Hello Everyone! Have you ever had the feeling that you wanted to do something that you knew was naughty? That happens to all of us some time or other. It's called "temptation." Where do you think temptation comes from? Do you think God is the one who makes us want to be naughty? Of course not! God is perfectly good and He always helps people to be good, not naughty. Never naughty! So what tempts us to be naughty? Temptation comes from inside us. It comes from our own feelings. I don't want you to be tricked my brothers and sisters. Doing the wrong thing just NEVER leads to anything good in the end. But every good thing comes down to us from our Heavenly Father, the Father of Lights, who never changes but is always good. Out of His goodness, He made us, the most special of all His creatures. So, my beloved, I want you all to be Quick to listen, Slow to speak, Slow to anger. Don't let yourself get angry too easily, because when a human being gets angry, they almost never do what our good God wants them to do. So, say "NO!" to naughtiness! Say "NO!" to doing bad things. And instead say "YES!" to Jesus and to the things Jesus teaches you deep in your heart. (James 1:13-21)

Be good!

Signed, James the Apostle

Do not love the world, nor the things which are in the world. The world shall pass away and all its desires; but he who does the will of God shall abide forever. Amen.

The Acts

A reading from the Acts of our fathers the pure apostles, who were invested with the grace of the Holy Spirit. May their blessing be with us all. Amen.

The Jews didn't like St Paul telling everyone about Jesus. They were so angry with St Paul that they started to beat him up. Poor St Paul! But the Roman soldiers heard the noise and came why on. Going to see what was they didn't know St Paul was being beaten, so, they arrested just him, just in case he was a criminal! But St Paul said to them, "Wait, give me a chance to talk to these people". The Soldiers agreed. "My brothers and my fathers, listen to me! So St Paul stood on the steps and spoke to the had been people who beating him: I am Jewish, just like you. I was the student of the Jewish Teacher, famous Gamaliel. I am just as keen as you are for the Laws God gave our fathers. I hunted down the Christians and put them into prison. Even the High Priest knows my work! But then one day, something amazing happened to me. I was on the road to Damascus, hunting for more Christians and suddenly, I was surrounded by the brightest light you could ever imagine! It was a light that came down from Heaven. I fell to the ground. I heard a Voice say: "Saul, Saul, why are you picking on Me?" "Who are You, Lord?" I asked. And the Voice answered, "I am Jesus of Nazareth." We were all trembling. We were all shaking with fear. The light had made me blind. "What should I do, Lord?" I asked. "Go to Damascus," He answered, "and there you will be told what to do." So my friends led me by the hand (I couldn't was I see anything anymore. really blind!) They led me on the road. They led me to Damascus. In Damascus, a good man called Ananias came to me. He said, "My brother Saul, see again." And suddenly, I could see!!! Then, he said to me, fathers "The God of our has chosen you. It is His voice you heard on the road." "God has chosen you to be His witness. God has chosen you to tell everyone about Him." "So what are you waiting for? Get up and be baptised! sins Wash away your in the name of the Lord!" (Chapter 21:40-22:16)

The word of the Lord shall grow, multiply, be mighty and be confirmed in the holy Church of God. Amen.

Holy Gospel

Stand up in the fear of God and listen to the Holy Gospel, A chapter from the Holy Gospel according to Saint Matthew, May his blessings be with us all, Amen

From the psalms of our teacher David the prophet and king, May his blessings be with us all, Amen

> To You, O Lord, I lift up my soul. O my God, I trust in You; Let me not be ashamed. Make known Your ways to me, O Lord, And teach me Your paths. Alleluia. Psalm 25:1-2,4

Blessed is He who comes in the Name of the Lord Our Lord, God and Saviour and the King of us all, Jesus Christ, the Son of the living God. Glory be to You forever more, Amen

"Do not lay up for yourselves treasures on earth, where moth and rust destroy and where thieves break in and steal; but lay up for yourselves treasures in heaven, where neither moth nor rust destroys and where thieves do not break in and steal. For where your treasure is, there your heart will be also. "The lamp of the body is the eye. If therefore your eye is good, your whole body will be full of light. But if your eye is bad, your whole body will be full of darkness. If therefore the light that is in you is darkness, how great is that darkness! "No one can serve two masters; for either he will hate the one and love the other, or else he will be loyal to the one and despise the other. You cannot serve God and mammon. "Therefore I say to you, do not worry about your life, what you will eat or what you will drink; nor about your body, what you will put on. Is not life more than food and the body more than clothing? Look at the birds of the into sow air, for they neither nor reap nor gather barns; yet your heavenly Father feeds them. Are you not of more value than they? Which of you by worrying can add one cubit to his stature? "So why do you worry about clothing? Consider the lilies of the field, how they grow: they neither toil nor spin; and yet I say to you that even Solomon in all his glory was not arrayed like one of these. Now if God so clothes the grass of the field, which today is, and tomorrow is thrown into the oven, will He not much more clothe you, O you of little faith? "Therefore do not worry, saying, 'What shall we eat?' or 'What shall we drink?' or 'What shall we wear?' knows that you need For after all these things the Gentiles seek. For your heavenly Father all these things. But seek first the kingdom of God and His righteousness, and all these things shall be added to you. Matthew 6:19-33

Glory be to God Forever, Amen

SECOND SUNDAY OF THE GREAT LENT

Holy Gospel

Stand up in the fear of God and listen to the Holy Gospel, A chapter from the Holy Gospel according to Saint Luke, May his blessings be with us all, Amen

From the psalms of our teacher David the prophet and king, May his blessings be with us all, Amen

> Be merciful to me, O God, be merciful to me! For my soul trusts in You; And in the shadow of Your wings I will make my refuge, Until these calamities have passed by. Alleluia. Psalm 57:1

Blessed is He who comes in the Name of the Lord Our Lord, God and Saviour and the King of us all, Jesus Christ, the Son of the living God. Glory be to You forever more, Amen

Then Jesus, being filled with the Holy Spirit, returned from the Jordan and was led by the Spirit into the wilderness, being tempted for forty days by the devil. And in those days He ate nothing, and afterward, when they had ended, He was hungry. And the devil said to Him, "If You are the Son of God, command this stone to become bread." But Jesus answered him, saying, "It is written, 'Man shall not live by bread alone, but by every word of God.' " Then the devil, taking Him up on a high mountain, showed Him all the kingdoms of the world in a moment of time. And the devil said to Him, "All this authority I will give You, and their glory; for this has been delivered to me, and I give it to whomever I wish. Therefore, if You will worship before me, all will be Yours." And Jesus answered and said to him, "Get behind Me, Satan! For it is written, 'You shall worship the Lord your God, and Him only you shall serve.' " Then he brought Him to Jerusalem, set Him on the pinnacle of the temple, and said to Him, "If You are the Son of God, throw Yourself down from here. For it is written: 'He shall give His angels charge over you, To keep you,' and, 'In their hands they shall bear you up, Lest you dash your foot against a stone.' "And Jesus answered and said to him, "It has been said, 'You shall not tempt the Lord your God.' " Now when the devil had ended every temptation, he departed from Him until an opportune time. Luke 4:1-13

Glory be to God Forever, Amen

Pauline

Paul, the servant of our Lord Jesus Christ, called to be an apostle, appointed to the Gospel of God. A reading from the Epistle of our teacher Paul to the Romans. May his holy blessings be with us. Amen.

St Paul the Apostle was writing a letter to the Christians who lived in the great city of Rome.

Dear Romans, Do you ever stop to think about other people being happy? Sometimes we do things that upset others. That's not good. We should always care about other people's feelings. Let's take the food you eat as an example. Every kind of food God made for us is pure and good. But some people believe they shouldn't eat certain kinds of food. Don't make fun of them! Don't eat that food in front of them either! That person might love God just as much as you do, and God is working in their heart, so don't spoil God's work by making fun of them. You have your own ideas between you and God. that's about food— If you feel guilty eating some food, don't eat it! But be patient with other people's ideas. Accept other people's ideas. I'll tell you something that is far, far more important than the kind of food you eat, do you know what it is? It is far more important to care about other people! Do whatever you can to make them happy, not just to make yourself happy. If you only try to please yourself; well, there's a word for that: SELFISH! Jesus was never selfish. He left Heaven to come to us and become one of us on earth. And He took all the bad stuff away from us and suffered it Himself instead of us. Wasn't that so kind? Wasn't that so caring? Wasn't that so UNSELFISH? When you read your many stories about Bible, you will find so how Jesus cares for us. It really does make you feel so much better, and it also means you never have to be scared. Jesus is looking after you. So I hope you all look after each other, and take care of each other, and be kind to each other. May God help you all to look after each other, so you can all pray with one heart, one mind, one mouth and glorify the God and Father of our Lord Jesus Christ. (Romans 14:19 to 15:7)

Bye for now!

Signed, Paul

The grace of God the Father be with you all, Amen.

Catholicon

The Catholic Epistle from the Epistle of our teacher St James. May his holy blessings be with us. Amen.

From James, My beloved brothers and sisters, you all know that Jesus loves everyone just the same don't you? But do you love everybody the same, just like Jesus? Or do you treat people differently? What about if a rich or important person comes to Church? Do you treat him really, really nicely? Good! But, what if a poor person comes to your Church? Do you treat him as nicely as you treated the rich person? Or do you treat him really badly, ignore him, or even insult him or make fun of him? Listen carefully now: God chose to love the poor people to be rich in faith, and to go to Heaven. If God treats them so nicely, how can you treat them so badly? And, it is usually the rich and important people who are greedy for money, and take people to court, and don't care about anyone else. So why do you treat the rich and important people so much better than you treat other people? If you really want to follow God's laws, listen to what He says: "You shall love your neighbour as you love yourself." If you do that, you are doing the right thing. But if you love some people more than others just because they are rich or important, then you are certainly doing the wrong thing. You are actually breaking God's law. That's right! If you break one law of God, then you are a law-breaker. You have saddened God, just as much as if you had broken any other law, like killing someone! So don't do the wrong thing. Love everyone just the same, just as Jesus loves all of us. If you show kindness and mercy to others, then God will show kindness and mercy to you. And we know how important it is for God to show us His mercy and if He didn't, we would all be in BIG trouble!!! (James 2:1-13)

Bye for now!

Signed,   James the Apostle

Do not love the world, nor the things which are in the world. The world shall pass away and all its desires; but he who does the will of God shall abide forever. Amen.

The Acts

St Paul was being judged in court. Do you know what crime he was being accused of? He was accused of telling people the Good News about Jesus! That's not a crime! So Paul stood up and said: "My brothers, I have always tried my hardest to do the right thing" But Ananias the High Priest told the guards to punch Paul in the mouth! Then Paul said: "Aren't you supposed to make people obey the law? Then why did you ask the guard to punch me for no reason? That's against the law!" The guards said to Paul, "How dare you talk back to the High Priest like that?!" "Is he the High Priest?" answered Paul. "I'm sorry, I didn't know who he was. Because God taught us not to talk back to those who are responsible for us." But Paul noticed something that was very interesting! Some of the people in the court were Sadducees—they didn't believe that people would rise from the dead and others in the court were Pharisees—they DID believe that people will rise from the dead. Then he had a brilliant idea, "Listen everyone!" he cried out in a loud voice; "I am a Pharisee too, and today I am being judged because I believe that people will rise from the dead!" Then the Sadducees started arguing with the Pharisees and the Pharisees started arguing with the Sadducees! "There is NO resurrection!" the Sadducees said angrily and "There IS a resurrection!" the Pharisees said even more angrily! And the Pharisees got up and shouted, "This man is innocent, leave him alone!" But the Sadducees got up and screamed, "No, he's guilty, punish him!" The Roman Army Commander saw how angry they were. He thought they might pull poor Paul to bits! So he sent his soldiers to rescue him and brought him to his headquarters. That night, in the quiet of a jail cell, the Lord came to Paul and comforted him. "Don't be worried or sad, Paul" Jesus said, "You stood up for Me today, here in Jerusalem. Soon, you will stand up for Me in Rome and tell the people there all about Me." And even though he was still in jail, St Paul felt so happy. He knew he was doing God's work, and that was all that mattered. (Chapter 23:1-11)

Holy Gospel

Stand up in the fear of God and listen to the Holy Gospel, A chapter from the Holy Gospel according to Saint Matthew, May his blessings be with us all, Amen

From the psalms of our teacher David the prophet and king, May his blessings be with us all, Amen

> Your face, O Lord, I will seek. Do not turn away. Your face from me;
> Be my helper; do not utterly cast me away, Nor forsake me, O God my
> saviour. Alleluia. Psalm 27:8-9

Blessed is He who comes in the Name of the Lord Our Lord, God and Saviour and the King of us all, Jesus Christ, the Son of the living God. Glory be to You forever more, Amen

Then Jesus was led up by the Spirit into the wilderness to be tempted by the devil. And when He had fasted forty days and forty nights, afterward He was hungry. Now when the tempter came to Him, he said, "If You are the Son of God, command that these stones become bread." But He answered and said, "It is written, 'Man shall not live by bread alone, but by every word that proceeds from the mouth of God.' " Then the devil took Him up into the holy city, set Him on the pinnacle of the temple and said to Him, "If You are the Son of God, throw Yourself down. For it is written: 'He shall give His angels charge over you,' and, 'In their hands they shall bear you up, Lest you dash your foot against a stone.' " Jesus said to him, "It is written again, 'You shall not tempt the Lord your God.' " Again, the devil took Him up on an exceedingly high mountain, and showed Him all the kingdoms of the world and their glory. "All these things I will And he said to Him, give You if You will fall down and worship me." Then Jesus said to him, and Him worship the "Away with you, Satan! For it is written, 'You shall Lord your God, only you shall serve.' "Then the devil left Him, and behold, angels came and ministered to Him. Matthew 4:1-11

Glory be to God Forever, Amen

THIRD SUNDAY OF THE GREAT LENT

Holy Gospel

MATINS

Stand up in the fear of God and listen to the Holy Gospel, A chapter from the Holy Gospel according to Saint Matthew, May his blessings be with us all, Amen

From the psalms of our teacher David the prophet and king, May his blessings be with us all, Amen

> Give ear to my prayer, O God, And do not hide Yourself from my supplication. Attend to me, and hear me; I am restless in my complaint, and moan noisily, Alleluia. Psalm 55:1-2

Blessed is He who comes in the Name of the Lord Our Lord, God and Saviour and the King of us all, Jesus Christ, the Son of the living God. Glory be to You forever more, Amen

"For the kingdom of heaven is like a landowner who went out early in the morning to hire laborers for his vineyard. Now when he had agreed with the laborers for a denarius a day, he sent them into his vineyard. And he went out about the third hour and saw others standing idle in the marketplace, and said to them, 'You also go into the vineyard, and whatever is right I will give you.' So they went. Again he went out about the sixth and the ninth hour, and did likewise. And about the eleventh hour he went out and found others standing idle, and said to them, 'Why have you been standing here idle all day?' They said to him, 'Because no one hired us.' He said to them, 'You also go into the vineyard, and whatever is right you will receive.' "So when evening had come, the owner of the vineyard said to his steward, 'Call the laborers and give them their wages, beginning with the last to the first.' And when those came who were hired about the eleventh hour, they each received a denarius. But when the first came, they supposed that they would receive more; and they likewise received each a denarius. And when they had received it, they complained against the landowner, saying, 'These last men have worked only one hour, and you made them equal to us who have borne the burden and the heat of the day.' But he answered one of them and said, 'Friend, I am doing you no wrong. Did you not agree with me for a denarius? Take what is yours and go your way. I wish to give to this last man the same as to you. Is it not lawful for me to do what I wish with my own things? Or is your eye evil because I am good?' So the last will be first, and the first last. For many are called, but few chosen." Matthew 20:1-16

Glory be to God Forever, Amen

Pauline

Paul, the servant of our Lord Jesus Christ, called to be an apostle, appointed to the Gospel of God. A reading from the Second Epistle of our teacher Paul to the Corinthians. May his holy blessings be with us. Amen.

St Paul the Apostle was writing a letter to the Christians who lived in the rich city of Corinth. Dear Corinthians, In olden times, God comforted His people. He said to them: "Do not worry! It is time for Me to hear you and to help you. This is the day I will save you." And guess what? Those words are for us too! This is the day that God will save us! My friends and I have tried to serve you the best we can. But it has not been easy. We have had to be really patient through all kinds of troubles. Sometimes, bad people hit us, or put us in jail without a reason. But we continued to have pure hearts, to be patient and kind, and to love them. God is our strength. He is like a suit of armour that protects us from any evil or danger. Because He is with us, we are not worried by anything. When people say bad things about us, we don't care. They say we are liars, They say no one knows us, but you (and others) listen to us! yet all our words are true! They say we are sad, yet look at how happy Jesus makes us! They say they will kill us, yet here we still are! They say we are poor, yet we have made lots of we gave them Jesus! people rich because They say we have nothing, yet all the world belongs to our Lord Jesus! Oh, people of Corinth— we have been really open and honest with you! We haven't tried to tie you up with too many rules. Now, do you think you can be open and honest with us? (2 Corinthians 6:2-13)

Bye for now!

Signed, Paul

The grace of God the Father be with you all, Amen.

Catholicon

The Catholic Epistle from the Epistle of our teacher St James. May his holy blessings be with us. Amen.

My little children, This is the Apostle James writing to tell you about something that is little, but very, very dangerous. I wonder if you can guess what it is? When you ride a horse, you put a little tiny 'bit' in the horse's mouth so you can make him go wherever you wish. And big huge ships can be steered by the tiny little rudder that pokes out from the back. A little tiny match can set a whole forest on fire! Well, this dangerous little thing can change being. big the whole life of a strong human Have you guessed what it is yet? It's the tongue! You see, we use our tongues to speak, and our little words can do so much damage! We use our tongues to pray to God, yet we use the same tongue to tease people who are made in the image of God! We use our tongue to say kind things and yet we use the same tongue to say mean, hurtful things! My little children, this should not be so. Does a spring pour out sweet water and bitter water from the same place? Does a fig tree bear olives? Can a grapevine bear figs? That's just crazy! But people find it so hard to control their tongues! We have tamed every kind of animal, or bird, or reptile, or even sea creatures! But we still seem to have so much trouble taming our tongue! Please, please, please be careful about what you say! (James 3:1-12)

Bye for now!

Signed, James the Apostle

Do not love the world, nor the things which are in the world. The world shall pass away and all its desires; but he who does the will of God shall abide forever. Amen.

The Acts

A reading from the Acts of our fathers the pure apostles, who were invested with the grace of the Holy Spirit. May their blessing be with us all. Amen.

St Paul was being judged in court. A clever Jewish man called Tertullus stood up and accused Paul in front of Felix the ruler, "Good ruler Felix," said Tertullus, "this man Paul is a big troublemaker! He confuses people with the strange things he says. He teaches them about this man from Nazareth called Jesus. That is not what Jews should be teaching! And he even wants to teach about Jesus in our synagogues, where we gather to pray our Jewish prayers. We tried to stop him, but then your soldiers came along and took him away from us, and arrested him before we could deal with him ourselves. So now, it is up to you to judge him, and I am sure you will agree with me that he is a troublemaker and should be punished." Then Felix, the ruler, looked at Paul, and nodded to him, giving him permission to answer. And Paul said, "Good judge, Felix, the truth is that I haven't been to their synagogues—Tertullus is making that up. But it is certainly true that I have been telling people about Jesus. I'm not at all ashamed about that! Jesus is the God of my fathers and their fathers! Their own Bible tells them about Jesus! They agree with me that everyone will rise from the dead and stand in front of God one day. Why are they upset with me? I didn't go to their synagogue, but I did go to the Big Temple, just like any Jewish man. I just went to pray and give donations— I didn't cause any trouble. And when they grabbed me and wanted to judge me, I just spoke to them about how we will all rise from the dead. They agree with me about that. So why are they upset?" So Felix thought about what Tertullus said, and what Paul answered. And then he made his decision Felix said: "Hmm. This is quite complicated! I want to think about it a bit more. In the meantime, Paul can go home, and meet anyone he likes, until I decide about this matter." (Chapter 24:1-23)

The word of the Lord shall grow, multiply, be mighty and be confirmed in the holy Church of God. Amen.

Holy Gospel

Stand up in the fear of God and listen to the Holy Gospel, A chapter from the Holy Gospel according to Saint Luke, May his blessings be with us all, Amen

From the psalms of our teacher David the prophet and king, May his blessings be with us all, Amen

> Do not remember our transgressions of old; Let Your mercies quickly overtake us, For we have become very poor. Help us, O God our saviour; Because of the glory of Your name.　　Alleluia. Psalm 79:8-9

Blessed is He who comes in the Name of the Lord Our Lord, God and Saviour and the King of us all, Jesus Christ, the Son of the living God. Glory be to You forever more, Amen

Then He said: "A certain man had two sons. And the younger of them said to his father, 'Father, give me the portion of goods that falls to me.' So he divided to them his livelihood. And not many days after, the younger son gathered all together, journeyed to a far country, and there wasted his possessions with prodigal living. But when he had spent all, there arose a severe famine in that land, and he began to be in want. Then he went and joined himself to a citizen of that country, and he sent him into his fields to feed swine. And he would gladly have filled his stomach with the pods that the swine ate, and no one gave him anything. "But when he came to himself, he said, 'How many of my father's hired servants have bread enough and to spare, and I perish with hunger! I will arise and go to my father, and will say to him, "Father, I have sinned against heaven and before you, and I am no longer worthy to be called your son. Make me like one of your hired servants." ' "And he arose and came to his father. But when he was still a great way off, his father saw him and had compassion, and ran and fell on his neck and kissed him. And the son said to him, 'Father, I have sinned against heaven and in your sight, and am no longer worthy to be called your son.' "But the father said to his servants, 'Bring out the best robe and put it on him, and put a ring on his hand and sandals on his feet. And bring the fatted calf here and kill it, and let us eat and be merry; for this my son was dead and is alive again; he was lost and is found.' And they began to be merry. "Now his older son was angry and would not go in. Therefore his father came out and pleaded with him. So he answered and said to his father, 'Lo, these many years I have been serving you; I never transgressed your commandment at any time; But as soon as this son of yours came, who has devoured your livelihood with harlots, you killed the fatted calf for him.' "And he said to him, 'Son, It was right that we should make merry and be glad, for your brother was dead and is alive again, and was lost and is found. Luke 15:11-32

Glory be to God Forever, Amen

FOURTH SUNDAY OF THE GREAT LENT

Holy Gospel

Stand up in the fear of God and listen to the Holy Gospel, A chapter from the Holy Gospel according to Saint Mattew, May his blessings be with us all, Amen

From the psalms of our teacher David the prophet and king, May his blessings be with us all, Amen

> Be of good courage, And He shall strengthen your heart, All you who hope in the Lord. Oh, love the Lord, all you His saints! For the Lord preserves the faithful, And fully repays the proud person. Alleluia. Psalm 31:24 & 7:23

Blessed is He who comes in the Name of the Lord Our Lord, God and Saviour and the King of us all, Jesus Christ, the Son of the living God. Glory be to You forever more, Amen

And Jesus answered and spoke to them again by parables and said: "The kingdom of heaven is like a certain king who arranged a marriage for his son, and sent out his servants to call those who were invited to the wedding; and they were not willing to come. Again, he sent out other servants, saying, 'Tell those who are invited, "See, I have prepared my dinner; my oxen and fatted cattle are killed, and all things are ready. Come to the wedding." ' But they made light of it and went their ways, one to his own farm, another to his business. And the rest seized his servants, treated them spitefully, and killed them. But when the king heard about it, he was furious. And he sent out his armies, destroyed those murderers, and burned up their city. Then he said to his servants, 'The wedding is ready, but those who were invited were not worthy. Therefore go into the highways, and as many as you find, invite to the wedding.' So those servants went out into the highways and gathered together all whom they found, both bad and good. And the wedding hall was filled with guests. "But when the king came in to see the guests, he saw a man there who did not have on a wedding garment. So he said to him, 'Friend, how did you come in here without a wedding garment?' And he was speechless. Then the king said to the servants, 'Bind him hand and foot, take him away, and cast him into outer darkness; there will be weeping and gnashing of teeth.' "For many are called, but few are chosen." Matthew 22:1-14

Glory be to God Forever, Amen

Pauline

Paul, the servant of our Lord Jesus Christ, called to be an apostle, appointed to the Gospel of God. A reading from the Epistle of our teacher Paul to the Ephesians. May his holy blessings be with us. Amen.

St Paul the Apostle was writing a letter to the Christians who lived in the city of Ephesus.

Dear Ephesians, I want you to be STRONG, for our Lord is very STRONG! But I don't mean strong in the muscles of your body. I mean strong in your heart and in your thinking. God makes us strong inside. He is like our armour, the armour that a soldier wears to battle. This armour of God helps us to fight against the devil and to win the battle! and all his evil, What is our armour? Put on the Belt of Truth. Jesus always told the Truth, and the Truth makes us strong. And the Breastplate of Righteousness. Jesus always did what was right and good. Doing good makes us strong. And the Boots of the Gospel of Peace. Jesus taught us His Gospel— His Good News— so we could have peace, and that makes us strong. And the Shield of Faith. When we believe in Jesus, and trust Him with our lives, nothing can ever really hurt us, so we are strong. And the Helmet of Salvation. Jesus saved us! This salvation protects our thoughts and our minds and makes us strong. And finally, the Spirit. Sword of the Jesus gave us His Holy Spirit, who fights our enemy, the devil for us, and makes us strong. Now you have the whole Armour of God! Now you are ready to fight against evil! Are you ready? But first, remember you are not fighting alone. We must always remember to pray for each other, for all our fellow soldiers of Christ. And that includes me, your friend Paul! Pray that God will always send us all the the right words to say. Pray that God will help me to be bold and brave, and to tell people how much Jesus loves them. Sometimes, people don't want to hear this. Sometimes, they get really angry when I tell them about Jesus. That is why they put me in jail! But I don't mind. I love Jesus and will always tell people how much He loves them. Because I know Jesus loves me, I am STRONG! Peace to all my brothers and sisters, and love with faith, from God the Father and the Lord Jesus Christ. God be be with all those who love our Lord Jesus Christ from all their hearts. Amen   (Ephesians 6:10-24)

Bye for now!

Signed, Paul

The grace of God the Father be with you all, Amen.

Catholicon

The Catholic Epistle from the Epistle of our teacher St James. May his holy blessings be with us. Amen.

From James, Give in to God! Stand up to the devil, and he will run away from you! Come closer to God and He will come closer to you. If you have done the wrong thing, tell God that you are sorry. Don't be all mixed up! Don't try to get away with doing the wrongthing! That's crazy! It is so much better to own up and confess before God. Be sad for your sins, so God can forgive you and make you happy again. He will lift you up high! Don't say bad things about each other -who made you the Judge??? There is only one true Judge— so leave the judging to Him. And don't be so proud as to say "I will do this," or "I am certainlygoing to do that." Our life is only short, and we are weak, like smoke that soon blows away in the wind; So it's better to say, "If God wills, I will do this or that." If you know how to do the right thing, and you still don't do it, that's bad: that's a sin.   (James 4:7-17)

Bye for now!

Signed, James the Apostle

Do not love the world, nor the things which are in the world. The world shall pass away and all its desires; but he who does the will of God shall abide forever. Amen.

The Acts

St Paul was still stuck in jail! Now, he was in a jail in a city called Caesarea. And it happened that while he was there, the Jewish King Agrippa and his wife Queen Bernice came to visit the Roman ruler, Festus. So Festus said to King Agrippa: "Hey, King Agrippa, maybe you can help me with something! I've got this prisoner in jail, and he's Jewish like you. And I don't know what to do with him!" "You see, King Agrippa, I didn't arrest Paul. He was brought in by some other Jewish people, who didn't like what he was saying." "And what has this Paul been saying, Festus?" asked King Agrippa. "He keeps talking about a man called Jesus, and he insists that this Jesus rose from the dead." "I'm a Roman," said Festus, "and I don't really understand your Jewish religion. But when I offered to send him back to court in Jerusalem, he said, no." "He wants to go to court in ROME! The capital of the Empire! He wants to go to court in front of the great Emperor Augustus Caesar himself!" "Well, Festus," said King Agrippa, "I think I'd like to hear this Paul for myself, if you don't mind." So the very next day, Festus the ruler, and King Agrippa and Queen Bernice sat on big thrones in the assembly hall, and they brought Paul in front of them. And Festus said, "I don't know what to do with this fellow! The other Jews want to kill him, but I can't find anything wrong with him" "And what's more, now he wants to go to Rome to speak in front of the Emperor himself!" "You're a Jew like Paul, King Agrippa. Maybe you can understand what he's saying, and help me decide what to do with him." And King Agrippa agreed, and said to St Paul, "Don't be afraid. Speak up. I want to hear what you have to say." Do you think St Paul was afraid to speak about Jesus? Of course not! And what did he say? Well, if you really want to know, you'll have to read it in your own Bible, because that's all we have time for now! (Chapter 25:13-26:1)

Holy Gospel

Stand up in the fear of God and listen to the Holy Gospel,A chapter from the Holy Gospel according to Saint John, May his blessings be with us all, Amen

From the psalms of our teacher David the prophet and king,May his blessings be with us all, Amen

> Let the heart of those who seek the Lord be glad; Seek the Lord and be strengthened; Seek His face continually. Remember the wonders He performed, Of His marvels and the judgments of His mouth. Alleluia. Psalms 105:3-5

Blessed is He who comes in the Name of the Lord Our Lord, God and Saviour and the King of us all, Jesus Christ, the Son of the living God. Glory be to You forever more, Amen

Therefore, when the Lord knew that the Pharisees had heard that Jesus made and baptized more disciples than John (though Jesus Himself did not baptize, but His disciples), He left Judea and departed again to Galilee. But He needed to go through Samaria. So He came to a city of Samaria which is called Sychar, near the plot of ground that Jacob gave to his son Joseph. Now Jacob's well was there. Jesus therefore, being wearied from His journey, sat thus by the well. It was about the sixth hour. A woman of Samaria came to draw water. Jesus said to her, "Give Me a drink." For His disciples had gone away into the city to buy food. Then the woman of Samaria said to Him, "How is it that You, being a Jew, ask a drink from me, a Samaritan woman?" For Jews have no dealings with Samaritans.

Jesus answered and said to her, "If you knew the gift of God, and who it is who says to you, 'Give Me a drink,' you would have asked Him, and He would have given you living water." The woman said to Him, "Sir, You have nothing to draw with, and the well is deep. Where then do You get that living water? Are You greater than our father Jacob, who gave us the well, and drank from it himself, as well as his sons and his livestock?" Jesus answered and said to her, "Whoever drinks of this water will thirst again, but whoever drinks of the water that I shall give him will never thirst. But the water that I shall give him will become in him a fountain of water springing up into everlasting life." The woman said to Him, "Sir, give me this water, that I may not thirst, nor come here to draw." Jesus said to her, "Go, call your husband, and come here."

The woman answered and said, "I have no husband." Jesus said to her, "You have well said, 'I have no husband,' for you have had five husbands, and the one whom you now have is not your husband; in that you spoke truly." The woman said to Him, "Sir, I perceive that You are a prophet. Our fathers worshiped on this mountain, and you Jews say that in Jerusalem is the place where one ought to worship." Jesus said to her, "Woman, believe Me, the hour is coming when you will neither on this mountain, nor in Jerusalem, worship the Father. You worship what you do not know; we know what we worship, for salvation is of the Jews. But the hour is coming, and now is, when the true worshipers will worship the Father in spirit and truth; for the Father is seeking such to worship Him. God is Spirit, and those who worship Him must worship in spirit and truth." The woman said to Him, "I know that Messiah is coming" (who is called Christ). "When He comes, He will tell us all things." Jesus said to her, "I who speak to you am He." And at this point His disciples came, and they marveled that He talked with a woman; yet no one said, "What do You seek?" or, "Why are You talking with her?" The woman then left her waterpot, went her way into the city, and said to the men, "Come, see a Man who told me all things that I ever did. Could this be the Christ?" Then they went out of the city and came to Him.

In the meantime His disciples urged Him, saying, "Rabbi, eat." But He said to them, "I have food to eat of which you do not know." Therefore the disciples said to one another, "Has anyone brought Him anything to eat?" Jesus said to them, "My food is to do the will of Him who sent Me, and to finish His work. Do you not say, 'There are still four months and then comes the harvest'? Behold, I say to you, lift up your eyes and look at the fields, for they are already white for harvest! And he who reaps receives wages, and gathers fruit for eternal life, that both he who sows and he who reaps may rejoice together. For in this the saying is true: 'One sows and another reaps.' I sent you to reap that for which you have not labored; others have labored, and you have entered into their labors." And many of the Samaritans of that city believed in Him because of the word of the woman who testified, "He told me all that I ever did." So when the Samaritans had come to Him, they urged Him to stay with them; and He stayed there two days. And many more believed because of His own word. Then they said to the woman, "Now we believe, not because of what you said, for we ourselves have heard Him and we know that this is indeed the Christ, the Savior of the world." John 4:1-42

Glory be to God Forever, Amen

FIFTH SUNDAY OF THE GREAT LENT

Holy Gospel

Stand up in the fear of God and listen to the Holy Gospel, A chapter from the Holy Gospel according to Saint Matthew, May his blessings be with us all, Amen

From the psalms of our teacher David the prophet and king, May his blessings be with us all, Amen

> Hear my prayer, O Lord, And let my cry come to You. Do not hide Your face from me in the day of my trouble; Incline Your ear to me; In the day that I call, answer me speedily. But You, O Lord, shall endure forever, And the remembrance of Your name to all generations. Alleluia. Psalms 102: 1-2,12

Blessed is He who comes in the Name of the Lord Our Lord, God and Saviour and the King of us all, Jesus Christ, the Son of the living God. Glory be to You forever more, Amen

"Hear another parable: There was a certain landowner who planted a vineyard and set a hedge around it, dug a winepress in it and built a tower. And he leased it to vinedressers and went into a far country. Now when vintage-time drew near, he sent his servants to the vinedressers, that they might receive its fruit. And the vinedressers took his servants, beat one, killed one, and stoned another. Again he sent other servants, more than the first, and they did likewise to them. Then last of all he sent his son to them, saying, 'They will respect my son.' But when the vinedressers saw the son, they said among themselves, 'This is the heir. Come, let us kill him and seize his inheritance.' So they took him and cast him out of the vineyard and killed him. "Therefore, when the owner of the vineyard comes, what will he do to those vinedressers?" They said to Him, "He will destroy those wicked men miserably, and lease his vineyard to other vinedressers who will render to him the fruits in their seasons."

Jesus said to them, "Have you never read in the Scriptures: 'The stone which the builders rejected Has become the chief cornerstone. This was the Lord's doing, And it is marvelous in our eyes'? "Therefore I say to you, the kingdom of God will be taken from you and given to a nation bearing the fruits of it. And whoever falls on this stone will be broken; but on whomever it falls, it will grind him to powder." Now when the chief priests and Pharisees heard His parables, they perceived that He was speaking of them. But when they sought to lay hands on Him, they feared the multitudes, because they took Him for a prophet. Matthew 21:33-46

Glory be to God Forever, Amen

Pauline LITURGY

Paul, the servant of our Lord Jesus Christ, called to be an apostle, appointed to the Gospel of God. A reading from the Second Epistle of our teacher Paul to the Thessalonians. May his holy blessings be with us. Amen.

St Paul the Apostle was writing a letter to the Christians who lived in the big city called Thessalonica.

Dear Thessalonian Today I want to tell you about the time when Jesus will come back to the world and when He will gather us all together with Him— what an exciting day that will be! But I have heard that some people are spreading a rumour that Jesus has already come back. Don't believe them! Before Jesus comes back, some other things lots of people in the Before Jesus comes, have to happen first: world will stop loving Jesus! Before Jesus comes, the Bad Man will try to trick people to pray to him as if he was God! This Bad Man is the exact opposite of Jesus Christ. He is the Antichrist. That means the opposite of Christ. Don't you remember that when I was with you I told you all this? But the right time has not yet come. For now, God is stopping the Antichrist from doing whatever he wants. But one day, God will let go, and then satan, will give the Antichrist the power to do miracles and wonders and amazing things. And then anyone who doesn't love God will be tricked by the Antichrist's lies and follow him. Because they love to do what is wrong, they will all be punished with the Antichrist. But don't worry, because after that, God will destroy our enemy, the Antichrist as easily as blowing away a dandelion! So I say "Thank You God!" because from the beginning you have believed in Jesus and you have loved doing good. So be strong! Be steady! Hold on to the traditions and everything I taught you about God. Now, may our Lord Jesus Christ Himself, and His you to do and to say your heart and help Heavenly Father, comfort everything that is good, because, do you know what? He loves us! (2 Thessalonians 2:1-17)

Bye for now!

Signed, Paul

The grace of God the Father be with you all, Amen.

Catholicon

The Catholic Epistle from the Second Epistle of our teacher St Peter. May his holy blessings be with us. Amen.

From Peter, Hello my beloved friends! I want to remind you about some very important things that will happen at the end of the world. How come He hasn't come back yet? Before the end, people will make fun of "Where is your Jesus? us and say things like, "See," they will say, "the world goes on like it always has; nothing changes. I bet He's never going to come back!" But they forget that God is in control of the whole world. In Noah's time, He flooded the whole world by His power, and all the evil men who made fun of Him suddenly died. Time is nothing to God. For God, one day is like a thousand years, and a thousand years are like one day! So Jesus has not forgotten to come back to the world! He wants to give everyone a chance to come back to Him and be good. Then, He will come back, all of a sudden! And this whole world will be quickly taken away. And He will make a new Heaven and a new Earth for those who are ready to meet Him. So if God is going to take away this world, don't you think we should try to be ready for Him when He comes? How can we get ready? Being ready means being good like God in everything we do. Being ready means not fighting with others. Being ready means being a peaceful person. Remember, God is being patient so we can have enough time to get ready. So start getting ready!!! My friend Paul has also written to you about the end of the world, Although his letters are a bit hard to understand sometimes, and some naughty people tried to use them to confuse you. So, I am making sure that you are not confused, so that no one can trick you: Keep doing what is right and good! No one knows when our Lord Jesus will come back to us. So always be ready. Keep growing in God's grace. Keep knowing Him better. Keep praising Him with joy. Glory be to Him, now and forever, amen. (2 Peter 3:1-18)

Bye for now!

Signed, Peter the Apostle

Do not love the world, nor the things which are in the world. The world shall pass away and all its desires; but he who does the will of God shall abide forever. Amen.

The Acts

Do you remember what we read last Sunday? Do you remember Festus, the ruler of Caesarea, and the Jewish King Agrippa and Queen Bernice who came to visit him? And do you remember how Festus asked King Agrippa to help him work out what to do with St Paul, who was in jail? Well, today, we will hear a little of what Paul said to Festus, King Agrippa, and Queen Berenice. Paul said: "So, King Agrippa, when Jesus appeared to me on the Road to Damascus, He told me to tell everyone just how much He loves us. And that is exactly what I did. I told both Jewish people and Gentiles—people who are not Jewish. I told them that we all need to repent—to stop doing bad things, and love God, and love one another. I was only telling them what is already in the Bible. I was telling them about the Messiah, the One that Moses and the prophets said would come, and rise from the dead, to save the world. But some of the Jewish people didn't like what I was saying! In fact, they wanted to kill me!" Then Festus said, "Paul, you have been reading too much! You are mad!" But Paul answered, "I'm not mad. King Agrippa has read Moses and the prophets. He knows I am speaking the truth. Don't you, King Agrippa?" King Agrippa answered, ve almost convinced me "You know what, you'to become a Christian!" Paul said, "I wish that everyone in the world would become a Christian!" So Festus and King Agrippa and Berenice went aside to discuss the case. They decided that Paul hadn't done anything wrong. In fact, if he hadn't insisted on speaking in front of Caesar, they could have set him free! So they put Paul back on a boat, and he continued his journey to Rome, to speak in front of the Emperor, Caesar. (Chapter 26:19-27:8)

Holy Gospel

Stand up in the fear of God and listen to the Holy Gospel, A chapter from the Holy Gospel according to Saint John, May his blessings be with us all, Amen

From the psalms of our teacher David the prophet and king, May his blessings be with us all, Amen

> He loves mercy and judgment; The earth is full of the Lord's mercy. By the word of the Lord the heavens were established, And all the host of them by the breath of His mouth. Alleluia. Psalm 33:5-6

Blessed is He who comes in the Name of the Lord Our Lord, God and Saviour and the King of us all, Jesus Christ, the Son of the living God. Glory be to You forever more, Amen

After this there was a feast of the Jews, and Jesus went up to Jerusalem. Now there is in Jerusalem by the Sheep Gate a pool, which is called in Hebrew, Bethesda, having five porches. In these lay a great multitude of sick people, blind, lame, paralysed, waiting for the moving of the water. For an angel went down at a certain time into the pool and stirred up the water; then whoever stepped in first, after the stirring of the water, was made well of whatever disease he had. Now a certain man was there who had an infirmity thirty- eight years. When Jesus saw him lying there, and knew that he already had been in that condition a long time, He said to him, "Do you want to be made well?" The sick man answered Him, "Sir, I have no man to put me into the pool when the water is stirred up; but while I am coming, another steps down before me." Jesus said to him, "Rise, take up your bed and walk." And immediately the man was made well, took up his bed, and walked. And that day was the Sabbath. The Jews therefore said to him who was cured, "It is the Sabbath; it is not lawful for you to carry your bed." He answered them, "He who made me well said to me, 'Take up your bed and walk.' " Then they asked him, "Who is the Man who said to you, 'Take up your bed and walk'?" But the one who was healed did not know who it was, for Jesus had withdrawn, a multitude being in that place. Afterward Jesus found him in the temple, and said to him, "See, you have been made well. Sin no more, lest a worse thing come upon you." The man departed and told the Jews that it was Jesus who had made him well. John 5:1-18

Glory be to God Forever, Amen

SIXTH SUNDAY OF THE GREAT LENT

Holy Gospel

MATINS

Stand up in the fear of God and listen to the Holy Gospel, A chapter from the Holy Gospel according to Saint Matthew, May his blessings be with us all, Amen

From the psalms of our teacher David the prophet and king, May his blessings be with us all, Amen

> Examine me, O Lord, and prove me; Try my mind and my heart. For Your lovingkindness is before my eyes, And I have walked in Your truth. Alleluia. Psalms 26:2-3

Blessed is He who comes in the Name of the Lord Our Lord, God and Saviour and the King of us all, Jesus Christ, the Son of the living God. Glory be to You forever more, Amen

"He who swears by the temple, swears by it and by Him who dwells in it. And he who swears by heaven, swears by the throne of God and by Him who sits on it. "Woe to you, scribes and Pharisees, hypocrites! For you pay tithe of mint and anise and cummin, and have neglected the weightier matters of the law: justice and mercy and faith. These you ought to have done, without leaving the others undone. Blind guides, who strain out a gnat and swallow a camel! "Woe to you, scribes and Pharisees, hypocrites! For you cleanse the outside of the cup and dish, but inside they are full of extortion and self-indulgence. Blind Pharisee, first cleanse the inside of the cup and dish, that the outside of them may be clean also. "Woe to you, scribes and Pharisees, hypocrites! For you are like whitewashed tombs which indeed appear beautiful outwardly, but inside are full of dead men's bones and all uncleanness. Even so you also outwardly appear righteous to men, but inside you are full of hypocrisy and lawlessness. "Woe to you, scribes and Pharisees, hypocrites! Because you build the tombs of the prophets and adorn the monuments of the righteous, and say, 'If we had lived in the days of our fathers, we would not have been partakers with them in the blood of the prophets.'

"Therefore you are witnesses against yourselves that you are sons of those who murdered the prophets. Fill up, then, the measure of your fathers' guilt. Serpents, brood of vipers! How can you escape the condemnation of hell? Therefore, indeed, I send you prophets, wise men, and scribes: some of them you will kill and crucify, and some of them you will scourge in your synagogues and persecute from city to city, that on you may come all the righteous blood shed on the earth, from the blood of righteous Abel to the blood of Zechariah, son of Berechiah, whom you murdered between the temple and the altar. Assuredly, I say to you, all these things will come upon this generation. "O Jerusalem, Jerusalem, the one who kills the prophets and stones those who are sent to her! How often I wanted to gather your children together, as a hen gathers her chicks under her wings, but you were not willing! See! Your house is left to you desolate; for I say to you, you shall see Me no more till you say, 'Blessed is He who comes in the name of the Lord!' "
Matthew 23:21-39

Glory be to God Forever, Amen

Pauline

LITURGY

Paul, the servant of our Lord Jesus Christ, called to be an apostle, appointed to the Gospel of God. A reading from the Epistle of our teacher Paul to the Colossians. May his holy blessings be with us. Amen.

St Paul the Apostle was writing a letter to the Christians who lived in the city of Colossae.

Dear Colossians, Being a Christian means that Jesus lives inside us! So we should be like Jesus! We should do our best to get rid of any bad things inside us. Things like being selfish, being jealous of other people and wanting to take things that are not ours. Maybe we used to do such should stop. These things hurt us, and they hurt other people. bad things before, but we So don't do any of these things: Don't get angry with each other, don't be mean to each other and never say bad things about God! Don't swear or say rude words and don't lie to anyone. Jesus made you a new person! You are now like Jesus! You are the Image of God! So don't go back to your bad old ways! We are all the Image of God! Whatever country you come from, whatever job you do, we are all God's children in Jesus. "Christ is all, And in all." Say it with me , "Christ is all, And in all." Be kind and gentle so here's what you should do, because you are the Image of God, and Jesus lives in you so be humble, and meek. Forgive each other just as Jesus forgave you. Be patient with each other, But most important of all, put on love, which will really make you good like Jesus. Let the peace of God rule in your hearts, for we are all one Body of Christ. Always be thankful. Let the Word of Christ always be in your thoughts and your hearts, for it will make you wise. Help each other to do what is good always. Sing beautiful songs to God together! Every single thing you do, do it in the Name of Christ. And remember to say "Thank You" to Jesus for everything. (Colossians 3:5-17)

Bye for now!

Signed, Paul

The grace of God the Father be with you all, Amen.

Catholicon

The Catholic Epistle from the First Epistle of our teacher St John. May his holy blessings be with us. Amen.

From John, My beloved brothers and sisters, Did you know that you and I share a very special secret? But it's the kind of secret that God wants us to tell everybody about! And here it is, are you ready? God has given us eternal life! That means that we can live forever with Him in Heaven! So if you know about Jesus, believe in Him, love Him and if Jesus lives inside you. You will get to live forever with Jesus in Heaven! So keep believing in Jesus. Keep loving Him more and more. Because He gives us more and more. Jesus hears every word we say to Him when we pray. Jesus answers our prayers. Especially when we pray for a something wrong. They brother or sister who is doing really need someone to pray for them! So they can stop being naughty! When you really love God, you just don't want to do anything wrong. And even though the devil might trick the whole world to do the wrong thing. He can never trick us — if we really, really love God. For God is true And Jesus is true And He protects us every day of our lives. (1 John 5:13-21)

God loves you!

Signed,   John the Beloved

Do not love the world, nor the things which are in the world. The world shall pass away and all its desires; but he who does the will of God shall abide forever. Amen.

The Acts

A reading from the Acts of our fathers the pure apostles, who were invested with the grace of the Holy Spirit. May their blessing be with us all. Amen.

Do you remember how St Paul was judged by Festus, King Agrippa and Queen Berenice? When Paul insisted on speaking to Emperor, Caesar, they sent him to Rome. But Paul's voyage to Rome was not a very easy one! One dark night, there was a big, big storm, and the sailors on the ship were very much afraid! The ship was getting too close to the rocks, and the water wasn't very deep. They thought there was going to be a big shipwreck! Some of the sailors tried to sneak a little boat over the side and wanted to jump into it and row away from the ship. But Paul said to the Captain of the ship, "If these sailors run away, the ship will be wrecked and the rest of us will die!" So they listened to Paul, and they cut the little boat loose and let if float away. And as the morning was beginning to dawn, Paul said to them, "Please have some food. We have been fighting this storm for fourteen days now, and you have hardly eaten! But I am sure the storm is almost over, and God will keep us all safe. Not even a hair of your head will be hurt." Then Paul took some bread in his hands. He gave thanks to God. He broke the bread. He ate the bread. And when all the scared they felt so much better, sailors saw him eat, and they started to eat too. And God kept them all safe, all 276 of them! (Chapter 27:27-37)

The word of the Lord shall grow, multiply, be mighty and be confirmed in the holy Church of God. Amen.

Holy Gospel

Stand up in the fear of God and listen to the Holy Gospel,A chapter from the Holy Gospel according to Saint John, May his blessings be with us all, Amen

From the psalms of our teacher David the prophet and king,May his blessings be with us all, Amen

> Hear me speedily, O Lord; My spirit faints within me; Turn not Your face from me. O Lord, hear my prayer; Give ear to my supplication in Your truth; Answer me in Your righteousness Alleluia. Psalm 143:7,1

Blessed is He who comes in the Name of the Lord Our Lord, God and Saviour and the King of us all, Jesus Christ, the Son of the living God. Glory be to You forever more, Amen

Now as Jesus passed by, He saw a man who was blind from birth. And His disciples asked Him, saying, "Rabbi, who sinned, this man or his parents, that he was born blind?" Jesus answered, "Neither this man nor his parents sinned, but that the works of God should be revealed in him. I must work the works of Him who sent Me while it is day; the night is coming when no one can work. As long as I am in the world, I am the light of the world." When He had said these things, He spat on the ground and made clay with the saliva; and He anointed the eyes of the blind man with the clay. And He said to him, "Go, wash in the pool of Siloam" (which is translated, Sent). So he went and washed, and came back seeing. [Then people asked him] "How were your eyes opened?" He answered and said, "A Man called Jesus made clay and anointed my eyes and said to me, 'Go to the pool of Siloam and wash.' So I went and washed, and I received sight." They brought him who formerly was blind to the Pharisees. Now it was a Sabbath when Jesus made the clay and opened his eyes. Then the Pharisees also asked him again how he had received his sight. He said to them,

"He put clay on my eyes, and I washed, and I see." Therefore, some of the Pharisees said, "This Man is not from God, because He does not keep the Sabbath." Others said, "How can a man who is a sinner do such signs?" And there was a division among them. They said to the blind man again, "What do you say about Him because He opened your eyes?" He said, "He is a prophet." So, they called the parents of him who had received his sight. And they asked them, saying, "Is this your son, who you say was born blind? How then does he now see?" His parents answered them and said, "We know that this is our son, and that he was born blind; but by what means he now sees we do not know, "or who opened his eyes we do not know. He is of age; ask him. He will speak for himself." His parents said these things because they feared the Jews, for the Jews had agreed already that if anyone confessed that He was Christ, he would be put out of the synagogue. So, they again called the man who was blind, and said to him, "Give God the glory! We know that this Man is a sinner." He answered and said, "Whether He is a sinner or not I do not know. One thing I know: that though I was blind, now I see." "I told you already, and you did not listen. Why do you want to hear it again? Do you also want to become His disciples?" Then they reviled him and said, "You are His disciple, but we are Moses' disciples. "We know that God spoke to Moses; as for this fellow, we do not know where He is from." The man answered and said to them, "Why, this is a marvellous thing, that you do not know where He is from; yet He has opened my eyes! "Now we know that God does not hear sinners; but if anyone is a worshiper of God and does His will, He hears him. "Since the world began it has been unheard of that anyone opened the eyes of one who was born blind. If this Man were not from God, He could do nothing." They answered and said to him, "You were completely born in sins, and are you teaching us?" And they cast him out. Jesus heard that they had cast him out; and when He had found him, He said to him, "Do you believe in the Son of God?" He answered and said, "Who is He, Lord, that I may believe in Him?" And Jesus said to him, "You have both seen Him and it is He who is talking with you." Then he said, "Lord, I believe!" And he worshiped Him.   John 9:1-41

Glory be to God Forever, Amen

PALM SUNDAY

Holy Gospel

Stand up in the fear of God and listen to the Holy Gospel, A chapter from the Holy Gospel according to Saint Luke, May his blessings be with us all, Amen

From the psalms of our teacher David the prophet and king, May his blessings be with us all, Amen

> Blessed be the Lord, Who daily loads us with benefits, The God of our salvation! Selah O God, You are more awesome than Your holy places. The God of Israel is He who gives strength and power to His people. Blessed be God! Alleluia. Psalm 68:19,35

Blessed is He who comes in the Name of the Lord Our Lord, God and Saviour and the King of us all, Jesus Christ, the Son of the living God. Glory be to You forever more, Amen

Then Jesus entered and passed through Jericho. Now behold, there was a man named Zacchaeus who was a chief tax collector, and he was rich. And he sought to see who Jesus was, but could not because of the crowd, for he was of short stature. So he ran ahead and climbed up into a sycamore tree to see Him, for He was going to pass that way. And when Jesus came to the place, He looked up and saw him, and said to him, "Zacchaeus, make haste and come down, for today I must stay at your house." So he made haste and came down, and received Him joyfully. But when they saw it, they all complained, saying, "He has gone to be a guest with a man who is a sinner."

Then Zacchaeus stood and said to the Lord, "Look, Lord, I give half of my goods to the poor; and if I have taken anything from anyone by false accusation, I restore fourfold." And Jesus said to him, "Today salvation has come to this house, because he also is a son of Abraham; for the Son of Man has come to seek and to save that which was lost." Luke 19:1-10

Glory be to God Forever, Amen

Pauline

Paul, the servant of our Lord Jesus Christ, called to be an apostle, appointed to the Gospel of God. A reading from the Epistle of our teacher Paul to the Hebrews. May his holy blessings be with us. Amen.

St Paul the Apostle was writing a letter to the Christians who were Hebrews—that means they were Jewish

Dear Hebrews,

You know how Hebrews offer animals as sacrifices in their temple? That was the agreement they made with God long ago. But now, we all have a new agreement: a "New Covenant" with God. We don't need to kill the poor animals anymore Our sacrifice now, is Jesus Christ Himself. Jesus gave Himself. He died on the Cross to save us all from dying. It is the Precious Blood of Jesus, which He shed on the Cross that saves us— not the blood of animals. The Hebrew High Priest just goes into the temple to pray for the people. But Jesus has gone into Heaven itself to save us all. And we are waiting for Jesus to come back to us again to take us home with Him! (Hebrews 9:11–28)

Bye for now!

Signed, Paul

The grace of God the Father be with you all, Amen.

Catholicon

The Catholic Epistle from the First Epistle of our teacher St Peter. May his holy blessings be with us. Amen.

Hello Everyone!

Our Lord, Jesus Christ died on the Cross to save us from everything that is bad. So of course, we should not do anything that is bad! Don't you think we have spent enough time doing the wrong thing? Sometimes other people want you to be bad with them and they are surprised when you tell them "no". Then they make fun of you! But do you know what? One day, they will have to stand in front of the Great Judge (that's Jesus) and they will have to explain all that bad stuff they did. I wouldn't want to be them! Would you? That's why Jesus went down to Hades and preached to the people down there who had died. He wanted to give them a chance to live! We never know when our end will come, so, please, always be ready, always be praying. And most important of all: Love one another, truly, from your heart, for "love will cover a multitude of sins"— if you love others, God will forgive their sins, and your sins too! So look after each other well, with great kindness, and do it happily, without grumbling and complaining about it. God has given each one of you their own special gifts, their own talents or abilities. Use them to serve each other, so that we all get the most out of the gifts God gave us. If your gift from God is being a good speaker, then speak the words of God! If your gift from God is to help others, then help as much as you can! That way, the goodness and love of God will spread far and wide, and everyone will glorify and praise God through Jesus Christ to whom belong the glory and the dominion forever and ever. Amen. (1 Peter 4:1–11)

Bye for now!

Signed, Peter the Apostle

Do not love the world, nor the things which are in the world. The world shall pass away and all its desires; but he who does the will of God shall abide forever. Amen.

The Acts

A reading from the Acts of our fathers the pure apostles, who were invested with the grace of the Holy Spirit. May their blessing be with us all. Amen.

Hi Everyone!

This is St Luke the Apostle, and I want to tell you some of the story of my exciting travels with St Paul. Paul was arrested and going to Rome to face the judge. But when we got to Rome, the judge was very busy. So Paul was allowed to stay in a house—but he wasn't allowed to leave it at all. So instead, Paul sent a message around to all the important Jewish people who lived in Rome. When they came to visit, he said to them: "My brothers, I want you to know that I haven't done anything wrong. The Romans judged me in Jerusalem, and they found that I haven't done anything wrong. "But when the Jews in Jerusalem complained, I said that they have to bring me to the King: Caesar himself, to settle the matter." So the Jewish people of Rome said to Paul: "This is all new news to us. Can you tell us some more? We'd like to understand what's going on." So they agreed on another day when they all came and listened to Paul speaking about Jesus, and how Moses and the prophets all prepared us for the coming of Jesus. Do you think that all the Jewish people in Rome believed Paul? Do you think they all wanted to follow Jesus and become Christians? Some people did. And some people didn't. So Paul said to the ones who didn't want to know Jesus: "If you don't want to know about Jesus, I will tell the Gentiles, the ones who are not Jewish. They will listen to me and follow Jesus." So Paul stayed in his house in Rome for two whole years. And he told everyone who came to see him about the love of Jesus, And all the beautiful things that Jesus said, and taught, and did. And about the Kingdom of God. And no one could stop him. (Chapter 28:11–31)

The word of the Lord shall grow, multiply, be mighty and be confirmed in the holy Church of God. Amen.

Holy Gospel

Stand up in the fear of God and listen to the Holy Gospel,A chapter from the Holy Gospel according to Saints. Matthew, Mark, and Luke. May their blessings be with us all, Amen

A chapter from the Holy Gospel according to Saint Matthew, May his blessings be with us all, Amen

From the psalms of our teacher David the prophet and king,May his blessings be with us all, Amen

Sound a trumpet in the new moon On this honourable day of our feast; Rejoice in God our helper; Rejoice greatly in the living God. Take up a psalm and sound a timbrel, a pleasant psaltery with a harp. Alleluia. Psalm 81:3,1–2

Blessed is He who comes in the Name of the Lord Our Lord, God and Saviour and the King of us all, Jesus Christ, the Son of the living God. Glory be to You forever more, Amen

Now when they drew near Jerusalem, and came to Bethphage, at the Mount of Olives, then Jesus sent two disciples, saying to them, "Go into the village opposite you, and immediately you will find a donkey tied, and a colt with her. "Loose them and bring them to Me. And if anyone says anything to you, you shall say, 'The Lord has need of them,'" and a very great multitude spread their clothes on the road; others cut down branches from the trees and spread them on the road. Then the multitudes cried out, saying: "Hosanna to the Son of David! 'Blessed is He who comes in the name of the Lord!' Hosanna in the highest!" Then Jesus went into the temple of God and drove out all those who bought and sold in the temple, and overturned the tables of the money changers and the seats of those who sold doves. And He said to them, "It is written, 'My house shall be called a house of prayer,' but you have made it a 'den of thieves.' " Then the blind and the lame came to Him in the temple, and He healed them. But when the chief priests and scribes saw the children crying out in the temple and saying, "Hosanna to the Son of David!" they were indignant and Jesus said to them, "Yes. Have you never read, 'Out of the mouth of babes and nursing infants You have perfected praise'?" Then He left them and went out of the city to Bethany, and He lodged there. Matthew 21:1–17

Glory be to God Forever, Amen

AND ALSO

A chapter from the Holy Gospel according to Saint Mark, May his blessings be with us all, Amen

So they went their way, and found the colt tied by the door outside on the street, and they loosed it. But some of those who stood there said to them, "What are you doing, loosing the colt?" And they spoke to them just as Jesus had commanded. So they let them go. Then they brought the colt to Jesus and threw their clothes on it, and He sat on it. And many spread their clothes on the road, and others cut down leafy branches from the trees and spread them on the road. Then those who went before and those who followed cried out, saying:

"Hosanna! 'Blessed is He who comes in the name of the Lord!' "Blessed is the kingdom of our father David That comes in the name of the Lord! Hosanna in the highest!" And Jesus went into Jerusalem and into the temple. So when He had looked around at all things, as the hour was already late, He went out to Bethany with the twelve. Mark 11:1–11

Glory be to God Forever, Amen

AND ALSO

A chapter from the Holy Gospel according to Saint Luke, May his blessings be with us all, Amen

Then, as He was now drawing near the descent of the Mount of Olives, the whole multitude of the disciples began to rejoice and praise God, with a loud voice for all the mighty works they had seen, saying: " 'Blessed is the King who comes in the name of the Lord!' Peace in heaven and glory in the highest!" And some of the Pharisees called to Him from the crowd, "Teacher, rebuke Your disciples." But He answered and said to them, "I tell you that if these should keep silent, the stones would immediately cry out." Now as He drew near, He saw the city and wept over it, saying, "If you had known, even you, especially in this your day, the things that make for your peace! "But now they are hidden from your eyes. For days will come upon you when your enemies close you in on every side, and level you to the ground" and He was teaching daily in the temple. But the chief priests, the scribes, and the leaders of the people sought to destroy Him, and were unable to do anything; for all the people were very attentive to hear Him. Luke 19:29–48

Glory be to God Forever, Amen

Stand up in the fear of God and listen to the Holy Gospel, A chapter from the Holy Gospel according to Saint John, May this blessings be with us all, Amen

From the psalms of our teacher David the prophet and king, May his blessings be with us all, Amen

It is fitting to sing a hymn to You in Zion, O God, And a vow shall be rendered to You in Jerusalem. Hear my prayer; To You all flesh shall come. Alleluia. Psalm 65:1–2

Blessed is He who comes in the Name of the Lord Our Lord, God and Saviour and the King of us all, Jesus Christ, the Son of the living God. Glory be to You forever more, Amen

The next day a great multitude that had come to the feast, when they heard that Jesus was coming to Jerusalem, took branches of palm trees, and went out to meet Him, and cried out: "Hosanna! 'Blessed is He who comes in the name of the Lord!' The King of Israel!" Then Jesus, when He had found a young donkey, sat on it; as it is written: "Fear not, daughter of Zion; Behold, your King is coming, Sitting on a donkey's colt." His disciples did not understand these things at first; but when Jesus was glorified, then they remembered that these things were written about Him and that they had done these things to Him. Therefore the people, who were with Him when He called Lazarus out of his tomb and raised him from the dead, bore witness. For this reason the people also met Him, because they heard that He had done this sign. The Pharisees therefore said among themselves, "You see that you are accomplishing nothing. Look, the world has gone after Him!" John 12:12–19

Glory be to God Forever, Amen

COVENANT OF THE HOLY THURSDAY

Holy Gospel

MATINS

Stand up in the fear of God and listen to the Holy Gospel, A chapter from the Holy Gospel according to Saint Luke , May his blessings be with us all, Amen

From the psalms of our teacher David the prophet and king, May his blessings be with us all, Amen

> The words of his mouth were smoother than butter, But war was in his heart; His words were softer than oil, Yet they were drawn swords. For it is not an enemy who reproaches me; Then I could bear it. Nor is it one who hates me who has exalted himself against me; Then I could hide from him.   Alleluia. Psalm 55:21,12

Blessed is He who comes in the Name of the Lord Our Lord, God and Saviour and the King of us all, Jesus Christ, the Son of the living God. Glory be to You forever more, Amen

Then came the Day of Unleavened Bread, when the Passover must be killed. And He sent Peter and John, saying, "Go and prepare the Passover for us, that we may eat." So they said to Him, "Where do You want us to prepare?"

And He said to them, "Behold, when you have entered the city, a man will meet you carrying a pitcher of water; follow him into the house which he enters. Then you shall say to the master of the house, 'The Teacher says to you, "Where is the guest room where I may eat the Passover with My disciples?" ' Then he will show you a large, furnished upper room; there make ready."

So they went and found it just as He had said to them, and they prepared the Passover. Luke 22: 7-13

Glory be to God Forever, Amen

Pauline

Paul, the servant of our Lord Jesus Christ, called to be an apostle, appointed to the Gospel of God. A reading from the First Epistle of our teacher Paul to the Corinthians. May his holy blessings be with us. Amen.

Dear Corinthians,

Do you know how Holy Communion started? It was Jesus Himself who taught His Disciples to pray and have Holy Communion. It all began one evening, a long time ago. Jesus was having His Last Supper with His Disciples, before He was arrested. Jesus took bread in His hands and when Jesus had prayed "thank You," to God the Father He broke the bread and said: "Take and eat; this is My Body which is broken for you; Remember Me when you do this." After supper, Jesus took the cup and said: "This cup is My Blood. It is my promise to you. Remember Me when you drink it." So, every time we eat this very special Bread And drink this very special Cup, We remember and tell the world that Jesus died and rose and is coming back again. But if you don't take Holy Communion seriously; if you don't respect the Body and Blood, you are not respecting Jesus Himself! Don't be like that! Each of us should not wait until we get into trouble. We should check ourselves if we're doing the wrong thing and fix it quick smart! And if you do get into trouble for doing the wrong thing, remember that it is only for your own good, so you can be a better person. So, when you all come together at Church to have Holy Communion, be respectful of Jesus' Body and Blood. And be respectful of each other too. I have more things I want to say to you, but they will have to wait until I come to visit you in Corinth. (1 Corinthians 11:23–34)

Bye for now!

Signed, Paul

The grace of God the Father be with you all, Amen.

Holy Gospel

Stand up in the fear of God and listen to the Holy Gospel, A chapter from the Holy Gospel according to Saint Matthew, May his blessings be with us all, Amen

From the psalms of our teacher David the prophet and king, May his blessings be with us all, Amen

> You prepare a table before me in the presence of my enemies. He who ate my bread, dealt deceptively with me. Alleluia. Psalm 23:5; 41:9

Blessed is He who comes in the Name of the Lord Our Lord, God and Saviour and the King of us all, Jesus Christ, the Son of the living God. Glory be to You forever more, Amen

When evening had come, He sat down with the twelve. Now as they were eating, He said, "Assuredly, I say to you, one of you will betray Me." And they were exceedingly sorrowful, and each of them began to say to Him, "Lord, is it I?" He answered and said, "He who dipped his hand with Me in the dish will betray Me. The Son of Man indeed goes just as it is written of Him, "but woe to that man by whom the Son of Man is betrayed! It would have been good for that man if he had not been born." Then Judas, who was betraying Him, answered and said, "Rabbi, is it I?" He said to him, "You have said it." And as they were eating, Jesus took bread, blessed and broke it, and gave it to the disciples and said, "Take, eat; this is My body." Then He took the cup, and gave thanks, and gave it to them, saying, "Drink from it, all of you. "For this is My blood of the new covenant, which is shed for many for the remission of sins. "But I say to you, I will not drink of this fruit of the vine from now on until that day when I drink it new with you in My Father's kingdom." Matthew 26:20–29

Glory be to God Forever, Amen

Holy Gospel

MATINS

Stand up in the fear of God and listen to the Holy Gospel, A chapter from the Holy Gospel according to Saint Mark, May his blessings be with us all, Amen

From the psalms of our teacher David the prophet and king, May his blessings be with us all, Amen

> Then the Lord awoke as from sleep, Like a mighty man who shouts because of wine. And He built His sanctuary like the heights, Like the earth which He has established forever. Alleluia. Psalm 78: 65,69

Blessed is He who comes in the Name of the Lord Our Lord, God and Saviour and the King of us all, Jesus Christ, the Son of the living God. Glory be to You forever more, Amen

Very early in the morning, on the first day of the week, they came to the tomb when the sun had risen. And they said among themselves, "Who will roll away the stone from the door of the tomb for us?" But when they looked up, they saw that the stone had been rolled away—for it was very large. And entering the tomb, they saw a young man clothed in a long white robe sitting on the right side; and they were alarmed. But he said to them, "Do not be alarmed. You seek Jesus of Nazareth, who was crucified. He is risen! He is not here. See the place where they laid Him. But go, tell His disciples—and Peter—that He is going before you into Galilee; there you will see Him, as He said to you."

So they went out quickly and fled from the tomb, for they trembled and were amazed. And they said nothing to anyone, for they were afraid. Now when He rose early on the first day of the week, He appeared first to Mary Magdalene, out of whom He had cast seven demons. She went and told those who had been with Him, as they mourned and wept. And when they heard that He was alive and had been seen by her, they did not believe. Mark 16:2-11

Glory be to God Forever, Amen

353

Pauline

Paul, the servant of our Lord Jesus Christ, called to be an apostle, appointed to the Gospel of God. A reading from the First Epistle of our teacher Paul to the Corinthians. May his holy blessings be with us. Amen.

Dear Corinthians,

Great news! Jesus Christ has risen from the dead! He died on the cross but He became alive again! Even better news!! Just like Jesus rose from the dead, so will we! So we don't have to be afraid of dying any more! Jesus is the Boss of the whole world. And at the end of the world, absolutely everything will listen to Jesus; Because Jesus listens to God the Father. And then, God shall be "All in all." We should always remember this. If Jesus hadn't risen from the dead, our lives would be very different! Maybe we wouldn't care about right and wrong. But instead, we look forward to rising with Jesus, and living with Him forever and ever. So we live every day getting ready for this. But maybe you are wondering: "How will we rise from the dead? What will we look like?" Well, you know how you plant a hard little seed in the ground, and it grows into a big beautiful plant with lots of delicious juicy fruits? The plant and the fruit are kind of the same as the hard little seed. But they are also just so much, much better! Same with us! Your body now is just like the hard little seed. But your body when you rise from the dead will be like the plant and the juicy fruit! God makes lots of different kinds of bodies! An animal is not a bird. A bird is not a fish. A fish is not the moon. The moon is not the sun. When we rise from the dead, we will have a special body, a SPIRITUAL body, even better than the bright shining sun! Adam and Eve were just made of dust. But when we rise from the dead, we will be just like Jesus! And we will live forever with Jesus! (1 Corinthians 15:23-50)

Bye for now!

Signed, Paul

> *The grace of God the Father be with you all, Amen.*

Catholicon

The Catholic Epistle from the First Epistle of our teacher St Peter. May his holy blessings be with us. Amen.

Hello Everyone! Are you keeping God's love safely sealed in your hearts? If you are, you will always be ready to politely answer anyone who asks you "Why do you trust God? Why do you depend so much on Him?" You will never be afraid of anyone. When bad people call you names, don't worry! Everyone sees your very good behaviour! Sometimes, life isn't fair. But it's so much better to be a good person than it is to be a bad person, even when things go terribly wrong. Things went very wrong indeed for Jesus. Remember how He was crucified on the Cross? That was very unfair. But because Jesus is good He turned the Cross into something wonderful! He saved the whole wide world! Even the people who had already died! From the Cross, Jesus went down into Hades and He set free all the people who were stuck there. Do you remember Noah and his ark? And how God brought them through the water, and saved life on earth? Jesus does the same thing for us, when we are baptised. God brings us through the water of baptism and saves our lives! Baptism saves us, because of that unfair thing that happened to Jesus: After Jesus died on the Cross He Went down to Hades. Then Jesus rose from the dead and He raised us with Him! And He went up to Heaven and He will take us to be there with Him one day! Because Jesus is the King of Heaven and all its angels. Won't that be wonderful? If Jesus did all that for us, don't you think that we should try extra hard to stay away from doing bad things? Lots of people waste their lives doing all kinds of bad things. And when you tell them that you don't want to join them, they think you're weird! But please don't worry about them. One day, EVERYONE will have to stand in front of Jesus and be responsible for what they have done. EVERYONE. That means those alive on the earth now; and those who were already dead; because Jesus went down into Hades so He could even tell the souls in Hades the Good News about how He saved them from death And us too (1 Peter 3:15–4:6)

Bye for now!

Signed, Peter the Apostle

Do not love the world, nor the things which are in the world. The world shall pass away and all its desires; but he who does the will of God shall abide forever. Amen.

The Acts

A reading from the Acts of our fathers the pure apostles, who were invested with the grace of the Holy Spirit. May their blessing be with us all. Amen.

Do you remember the story of how the Holy Spirit came down upon the disciples of Jesus like many little flames of fire? One of those disciples was St Peter. And he went outside, right away, and began to speak the people standing there: "Hey! Everyone! Listen to me You all saw Jesus, and how he did lots of miracles right in front of your eyes. Remember Him? "That's right! Jesus is the one you arrested and crucified on the cross. Well, guess what happened to Him? "Jesus is alive! Jesus rose from the dead! Death wasn't strong enough to hold on to Him! Jesus has beaten death! Just like the Psalm says "The Lord is always right in front of me. Because He is with me I am never scared of anything at all. "So, my heart is always happy; And my tongue is always saying joyful things. "And my body will rest in hope. For God will not leave me when I die. God will not let His Holy One (that means Jesus) in the grave. "God has shown me the way of life. I am full of happiness because I am with God forever and forever." (Chapter 2:22–28)

The word of the Lord shall grow, multiply, be mighty and be confirmed in the holy Church of God. Amen.

Holy Gospel

Stand up in the fear of God and listen to the Holy Gospel,A chapter from the Holy Gospel according to Saint John, May his blessings be with us all, Amen

From the psalms of our teacher David the prophet and king,May his blessings be with us all, Amen

> This is the day the Lord made; Let us greatly rejoice, and be glad therein. O Lord, save us now; O Lord, prosper us now. God is the Lord, and He revealed Himself to us. Alleluia. Psalm 118:24–25,27

Blessed is He who comes in the Name of the Lord Our Lord, God and Saviour and the King of us all, Jesus Christ, the Son of the living God. Glory be to You forever more, Amen

Now the first day of the week Mary Magdalene went to the tomb early, while it was still dark, and saw that the stone had been taken away from the tomb. Then she ran and came to Simon Peter, and to the other disciple, whom Jesus loved, and said to them, "They have taken away the Lord out of the tomb, and we do not know where they have laid Him." Peter therefore went out, and the other disciple, and were going to the tomb. So they both ran together, and the other disciple outran Peter and came to the tomb first. And he, stooping down and looking in, saw the linen cloths lying there; yet he did not go in. Then Simon Peter came, following him, and went into the tomb; and he saw the linen cloths lying there, and the handkerchief that had been around His head, not lying with the linen cloths, but folded together in a place by itself. Then the other disciple, who came to the tomb first, went in also; and he saw and believed. For as yet they did not know the Scripture, that He must rise again from the dead. Then the disciples went away again to their own homes. But Mary stood outside by the tomb weeping, and as she wept she stooped down and looked into the tomb. And she saw two angels in white sitting, one at the head and the other at the feet, where the body of Jesus had lain. Then they said to her, "Woman, why are you weeping?" She said to them, "Because they have taken away my Lord, and I do not know where they have laid Him." Now when she had said this, she turned around and saw Jesus standing there, and did not know that it was Jesus. Jesus said to her, "Woman, why are you weeping? Whom are you seeking?" She, supposing Him to be the gardener, said to Him, "Sir, if You have carried Him away, tell me where You have laid Him, and I will take Him away." Jesus said to her, "Mary!" She turned and said to Him, "Rabboni!" (which is to say, Teacher). Jesus said to her, "Do not cling to Me, for I have not yet ascended to My Father; "But go to My brethren and say to them, 'I am ascending to My Father and your Father, and to My God and your God.' " Mary Magdalene came and told the disciples that she had seen the Lord, and that He had spoken these things to her. John 20:1–18

Glory be to God Forever, Amen

HOLY
PENTECOST

FIRST SUNDAY OF THE HOLY PENTECOST

Holy Gospel

MATINS

Stand up in the fear of God and listen to the Holy Gospel, A chapter from the Holy Gospel according to Saint John, May his blessings be with us all, Amen

From the psalms of our teacher David the prophet and king, May his blessings be with us all, Amen

> Oh, sing to the Lord a new song! Sing to the Lord, all the earth. Sing to the Lord, bless His name; Proclaim the good news of His salvation from day to day. Alleluia. Psalm 96:1-2

Blessed is He who comes in the Name of the Lord Our Lord, God and Saviour and the King of us all, Jesus Christ, the Son of the living God. Glory be to You forever more, Amen

After these things Jesus showed Himself again to the disciples at the Sea of Tiberias, and in this way He showed Himself: Simon Peter, Thomas called the Twin, Nathanael of Cana in Galilee, the sons of Zebedee, and two others of His disciples were together. Simon Peter said to them, "I am going fishing." They said to him, "We are going with you also." They went out and immediately got into the boat, and that night they caught nothing. But when the morning had now come, Jesus stood on the shore; yet the disciples did not know that it was Jesus. Then Jesus said to them, "Children, have you any food?" They answered Him, "No."

And He said to them, "Cast the net on the right side of the boat, and you will find some." So they cast, and now they were not able to draw it in because of the multitude of fish. Therefore that disciple whom Jesus loved said to Peter, "It is the Lord!" Now when Simon Peter heard that it was the Lord, he put on his outer garment (for he had removed it), and plunged into the sea. But the other disciples came in the little boat (for they were not far from land, but about two hundred cubits), dragging the net with fish. Then, as soon as they had come to land, they saw a fire of coals there, and fish laid on it, and bread. Jesus said to them, "Bring some of the fish which you have just caught." Simon Peter went up and dragged the net to land, full of large fish, one hundred and fifty-three; and although there were so many, the net was not broken. Jesus said to them, "Come and eat breakfast." Yet none of the disciples dared ask Him, "Who are You?"—knowing that it was the Lord. Jesus then came and took the bread and gave it to them, and likewise the fish. This is now the third time Jesus showed Himself to His disciples after He was raised from the dead. John 21:1-14

Glory be to God Forever, Amen

Pauline

Paul, the servant of our Lord Jesus Christ, called to be an apostle, appointed to the Gospel of God. A reading from the Epistle of our teacher Paul to the Ephesians. May his holy blessings be with us. Amen.

St Paul the Apostle was writing a letter to the Christians who lived in the busy city of Ephesus. Dear Ephesians, Do you truly understand what it means to follow Jesus? It means we have to leave our old selves behind with all our mistakes and naughtiness, And become new every day, being just like Jesus, doing good things. So, we should leave behind Always tell the truth us things like Lying to each other, for we are all members of the Body of Jesus. Getting Angry. If you do lose your temper don't hurt anyone with your words or actions, and don't stay angry for long. Stealing. We shouldn't be TAKING should be GIVING to from others. We help others!Work hard so you can earn enough to help others. Bad Words. Only let good words come out of your mouth, words that help others, not words that hurt others. You are filled with God's Holy Spirit! Don't make Him sad. He is sad when you are bitter, angry, mean, or make trouble. But you make the Holy Spirit who lives in you really happy when you are kind, gentle and forgiving, just as Jesus forgave you. Isn't it so much nicer to make God and other people happy? (Ephesians 4:20-32)

Bye for now!

Signed, Paul

The grace of God the Father be with you all, Amen.

Catholicon

The Catholic Epistle from the First Epistle of our teacher St John. May his holy blessings be with us. Amen.

From John,

My beloved brothers and sisters, do you remember the most important commandment God has given us? The most important commandment, from long ago, and forevermore, is LOVE! We must love God, and love one another. That is what Jesus taught us. If you don't love other people, you are like a person who lives in darkness. You will always stumble and fall. The light of Jesus is much stronger than the darkness. But if you love other people, you are like a person who lives in the light. You will never stumble or fall! I wanted to write these things to you, O little children Because God has forgiven your sins. I wanted to write these things to you, O parents Because you have known God very well. I wanted to write these things to you, O young people Because you have beaten the devil. I wanted to write these things to you, O little children Because you are friends with the Father. I wanted to write these things to you, O parents Because you are friends with God. I wanted to write these things to you, O young people Because you are strong, and God's word lives in you, and you have beaten the devil. If you are selfish, and just you won't be able to truly love God. God teaches us love the things in the world, to NOT be selfish. So we don't really care that much about those selfish things everyone else goes crazy about. This world is going to end one day. But our love for God is forever! (1 John 2:7-17)

God loves you!

Signed,   John the Beloved

Do not love the world, nor the things which are in the world. The world shall pass away and all its desires; but he who does the will of God shall abide forever. Amen.

The Acts

St Paul was waiting for his friends from overseas to join him in the great city of Athens, the capital of the country called Greece. While he was there he would go down to the marketplace of Athens and talk to whomever he might find there. Some were Jews, like him. Some were Greeks. The Greeks worshipped their own gods in their own temples, with statues. But some of them were really curious about the things that Paul was saying. So they invited Paul to a public place called the Areopagus [aer-ee-oh-pay-guss] for a discussion. They loved talking about new ideas! This is what Paul said to them: "Men of Athens! I noticed you have many altars to all your gods. But one of them caught my eye. On this altar is written: To the Unknown God. Let me tell you about the real God you don't know yet. The real God is the One who made the whole world and everything in it. Including all of us, wherever we come from! We are all His children. So we should all look for Him, try to know Him better. But actually, He is not very far from us at all. Your own poets said: "In Him we live, and move, and have our being." He is all around us! God is not made of gold or silver, like your statues. He is bigger than the whole world, and He loves us all. Don't you want to love Him back? Don't you want to stop all your sins? One day, we will rise from the dead like Jesus, and Jesus will come back and judge the whole world." Some of the Greeks laughed at Paul. But some of them believed what he told them, including Dionysius the Areopagite and a lady called Damaris. (Chapter 17:16-34)

Holy Gospel

Stand up in the fear of God and listen to the Holy Gospel,A chapter from the Holy Gospel according to Saint John, May his blessings be with us all, Amen

From the psalms of our teacher David the prophet and king,May his blessings be with us all, Amen

Sing a new song to the Lord, For He did wondrous things; Shout aloud to God, all the earth; Sing and greatly rejoice, and sing psalms. Alleluia Psalm 98:1,4

Blessed is He who comes in the Name of the Lord Our Lord, God and Saviour and the King of us all, Jesus Christ, the Son of the living God. Glory be to You forever more, Amen

Then, the same day at evening, being the first day of the week, when the doors were shut where the disciples were assembled, for fear of the Jews, Jesus came and stood in the midst, and said to them, "Peace be with you." When He had said this, He showed them His hands and His side. Then the disciples were glad when they saw the Lord. So Jesus said to them again, "Peace to you! As the Father has sent Me, I also send you." And when He had said this, He breathed on them, and said to them, "Receive the Holy Spirit. "If you forgive the sins of any, they are forgiven them; if you retain the sins of any, they are retained." Now Thomas, called the Twin, one of the twelve, was not with them when Jesus came. The other disciples therefore said to him, "We have seen the Lord." So he said to them, "Unless I see in His hands the print of the nails, and put my finger into the print of the nails, and put my hand into His side, I will not believe." And after eight days His disciples were again inside, and Thomas with them. Jesus came, the doors being shut, and stood in the midst, and said, "Peace to you!" Then He said to Thomas, "Reach your and put it into reach your at My hands; finger here, and look and hand here, My side. Do not be unbelieving, but believing." And Thomas answered and said to Him, "My Lord and my God!" Jesus said to him, "Thomas, because you have seen Me, you have believed. Blessed are those who have not seen and yet have believed." And truly Jesus did which are not written in this book; many other signs in the presence of His disciples, but these are written that you may believe that Jesus is the Christ, the Son of God, and that believing you may have life in His name. John 20:19-31

Glory be to God Forever, Amen

SECOND SUNDAY OF THE HOLY PENTECOST

Holy Gospel

Stand up in the fear of God and listen to the Holy Gospel, A chapter from the Holy Gospel according to Saint John, May his blessings be with us all, Amen

From the psalms of our teacher David the prophet and king, May his blessings be with us all, Amen

> The works of the Lord are great, Studied by all who have pleasure in them. His work is honorable and glorious, And His righteousness endures forever. He has made His wonderful works to be remembered; The Lord is gracious and full of compassion. . Alleluia Psalm 111:2-4

Blessed is He who comes in the Name of the Lord Our Lord, God and Saviour and the King of us all, Jesus Christ, the Son of the living God. Glory be to You forever more, Amen

When the people therefore saw that Jesus was not there, nor His disciples, they also got into boats and came to Capernaum, seeking Jesus. And when they found Him on the other side of the sea, they said to Him, "Rabbi, when did You come here?" Jesus answered them and said, "Most assuredly, I say to you, you seek Me, not because you saw the signs, but because you ate of the loaves and were filled. Do not labor for the food which perishes, but for the food which endures to everlasting life, which the Son of Man will give you, because God the Father has set His seal on Him." Then they said to Him, "What shall we do, that we may work the works of God?" Jesus answered and said to them, "This is the work of God, that you believe in Him whom He sent." Therefore they said to Him, "What sign will You perform then, that we may see it and believe You? What work will You do? Our fathers ate the manna in the desert; as it is written, 'He gave them bread from heaven to eat.'" Then Jesus said to them, "Most assuredly, I say to you, Moses did not give you the bread from heaven, but My Father gives you the true bread from heaven. For the bread of God is He who comes down from heaven and gives life to the world." John 6: 24-33

Glory be to God Forever, Amen

Pauline

Paul, the servant of our Lord Jesus Christ, called to be an apostle, appointed to the Gospel of God. A reading from the Epistle of our teacher Paul to the Ephesians. May his holy blessings be with us. Amen.

St Paul the Apostle was writing a letter to the Christians who lived in the busy city of Ephesus. Dear Ephesians, Do you know that we are all God's Family? Each one of us is like one brick in the big, big house that God built! All of us bricks are built on top of the strong foundation, which is Jesus Himself, and His apostles and prophets. And do you know Who lives in this big, big house that is made up of us? Can you guess? Yes, it is God Himself! House or Temple of All of us are the God's Holy Spirit. God has been very kind to me. He has taught me so much about how much He loves everybody in the world. And now I want you all to know it too! It doesn't matter whether you are a Jew or not. All of us are God's children. All of us are part of God's House. All of us are part of the Body of Christ. Out of His kindness, God gave little me the big job of telling people about His love, especially the people who are not Jewish, people like you, the Gentiles. Because this is the secret of God—His mystery: From the beginning of the world, God has loved us all! And now, you all know this great and beautiful secret! It is our job—all of us— to tell the whole world about this incredible beautiful mystery. Even the angels in heaven are amazed and astounded when they see the Church, this House of God, filled with God's love! (Ephesians 2:19-3:10)

Bye for now!

Signed, Paul

The grace of God the Father be with you all, Amen.

Catholicon

The Catholic Epistle from the First Epistle of our teacher St John. May his holy blessings be with us. Amen.

From John,

My beloved brothers and sisters, Did you know that you and I share a very special secret? But it's the kind of secret that God wants us to tell everybody about! And here it is, are you ready? God has given us eternal can live forever with That means that we life! Him in Heaven! So if you know about Jesus, believe in Him, love Him and if Jesus lives inside you. You will get to live forever with Jesus in Heaven! Because He gives us more and more. So keep believing in Jesus. Keep loving Him more and more. Jesus hears every word we say to Him when we pray. Jesus answers our prayers. Especially when we pray for a brother or sister who is doing something wrong. They really need someone to pray for them! So they can stop being naughty! When you really love God, you just don't want to do anything wrong. And even though the devil might trick the whole world to do the wrong thing. He can never trick us — if we really, really love God. For God is true And Jesus is true And He protects us every day of our lives. (1 John 5:10-20)

Bye for now!

Signed, John the Beloved

Do not love the world, nor the things which are in the world. The world shall pass away and all its desires; but he who does the will of God shall abide forever. Amen.

The Acts

Hello everyone. My name is St Luke, and I am the one who wrote the Book of Acts. Today, I want to tell you a little more of the story of St Paul. I was travelling with Paul. We went to lots of new places—Macedonia, and Greece, and Philippi, and Troas. And we had lots of helpers travelling with us, telling people all about Jesus. One Sunday, we were in Troas, and we came together to pray, have communion, and talk. Paul spoke and spoke and they listened and listened, so happy to learn more about Jesus' love. Before anyone realised, it was already midnight! It was way past the bedtime of a boy called Eutychus [Yoo-tie-kuss]. They were on the third floor and Eutychus was sitting somewhere that was not very clever. Eutychus was sitting on the window sill. And the window was open. And Eutychus fell asleep! OH! Be careful Eutychus! Oh no! Eutychus fell out the window! How awful! Everyone rushed downstairs. Is he hurt? Is he alive? Oh no! Oh no! Eutychus was dead. But Paul went through all the people, and he picked up Eutychus. Paul hugged him. Paul prayed for him. Then, a miracle happened, Eutychus came back to life! He was alive again! Everyone was so happy! Then we all went back inside, and had something to eat, which we needed after a shock like that! And we kept listening to Paul all through the night, all the way to morning. The things he was telling us about Jesus were just so beautiful. We didn't want him to stop! And in the morning, Paul left to get on a ship to continue his adventures. (Chapter 20:1-12)

Holy Gospel

Stand up in the fear of God and listen to the Holy Gospel, A chapter from the Holy Gospel according to Saint John, May his blessings be with us all, Amen

From the psalms of our teacher David the prophet and king, May his blessings be with us all, Amen

> He sent redemption to His people; He commanded His covenant forever; Holy and fearful is His name. The beginning of wisdom is the fear of the Lord. Alleluia. Psalm 111:9-10

Blessed is He who comes in the Name of the Lord Our Lord, God and Saviour and the King of us all, Jesus Christ, the Son of the living God. Glory be to You forever more, Amen

And Jesus said to them, "I am the bread of life. He who comes to Me shall never hunger, and he who believes in Me shall never thirst. But I said to you that you have seen Me and yet do not believe. All that the Father gives Me will come to Me, and the one who comes to Me I will by no means cast out. not to do My own will, For I have come down from heaven, but the will of Him who sent Me. This is the will of the Father who sent Me, that of all He has given Me I should lose nothing, but should raise it up at the last day. And this is the will of Him who sent Me, that everyone who sees the Son and believes in Him may have everlasting life; and I will raise him up at the last day." about Him, because He said, "I am the bread which came down from heaven." The Jews then complained And they said, "Is not this Jesus, the son of Joseph, whose father and mother we know? How is it then that He says, 'I have come down from heaven'?" Jesus therefore answered and said to them, "Do not murmur among yourselves, no one can come to Me unless the Father who sent Me draws him; and I will raise him up at the last day. It is written in the prophets, 'And they shall all be taught by God.' Therefore everyone who has heard and learned from the Father comes to Me. John 6:35-45

Glory be to God Forever, Amen

THIRD SUNDAY OF THE HOLY PENTECOST

Holy Gospel

Stand up in the fear of God and listen to the Holy Gospel, A chapter from the Holy Gospel according to Saint John, May his blessings be with us all, Amen

From the psalms of our teacher David the prophet and king, May his blessings be with us all, Amen

> Then I called upon the name of the Lord: "O Lord, I implore You, deliver my soul!" Gracious is the Lord, and righteous; Yes, our God is merciful. Alleluia. Psalm 116:4-5

Blessed is He who comes in the Name of the Lord Our Lord, God and Saviour and the King of us all, Jesus Christ, the Son of the living God. Glory be to You forever more, Amen

Then Jesus said to them again, "I am going away, and you will seek Me, and will die in your sin. Where I go you cannot come." So the Jews said, "Will He kill Himself, because He says, 'Where I go you cannot come'?" And He said to them, "You are from beneath; I am from above. You are of this world; I am not of this world. Therefore I said to you that you will die in your sins; for if you do not believe that I am He, you will die in your sins." Then they said to Him, "Who are You?" And Jesus said to them, "Just what I have been saying to you from the beginning. I have many things to say and to judge concerning you, but He who sent Me is true; and I speak to the world those things which I heard from Him." They did not understand that He spoke to them of the Father. Then Jesus said to them, "When you lift up the Son of Man, then you will know that I am He, and that I do nothing of Myself; but as My Father taught Me, I speak these things. And He who sent Me is with Me. The Father has not left Me alone, for I always do those things that please Him." As He spoke these words, many believed in Him. John 8:21-30

Glory be to God Forever, Amen

Pauline

LITURGY

St Paul the Apostle was writing a letter to the Christians who lived in the city of Colossae. Dear Colossians, Being a Christian means that Jesus lives inside us! Jesus died on the Cross, rose from the dead, and went up to Heaven! But Jesus lives inside our hearts and minds. So our hearts and minds should be where Jesus is. We should always be thinking about heavenly things, just like Jesus. We should do our best to get rid of any bad things inside us. Things like, being selfish, being jealous of other people and wanting to take things that are not ours. Maybe we used to do such should stop. These things hurt us, and they hurt other people. bad things before, but we so don't do any of these things: Don't get angry with each other, don't be mean to each other and ever say bad things about God! Don't swear or say rude words and don't lie to anyone. Jesus made you a new person! You are now like Jesus! You are the Image of God! So don't go back to your bad old ways! We are all the Image of God! Whatever country you come from, whatever job you do, we are all God's children in Jesus. "Christ is all, and in all." Say it with me, "Christ is all, And in all." Be kind and gentle, so here's what you should do, because you are the Image of God, and Jesus lives in you, be humble, and meek. Forgive each other just as Jesus forgave you! Be patient with each other, But most important of all, put on love, which will really make you good like Jesus. Let the peace of God rule in your hearts, for we are all one Body of Christ. Always be thankful. Let the Word of Christ always be in your thoughts and your hearts, for it will make you wise. Help each other to do what is good always. Sing beautiful songs to God together! Every single thing you do, do it in the Name of Christ. And remember to say "Thank You" to Jesus for everything. (Colossians 3:1-17)

Bye for now!

Signed, Paul

> *The grace of God the Father be with you all, Amen.*

Catholicon

The Catholic Epistle from the First Epistle of our teacher St John. May his holy blessings be with us. Amen.

My little children, Sometimes, when you are good and do the right thing, other people don't like you. But don't be surprised! We love everyone, just like Jesus loved everyone. He even died for us— that's how much He loves us! So if you don't love other people, you are not really following Jesus, are you? This is what love looks like: If you see someone who is poor, and you have something you could give them, you will give it to them! If you are selfish and don't help other people, how can you say that you love them? So, let's not just SAY that we love each other, let's SHOW that we love each other in everything we SAY and everything we THINK and everything we DO. If we really love like this, then our hearts won't ever be worried. And even when we feel guilty, we know that God will never stop loving us! answers our prayers, especially We know that God if we keep His commandments and do what makes Him happy. Do you know what His commandment is? That we should believe in the name of His Son Jesus Christ and that we should love one another. Whoever keeps God commandments is living in God and God lives in him; That's how we know that God is living inside us— because His Holy Spirit inside us helps us to obey Him! (1 John 3:13-24)

God loves you!

Signed, John the Beloved

Do not love the world, nor the things which are in the world. The world shall pass away and all its desires; but he who does the will of God shall abide forever. Amen.

The Acts

A reading from the Acts of our fathers the pure apostles, who were invested with the grace of the Holy Spirit. May their blessing be with us all. Amen.

God had sent St Peter the Apostle to talk to a very kind Roman soldier, a centurion, whose name was Cornelius. Peter said: It seems, Cornelius, that you have heard what is being said about Jesus of Nazareth. How he was baptised by John the Baptist, and how the Holy Spirit appeared above Him, and how He helped people, and healed them. We saw all this with our own eyes! And we saw how they crucified Him on the Cross, and we saw Him when He came back to life again on the third day! He even ate and drank with us, after he rose from the dead! He told us that we must preach about Him— we must tell everyone that Jesus is the Lord of all the world, the living and the dead. As the old prophets said, whoever believes in Him will have their sins forgiven. (Chapter 10:37-43)

The word of the Lord shall grow, multiply, be mighty and be confirmed in the holy Church of God. Amen.

Holy Gospel

Stand up in the fear of God and listen to the Holy Gospel,A chapter from the Holy Gospel according to Saint John, May his blessings be with us all, Amen

From the psalms of our teacher David the prophet and king,May his blessings be with us all, Amen

> The Lord remembered us and blessed us; He blessed the house of Israel; He blessed the house of Aaron; He blessed those who feared the Lord, The least with the greatest. Alleluia Psalms 115:12-13

Blessed is He who comes in the Name of the Lord Our Lord, God and Saviour and the King of us all, Jesus Christ, the Son of the living God. Glory be to You forever more, Amen

Now Jesus learned that the Pharisees had heard that he was gaining and baptizing more disciples than John— although in fact it was not Jesus who baptized, but his disciples. So he left Judea and went back once more to Galilee. Now he had to go through Samaria. So he came to a town in Samaria called Sychar, near the plot of ground Jacob had given to his son Joseph. Jacob's well was there, and Jesus, tired as he was from the journey, sat down by the well. It was about noon.

When a Samaritan woman came to draw water, Jesus said to her, "Will you give me a drink?" (His disciples had gone into the town to buy food.)The Samaritan woman said to him, "You are a Jew and I am a Samaritan woman. How can you ask me for a drink?" (For Jews do not associate with Samaritans.) Jesus answered her, "If you knew the gift of God and who it is that asks you for a drink, you would have asked him and he would have given you living water." "Sir," the woman said, "you have nothing to draw with and the well is deep. Where can you get this living water? Are you greater than our father Jacob, who gave us the well and drank from it himself, as did also his sons and his livestock?" Jesus answered, "Everyone who drinks this water will be thirsty again, but whoever drinks the water I give them will never thirst. Indeed, the water I give them will become in them a spring of water welling up to eternal life."

The woman said to him, "Sir, give me this water so that I won't get thirsty and have to keep coming here to draw water." He told her, "Go, call your husband and come back." "I have no husband," she replied. Jesus said to her, "You are right when you say you have no husband. The fact is, you have had five husbands, and the man you now have is not your husband. What you have just said is quite true." "Sir," the woman said, "I can see that you are a prophet. Our ancestors worshiped on this mountain, but you Jews claim that the place where we must worship is in Jerusalem."

"Woman," Jesus replied, "believe me, a time is coming when you will worship the Father neither on this mountain nor in Jerusalem. You Samaritans worship what you do not know; we worship what we do know, for salvation is from the Jews. Yet a time is coming and has now come when the true worshipers will worship the Father in the Spirit and in truth, for they are the kind of worshipers the Father seeks. God is spirit, and his worshipers must worship in the Spirit and in truth."

The woman said, "I know that Messiah" (called Christ) "is coming. When he comes, he will explain everything to us." Then Jesus declared, "I, the one speaking to you—I am he."

Just then his disciples returned and were surprised to find him talking with a woman. But no one asked, "What do you want?" or "Why are you talking with her?" Then, leaving her water jar, the woman went back to the town and said to the people, "Come, see a man who told me everything I ever did. Could this be the Messiah?" They came out of the town and made their way toward him. Meanwhile his disciples urged him, "Rabbi, eat something." But he said to them, "I have food to eat that you know nothing about." Then his disciples said to each other, "Could someone have brought him food?" "My food," said Jesus, "is to do the will of him who sent me and to finish his work. Don't you have a saying, 'It's still four months until harvest'? I tell you, open your eyes and look at the fields! They are ripe for harvest. Even now the one who reaps draws a wage and harvests a crop for eternal life, so that the sower and the reaper may be glad together. Thus the saying 'One sows and another reaps' is true. I sent you to reap what you have not worked for. Others have done the hard work, and you have reaped the benefits of their labor."

Many of the Samaritans from that town believed in him because of the woman's testimony, "He told me everything I ever did." So when the Samaritans came to him, they urged him to stay with them, and he stayed two days. And because of his words many more became believers. They said to the woman, "We no longer believe just because of what you said; now we have heard for ourselves, and we know that this man really is the Savior of the world."

Glory be to God Forever, Amen

FOURTH SUNDAY OF THE HOLY PENTECOST

Holy Gospel

Stand up in the fear of God and listen to the Holy Gospel, A chapter from the Holy Gospel according to Saint John, May his blessings be with us all, Amen

From the psalms of our teacher David the prophet and king, May his blessings be with us all, Amen

> You are my God, and I will praise You; You are my God, I will exalt You. I will praise You, For You have answered me, And have become my salvation. Alleluia Psalms 118:28,21

Blessed is He who comes in the Name of the Lord Our Lord, God and Saviour and the King of us all, Jesus Christ, the Son of the living God. Glory be to You forever more, Amen

Most assuredly, I say to you, if anyone keeps My word he shall never see death." Then the Jews said to Him, "Now we know that You have a demon! Abraham is dead, and the prophets; and You say, 'If anyone keeps My word he shall never taste death.' Are You greater than our father Abraham, who is dead? And the prophets are dead. Who do You make Yourself out to be?"

Jesus answered, "If I honor Myself, My honor is nothing. It is My Father who honors Me, of whom you say that He is your God. Yet you have not known Him, but I know Him. And if I say, 'I do not know Him,' I shall be a liar like you; but I do know Him and keep His word. Your father Abraham rejoiced to see My day, and he saw it and was glad." Then the Jews said to Him, "You are not yet fifty years old, and have You seen Abraham?" Jesus said to them, "Most assuredly, I say to you, before Abraham was, I AM." Then they took up stones to throw at Him; but Jesus hid Himself and went out of the temple, going through the midst of them, and so passed by. John 8:51-59

Glory be to God Forever, Amen

Pauline LITURGY

St Paul the Apostle was writing a letter to the Christians who lived in the busy city of Thessalonica. Dear Thessalonians, I always thank God that you are following Jesus, who loved you and made you holy by His Holy Spirit. So be strong, my brothers and sisters, and hold on tight to the traditions— the things you learned in Church and in the Bible. And may our Lord Jesus Christ and God our Father who loved us and always comforts us, comfort you too and help you to do every kind of good deed. Finally, my brothers and sisters, pray for us, so that we can spread the word of God to others, just as we have with you. And pray that God will save us from bad people because there are people who are not very nice. But God is so kind! He cares for us so much! you strong, and guard He will always make and protect you from any evil. And we know that you love God so much. and will always do— Because of this love, you already do— the things we learned from Jesus. May God always guide your hearts to love Him more and more, and to be patient just like Jesus. (2 Thessalonians 2:13-3:5)

Bye for now!

Signed, Paul

Catholicon

The Catholic Epistle from the First Epistle of our teacher St John. May his holy blessings be with us. Amen.

My Beloved, Let us love one another for love is of God and everyone who loves is born of God. Anyone who does not love, Does not know God. For God is love. Say it with me now: God is love. Because God sent to us His Only-Begotten Son, Jesus Christ, to give us life. And how do we know that God loves us so? Where does love come from? We love God, because He first loved us, and sent His Son Jesus Christ to save us from our sins. My little children, If God loves us SO much then we also should love each other! Nobody has ever actually seen God, but if we truly love each other, God truly lives inside us! Do you want to know how you can tell if you area good follower of God? Well, if you have the Holy Spirit living in you, you are a good Jesus Follower. (1 John 4:7-13)

Bye for now!

Signed, John the Beloved

Do not love the world, nor the things which are in the world. The world shall pass away and all its desires; but he who does the will of God shall abide forever. Amen.

The Acts

One day, in a city called Lystra, Paul was preaching to a large group of people, telling them all about Jesus. As he was speaking, he noticed something very sad indeed! There was a crippled man who had never been able to walk, even when he was a little boy! And this man was listening oh so carefully to Paul! So Paul looked at him very hard, and said loudly, "Stand up straight on your feet!" And guess what happened next? The crippled man jumped up suddenly and walked on his feet! He was healed! His feet were normal and healthy! Now the people Paul was talking to weren't Christians. They got a funny idea when they saw him heal the crippled man. They thought Paul was a god! Oh dear! They thought Paul was the Greek god Hermes (Her-mees), because he was a clever speaker! And they thought that the apostle Barnabas was Zeus (Zoos), the king of the gods! Oh dear, oh dear! And the pagan priest of Zeus even brought some cows and flowers to sacrifice to Paul and Barnabas! Oh dear, oh dear, oh dear! Well, Paul had to do something, and pretty quick! So he started to speak to the people "Hey everybody, listen to me. We are just men like you! We are not gods! "There is just One True God — not Zeus or Hermes—but the God who made heaven, earth, sea, and everything in them." "And God shows everyone in the world just how much He loves us all, by giving us rain from heaven so the fruits will grow, and filling our hearts with food and gladness." Then some Jews came along, and convinced the crowd to let them take Paul away. But they wanted to hurt Paul. They threw stones at him, until he was almost dead! Poor, poor Paul! They left him lying on the ground outside the city. But when the other Christians found him, he got up! He was OK! Hooray! And he went to more cities to tell people about Jesus. And one day, he even came back to Lystra again. He was so brave. He said, "Don't be afraid. Even if things go wrong for us, we know we are heading for the kingdom of God". And Paul and the others chose priests for every church, and they prayed and fasted with them, and then they left them in God's loving care. (Chapter 14:8-23)

Holy Gospel

Stand up in the fear of God and listen to the Holy Gospel, A chapter from the Holy Gospel according to Saint John, May his blessings be with us all, Amen

From the psalms of our teacher David the prophet and king, May his blessings be with us all, Amen

> The Lord is my strength and my song, And He became my salvation. The sound of exceeding joy and salvation is in the tents of the righteous; The right hand of the Lord worked its power; The right hand of the Lord exalted me; The right hand of the Lord worked its power. Alleluia. Psalm 118:14-16

Blessed is He who comes in the Name of the Lord Our Lord, God and Saviour and the King of us all, Jesus Christ, the Son of the living God. Glory be to You forever more, Amen

Then Jesus said to them, "A little while longer the light is with you. Walk while you have the light, lest darkness overtake you; he who walks in darkness does not know where he is going. While you have the light, believe in the light, that you may become sons of light." These things Jesus spoke, and departed, and was hidden from them. But although He had done so many signs before them, they did not believe in Him. Nevertheless even among the rulers many believed in Him, but because of the Pharisees they did not confess Him, lest they should be put out of the synagogue; of God. for they loved the praise of men more than the praise Then Jesus cried out and said, "He who believes in Me, believes not in Me but in Him who sent Me. And he who sees Me sees Him who sent Me. I have come as a light into the world, that whoever believes in Me should not abide in darkness. And if anyone hears words and does not believe, I do not judge him; for I did not come to judge the world but to save the world. He who rejects Me, and does not receive My words, has that which judges him— the word that I have spoken will judge him in the last day. For I have not spoken on My own authority; but the Father who sent Me gave Me a command, what I should say and what I should speak. And I know that His command is everlasting life. Therefore, whatever I speak, just as the Father has told Me, so I speak." John 12:35-50

Glory be to God Forever, Amen

FIFTH SUNDAY OF THE HOLY PENTECOST

Holy Gospel

Stand up in the fear of God and listen to the Holy Gospel, A chapter from the Holy Gospel according to Saint John, May his blessings be with us all, Amen

From the psalms of our teacher David the prophet and king, May his blessings be with us all, Amen

> Bless the Lord, O house of Israel! Bless the Lord, O house of Aaron! Alleluia. Psalm 135:19

Blessed is He who comes in the Name of the Lord Our Lord, God and Saviour and the King of us all, Jesus Christ, the Son of the living God. Glory be to You forever more, Amen

Abide in Me, and I in you. As the branch cannot bear fruit of itself, unless it abides in the vine, neither can you, unless you abide in Me. "I am the vine, you are the branches. He who abides in Me, and I in him, bears much fruit; for without Me you can do nothing. If anyone does not abide in Me, he is cast out as a branch and is withered; and they gather them and throw them into the fire, and they are burned. If you abide in Me, and My words abide in you, you will ask what you desire, and it shall be done for you. By this My Father is glorified, that you bear much fruit; so you will be My disciples. John 15:4-8

Glory be to God Forever, Amen

Pauline

Paul, the servant of our Lord Jesus Christ, called to be an apostle, appointed to the Gospel of God. A reading from the Epistle of our teacher Paul to the Hebrews. May his holy blessings be with us. Amen.

St Paul the Apostle was writing a letter to the Jews or Hebrews everywhere. Dear Hebrews, We have a very special gift In the Old Testament, from Jesus. There was a special place in the Temple called the Holy of Holies. Only the High Priest was allowed to meet God in the Holy of Holies. But now, Jesus is our High Priest, and He has opened the curtain to the Holy of Holies for all of us! But we have to have pure hearts to go in there! So let's clean our hearts and bodies, trust Jesus, love one another and share our lives together. In the Old Testament, anyone who didn't follow God' was punished! We don't want s commands to be punished! So don't forget your love for Jesus, and how you joyfully put up with the bad treatment you suffered from nasty people, because you love Jesus. You knew that it didn't matter if you lost anything here on earth, because you have a much more precious treasure in heaven with Jesus. So please be patient in your suffering. Jesus is not far from you, and He will reward your suffering. A good person trusts God That's what these words mean: "The just shall in everything in their lives. live by faith." So please, don't stop trusting God. (Hebrews 10:19-38)

Bye for now!

Signed, Paul

> *The grace of God the Father be with you all, Amen.*

Catholicon

The Catholic Epistle from the First Epistle of our teacher St Peter. May his holy blessings be with us. Amen.

Hello Everyone! Do you know why Jesus went down to Hades after He died on the Cross and preached to the people down there who had already died? He wanted to give them a chance to live! We never know when our end will come, so, please, always be ready, always be praying. And most important of all: Love one another, truly, from your heart, for "love will cover a multitude of sins"— if you love others, God will forgive their sins, and your sins too! So look after each other well, with great kindness, and do it happily, without grumbling and complaining about it. God has given each one of you own talents or abilities. their own special gifts, their Use them to serve each other, so that we all get the most out of the gifts God gave us. If your gift from God is being a good speaker, then speak If your gift from God the words of God! is to help others, then help as much as you can! That way, the goodness and love of God will spread far and wide, and everyone will glorify and praise God through Jesus Christ to whom belong the glory and the dominion forever and ever. Amen. Oh, and there's one more thing! My beloved, don't be surprised if people treat you badly, because you follow our Lord Jesus. Be happy that you got to share with Jesus in His suffering. That means that you will also share in His glory and joy when He comes again! What a blessing it is to That just means that suffer with Jesus! God's Holy Spirit Is filling your heart. What could be nicer?!? Others may not like Jesus, but in you, they will see how beautiful Jesus really is! (1 Peter 4:6-14)

Bye for now!

Signed, Peter the Apostle

Do not love the world, nor the things which are in the world. The world shall pass away and all its desires; but he who does the will of God shall abide forever. Amen.

The Acts

A reading from the Acts of our fathers the pure apostles, who were invested with the grace of the Holy Spirit. May their blessing be with us all. Amen.

Do you remember St Paul the Apostle? Well, before he changed his name, he was called Saul. And he was NOT a nice man. Saul travelled around the land, arresting Christians, and bringing them to Jerusalem to be judged and sometimes even killed! One day, as he was travelling on the road to a place called Damascus, he didn't just find Christians, He found Jesus Christ Himself! While Saul was riding on his horse, suddenly, a bright light from heaven shone all around him! Saul fell off his horse! Then Saul heard loud voice, "SAUL, SAUL, WHY ARE YOU HURTING ME?" "Who are you Lord?" Saul answered, shaking and scared. "I AM JESUS." "What do you want me to do, Lord?" asked Saul. "GET UP AND GO TO THE CITY, THERE YOU WILL FIND OUT." When Saul opened his eyes, the Light was gone. But Saul was blind! For three days, his friends had to lead him by the hand. And he couldn't eat or drink. But in the city of Damascus Saul met a Christian called Ananias. God sent Ananias to help Saul see again by praying for him. Ananias was scared of Saul! But he obeyed God. He went and found Saul. He laid his hands on Saul. He prayed for Saul. And suddenly, as Ananias was praying, something like fish-scales fell out from Saul's eyes. Saul could see again! Now, Saul, who used to go around arresting Christians said: "I want to be a Christian!" So they baptised him, and he was filled with the Holy Spirit, and he began to tell everyone that Jesus really is the Son of God. (Chapter 9:1-20)

The word of the Lord shall grow, multiply, be mighty and be confirmed in the holy Church of God. Amen.

Holy Gospel

Stand up in the fear of God and listen to the Holy Gospel, A chapter from the Holy Gospel according to Saint John, May his blessings be with us all, Amen

From the psalms of our teacher David the prophet and king, May his blessings be with us all, Amen

> Give thanks to the Lord, for He is good, For His mercy endures forever;
> Give thanks to the God of gods, For His mercy endures forever; Alleluia.
> Psalm 136:1-2

Blessed is He who comes in the Name of the Lord Our Lord, God and Saviour and the King of us all, Jesus Christ, the Son of the living God. Glory be to You forever more, Amen

Let not your heart be troubled; you believe in God, believe also in Me. In My Father's house are many mansions; if it were not so, I would have told you. I go to prepare a place for you. And if I go and prepare a place for you, I will come again and receive you to Myself; that where I am, there you may be also. And where I go you know, and the way you know." and how can we know the way?" Thomas said to Him, "Lord, we do not know where You are going, Jesus said to him, "I am the way, the truth, and the life. No one comes to the Father except through Me. "If you had known Me, you would have known My Father also; and from now on you know Him and have seen Him." Philip said to Him, "Lord, show us the Father, and it is sufficient for us." Jesus said to him, "Have us 'Show how so has known Me, Philip? He not long, I been with you so and yet you have who has seen Me seen the Father; can you say, the Father'? Do you not believe that I am in the Father, and the Father in Me? The words that I speak to you I do not speak on My own authority; but the Father who dwells in Me does the works. Believe Me that I am in the Father and the Father in Me, or else believe Me for the sake of the works themselves. John 14:1-11

Glory be to God Forever, Amen

SIXTH SUNDAY OF THE HOLY PENTECOST

Holy Gospel

Stand up in the fear of God and listen to the Holy Gospel, A chapter from the Holy Gospel according to Saint John, May his blessings be with us all, Amen

From the psalms of our teacher David the prophet and king, May his blessings be with us all, Amen

> Praise the Lord! For it is good to sing praises to our God; For it is pleasant, and praise is beautiful. The Lord builds up Jerusalem; He gathers together the outcasts of Israel. Alleluia. Psalm 147:1-2

Blessed is He who comes in the Name of the Lord Our Lord, God and Saviour and the King of us all, Jesus Christ, the Son of the living God. Glory be to You forever more, Amen

Philip said to Him, "Lord, show us the Father, and it is sufficient for us." Jesus said to him, "Have I been with you so long, and yet you have not known Me, Philip? He who has seen Me has seen the Father; so how can you say, 'Show us the Father'? Do you not believe that I am in the Father, and the Father in Me? The words that I speak to you I do not speak on My own authority; but the Father who dwells in Me does the works. Believe Me that I am in the Father and the Father in Me, or else believe Me for the sake of the works themselves. "Most assuredly, I say to you, he who believes in Me, the works that I do he will do also; and greater works than these he will do, because I go to My Father. And whatever you ask in My name, that I will do, that the Father may be glorified in the Son. If you ask anything in My name, I will do it. John 14:8-14

Glory be to God Forever, Amen

Pauline

Paul, the servant of our Lord Jesus Christ, called to be an apostle, appointed to the Gospel of God. A reading from the First Epistle of our teacher Paul to the Corinthians. May his holy blessings be with us. Amen.

St Paul the Apostle was writing a letter to the Christians who lived in the rich city of Corinth. Dear Corinthians, What should we say to God, who helps us to beat sin and evil? Why, THANK YOU, of course! So, my dear brothers and sisters, always be strong. Don't let anything scare you. Keep doing God's work. Remember that God will always bring good out of everything you do for Him. And please remember what I asked you to do— when you come together every Sunday, collect some money for the poor and needy people. When I come to visit you, you can tell me who you trust, and I will give the money to them to take to the poor people back home in Jerusalem. I might be going to Jerusalem myself, by the way, so maybe they can just come with me. I am hoping to come to your area soon. I might stay with you for a while. If it is winter, I might stay with you until it is warm enough to travel again. I didn't want to come now and just breeze quickly through Corinth. When I come later, I will have lots of time to spend with you! And then I will visit your neighbours in the city of there until Pentecost. Ephesus, and stay (1 Corinthians 15:57-16:8)

Bye for now!

Signed, Paul

The grace of God the Father be with you all, Amen.

Catholicon

The Catholic Epistle from the First Epistle of our teacher St Peter. May his holy blessings be with us. Amen.

My little children, This is the Apostle Peter writing to all of you who love God And who are the special children of God the Father, Made holy by the Holy Spirit, And washed clean by the Blood of Jesus Christ. We have a lot to thank God for— He gave us hope when Jesus rose from the dead. He opened the way for us to go to Heaven and to live there forever and ever and ever. And His power protects us all our lives. Even when things go a bit wrong for us. Now I've heard that you have been having a hard time lately. I have heard that some evil people are attacking you because you are Christian. Don't be sad about this but Be HAPPY! All these attacks will only make your faith stronger, just like gold is made stronger by being heated in the flames of fire. Even though you have never met Jesus yourselves, you have believed in Him. And this has given you so much JOY! Because the prophets from olden times really wanted to see the Saviour—but they couldn't and the Angels really wanted to know about the Saviour—but they couldn't! But now, we get to know Him, because we have heard the Gospel, the story of Jesus Christ. (1 Peter 1:2-12)

Bye for now!

Signed, Peter the Apostle

Do not love the world, nor the things which are in the world. The world shall pass away and all its desires; but he who does the will of God shall abide forever. Amen.

The Acts

Hello everyone. My name is St Luke, and I am the one who wrote the Book of Acts. Today, I want to tell you a little more of the story of St Paul. I was travelling with Paul. We went to lots of new places — Macedonia, and Greece, and Philippi, and Troas. And we had lots of helpers travelling with us, telling people all about Jesus. One Sunday, we were in Troas, and we came together to pray, have communion, and talk. Paul spoke and spoke and they listened and listened, so happy to learn more about Jesus' love. Before anyone realised, it was already midnight! It was way past the bedtime of a boy called Eutychus [Yoo-tie-kuss]. They were on the third floor and Eutychus was sitting somewhere that was not very clever. Eutychus was sitting on the window sill. And the window was open. And Eutychus fell asleep! OH! Be careful Eutychus! Oh no! Eutychus fell out the window! How awful! Everyone rushed downstairs. Is he hurt? Is he alive? Oh no! Oh no! Eutychus was dead. But Paul went through all the people, and he picked up Eutychus. Paul hugged him. Paul prayed for him. Then, a miracle happened, Eutychus came back to life! He was alive again! Everyone was so happy! Then we all went back inside, and had something to eat, which we needed after a shock like that! And we kept listening to Paul all through the night, all the way to morning. The things he was telling us about Jesus were just so beautiful. We didn't want him to stop! And in the morning, Paul left to get on a ship to continue his adventures. He was hurrying to get to Jerusalem in time for the great feast of Pentecost! (Chapter 20:1-16)

Holy Gospel

Stand up in the fear of God and listen to the Holy Gospel, A chapter from the Holy Gospel according to Saint John, May his blessings be with us all, Amen

From the psalms of our teacher David the prophet and king, May his blessings be with us all, Amen

> Praise the Lord, O Jerusalem; Praise your God, O Zion. His wind shall blow, and the waters shall flow. Alleluia. Psalm 147:12,18

Blessed is He who comes in the Name of the Lord Our Lord, God and Saviour and the King of us all, Jesus Christ, the Son of the living God. Glory be to You forever more, Amen

"And in that day you will ask Me nothing. Most assuredly, I say to you, whatever you ask the Father in My name He will give you. Until now you have asked nothing in My name. Ask, and you will receive, that your joy may be full. These things I have spoken to you in figurative language; but the time is coming when I will no longer speak to you in figurative language, but I will tell you plainly about the Father. In that day you will ask in My name, and I do not say to you that I shall pray the Father for you; for the Father Himself loves you, because you have loved Me, and have believed that I came forth from God. I came forth from the Father and have come into the world. Again, I leave the world and go to the Father." His disciples said to Him, "See, now You are speaking plainly, and using no figure of speech! Now we are sure that You know all things, and have no need that anyone should question You. By this we believe that You came forth from God." Jesus answered them, "Do you now believe? Indeed the hour is coming, yes, has now come that you will be scattered, each to his own, and will leave Me alone. And yet I am not alone, because the Father is with Me. These things I have spoken to you, that in Me you may have peace. In the world you will have tribulation; but be of good cheer, I have overcome the world." John 16:23-33

Glory be to God Forever, Amen

FEAST OF THE ASCENSION

Holy Gospel

MATINS

Stand up in the fear of God and listen to the Holy Gospel, A chapter from the Holy Gospel according to Saint Mark, May his blessings be with us all, Amen

From the psalms of our teacher David the prophet and king, May his blessings be with us all, Amen

> You have ascended on high, You have led captivity captive; You have received gifts among men, Even from the rebellious, That the Lord God might dwell there. Blessed be the Lord, Who daily loads us with benefits, The God of our salvation! Selah   Alleluia. Psalm 68:18-19

Blessed is He who comes in the Name of the Lord Our Lord, God and Saviour and the King of us all, Jesus Christ, the Son of the living God. Glory be to You forever more, Amen

After that, He appeared in another form to two of them as they walked and went into the country. And they went and told it to the rest, but they did not believe them either. Later He appeared to the eleven as they sat at the table; and He rebuked their unbelief and hardness of heart, because they did not believe those who had seen Him after He had risen. And He said to them, "Go into all the world and preach the gospel to every creature. He who believes and is baptized will be saved; but he who does not believe will be condemned. And these signs will follow those who believe: In My name they will cast out demons; they will speak with new tongues; they will take up serpents; and if they drink anything deadly, it will by no means hurt them; they will lay hands on the sick, and they will recover." So then, after the Lord had spoken to them, He was received up into heaven, and sat down at the right hand of God. And they went out and preached everywhere, the Lord working with them and confirming the word through the accompanying signs. Amen. Mark 16:12-20

Glory be to God Forever, Amen

Pauline

Paul, the servant of our Lord Jesus Christ, called to be an apostle, appointed to the Gospel of God. A reading from the First Epistle of our teacher Paul to Timothy. May his holy blessings be with us. Amen.

St Paul the Apostle was writing a letter to his good friend Timothy.

Dear Timothy, I want you to remind your deacons that if they do their service very well, they will really help people to know Jesus. I wanted to write to you and give you some advice, but I hope that soon I will come to visit you. Until then, I wrote this letter to remind you how we should all live and behave in the Church, which is the House of God. Our God is the living God! Our God is the God of Truth! Everything that is true comes from our God. And this is the great Mystery, the most amazing thing EVER: God became a Human Being (that's Jesus) and the Holy Spirit told us who He really is. And the angels saw Him and people preached about Him throughout the world. Many people believed in Him and He went up to Heaven in glory. (1 Timothy 3:13–16)

Bye for now!

Signed, Paul

> *The grace of God the Father be with you all, Amen.*

Catholicon

The Catholic Epistle from the First Epistle of our teacher St Peter. May his holy blessings be with us. Amen.

Hello Everyone! Are you keeping God's love safely sealed in your hearts? If you are, you will always be ready to politely answer anyone who asks you "Why do you trust God? Why do you depend so much on Him?" You will never be afraid of anyone. When bad people call you names, don't worry! Everyone sees your very good behaviour! Sometimes, life isn't fair. But it's so much better to be a good person than it is to be a bad person, even when things go terribly wrong. Things went very wrong indeed for Jesus. Remember how He was crucified on the Cross? That was very unfair. But because Jesus is good He turned the Cross into something wonderful! He saved the whole wide world! Even the people who had already died! From the Cross, Jesus went down into Hades and He set free all the people who were stuck there. Do you remember Noah and his ark? And how God brought them through the water, and saved life on earth? Jesus does the same thing for us, when we are baptised. God brings us through the water of baptism and saves our lives! Baptism saves us, because of that unfair thing that happened to Jesus: After Jesus died on the Cross He Went down to Hades. Then Jesus rose from the dead and He raised us with Him! And He went up to Heaven and He will take us to be there with Him one day! Because Jesus is the King of Heaven and all its angels. Won't that be wonderful? (1 Peter 3:15-22)

Bye for now!

Signed, Peter the Apostle

Do not love the world, nor the things which are in the world. The world shall pass away and all its desires; but he who does the will of God shall abide forever. Amen.

The Acts

A reading from the Acts of our fathers the pure apostles, who were invested with the grace of the Holy Spirit. May their blessing be with us all. Amen.

The Book of Acts in the Bible was written by St Luke the apostle, to his friend Theophilus [Thee-OFF-ill-us]. In it, Luke continues the story of what happened to the followers of Jesus, after He had suffered on the Cross, risen from the dead, and spent forty days with them. Jesus gathered His followers and told them not to leave Jerusalem, because He was going to send them the Holy Spirit! They asked Jesus if He was going to bring back the Kingdom of Israel. But Jesus told them to be patient. The Holy Spirit would soon come upon them and fill them with His power, so that they would go all over the world to tell everyone about Jesus. When Jesus finished speaking, something amazing happened. Jesus was taken up into the sky, until He disappeared into a cloud! And as His followers stood there looking up, two men in white clothes appeared and said to them, Don't worry! This same Jesus, who was taken up from you into heaven, will come back to you in the same way from heaven. So the followers of Jesus left the Mountain of Olives and went back home to Jerusalem, just like Jesus had asked them to.

The Disciples were there: Peter, James, John, and Andrew; Philip and Thomas; Bartholomew and Matthew; James the son of Alphaeus and Simon the Zealot; and Judas the son of James. And St Mary, the Mother of Jesus was there, and His women followers, and His relatives. They all prayed together and waited and waited And waited (Chapter 1:1–14)

The word of the Lord shall grow, multiply, be mighty and be confirmed in the holy Church of God. Amen.

Holy Gospel

Stand up in the fear of God and listen to the Holy Gospel,A chapter from the Holy Gospel according to Saint Luke, May his blessings be with us all, Amen

From the psalms of our teacher David the prophet and king,May his blessings be with us all, Amen

> Lift up the gates, O you rulers, And be lifted up, you everlasting doors, And the King of glory shall enter. Who is this King of Glory? The Lord of hosts, He is the King of glory. Alleluia. Psalm 24:9–10

Blessed is He who comes in the Name of the Lord Our Lord, God and Saviour and the King of us all, Jesus Christ, the Son of the living God. Glory be to You forever more, Amen

Now as they said these things, Jesus Himself stood in the midst of them, and said to them, "Peace to you." But they were terrified and frightened, and supposed they had seen a spirit. And He said to them, "Why are you troubled? And why do doubts arise in your hearts? Behold My hands and My feet, that it is I Myself. Handle Me and see, for a spirit does not have flesh and bones as you see I have." When He had said this, He showed them His hands and His feet. But while they still did not believe for joy, and marvelled, He said to them, When He had said this, He showed them His hands and His feet. But while they still did not believe for joy, and marvelled, He said to them, "Have you any food here?" So they gave Him a piece of a broiled fish and some honeycomb. And He took it and ate in their presence. Then He said to them, "These are the words which I spoke to you while I was still with you, that all things must be fulfilled "which were written in the Law of Moses and the Prophets and the Psalms concerning Me." And He opened their understanding, that they might comprehend the Scriptures. Then He said to them, "Thus it is written, and thus it was necessary for the Christ to suffer and to rise from the dead the third day, "and that repentance and remission of sins should be preached in His name to all nations, beginning at Jerusalem. And you are witnesses of these things. " Behold, I send the Promise of My Father upon you; but tarry in the city of Jerusalem until you are endued with power from on high." And He led them out as far as Bethany, and He lifted up His hands and blessed them. Now it came to pass, while He blessed them, that He was parted from them and carried up into heaven. And they worshiped Him, and returned to Jerusalem with

great joy, and were continually in the temple praising and blessing God. Amen.
Luke 24:36-53

Glory be to God Forever, Amen

SEVENTH SUNDAY OF THE HOLY PENTECOST

Holy Gospel

Stand up in the fear of God and listen to the Holy Gospel, A chapter from the Holy Gospel according to Saint John, May his blessings be with us all, Amen

From the psalms of our teacher David the prophet and king, May his blessings be with us all, Amen

> You send forth Your Spirit, they are created; And You renew the face of the earth. May the glory of the Lord endure forever; May the Lord rejoice in His works. Alleluia. Psalm 104:30-31

Blessed is He who comes in the Name of the Lord Our Lord, God and Saviour and the King of us all, Jesus Christ, the Son of the living God. Glory be to You forever more, Amen

If you ask anything in My name, I will do it. "If you love Me, keep My commandments. And I will pray the Father, and He will give you another Helper, that He may abide with you forever— the Spirit of truth, whom the world cannot receive, because it neither sees Him nor knows Him; but you know Him, for He dwells with you and will be in you. I will not leave you orphans; I will come to you.

"A little while longer and the world will see Me no more, but you will see Me. Because I live, you will live also. At that day you will know that I am in My Father, and you in Me, and I in you. He who has My commandments and keeps them, it is he who loves Me. And he who loves Me will be loved by My Father, and I will love him and manifest Myself to him." Judas (not Iscariot) said to Him, "Lord, how is it that You will manifest Yourself to us, and not to the world?" Jesus answered and said to him, "If anyone loves Me, he will keep My word; and My Father will love him, and We will come to him and make Our home with him. He who does not love Me does not keep My words; and the word which you hear is not Mine but the Father's who sent Me. "These things I have spoken to you while being present with you. But the Helper, the Holy Spirit, whom the Father will send in My name, He will teach you all things, and bring to your remembrance all things that I said to you. Peace

I leave with you, My peace I give to you; not as the world gives do I give to you. Let not your heart be troubled, neither let it be afraid. You have heard Me say to you, 'I am going away and coming back to you.' If you loved Me, you would rejoice because I said, 'I am going to the Father,' for My Father is greater than I. "And now I have told you before it comes, that when it does come to pass, you may believe. I will no longer talk much with you, for the ruler of this world is coming, and he has nothing in Me. But that the world may know that I love the Father, and as the Father gave Me commandment, so I do. Arise, let us go from here. Abide in Me, and I in you. As the branch cannot bear fruit of itself, unless it abides in the vine, neither can you, unless you abide in Me. John 14:26-15:4

Glory be to God Forever, Amen

Pauline

Paul, the servant of our Lord Jesus Christ, called to be an apostle, appointed to the Gospel of God. A reading from the First Epistle of our teacher Paul to the Corinthians. May his holy blessings be with us. Amen.

St Paul the Apostle was writing a letter to the Christians who lived in the rich city of Corinth. Dear Corinthians, I need to tell you about you can understand the special gifts that the Holy Spirit gives to His Children, so them better. The Holy Spirit would never make someone hate Jesus! And no one can follow Jesus, unless the Holy Spirit helps him. There is only One God. There is only One Holy Spirit. But the One Holy Spirit of God gives lots of different kinds of gifts, so everyone can benefit. To one person, the Spirit gives the gift of speaking words to teach and help others. To another, the gift of healing, or doing miracles or prophecy, or dealing with spirits, or speaking and understanding different languages. But all these gifts come from the One Holy Spirit of God. Just think about your body. It has lots of different parts. But they are all still just one body, aren't they? No matter where you came from, you are all the one the Holy Spirit made When Body of Jesus. you were baptised, you a part of the Holy Body of Jesus. And we all need each other! Every part of a body needs all the other parts. Imagine if the foot says, "Woe is me! I wish I were a hand!" Wouldn't that be silly? The body needs both the hand

AND the foot! If our ears wanted to be eyes, we would never hear anything! But God gave each of us our own special gift, just as He pleased, so we could all work together. What good would it do you if your whole body was just made of eyes!?! Wouldn't that be weird? Every part of the body NEEDS every other part. Don't think that some parts matter morethan others. Every part is important, no matter what it does. That is why we should care just as much about every single person, whatever their gifts might be. No one matters more than anyone else. If one part is happy, the whole body is happy. And if one part of the body is hurt, the whole body is hurt. Now, you are all the parts of the Body of Jesus. Everyone of you is just as important to Him. But God has given every part a different job: Some are apostles. Some are prophets. Some are teachers. Some work miracles. Some make sick people better. Different languages. Some organise things. Some help the needy. Some speak with Everyone has their own job. Does everyone get to work miracles? Of course not! Does everyone get to be an apostle? Of course not! They don't need to, because we all have each other, And each one has their own special gift from God. If you really want lovely gifts from God, I will show you how, but that's for another time. (1 Corinthians 12:1-31)

Bye for now!

Signed, Paul

The grace of God the Father be with you all, Amen.

Catholicon

The Catholic Epistle from the the First Epistle of our teacher St John. May his holy blessings be with us. Amen.

Hello Everyone! We Christians have a very, very special gift from God: His Holy Spirit lives in us! The Holy Spirit helps us to know what is true and what is a lie. If anyone says that Jesus is NOT the Christ, the One who saves us all that's a lie! And if anyone doesn't believe in Jesus, They don't believe in God the Father either! If you believe in Jesus, you believe in God the Father too. You will live safely in the love of the Son and of the Father. From the beginning, you have learned the truth about God, about Jesus His Son, and about eternal life— living forever. Also, you were filled with the Holy Spirit when you were when you hear something Spirit who lives in you baptised, and the Holy helps you to feel that's not true about God. So if you let God's truth live inside you, you will also live in God! And when Jesus comes back at the end of the world, you will be so happy, not scared at all! If you do good things, you are God's child because He is good. Isn't it amazing how much God loves us? He loves us so much He even called us His own children! That's why the world doesn't know us— because they don't know the Father. (1 John 2:20-3:1)

God loves you!

Signed, John the Apostle

Do not love the world, nor the things which are in the world. The world shall pass away and all its desires; but he who does the will of God shall abide forever. Amen.

The Acts

Soon after Jesus had ascended to Heaven, His Disciples got together to pray on the day of Pentecost. Suddenly, a sound like a mighty wind filled the whole house! And a little flame of fire appeared on top of each of their heads! These were the signs that the Holy Spirit had come to them, just as Jesus had promised! And each of the Disciples began to speak a different language! Now lots of people from all over the world were visiting Jerusalem for the Feast of Pentecost. When they heard the noise, they came to see what was happening. And each person heard a Disciple speaking in his own language, saying beautiful things about God! What on earth is going on here, they asked? Some people said, "Oh, they must be drunk." But the Disciple Peter told them with a loud voice: "Hey, everyone. Listen to me! We're not drunk! (It's too early for that anyway—it's only 9 o'clock in the morning). No, today, God has done a big, big miracle! In the Bible, a long, long time ago, the prophet Joel said that a day would come when people would be filled with God's Holy Spirit. And they would speak amazing things that the Holy Spirit tells them. That's what's happening right here, right now! And whoever turns to God and calls upon God's name will be saved!" (Chapter 2:1-21)

Holy Gospel

Stand up in the fear of God and listen to the Holy Gospel,A chapter from the Holy Gospel according to Saint John, May his blessings be with us all, Amen

From the psalms of our teacher David the prophet and king,May his blessings be with us all, Amen

> God ascended with a shout, The Lord with the sound of the trumpet.
> For God is King of all the earth. Alleluia. Psalm 47:5,7

Blessed is He who comes in the Name of the Lord Our Lord, God and Saviour and the King of us all, Jesus Christ, the Son of the living God. Glory be to You forever more, Amen

"But when the Helper comes, whom I shall send to you from the Father, the Spirit of truth who proceeds from the Father, He will testify of Me "And these things I did not say to you at the beginning, because I was with you. "But now I go away to Him who sent Me, and none of you asks Me, 'Where are You going?' But because I have said these things to you, sorrow has filled your heart. Nevertheless I tell you the truth. It is to your advantage that I go away; for if I do not go away, the Helper will not come to you; but if I depart, I will send Him to you. And when He has come, He will convict the world of sin, and of righteousness, and of judgment: of sin, because they do not believe in Me; of righteousness, because I go to My Father and you see Me no more; of judgment, because the ruler of this world is judged. "I still have many things to say to you, but you cannot bear them now. However, when He, the Spirit of truth, has come, He will guide you into all truth; for He will not speak on His own authority, but whatever He hears He will speak; and He will tell you things to come. He will glorify Me, for He will take of what is Mine and declare it to you. All things that the Father has are Mine. Therefore I said that He will take of Mine and declare it to you. John 15:26-16:15

Glory be to God Forever, Amen

www.ingramcontent.com/pod-product-compliance
Lightning Source LLC
Chambersburg PA
CBHW081114160426
42814CB00035B/318